THE
BUSINESS-TO-BUSINESS
DIRECT
MARKETING
HANDBOOK

ROY G. LJUNGREN

amacom

American Management Association

This book is available at a special
discount when ordered in bulk quantities.
For information, contact Special Sales Department,
AMACOM, a division of American Management Association,
135 West 50th Street, New York, NY 10020.

Library of Congress Cataloging-in-Publication Data

Ljungren, Roy G.
    The business-to-business direct marketing handbook.

    Includes index.
    1. Direct marketing.   2. Industrial marketing.
3. Telemarketing.   I. American Management Association.
II. Title.
HF5415.126.L57   1989   658.8'4   89–47707
ISBN 0–8144–5834–3

Printing Number

10   9   8   7   6   5   4   3   2   1

PREFACE

Direct marketing, viewed from the desk of the business-to-business marketer, consists of two separate functions: a sales support function and a mail order function, which is a complete selling function. What brings the two together here is that they both share common markets and media—direct mail and telemarketing. They also employ similar direct response techniques.

Many fine books cover consumer direct marketing. This book, however, is dedicated solely to the business-industrial segment. Consumer direct marketing is virtually all mail order and is concerned with a marketplace that is very different from that of business. Further, business-to-business direct marketing uses are quite different from the consumer variety. And although we occasionally hear otherwise, there are strategic differences between the two in virtually every major direct marketing category.

From the start of my career, business-to-business direct mail has always fascinated me. I have been responsible for the mailing of over 130 million pieces of direct mail, and have used every offer, creative approach, and business market segment you can imagine. This does not appear to be much of a feat until you realize that most of those mailings were to market segments of less than 25,000. That's a lot of planning, a lot of campaigns, and a lot of results.

I have learned that telemarketing in concert with direct mail makes both approaches more effective. That lesson began when I answered my phone at the NCR Corporation one day in 1975. I was asked if I would like to listen to a taped message about telephone marketing from Murray Roman. I was intrigued. His live callback the next day resulted in my arranging for a meeting, four weeks later, in a small auditorium in Dayton, Ohio. Eight market division heads listened to Murray Roman discuss the advantages of telemarketing. I was hooked. NCR signed up two of its sales divisions for trials a week later. The first program grossed several million dollars, and success increased steadily.

This handbook draws on my own direct marketing experience along with that of many others who have learned to use direct marketing successfully. My objective in writing this book has been to sort out in one volume what the business-to-business marketer must specifically know to experience success with direct marketing.

The book is in three parts. Part I covers the essentials—sales support and mail order, market segmentation and targeting, business lists, and the marketing data base. Part II addresses all aspects of managing the direct marketing effort. In Part III, various business-to-business direct marketing strategies are examined. This part also contains mini case studies, which are examples of award-winning direct marketing campaigns illustrating a variety of successful strategies.

CONTENTS

Part III
DIRECT MARKETING STRATEGIES

PART I

Direct Marketing Mix

1

OVERVIEW

BUSINESS-TO-BUSINESS DIRECT MARKETING—A DEFINITION

For many business-to-business marketers, the term *direct marketing* is synonymous with *direct advertising.* For other people, especially marketers of consumer goods, direct marketing means selling by catalog or solo mail, commonly called mail order selling. But direct marketing has a broader definition, particularly in the business-to-business arena, that includes other types of prospect and customer transactions and communications (see Appendix 1).

Business-to-business direct marketing encompasses the much broader concept of sales support. Sales support direct marketing is the business-to-business marketer's link between advertising goals and field sales activity.

For the purpose of this book, business-to-business direct marketing refers to any form of communication that is sent from the seller directly to the buyer *and* that employs some sort of response technique. For both sales support and mail order marketing, the communications media of choice have been direct mail and telephone, used separately or together. In the case of business-to-business mail order, some use is made of print advertising and, to a much lesser extent, TV, radio, and selected electronic media.

The terms *direct response* and *direct response advertising* are used often as synonyms for direct marketing. These terms refer to customers or prospects taking some form of overt action in response to a promotion, such as placing an order in the case of mail order selling, or calling an 800 number for more information in the case of a sales support promotion. A large part of the growing appeal of the direct response form of direct marketing is the opportunity that the marketer has to define objectives in realistic, measurable terms and then to test them. Reactions can be measured for different offers, different messages using different lists—all in small samples—before the marketer is committed to a total campaign and a large expenditure.

However, direct marketing also involves other promotions that provide an indirect response, such as the modification of attitudes or opinions, which result in direct action at a later time. Since direct and indirect response campaigns support one another, the business-to-business marketer should integrate both into the advertising mix.

Figure 1-1 outlines six broad categories in which business-to-business direct marketing can be grouped.

GROWTH OF DIRECT MARKETING IN THE BUSINESS SECTOR

Direct marketing is not new for the business-to-business marketer. In fact, in 1900, John H. Patterson, founder of the National Cash Register Company (now known as NCR Corporation) mailed 6 million pieces of direct mail advertising to support his expanding field sales organization. He referred to direct mail as the "strong right arm of selling."

Over the years, the only use of direct mail for some industrial firms was to send copies of their print advertisements to customers to keep them informed. Some firms also mailed brochures, sales literature, or self-mailers as reminders or as information. Many of these mailing pieces seemed to have no clear objectives.

Figure 1-1. Categories of business-to-business direct marketing.

Sales Support	
Inquiry generation	To identify prospects among group of suspects
Pre-qualified prospect penetration	To bring together at a face-to-face meeting a salesperson and a prospect who has already been qualified
Awareness	To build positive customer and prospect perceptions and opinions toward companies and products
Reinforced selling	To reinforce the planned sales call
Research	To gather information
Mail Order	To sell directly without a face-to-face sales call

And if any inquiries were generated from the mailings (or any source for that matter), they were sent directly to the sales force for follow-up, with no qualifying procedures.

Knowledgeable marketers today are accelerating their use of sophisticated direct mail and telemarketing methods to help increase sales. A 1985 Stephan Direct survey indicates that average business executives receive 44 pieces of unsolicited mail each week while presidents, general managers, and division heads get more than 200 pieces. The amount of mail received by businesspeople is in direct proportion to the importance of their job titles within the company.

Computer & Electronics Marketing Magazine, in its January 1986 issue, reported the results of a recent study by Techvantage, a marketing and research firm. The results are fairly typical of the quantity and type of mail received by businesspeople: They show that marketing information systems managers receive 54 pieces of promotional mail a week, applications managers receive 61 pieces, and data processing managers get 41. Of this mail, 45 percent consists of seminar and presentation offerings, 19 percent of hardware and software products, and 14 percent of specific promotional pieces.

Direct mail continues to grow every year. A study released by the New York advertising agency of Doyle Dane Bernbach in 1986 showed direct mail increasing at a faster rate than TV in terms of national advertising dollars. In the business sector, at least part of the attraction is that through direct mail, the marketer has a medium that can communicate to buyers and influencers one at a time. It's the "me-to-you" medium.

Without question, it is the combination of the personal and the business communication aspects of direct mail, along with the added dimension of telephone marketing, that has made direct marketing so successful in business-to-business applications. However, before successful media and creative strategies can be developed, it is helpful for marketers to know the business-to-business differences when compared with consumer direct marketing.

BUSINESS VS. CONSUMER PERSPECTIVES

The buying behavior of businessmen and businesswomen is different from that of consumers. In business purchases the average industrial sale is higher and often more complex. Purchasers are more serious and act less on impulse. And they are more informed and knowledgeable about the products they buy. Business buyers are more careful about spending their firms' money, particularly since they must justify their purchasing decisions to others.

Business buyers scrutinize ad copy for performance facts, comparisons, "reasons why," demonstrations, trial runs, and test results. Therefore, business-to-business direct mail gets higher readership and attention than consumer mail. Accordingly, direct mail formats and copy are less like advertising and more businesslike. Telephone scripts are also more pinpointed, and communicators talk knowledgeably about the buyer's particular line of business. The higher-ticket products allow for a higher contribution of dollars for direct marketing promotion.

Business-to-business marketers target their marketplace more precisely with mailings and telephone calls. List usage is usually limited to compiled and in-house lists, except, of course, for marketers who have mail order objectives. And even though there are many business lists available, a look at the *Direct Mail Lists Rates and Data* directory, published by Standard Rate & Data Service, Inc. (SRDS), will show that the average market segment is relatively small. As a result, there is limited pretesting.

The vast majority of business-to-business marketers operate with a small, unique customer base, some with as few as 50 customers and most with no more than 5,000 names on their customer list. And, of course, the nature of their products dictates that their marketing techniques be quite different from those used for a mass market. Industrial products, for instance, which make up a sizable segment of business-to-business sales, are often conceived and designed for special technological needs and uses. They often produce highly profitable sales, but many of the products require a technically oriented marketing approach, and many require one-on-one contact with salespeople.

WHY USE DIRECT MARKETING?

Marketing industrial products was relatively inexpensive in the 1970s while costs for data processing were out of reach for all but the largest companies. In the late 1980s, the picture has been reversed, with marketing and selling costs becoming burdensome. Added to this are the steady flow of new products coming into the marketplace and markets that shift as well as fragment. Mass marketing is no longer a viable method for the business-to-business marketer, since the masses contain too many nonprospects. Segmentation is now the name of the game.

The challenge for the business-to-business marketer today is to reduce the cost of selling. Two of the most practical ways to do this is to increase the salesperson's productivity or to switch to a more cost-effective selling channel. Direct marketing can assist with both objectives by properly integrating sales support direct marketing into the marketing mix and by performing feasibility studies and tests to determine which products, if any, could possibly be sold profitably by mail order.

Direct marketing can also find prospects, qualify them, and reinforce the salesperson's selling efforts. It can help salespeople get in to see decision makers who previously have had their doors closed. It can broaden the awareness of prospects and customers for a company and its products and services, and serve as a reminder that the company wants to do business with them. And because direct mail and telemarketing techniques can be measured and adjusted to appeal to the needs and expectations of the customer, they have proved very effective in achieving those objectives.

Pressure is mounting as companies cut personnel and operate with leaner staffs. And with stiff competition facing most business-to-business marketers, companies are having to make better decisions faster. Business-to-business marketers must get new customers at less cost while building strong relationships with current customers without the high costs.

At the same time, more company managements are requiring quantitative documentation that their advertising and direct marketing efforts are paying off. They are looking for proof of effectiveness and material contributions to the corporation's goals and marketing objectives. The fact that direct marketing is accountable and measurable is why it is moving into the business-to-business marketer's spotlight. Costs can be directly related to sales. The goals of direct marketing are short-range because the prospect is motivated to take a specific action right away.

One of the big advantages of direct marketing for the small marketer is that its cost per prospect reached is not that much greater than that paid by the large marketer. The smaller marketer may not be able to afford the dollars it takes for advertising in trade or business publications to build and maintain an image in a limited marketplace. But with direct marketing, marketers of any size can affordably reach at least the most important segments of their target market with enough communications to make a substantial impression.

While direct marketing has emerged as an integral part of the overall marketing mix in many major companies, it has become a catalyst in establishing marketing information systems that generate huge amounts of information readily and inexpensively. These systems not only support direct marketing operations—both sales support and mail order—but additionally benefit all sales and marketing groups within the company. For instance, as end users of the data base, they obtain precise customer profiles that help salespeople develop more pinpointed selling approaches. Also, customer buying cycle data improve the timing of sales callbacks.

And the use of direct marketing as a significant part of the mix for business-to-business marketers has escalated because the growing need for information has fortunately coincided with the computer's ability to make this information accessible and affordable. Managements involved in direct marketing continually gather more and more information about their target markets—what customers buy, how much they pay, how often they buy, why they buy, and who makes the buying decisions. As the data base grows, so does the marketers' ability to pinpoint the right customers and prospects at the right time with messages that say the right things.

2

SALES SUPPORT DIRECT MARKETING

DETERMINING OBJECTIVES

Sales support direct marketing is a particularly valuable tool for the business-to-business marketer, since it has a variety of uses and can be tailored to meet any number of promotional objectives. A successful sales support campaign implemented within the framework of overall marketing, sales, and advertising plans can help the marketer reach that most elusive of goals—a program that represents the optimum use of all marketing and selling tools. Before that goal can be reached, however, the marketer must have a thorough understanding of the uses of sales support direct marketing.

Two essentials for creating successful marketing programs are (1) having the product marketing and sales objectives, strategies, and tactics detailed by product and by market and (2) having the advertising and promotion spelled out before sales-support direct-marketing planning is prepared. If marketing or sales objectives are not clear-cut, or are in flux, direct marketing efforts tend to go astray. Sales-support direct-marketing planners, because of their early need for detailed product forecasts and market definition, often become the catalysts in getting marketing and sales management to finalize their objectives. Marketing and sales functions must be formalized and commitments must be made before direct marketing strategies and tactics can be planned. (An exception to this is when using direct marketing for research. In this case, direct mail may be sent out in advance of a final marketing plan to help determine product feasibility or to identify the best markets or market segments.)

8

When determining the objectives to be accomplished by sales support direct marketing, the planner must look beyond the immediate marketing and sales objectives and analyze other operational areas of the company and its competitors. A useful outline of key areas that direct marketing planners should investigate before establishing objectives is provided in Figure 2-1.

Figure 2-1. Key areas for business-to-business marketers to investigate before establishing objectives.

Products

1. All specific products or services, and their particular applications in each industry served.
2. Principal sales points or competitive advantages for each.
3. Their market acceptance: company's share of each market.
4. Company's special areas of capability which have a market in the industry.
5. Types of organizations using your products or services.
6. Relative importance of each customer group, in terms of percent of the total market potential.
7. Seasonal trends for each significant market.
8. Buying habits and buying trends in each.
9. Types of individuals, by title and function, with direct influence on the evaluation, specification, or purchase of each product or service.
10. General conditions and habits of mind surrounding purchase.
11. Exact need fulfilled by the purchase: what are the needs, feelings, and desires involved?
12. Preconceived ideas, prejudices, false or true notions which impede or aid the purchase.
13. Standing of your products in the buyer's mind.
14. Main factors that limit your market.
15. Production trend and outlook for next quarter, next year.
16. Are new products being developed? What? For which market or uses?

The Company and Its Sales Policies

1. Reputation: how long and well established.
2. Do you sell through distributors, manufacturer's representatives, dealers, company sales staff, or a combination of these?
3. Number in each category.
4. Exclusivity of representation policy, if any.
5. Geographic emphasis of distribution and sales, if any.

Source: Edward N. Mayer and Roy G. Ljungren, *The Handbook of Industrial Direct Mail Advertising,* Business Professional Advertising Association, New York, 1984. Used by permission of BPAA.

(continues)

Figure 2-1 *(continued)*

6. Seasonal emphasis of distribution and sales, if any. 7. Any projected change in emphasis on areas, markets, or products? 8. Price and discount policies: what and whether they vary from the industry's policies. 9. Are foreign markets important? Which? The Company's Advertising 1. Current detailed ad schedule: space, direct mail, other.	2. Amount of current budget. 3. Basis of its determination: percentage of sales, task accomplishment, or otherwise. 4. Nature and size of various mailing lists: how classified, developed, and maintained. 5. Size of each competitor's budget, relative to his share of the market and relative to your own company's budget. 6. Major objectives of competitor's advertising. 7. Each competitor's primary advantages in each market.

After analysis most marketers realize that many sales-support direct-marketing campaigns may be needed to accomplish different objectives for each product in each market. Although there are dozens of ways that sales support direct marketing can be profitably employed, five major business-to-business uses or functions are those that were listed in Chapter 1:

1. Identifying qualified prospects from broad suspect markets—the most important and most prevalent use
2. Targeting prequalified prospects with an objective of getting customers and prospects to agree to a face-to-face meeting with the marketer's salespeople
3. Aiming pure advertising communication at getting mind share or awareness level increases among target audiences with a specific end goal of getting the product specified
4. Strengthening a planned sales call by providing specific support, usually in the form of direct mail, to reinforce the salesperson's activities with those prospects currently being called on
5. Doing research in the form of a mail or telephone questionnaire

A more comprehensive listing of uses for business-to-business direct marketing is shown in Figure 2-2. The rest of this chapter examines the five major uses and the response techniques they employ.

INQUIRY GENERATION

Defining an Inquiry

Because the terms *sales inquiry* and *sales lead* have been used interchangeably in the field of business-to-business marketing, there is confusion in the minds of

Figure 2-2. Uses for business-to-business direct marketing where direct mail and telemarketing are the main media.

Identifying market segments for targeting

Securing inquiries for further follow-up

Qualifying inquiries for a salesperson's follow-up

Reinforcing a planned sales call

Maintaining contact with prospects between salesperson's calls

Further selling prospective customers after a demonstration or salesperson's call

Bringing potential buyer to sales office or seminar

Building business relationships, goodwill

Building company and product image

Announcing a new product, new policy, or expansion

Opening doors for salespeople

Introducing a new product

Researching products, markets, and competition

Securing new dealers

many sales and marketing personnel. Perhaps the best way to decide whether to classify a response as an inquiry or a lead is to make the classification dependent on whether the offer in the direct marketing campaign has prequalified the inquirer. Qualified inquirers are identified by the extent to which they meet certain criteria; only then can they be said to have sales value and be treated as bona fide sales leads. Not every sales inquiry can be considered a sales lead, since some inquiries will never lead to a sale. For example, a small flow of inquiries continually arrives in any business-to-business company's mailbox from the general public, mostly from students and librarians seeking information. Marketers, being good corporate citizens, usually reply courteously to these inquirers. Some of the inquiries that come from publication reader response cards are also not from serious inquirers. In fact, one publisher throws away response cards that are returned with over ten item numbers checked.

Another nonproductive type of inquiry comes from competitors who seek intelligence to counteract competitive marketing strategy. Some marketers ignore this, while others actually exchange promotional materials within their industry.

The specific industry custom determines the disposition of this type of inquiry.

The more highly prized inquiries come from mailings to current customers, or prospects who attend demonstration meetings or company-sponsored seminars. In addition to direct mail and telemarketing, typical inquiry sources for the business-to-business marketer include (in order of value):

- Business trade shows
- Random white mail (no identifiable promotion source)
- Advertisements in trade and business publications
- Card deck mailings
- Product publicity

When an Inquiry Becomes a Lead

An inquiry becomes a lead when the inquirer specifically states a desire to see a salesperson or attends a seminar, demonstration, or other sales event, or when field sales management or salespeople have agreed beforehand that a specified offer will produce a qualified prospect inquiry worth a personal sales call. Focus group research interview sessions with typical field people can help the direct mail planner determine what the offer should be. An inquiry can also become a lead when it comes from someone easily recognized by name, title, or company as an important prospect that has use for the product.

The degree of value any sales inquiry will have in the minds of salespeople depends on their perception of how easily they can turn the inquiry into a sale. Some marketers have a firm policy stating that all trade and business publication reader response cards, trade show inquiries, and raw inquiries from direct mail should be sent directly to the field organization for their follow-up. They justify this action with the logic that salespeople are best equipped to weed out the nonprospects. Yet, this is a poor policy for today's lead-generation programs, since inquiry qualification can be performed more effectively, faster, more thoroughly, and at less cost by professional inquiry qualification personnel at a central location.

To get optimum closure rates the direct mail planner must give the salespeople more than the inquirer's name and address. They need to know what the prospect wants and what is needed. The better the prospect profile the marketer can give to the salesperson along with the inquiry, the better the chance that the salesperson will actually make the sales call. Also, the more the salespeople know about prospects before the calls, the better they will be able to prepare more specific and successful customer presentations.

Qualifying Responses

The best inquiries a marketer can get are from prospects who request a salesperson to call because these prospects have identified themselves as being highly interested in what the salesperson has to say. If the prospects like what they hear the salesperson may be rewarded with an order on the first call. The worst kind of inquiries are from those who do not even have an application for the product but want to see a salesperson anyway. These inquiries cost the marketer greatly in the salesperson's time. For some marketers there never seem to be enough good inquiries and there are almost always too many bad ones. The business-to-business inquiry-generation program aims, of course, at getting a maximum number of the former and a minimum number of the latter.

Because the ideal inquiry cannot be generated in large enough quantities from a direct mailing to satisfy most business-to-business marketers' objectives, they aim for an inquiry of lesser quality to be qualified in a subsequent step in the lead-generation program. Actually, for many marketers this can be the most profitable strategy in the long run.

The marketer has a number of tools available with which to fine-tune the quality of responses to a given campaign. Since direct mail is such a large part of direct marketing strategy, mailing lists obviously are one of the most important qualifiers. Other techniques, such as lead hardeners and softeners, telemarketing, and bounce-back cards are also effective.

Lists

For any response mailing, the more qualified the list is to begin with—that is, the more demographic, geographic, and behavioral information (known as *selects*) requested—the greater the number of quality inquiries that will be generated. However, the inquiry-generation planner usually finds that the more qualified lists are more expensive to assemble from the list rental market and also, of course, are smaller in size.

Business-to-business marketers have a wide range of market segments available to them in the lists they can rent or compile. At one end of this range are very general groups of businesses with few, if any, characteristics that match those of the marketer's best customers. At the other end are selected lists of prospects who have a high degree of "best-customer" geographic, demographic, and behavioral characteristics (such as number of employees, annual revenue, standard industrial classification [SIC] category, past purchase types and amounts).

Companies at the high end of the range are, as may be expected, labeled as more highly qualified prospects. Inquiries that result from mailings to these names have the best chance of meeting the criteria that sales management has established for a bona fide sales lead, thus eliminating the need to further qualify the inquiry before passing it on to the sales force for follow-up. It has been established that when a marketer mails randomly to a nonqualified mass suspect market list with little regard for prospect characteristics (except they may all fit within a two-digit SIC code), the inquiries that result will have a lower sales close ratio than those from an identical mailing to a list or list segment that contains numerous characteristics of the "best customer profile." (See Chapter 5 for more information on business lists.)

In addition to the list, marketers can use so-called lead hardeners and softeners to control the quantity and quality of response. These techniques relate mostly to direct mail, although some apply to direct response print ads.

Lead Softeners

Business-to-business marketers use inquiry softeners to improve response from inquiry-generation campaigns. They accomplish this for the most part by making the offer, message, and invitation to action less selective and more personal.

Offers Regulating the value and importance of the offer to the prospect has the most impact on who responds to a mailing. The more general the offer, the less chance it has of attracting a narrow audience that may have specific goals.

Premiums and giveaways used as offers, especially if they have significant value, can increase the number of inquiries that result from a direct response effort. Premiums, or contests and sweepstakes with worthwhile prizes that are independent of the offer, can be an extra incentive that can hype response. In the context of sales support direct marketing, such softeners are only practical when used in mailings to highly qualified or prequalified lists.

Offers of free literature, especially industry-generic and product-generic, relate only to the prospect's broad interest and bring in the softest inquiries. (Chapter 7 details the range of specific offers that increase responses.)

Message Although the offer is virtually always the most influential of all the lead qualification strategies, the creative interpretation of the offer in the mailing can maximize or minimize the effect that it will have on the prospect. Also, the reader's perception of the value of an offer can be enhanced or diminished depending on the emphasis placed on it by the copy and graphics. Dedicating the entire copy/graphics message to only the offer will usually increase responses. Emphasizing the offer in the P.S. of a letter can also improve response.

How the offer is integrated into the message also helps control the response action. For instance, in an attempt to fine-tune for the optimum quantity/quality inquiry mix from a mailing to a broad suspect list, an inquiry-generation planner may harden a soft primary offer of an industry/generic book by burying the offer halfway or three-quarters of the way into the copy. This technique tends to focus the value and impact of the offer or premium on those in the audience who are the better prospects—those who show enough interest in the subject message to continue to read much of the message.

More responses usually result from inquiry mailings that do not elaborate on the product or service. They only whet the reader's appetite for more information.

Invitations to action Business-to-business marketers commonly use the following action response softeners to make it simple and convenient for readers to respond:

- Use of the prospect's name and address on the reply card or action response form.
- A reply card that is detached from the mailing piece or letter.
- Limiting the offer to only one option. The fewer decisions the reader is asked to make, the better.
- A postage-paid reply card or envelope.

Personalization Using a personal name on an envelope will improve response if the name list used is current. The use of a processed or computerized personal letter or note in a mailing also increases response.

Lead Hardeners

Lead hardeners are, in most respects, the reverse of lead softeners. The following hardener techniques in inquiry-generation offers, messages, and invitations to action produce fewer inquiries but are more likely to turn into a sale.

Offers   The more relevant the offer is to the product or service, the better the inquiry. Literature with a highly specific title germane to the product will attract only those readers who are interested in that narrow subject. Also, asking a prospect to pay for a descriptive booklet discourages literature seekers and singles out the serious prospects.

For prospects to qualify for a free survey or analysis a marketer may include on the reply form a series of questions for the prospect to answer. Of course, only higher quality hard inquiries result from this offer technique, especially when the answers are confidential. The offer to "have a salesman call me at this number on this date" is the ultimate hardener. In fact, any mention in the inquiry-generation mailing that a salesperson will call in response to the inquiry will turn off many would-be responders, including some highly interested and some mildly interested prospects. However, those who do respond, who know they will be called on by a salesperson, are probably at a critical stage in their buying behavior cycle. Exceptions prevail when high value premiums are prominently offered.

Message   The more product features, functions, and benefits described in the inquiry-generation direct-mail package, the higher the quality of the inquiry that will result. When descriptive product application and case history booklets relevant to the prospect's business are included in the mailing package, response will be limited mostly to those serious prospects seeking additional information. These prospects are closer to the threshold of taking buying action. The mention of price also is a powerful inquiry hardener.

Invitations to action   Making it difficult for a prospect to respond reduces the number of respondents to those most persistent or those with an urgent need. Asking prospects to request more information on their company letterhead can slow inquiries to a trickle, resulting in very hard, high-quality inquiries.

Other deterrents to response that have the effect of raising inquiry quality include:

- The use of a reply form that requires prospects to enter their names, addresses, and telephone numbers
- A request that prospects place their own stamp on the reply card or envelope
- The use of multiple-option offers in a mailing, which hinders readers' decision making

Generally, the more options the fewer the responses.

To some marketers, the use of lead hardeners and softeners may mean that inquiries from a mailing can go directly to the salesforce without further qualification, and will result in an acceptable sales close rate and cost. But for other marketers it may mean that inquiries will have to be further qualified by tele-marketing, additional direct mailings, or fulfillment package bounce-back cards before being passed on to the sales force.

Telemarketing

The basic functions of telephone marketing for inquiry qualification are to eliminate all nonprospects who have responded and to rank all prospects by degree of quality. This task should be performed by experienced outbound telemarketing communicators who call inquirers to ask very specific questions. The answers they get will determine whether the inquiry is worth more follow-up by direct mail or a telephone callback at a specified future time, or if the inquirer would be receptive to a visit by a salesperson.

Following are some key pieces of information that the telephone representative should try to identify:

- If the prospect intends to buy a particular product or service within a specified time period
- Who the key decision maker is within the prospect organization
- The size of the budget and whether it has been approved
- The prospect's application for the product
- The prospect's familiarity with the marketer's complete product line
- The competition under consideration
- Past use of product or similar products
- Purchase objectives
- Purchase selection guidelines
- Interest in testing the product
- Need for salesperson to call
- Actual commitment to see a salesperson

Trained telemarketing representatives, prepared with the right questions and replies to the inquirers' responses, have the best chance of eliciting a vast amount of meaningful information. This information not only can be passed directly on to salespeople for pinpointed follow-up but also enhances the marketer's prospect data base. (See Chapter 11 for more on telemarketing.)

The "Bounce-back" Card

Some marketers rely on the fulfillment package to further qualify inquiries. Designated offer material and another action response vehicle, usually a reply card "bounce-back," are sent to those inquirers who have responded to specific offers in inquiry-generation media. The purpose of the bounce-back card is to single out the more highly interested prospects. Prospects who respond to this fulfillment mailing are then passed on to the salespeople as qualified leads.

The number of inquiries that become qualified in this way will depend on the following key factors:

1. *Information given to the reader in the fulfillment material.* It must be persuasive, believable, and include enough facts to identify responders who will be seriously interested.

2. *The amount of information the prospect is asked to provide in the bounce-back card or form.* Generally the more information requested of the reader, the fewer cards that will be returned. Those returned, however, will provide valuable prospect profile data that identifies potential buyer status.

3. *Additional mailings to those inquirers who have not returned the bounce-back cards.* The evidence is positive that follow-up mailings to inquirers can pay off. A study in a *New Equipment Digest* article ("Profiting From Industrial Advertising Sales Leads," 1984, page 76) concludes, "You can almost double the number of leads you are able to qualify by making just one additional mailing after the initial fulfillment of the inquiry." Even more qualification cards will be returned when inquirers are asked to check the address label for any changes rather than fill out the name and address themselves. Figure 2-3 typifies a two-mailing bounce-back qualification procedure.

Many marketers feel they don't get enough bounce-back card leads. Too many potential purchasers will not respond, so increasing numbers of marketers employ the more personal, in-depth telemarketing techniques to qualify inquiries.

Field-Initiated Inquiry-Generation Programs

Making Programs Available From Headquarters
Periodically sending direct mail materials to salespeople and expecting them to somehow fit these materials into their current sales strategy has proven to be a futile exercise, especially for uninitiated business-to-business advertising managers. Highly organized, centrally coordinated direct mail programs seem to work best. These are structured long-term programs that include a collection of single mailing pieces or series of pieces designed to generate prospect inquiries for the products, systems, or services sold by the company or division.

The direct mail campaigns are created by professional business-to-business direct mail writers and designers and are tested in the mail before they are made available for field use. These campaigns are in envelopes or on magnetic tape at

Figure 2-3. A typical two-mailing bounce-back qualification procedure.

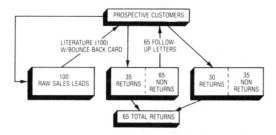

Source: Excerpt from "Profiting from Industrial Advertising Sales Leads," published by *New Equipment Digest* magazine, Penton/IPC Publishing, Cleveland, 1984. Used by permission.

a central location ready for processing and mailing to prospects in sales territories as requested by the field salespeople. Programs of this type permit the salespeople to integrate inquiry-generation direct mail into their own individual selling strategy on a day-to-day, week-to-week basis. With this procedure, the marketer controls the professionalism in the use of the medium by the field sales force, including the actual mailings made from a central facility.

There are two major conditions needed for this program to be successful. First is that headquarter's management provide field salespeople with a large enough collection of lead-building direct mail campaigns from which they can choose mailings that fit their own sales needs for the time period they specify. For some smaller sales organizations there may be a dozen appropriate campaigns "on the shelf." For larger companies, with multiple products and applications in multiple markets, dozens of campaigns may be in demand by the sales force.

The second condition needed for this centralized program to succeed is an easy procedure. The way to encourage salespeople to participate in a program like this is to establish ways that make it very simple to participate. Headquarters makes it easy when it takes the work of creating, producing, mailing, and fulfilling of direct mail materials out of the salesperson's hands and has these valuable services performed by a central service (either in-house or by a direct mail service firm). It is easy when local sales offices can elect to have one or more campaigns mailed to one or more target lists that they determine on the dates that they specify.

Lists

An important advantage of a centrally controlled field-initiated lead program is that sales offices can have access to the most current and appropriate lists. The home office direct-marketing planner can be of material help to the sales force by arranging with a major business list supplier to make local sales territory prospect lists available. List suppliers can extract from their compiled data banks or data bases specific SIC segments and other demographic selections for each of the marketer's sales territories. These then become lists for the sales offices to use for their own inquiry-building programs. Before initiating a mailing, salespeople should get a copy of the lists to examine, removing any names known to be nonprospects.

Field salespeople, of course, should be encouraged to develop their own lists for prospecting. However, very few will come up with better than average lists. When arranging for local mailings on their own, salespeople often resort to the Yellow Pages to compile their lists of prospects. There are four good reasons why salespeople should not use this directory for building a list:

1. There is much duplication.
2. There are no zip codes.
3. Some listings are not current.
4. Addresses can be incomplete.

Since Yellow Pages directories are only published annually, they can be more than 10 percent outdated at time of issue.

Some salespeople can, of course, come up with very good lists, but, as most business-to-business direct marketers will attest, only a small fraction of an average sales force has the aptitude, interest, and discipline to compile and maintain a good list.

Because the list quantity requirements of many local sales offices are small, minimum order charges make direct ordering by these local sales offices unaffordable. However, a central coordinator may arrange to have files and updates on an annual rental basis in the home office to expedite field-initiated direct mail requests.

Centralized systems give the salespeople free reign in determining target markets, mailings, and mailing dates. The fewer restrictions the better, but some mailing quantity guidelines are necessary to protect the salespeople from their own unbridled enthusiasm. Too many pieces mailed at one time can result in too many inquiries. For instance, if a two-person sales office requests the mailing of 4,000 pieces that produces a 3 percent response, 120 inquiries could be generated within a two-week period. Two salespeople cannot reasonably follow up this many leads. It is unrealistic to assume that salespeople can handle more than one or two new inquiries per day. One or two a week may be more appropriate for some organizations.

Pitfalls of Locally Controlled Programs

Some marketers encourage their field sales offices to initiate their own lead-building direct mail programs locally. Mailings may be prompted by a special binder sent to the salespeople by the home office containing suggested letters with guidelines on how and when salespeople may want to use them in mailings from their local offices. Aside from furnishing the letters, there is minimal intervention from the home office's advertising or marketing department.

About 10 to 15 percent of field sales organizations have experienced success with the use of direct mail and have learned to use it profitably. These salespeople know how to canvass by mail as well as communicate with current customers with the objective of keeping them sold. They instinctively know how to prepare their own direct mail and when to use it regardless of who controls the system. But most salespeople have little aptitude and little time for creating sales-support direct-mail advertising. Most find it much easier to make phone calls than to write letters.

The most common reason locally controlled direct mail programs fail to get the results expected is the lack of expertise of the field sales force in direct mail. Choosing an offer, developing a creative approach, and securing a mailing list may, on the surface, appear relatively easy to do, but one major mistake in any of these three areas can render the whole effort valueless.

The typical direct mailing originating from a field sales office is a letter, most often having multiple objectives. Although these letters purport to have lead-building objectives, they often more closely resemble sales presentations and image builders rather than prospect identifiers. Salespeople are not usually trained in the techniques of writing lead-generation direct mail.

Poor results also follow if the letters are sent to the wrong market segments or if a field salesperson rewrites direct mail letters and other materials professionally created by the advertising agency or headquarter's staff to fit his or her particular audience. This same lack of expertise is usually why there is no feedback on results. It is a major weakness of a system that is not controlled by a central coordinating responsibility.

Dealer Inquiry-Generation Programs

Some marketers who sell through dealers have special direct marketing programs similar to central field-initiated programs. Only appropriate for the sales of higher ticket items, these programs are centrally planned, controlled, and designed specifically for dealer organizations to use at the local level. They can enhance the relationship marketers have with their dealers.

These ongoing programs center around matching mailing list data with basic business list files such as those provided by Dun's Marketing Services. The marketer arranges with a list supplier to prepare a prospect availability report that will help assign geographic areas of sales responsibility.

The procedure in its basic form is simple. A list supplier provides the marketer with a list of counties nationwide. The marketer assigns a number for each county where there is assigned dealer representation. The list organization then prints out a prospect availability report for each dealer. From this report the marketer can learn what the prospect potential is in raw numbers in each marketing area.

As an added benefit the data indicate specific territories with weak or no sales coverage, which the marketer can then fill. The report lists the number of prospects available in the compiled universe. They are segmented into subgroups by type of business, size of company, title, or any of over a dozen different categories. A minimum of 50,000 names is fairly standard for a prospect report.

Participation by dealers is optional, and those who do participate can order inquiry-generation and other sales-support direct-mail campaigns and telemarketing scripts from the marketer. The list house provides mailing labels, manuscript listings, or three- by five-inch cards that include telephone numbers for dealer telephone follow-up to the mailing campaigns.

The cost of most programs of this type is shared 30 percent to 50 percent by the dealer and the marketer. This helps motivate the dealer to become involved, which in turn improves lead/sales conversion ratios. There is a base list charge on a per thousand basis. Additional charges are made for unlimited list use for 12 months, mailing labels and manuscript list, extra copies, telephone numbers, and a tape update if required. A total charge to a marketer for a prospect availability report involving 100,000 names and the necessary labels for four mailings plus a manuscript list can be over $150 per thousand, so when averaged for a four-time mailing, each mailing may run over $40 per thousand.

The value of such a program to an individual dealer depends, of course, on whether it meets the dealer's objectives. A simple feasibility analysis developed beforehand can reveal if there is a profit potential.

Card Decks for Inquiry Generation

Card decks are postcard-size cards in polypacks with 25 or more cards per pack. Most of the more than 650 deck publishers strive for 100 cards per pack and target nonconsumer market segments. When the audience targeted by the deck publishers resembles the marketer's customer profile, the marketer has the best chance of succeeding in getting inquiries with card decks.

A growing number of business-to-business marketers use card decks to generate inquiries. However, since it is only a marginal supplementary inquiry-generating medium, the card deck accounts for only a small fraction of inquiry volume for any one marketer. Inquiries generated from these response cards should be further qualified before being turned over to the sales force for follow-up. Qualification by telephone, or bounce-back card from the fulfillment package or another mailing, is necessary because of the low-quality inquiries these decks generate.

Card decks don't work for every marketer. But cost per inquiry can be affordable especially to those marketers who have generic business products. A successful card deck may be mailed four times or more a year. Readership depends on the headline and graphics. The top card in the deck gets best readership. Magazine publishers, book publishers, and other direct marketers find it advantageous to use the inquiries from advertising in these decks to add names to their own mailing lists.

PREQUALIFIED PROSPECT PENETRATION

Some inquirers who want further information by mail or telephone but do not want to see a salesperson (or want to maintain a low profile for other reasons) may still be excellent prospects. Especially when qualified by salespeople, these inquirers are logical candidates for prequalified prospect penetration, or door-opener direct-marketing campaigns. These campaigns attempt to set up serious face-to-face situation meetings between the marketer and the prospect.

It is important to distinguish between a highly qualified list of prospects and a prequalified list of prospects. Highly qualified prospects have not yet expressed an interest in the marketer's offer, product, or service, although they have the credentials in their profile that make them better than average candidates for sales. Mailings to this group are to identify interested prospects, as discussed in the previous section on inquiry generation.

Prequalified prospects are lists of bona fide prospects proven because they responded to a previous contact through direct mail, telephone, trade show, seminar, or personal field visit in ways that identify them as good potential customers. These are prequalified as key prospects, but for one reason or another, the salespeople have not been able to move them forward in the buying process.

Even though prequalified prospects may be few in number in any sales territory, their potential value to the marketer can be extremely high. Since this group of prospects does not respond to standard inquiry-generation offers, the marketer is challenged to use campaign techniques that overcome the barriers that prevent the salesperson from setting up a face-to-face meeting.

A series of three or more high-impact dimensionals is most often used to get needed attention and readership. The cost per prospect for these mailings and accompanying telephone follow-up is usually very high, especially when compared to inquiry-generation mailings. However, resulting incremental sales can net a marketer 50 times their promotional cost. Thus the marketer willingly will spend $50 to $100 per prospect to implement the campaign.

AWARENESS DIRECT MAIL ADVERTISING

Use of direct marketing in business-to-business extends beyond lead-getting functions into a concept called *relationship marketing.* Although only recently articulated in direct marketing industry literature, direct marketing has always been a strategic marketing objective for most business-to-business marketers. The objective of sales-support direct-mail awareness advertising or direct advertising is to build mind share through continuous mailings that foster solid relationships with customers and potential customers.

Awareness direct mail advertising is pure advertising that uses direct marketing media to accomplish its objectives. Whenever there is an advertising objective to get a greater share of mind, there is an opportunity to use awareness direct mail. Indeed, a continuing long-range objective all marketers should have is constant communication with their customers and key prospects to help salespeople establish and maintain healthy, long-term buyer-seller relationships.

The need for awareness direct mail advertising is highlighted by the fact that the customer and prospect marketplace has a short memory. Of the many studies done on "forgetfulness," the McGraw-Hill survey of manager's recall of advertisements is typical. Figure 2-4 shows that messages could not be remembered by 73 percent of the readers even with aided recall after 21 days.

Continuity is the key to its success. Awareness direct mail campaigns are scheduled mailings. Almost always in a series, similar to publication advertising campaigns, they are made in waves of usually no less than three in a three-month period. Weekly, biweekly, or monthly mailings for longer periods are best for many sales objectives.

General advertising goals for increasing awareness are mostly based on the reach and frequency parameters used in broad-based advertising planning. This kind of mass communication is too costly for business-to-business direct mail use. Therefore, some marketers prematurely dismiss the employment of direct mail as a viable awareness advertising medium. And, indeed, the cost of an advertisement per thousand (CPM) in a trade or business publication may be ten or fifteen times less than the cost of each thousand pieces of direct mail. But the *cost per reader* is the key figure. A comparison of the readership of publication ads and direct mail advertising shows that the cost per prospect reached in terms of readership can actually be less for direct mail (see Table 2-1).

Awareness direct mail is used most often to supplement print or other advertising programs. These mailings may be directed to all those best prospects in a sales territory who someday may be customers or sent when marketers want to ensure that specific sales messages get read by highly important segments of the marketplace.

Awareness campaigns are also sent to key customers and prospects located in geographic territories. Since many trade publications do not have regional editions, the marketer fills this need for image or product advertising with awareness direct

Figure 2-4. The curve of forgetting.

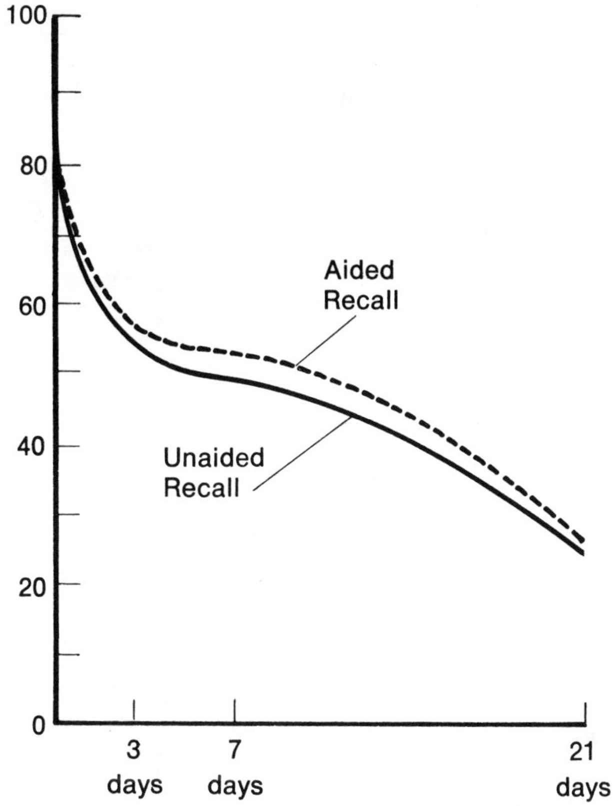

100 = 8 ads studied
Unaided Recall was 53% three days later,
49% one week later,
25% three weeks later.
Aided Recall was 55% three days
later, 53% one week later, 27%
three weeks later.

Source: McGraw-Hill Manager's Survey, McGraw-Hill Research Laboratory of Advertising Performance #5260.1, 1977. Used by permission.

mail advertising. Smaller companies that do not have national distribution find that advertising in national publications is wasteful. Awareness direct mail may be the only appropriate medium for these marketers since they can target any geographic or demographic segment they wish.

Awareness direct mail does its job best when sent to narrow and very selective target markets. For instance, an electrical components manufacturer may have a prospect marketplace of 30,000 consulting engineers targeted with a new product advertising program consisting of an eight-time ad schedule in one business and two monthly trade publications. An efficient buy for the marketer may reach 80 percent of the marketplace four times. To make sure that the most important

Table 2-1. Comparative cost per reader of trade publication
ad and direct mail piece.

Trade Publication		Direct Mail Piece	
Circulation	100,000	List	100,000
Issue exposure (80% of circulation)	80,000	Deliverable names (5% nixies)	95,000
Starch readership score (Read most, 12%)	9,600	Average readership (69%)	65,550
Cost for ad: page rate and preparation	$9,000	Cost in the mail	$450/M
Cost per reader	$0.94	Cost per reader	$0.69

people do not miss the ad messages, product-awareness direct-marketing campaigns containing similar messages may be sent to those 300, 1,200, or 5,000 key customers and prospects as added promotional support.

Before-and-after surveys measure the impact of an awareness direct mail program. A representative sample of the list used for the campaign will be asked questions that relate to the message before the campaign is mailed. The same questions are then asked of a different sample after all the mailings have been received. The changes in the responses from the first to the second survey can usually provide a reasonable measure of the impact of the campaign.

REINFORCED SELLING PROGRAMS

Another use of direct marketing that works well for the business-to-business marketer is to reinforce a planned sales call. Precall and postcall direct mail to prospects increases the salesperson's productivity on each face-to-face sales call. The objective of reinforced selling direct mail is based on what clinical psychologists have learned—most lasting impressions are received through the eye rather than the ear. Prospects are far more likely to remember what the salesperson has said when they can also read about it. This reinforced selling technique enables a salesperson to keep the number of contacts per prospect high while keeping the number of actual sales calls to a minimum, thus helping to control the cost of selling.

At any point a salesperson has about ten, fifteen, or perhaps twenty-five good potential customers to call on with the ultimate goal of closing a sale with each one. These are the salesperson's best prospects, many coming from direct-mail lead-generation efforts. Under pressure to meet and exceed sales quotas, the major portion of the salesperson's time and energy goes into selling efforts on those prospects. Salespeople employ all available tools and resources that can assist in bringing those potential sales to a close. To presell the prospect some send letters or literature with background information and reasons to buy the product. And salespeople also communicate with current customers with the objective of keeping them sold.

These individual efforts can be strengthened with a planned program of continuing sales messages that reinforce in writing what salespeople communicate to the prospect during their sales calls. These mailings are particularly helpful when:

- Products require a great deal of technical explanation
- A salesperson must make many calls a day to low potential prospects
- Weak sales territories need to be strengthened
- Prospects are in remote geographic areas

Like the field-initiated inquiry-generation program described earlier, reinforced selling programs can rely on the field salespeople to prepare their own material or can be centrally coordinated. Some companies have prepared dozens of different sample letters to cover many selling situations. These are housed in special binders for the salesperson's reference. These letters provide salespeople with professional guidance and ideas for them to adapt in the preparation of their own letters and other mail materials.

Some business-to-business marketers produce large quantities of printed direct mail materials with reinforced selling messages for field salespeople to mail out locally to key prospects they are currently calling on. The most successful reinforced selling programs are those centrally organized and integrated into the marketer's long-range strategic marketing plan. In these programs not only are the campaigns prepared by the marketer's central facility but mailed as well to the key prospect names.

DIRECT MAIL IN RESEARCH

Planners cannot expect to win too often shooting from the hip. And the need for research, of course, is not limited to any one segment in business. In most organizations, product or market research may be performed by various areas of management—a research director, marketing task force, product director, or general manager. But in some smaller companies there is usually little or no research available on which the direct marketing planner can base promotion strategies. The mail questionnaire sent to limited segments of the universe can help fill in the blanks. However, qualitative focus research sessions often precede the quantitative mail research surveys because new ideas and approaches that frequently result from focus sessions can affect the questions used in the questionnaire.

Asking questions of customers, prospects, and suspects through mail questionnaires has become a useful and relatively inexpensive method to learn more about the decision maker's company, product preferences, purchasing methods, and behavior. Research professionals aim for a response of at least 50 percent in order to have confidence that reliable projections can be made.

A follow-up telephone survey to samples of mail survey respondents and non-respondents provides a quality check on the questionnaire results, helping to remove any serious bias. Focus interview sessions are also used as a quality check of the mail questionnaire survey results.

Questionnaires are used to determine which product strategies to pursue first, which features and benefits to stress, which creative strategy is best, which customer profiles to target, and what the trends are in the marketplace. Although mail questionnaires do not have the in-depth quality aspect of personal interviews, surveys and mail questionnaires allow responses to come from a wider distribution with less geographic bias and without interview bias.

Incentives to Respond

A special incentive is often provided along with the questionnaire to increase response. Money is one of the most effective. A dollar bill taped to the letter accompanying the questionnaire continues to generate high response. As inflation shrinks the dollar, even higher denominations may be required to raise response to acceptable levels. The actual amount of money is not what provides the incentive as such, but rather the perceived value of coins or dollar bills and the guilt the reader associates with keeping the money while throwing away the questionnaire.

Functional items that may have use in an office, such as small keychains, knives, rulers, and pens, also do well in building response. Whatever premium is used, it should be tasteful, mailable, and light enough not to incur unreasonable postage. Some mailers offer to make a donation to the reader's favorite charity as an inducement to respond. Others use contests and offer cash prizes to randomly selected winners. When applicable, offers of a copy of the survey results can motivate readers to respond.

A successful direct mail questionnaire mailing begins with the use of the proper creative techniques in the cover letter, the printed questionnaire, and the reply vehicle.

The Cover Letter

The letter (on white stock) should be short and personalized if practical. A one-line salutation is as good as the company's full inside address. Copy contained in three or four paragraphs should be warm and friendly and in the style of a personal letter written from one businessperson to another. And it should mention the importance of the survey to the reader, giving the reader a reason to respond. It is interesting to observe how many businesspeople will respond to a "request for a favor." Copy emphasis should be on the value the survey will have in adding to the bank of knowledge in the industry, if it applies.

The letter should tell the reader exactly what to do. ("Simply place the completed questionnaire in the preaddressed and stamped envelope.") A guarantee of the confidentiality of the information requested must be mentioned in the letter. The P.S. can be used to highlight the premium if there is one. The premium usually is described as a token, something that may be "given to a youngster you know," sent in appreciation for participating in the survey.

The signature on the letter can be important if the organization sponsoring the survey is a prestigious name in the industry. A "blind" survey is used when the appearance of the marketer's name may bias results. To lend credibility to the questionnaire and get more response, a marketer may arrange for the survey to be made in conjunction with an industry association. In this case, the association's name may appear on the letterhead.

The same layout principles used for effective direct mail letters certainly apply to the letter that accompanies a survey questionnaire. (See Chapter 8 for more on direct mail letters.) Liberal white space in left- and right-hand margins and at the bottom is always appropriate. If a marketer wants a reader to take time to complete and return a questionnaire, it should be perceived as a quality survey enhanced by good cover letter reproduction and paper stock.

The Printed Questionnaire Form

In their eagerness to gather a great deal of information at one time from a single survey, some marketers load the form with more questions than an average respondent will answer in one sitting. When more questions are asked, fewer questionnaires will be returned. Five or six simple, easy-to-understand questions are ideal. Open-ended questions make it difficult for the reader to answer. However, where open-ended questions cannot be avoided, providing limited space in which a response can be written minimizes their formidable appearance. True/false, multiple choice, and one-word answers are best. When multiple choice answers are asked for, including a space for "other" brings in added information without affecting the response.

In an attempt to make sure questions are not ambiguous, writers new to the task often construct complex and verbose questionnaires. Also, leading questions and bias have a tendency to creep in when questionnaires are not constructed by a research professional. If mail questionnaires or telephone survey approaches are prepared by nonresearch personnel, it will be money well spent by the marketer to have the questions examined by a professional with survey expertise.

Questionnaires can be of any size but the smaller sizes give the appearance of being easier to fill out. A color paper stock for the questionnaire that is different from the letter and envelope usually pulls more response. Graphics, if needed at all, should not be used for decoration but only to enhance an understanding of the questions. To ensure a contemporary appearance and to make it inviting to the reader, it is best to get input from a professional layout artist.

When longer questionnaires are necessary, it is especially helpful to include a first or second question that would be of special interest to the reader even though the answers may be of no use to the marketer. Also, questionnaire response usually suffers when the reader is asked to indicate a ranking of items, when questions of a highly confidential nature about company finances are asked, when technical terminology or jargon is used, and when respondents are asked to identify themselves. Questions that can provoke more general answers or ranges of choice are best.

The Reply Vehicle

The letter, questionnaire, and number 9 return envelope, which ensures privacy, should be placed in a white number 10 envelope with first-class postage. Postage stamps affixed to the envelope give the impression of being more personal, less commercial, and seem to work better than prepaid printed indicia. Air-mail postage, when appropriate, helps indicate urgency. Response can be increased when respondents get advance notice that a questionnaire will be coming.

SPECIAL CONSIDERATIONS FOR LEAD-GENERATION PROGRAMS

There are a number of key factors the business-to-business marketer must analyze when structuring a lead-generation program. These are:

- Prospects' buying behavior cycle
- Number of leads to generate
- Mailing frequency
- Acceptable cost per lead
- Acceptable promotion and selling cost per sale

Buying Behavior Cycle

A primary objective of most inquiry-generation campaigns is to select from the customer and prospect marketplace those who are at the stage in their buying behavior cycle when it would be most appropriate for a salesperson to make a call. This will vary depending on an individual marketer's selling strategy. At any point in time, decision makers are at one stage or another in this cycle. (For supplies and similar products, of course, the marketer knows the prospect has a continuing need that is filled through ordering schedules triggered periodically.) It is important for the direct mail planner to recognize the various stages and apply the most favorable direct marketing programs to develop inquiries.

1. *Need.* The cycle usually starts when decision makers begin to realize they have a need for the product or service. It is possible that an appropriately convincing direct mail piece followed by an equally convincing telemarketing call could be what provoked a prospect into realizing he or she has a need. However, establishing a need in the prospect's mind is not the objective of business-to-business lead-generation direct mail. Developing what amounts to primary demand for a product or service requires time and is usually most successfully initiated by market leaders. Awareness direct marketing and advertising campaigns most often assist in getting this job done before lead-building efforts begin.

2. *Want.* The want stage develops when decision makers realize some action will have to be taken at a future date. This is when prospective buyers think generally about what the want is and what must be done to satisfy it.

3. *Covert action.* During the covert action period decision makers get serious, seek information, and develop approximate purchase timetables.

4. *Overt action.* The overt action stage begins when the decision makers get to the threshold of taking buying action. This occurs when they start talking to suppliers and vendors, arranging for proposals and quotations. Salespeople really appreciate sales leads that identify specific prospects who are at this stage—those who are serious and ready to buy.

For complex industrial products or systems, the realization of the need might come a year or even two before buying action is taken. And for others, buying action may come six months or only one month after the need is realized.

Sophisticated marketers prepare their own marketplace buying behavior analyses for their own products. Direct mail planners lean on these to come up with the kind of offers, copy approaches, and formats needed to generate the right number and quality of inquiries for the different stages from their specific target list segments. Some products dictate the need to get salespeople into the prospect's place of business as early as possible in the cycle, when the decision maker first identifies the want. Aggressive use of direct mail and telemarketing, integrated with personal selling efforts of field salespeople, can accelerate the movement of the cycle.

Different kinds of offers will identify prospects at different stages. If the marketer wants to provoke response from decision makers early in the cycle—those who have recently found they have a need for the product or service—some generic or elementary but pertinent information can be chosen as the offer. When inquiries come from potential first-time users of the product, chances are they will be looking for some basic information found in booklets and general sales literature that discuss benefits and functions. When further along in the cycle they seek more specific "Here's what we can do for you" offers.

Marketers who sell high-cost products, such as complex hardware and software systems that involve a lengthy selling process, will include offers of surveys, extensive demonstrations, proposals, and trial runs to get inquiries coming in at the early stages of the buying behavior cycle. That is when many of these decision makers lock in their choices of vendor candidates, and for some marketers it pays to be involved that long. But, for marketers of lower-priced products, the selling expense is prohibitive. These marketers need to identify in their marketplaces those buyers closer to placing an order. A product-specific or company-specific offer will bring in that type of inquirer.

Lead Generation in a Lead-Building Program

The development of too many leads for a sales organization to follow results in irritated salespeople, and even more damaging, mishandled customers and prospects. For some organizations, especially those selling high-ticket items or systems that involve a great amount of presale or postsale time, leads can be followed only when time permits. As many leads as can be handled without waste should be the goal.

Field sales managers are in the best position to tell the lead-generation planner the number of sales leads that can be handled adequately in individual sales territories because they know the salespeople's capabilities, which can vary widely within a company as well as from one company to another. The better salespeople are much more adept, of course, at converting leads into sales.

A survey of field sales management needs by the lead program planner is a vital preliminary step in lead-generation program development. This survey should spell out specific offers and creative approaches that generate a range of inquiry quality. The survey should also focus on the differences of lead costs and how they relate to quantity versus quality. Salespeople themselves are usually not that interested in lead costs or promotion costs per product sold since they don't control the profit center. But the sales manager is interested. The lead program planner and sales management must agree on the specific inquiry quality that will result from the response promotions and qualification procedures.

An effective method of getting sales management's understanding and agreement on the optimum level of inquiry quality is to simulate a half dozen or more business reply cards or other response promotion formats with different offers ranging from high to low quality, and then to review each with field sales managers, asking which in the array would produce a sales lead that the manager would accept. Without this input the planner may have difficulty committing to a specified number of the kind of leads the field sales force would want for follow-up.

Mailing Frequency

It is important for marketers planning their inquiry-generation programs to know how many times mailings can continue to produce profitable responses from the same prospect marketplace. The only sure way to determine this is through experience or testing various time intervals. The frequency of inquiry-generation mailings may be influenced by interest turnover of the product.

Normally, products in their introductory stages develop more marketplace interest. When the product's life cycle is in the ascent or descent stage, it is difficult to get a good reading on the number of mailings that can be made during a predetermined future period. Most expendable products such as business supplies have high interest turnover. Here buying frequency is greater since purchases are made perhaps every few months. Another reason buying frequency and interest turnover can be high is because every week in every market there are those buyers who are unhappy with their present supplier. However, marketers who sell high-cost, long-term-use products, such as scientific or multipurpose computer systems, naturally find buying frequency low.

Interest turnover of a product is also affected by personnel changes in prospective customer companies. New replacement buyers are eager to investigate new sources and respond positively to lead-building offers.

Analyzing the Cost Effectiveness of Lead-Generation Programs

For some marketers the cost of generating leads, along with concomitant selling costs, may be too high to sustain an ongoing lead-generation direct-marketing program. Therefore, determining the feasibility of such a program must be done for each major product family at an early stage. Some business marketers are able to generate acceptable inquiries from trade and business publications and postcard decks on a continuing basis. However, direct mail is the predominant medium for most business-to-business marketers for inquiry generation.

Before implementing an ongoing program the marketer first looks at:

- *Cost per thousand direct mail pieces.* Although direct mail has had a reputation of being a high cost per inquiry medium, its efficiency makes it cost effective for most programs. And the average cost per inquiry is only about one-tenth of the cost of a personal sales call.
- *Anticipated response.* A high response can be meaningless in some sales-support lead-generation programs. The objectives of the program will determine the kind of response wanted. The number of inquiries that can convert to a sale is the measure of their real value to the marketer.
- *Closure rate.* It takes more than one inquiry to make a sale. The closure rate is dependent on the quality of the sales force as well as the quality of the lead.
- *Average unit selling price of the product.* This figure is the average amount that comes from one sale as a result of the promotion.

In some companies an average sale may consist of three or four product units and include accessories and supplies. For others a single product per sale may be average. There are many products that cannot be sold profitably by salespeople even with a sales lead program because the selling price of the product cannot cover selling costs and allow a profit (see Table 2-2).

For example, a marketer may get a 2.4 percent response on a $450 per thousand direct mail effort, and a closure rate by the salespeople of one sale out of eight

Table 2-2. Sample of selling and lead cost.

Unit selling price	$3,000
Sales calls needed to make a sale (lead/sales conversion ratio ⅛)	8
Lead response expected (2.4%)	24
Total mailing pieces needed to produce required leads	1,000
Direct mail cost per thousand	$450
Direct mail lead cost per sale ($18.75 × 8 leads)	$150
Lead cost as a percentage of selling price	5%
Cost of personal sales call	$245
Calls needed to convert 10 leads into 1 sale (8 + 2 extra)	10
Sales cost, personal sales calls	$2,450
Total selling and lead cost	$2,600
Selling and lead cost as a percentage of selling price	87%

inquiries. Computed on an average unit sale price of $3,000, this promotion would result in a direct mail cost per sale of $150 or 5 percent of the unit selling price. On the surface, this appears acceptable until the cost of the salesperson's face-to-face follow-up calls is included. If $245 is assumed as an average cost of a salesperson's call, a total of $2,450 in selling costs would have to be allocated for the sales calls on eight prospects to find the one who will buy, plus two more calls needed to complete the sale. In this example it is obvious that it takes a total of $2,600 in promotional and personal selling costs to sell one $3,000 product ($2,450 plus $150). That amounts to 87 percent of the selling price. The personal selling effort is the dominant cost as it is in most lead-to-sales equations. The cost of personal sales calls averages around $1,000 per sale. Cost of selling is the largest single item of expense for many marketers today.

In the example the personal selling cost could no doubt have been cut in half by using telephone marketing inquiry qualification. If all direct mail inquiries were qualified by telephone with an objective of weeding out the worst half before sending them to the salespeople, one sale out of four inquiries could be expected. And this could have been accomplished with an additional cost for qualification of about $15 per inquiry, or $120 per sale, resulting in a selling and lead cost totaling 58 percent of the selling price.

A review of another example in Table 2-3 will illustrate this strategy in more depth and with a higher unit price, providing additional figures that have a direct relationship to the feasibility of a projected lead-generation program. Each item in the table is discussed below.

1. *Unit selling price.* Higher profit margins on higher-priced industrial products allow marketers of these products to justify higher cost prospecting. The unit selling price used in the example is a hefty $30,000, although it is at the low end of most capital equipment price ranges.

2. *Sales volume objective.* This dollar value may be a quarterly, semiannual, or annual objective and should be computed for the entire sales force and any segment in it. In most companies individual sales volume quotas will vary. In the example, it is assumed that a sales objective for one salesperson is $162,500 during the plan period.

3. *Sales needed to reach objective.* The number of sales required to reach the marketing objective is found simply by dividing the sales volume objective by the unit selling price. In the example, 5.4 sales will be needed.

4. *Number of leads needed to make one sale.* This figure is more difficult to assess. The number of prospects called on in order to make a sale depends on the quality of the lead in relation to the quality of the sales organization. Once a lead program is well underway, experience will indicate more on-target assumptions. Usually, the higher the unit price, the longer it takes to close a sale. In the example, the assumption is that one sale will result from following up on each of the 10 sales leads.

5. *Number of leads needed.* Multiplying the individual sales objective of 5.4 sales by the number of sales calls it will take to make one sale gives the number of leads needed to reach the objective. In the example, the goal is 54 leads.

Table 2-3. Sample of sales-lead program-feasibility analysis.

Key Objectives and Assumptions	
Unit selling price	$30,000
Sales volume objective	$162,500
Sales needed to reach objective	5.4
Sales calls needed to make a sale (lead/sales conversion ratio 1/10)	10
Leads needed to reach objective	54
Response expected	2%
Total mailing pieces needed to produce required leads	2,700
Times a 2% response can be produced when mailing to market segment within plan period	4
List size required	675
Direct mail cost per thousand	$500
Total direct mail cost	$1,350
Cost per lead	$25
Cost of personal sales calls	$245
Calls needed to convert 10 leads into 1 sale (10 + 2 extra)	12
Sales cost, personal sales calls	$2,940
Cost per 10 leads	$250
Total selling and lead cost	$3,190
Selling and lead cost as a percentage of selling price	10.6%

6. *Percent response expected.* Most direct marketing professionals won't venture a guess about response for an average mailing because any number of variables can cause it to fluctuate from .05 percent to 4 percent or 8 percent, or higher. Yet, experience gained from mailing enough similar offers to the same or similar marketplaces will provide the marketer with average response rate guidelines. The first-time mailer will of necessity do more testing at the start. In the example, the marketer assumes that a 2 percent response rate can be expected as a result of mailing a very specific offer to a well-defined marketplace.

7. *Total mailing pieces needed.* Dividing 54 leads by the anticipated response rate of 2 percent provides the planner with the number of mailing pieces it will take to accomplish the objective. In the example, 2,700 pieces will be needed.

8. *Frequency of mailing.* Another important estimate is the number of times a mailing effort to the same market segment can produce the same response within a plan period. The marketer's experience during the first year of the program can establish valuable mailing frequency guidelines. In the example, four is considered a reasonable number of mailings that can be made to the same list, each time producing a 2 percent response.

9. *List size.* Dividing the total number of mailing pieces needed by the mailing frequency required to reach the inquiry objective, the marketer determines the list size needed. In the example, a universe of 675 prospects mailed four times during the plan period will produce the number of inquiries a salesperson needs to reach the sales volume objective. Mailings would be spaced evenly, weekly or semiweekly, throughout the plan period to ensure an even flow of inquiries. If the plan period is for twelve months, then the list of 675 prospects would turn over every three months.

10. *Direct mail cost.* The example shows a $500/thousand cost of direct mail, which covers all costs—creativity, printing, lists, overhead, postage, and mailing. These costs also reflect elaborateness of the package, degree of personalization, quantity of mailing pieces, and class of postage. The total direct mail cost is simply the result of applying the direct mail cost per thousand to the number of mailing pieces needed to produce the required inquiries. In the example the total direct mail cost is $1,350. The cost of an inquiry is found by dividing the total direct mail cost by the number of inquiries needed. In the example the cost of an inquiry is $25.

11. *Cost of a personal sales call.* Two business publishers—Sales Marketing and Management (SM&M) and McGraw-Hill—conduct and publish surveys periodically on the cost of the face-to-face personal sales call. SM&M figures do not include the cost of field sales management and therefore are lower than McGraw-Hill's totals. The McGraw-Hill 1987 survey results reported $251.63 as the cost of an average sales call (see Figures 2-5 and 2-6). Experienced marketers know the personal sales call cost figures for their own sales organization. As seen from the McGraw-Hill survey, this figure varies, depending on size of company, geographic location, products sold, and the complexity of the specific selling process in particular industries. In Table 2-3 a sales call cost of $245 is used.

12. *Total sales calls.* Once a sale is made it often takes more calls to follow through on the sale. In Table 2-3 two calls have been added to the ten original calls. A total of twelve calls, then, are estimated as needed to make the sale. (For the sake of clarity, the table presents an oversimplification of the actual selling process. Most often, if ten inquiries are followed up by salespeople with face-to-face calls, perhaps four or five inquiries will be pursued, requiring one or more additional calls before a sale to one of them is concluded.)

13. *Total personal sales call costs.* Twelve sales calls at $245 result in a total personal sales call cost of $2,940.

14. *Cost for ten sales inquiries.* The total cost for ten sales leads at $25 each is $250.

15. *Total selling and inquiry costs.* Personal sales call costs of $2,940 for one sale added to the cost of the ten inquiries of $250 equals $3,190 for selling and inquiry cost.

16. *Selling and inquiry cost as a percentage of selling price.* Dividing the total selling and inquiry cost by the unit selling price and multiplying by 100 represents the total selling and promotion costs as a percentage of the selling price. The figure given in the table is 10.6 percent, which can be affordable for many marketers.

Figure 2-5. Increase in cost of a business-to-business industrial sales call.

The cost of a face-to-face sales call on a business-to-business company rose to $251.63 in 1987. A McGraw-Hill Research analysis of 797 vice presidents of sales and sales managers shows that personal selling costs increased 9.5% between 1985 and 1987.

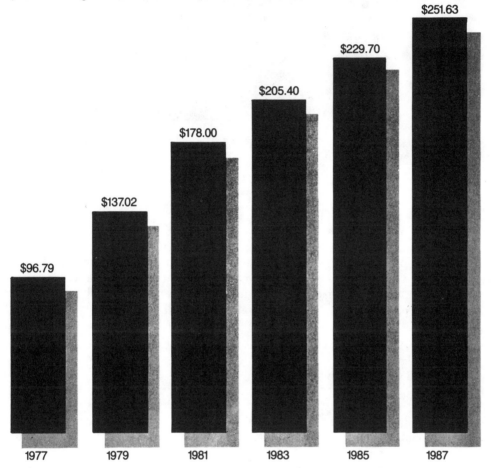

Note: Survey based on an nth sample of vice-presidents of sales and sales managers in industrial companies drawn from the circulation list of *Business Marketing* magazine.

Source: McGraw-Hill Research Laboratory of Advertising Performance #8013.9, 1987 "Cost of an Industrial Sales Call" survey. Used by permission of McGraw-Hill Publications Company.

Yet, this analysis is only the first half of the lead-generation process for those business-to-business marketers who want to get more productivity from their field-selling organization. If salespeople have only a one-out-of-ten sales/lead closure rate, perhaps it is because they are following up raw inquiries rather than bona fide sales leads.

Inquiry qualification is the second half of the lead-generation process. Direct mail coupled with telemarketing qualification strategies allow emphasis to be

Figure 2-6. Size of sales force impacts on face-to-face selling costs.

Economies of scale are evident with larger sales forces. As the size of the sales force increases, the cost per call decreases. The chart below shows average sales call costs by size of sales force for 1985 and 1987.

Size of Sales Force	Cost of Business-to-Business Sales Call (1985)	(1987)
Fewer than 10	$254.40	$281.00
10-50	$202.10	$225.80
More than 51	$176.10	$179.70
Average	$229.70	$251.63

Source: McGraw-Hill Research Laboratory of Advertising Performance #8013.9, 1987 "Cost of an Industrial Sales Call" survey. Used by permission of McGraw-Hill Publications Company.

concentrated on the most potentially profitable segments of the market in ways not available with other media. However, the degree of qualification is critical here. If qualification standards are too high, conversion rates will improve substantially, but the number of resulting sales leads will be very low. In Table 2-3 the objective set for inquiry qualification is to enable the salesperson to close the same number of sales but at almost half the personal selling cost.

Telemarketing Lead-Qualification Costs

The marketer may elect to put a telemarketing lead-qualification plan to work using professional telephone communicators to call all 54 inquirers resulting from the direct mail campaign. Their goal would be to determine the 27 most qualified inquirers out of the 54.

When the telemarketing communicators identify the half that are the better leads, these would then be turned over to the sales organization with the expectation that one out of five instead of one out of ten could be converted (see Table 2-4). The salesperson's productivity is doubled.

Telemarketing lead-qualification costs at $15 per call to the 54 inquirers total $810. When this qualification cost is divided by the number of sales needed to reach the sales volume objective, 5.4, telemarketing qualification costs per sale total $150. Sales lead and qualification cost per sale then becomes $400 when this figure is added to the direct mail inquiry cost of $250.

Table 2-4 shows how applying telemarketing inquiry qualification cuts sales call costs almost in half. Personal sales calls to follow up five leads plus two extra sales calls to solidify the sale now total $1,715 ($245 × 7 = $1,715). This, added to the lead cost per sale of $400, results in total costs for selling and lead

Table 2-4. Feasibility analysis for telemarketing
inquiry qualification.

Objective: Identify the 50% of the inquiries *that are most qualified in Table 2-3.*	
Cost of telemarketing 54 calls @ $15	$810
Telemarketing cost per lead	$30
Telemarketing cost per sale	$150
Direct mail inquiry cost per sale	$250
Sales lead and qualification cost per sale	$400
Sales call cost (7 × $245)	$1,715
Total direct marketing and sales call costs	$2,115
Selling and lead cost as a percentage of selling price	7.5%

generation of $2,115. The net savings per sale of $1,075 ($3,190 − $2,115) could logically be credited to the qualification procedure.

Of course, identifying specifically the better half of direct mail inquiries is not the only way, nor is it necessarily the best way, to use telemarketing qualification strategy. Most marketers consider it more practical to establish specific telemarketing qualification criteria that will single out the optimum quality/quantity sales leads to be turned over to the sales force.

Table 2-4 does make it obvious, however, that inquiry qualification—whether performed up front in the original inquiry development mailing or performed as a second or subsequent step in the sales lead-generation process—is the key to improving the salesperson's productivity and the company's profit.

Ultimate refinement of the inquiries through qualification techniques can theoretically disqualify all inquirers except those ready to make a purchase, giving the salesperson following up a 100 percent hit record. However, the lead planner should not screen the inquiries so finely that prospects who are close but not at the buying threshold never get exposed to the selling talents of the salespeople. This would, in effect, render the salesperson little more than an order taker.

SUMMARY

Direct marketing planners must analyze products and markets as well as current marketing, sales, and advertising objectives. The major uses of sales support direct marketing are:

- Identifying prospects
- Getting prequalified prospects to agree to a sales call
- Building company and product awareness
- Reinforcing a planned sales call
- Research

Inquiries must be qualified by meeting certain established criteria to increase their chances of being converted into a sale when in the hands of a salesperson. Even though there are many business lists to choose from, the more qualified lists are smaller and more expensive to assemble. Mail planners can fine-tune mailings by using hardener and softener techniques that will generate the optimum quantity and quality of inquiries.

"Bounce-back" cards included in fulfillment packages sent to inquirers single out the more highly interested prospects when returned. Telemarketing inquiry qualification gets a vast amount of meaningful information from the prospect. This determines the quality level of the inquiry, and when sufficiently qualified, increases the salesperson's interest in following up.

Before planning an ongoing lead-generation program, the business-to-business marketer first makes an analysis of key factors:

- Quality of inquiry to be identified
- Prospect's buying behavior cycle
- Number of sales leads to generate
- Mailing frequency
- Acceptable promotion and selling cost per sale

The initiation of field sales in lead-development and reinforced-selling direct-mail programs is most successful when the programs are centrally organized. This takes the creating, producing, mailing, and fulfillment out of the salespeople's hands but lets them determine what gets mailed, when it gets mailed, and to whom it gets mailed.

Indirect-response sales-support direct marketing helps sales people maintain healthy long-term buyer-seller relationships through direct mail opportunities to build name and product awareness in key target markets. Reinforced-selling direct-mail programs help reduce the cost of selling by supplementing personal sales calls to prospects who are close to the buying threshold.

The mail questionnaire is a valuable, inexpensive marketing research tool used by business-to-business marketers to learn more about the customer's company, product, preferences, and purchasing methods.

3

MAIL ORDER DIRECT MARKETING

Historically, the greatest use of mail order direct marketing has been by direct response marketers making mass mailings to millions of consumers. Their counterparts in business-to-business firms who have mass markets across the entire business spectrum are relatively few in number, but they are growing. In fact, even though mail order direct marketing has been used as a distribution channel for many years, it is only recently that business-to-business marketers have learned the techniques for using it with maximum effect.

WHO THE PLAYERS ARE

There are basically four groups of business-to-business mail order marketers:

1. Business supplies mail order specialty marketers who sell software, forms, furniture, and office specialties, mainly through catalogs.
2. Business service mail order specialty marketers who sell information, communication, air freight services, and trade publication subscriptions. These firms generally use solo mail and, like the business supplies group, they sell across horizontal markets.
3. Industrial maintenance, medical-pharmaceutical, and industry-specific products.
4. Divisions and business units of multichannel companies that can no longer

afford salespeople to sell supplies, accessories, aftermarket, and other low-end products—the largest group of the four.

The last two groups target both vertical and horizontal customer and prospect markets mostly through catalogs.

TYPES OF MAIL ORDER MARKETERS

Solo Mail Order

The two main formats for mail order direct mail are solo direct mail and catalogs. Solo mail attempts to sell only one item or a small group of related items in the one mailing package. Each mailing must pay its way by the profit projections resulting from orders received. Solo mail order direct mail continues as the dominant mail use found in the businessperson's in-box.

For business-to-business mail order offers to be worthwhile the individual marketer must earn a large enough profit in a reasonably sized market in relation to overall marketing goals. For instance, a small specialty marketer may be very satisfied with the sales results generated from two or three mailings to a narrow marketplace if they provide the bulk of his or her total annual business. The same effort for a multichannel marketer in the context of the total operation may not be worth the time and effort of management.

The mail order channel with its continuing contacts often helps the multichannel manufacturer get "mind-share" among those who receive these promotions. These contacts, in effect, presell prospects by implication on the value of the marketer's other products that may be sold by a different distribution channel.

Catalogs

Catalogs essentially have the same marketing objectives as solo mailings but, of course, include any number of products for the buyer to select from the one mailing. There are two kinds of business-to-business mail order catalog marketers. One is the mail order specialty marketer whose only channel of selling is through catalogs. Other catalogers are marketers who in effect run divisions or business units of multichannel business-to-business companies. These companies sell the same or different products through several distribution channels to the same or different markets. However, even though the mail order catalog operation in these organizations initially or subsequently becomes a separate distribution channel, it remains as only one selling strategy of a larger division or corporate marketing plan.

Prime examples of these business-to-business catalogers are the high-tech marketers, such as IBM, DEC, and NCR, and the information and communication companies such as McGraw-Hill and AT&T. Their direct marketing strategies, although influenced by their profit center discipline, also have to conform to the corporate marketing plan. With some companies this can be restrictive.

One Fortune 500 corporation after another had been finding it no longer could afford to sell supply items to its gigantic user base except through sales office walk-ins, threatening loss of share of this important aftermarket. Catalog programs not only reestablished the supply businesses as profitable for many of these companies but in the process profit opportunities were expanded by their marketing other manufacturers' related products wherever appropriate through these catalogs.

Often business-to-business catalogs start out with a single product line as originally sold or distributed by the company before the mail order channel is used. If successful, other related third-party lines are added. The NCR catalog is an example. It began with paper and ink ribbons for retail cash registers, and expanded into magnetic tape and assorted computer supplies in multicatalog releases of 120 pages, selling office furniture, retail marking devices, and a broad line of data processing, business-oriented supplies.

Creating a new channel of selling through catalogs that does not somehow disrupt existing channels is unusual, however. Conflicts can arise when a multi-channel marketer attempts to sell the same products in a catalog that the sales-people continue to sell in conjunction with the sale of standard line, higher-priced products. To prevent antagonizing a valuable sales force, some marketers design special commission systems that reward salespeople on catalog sales in their territory or assigned accounts.

Digital Equipment Corporation, for instance, had as an objective for its catalog operation the development of an easy way for customers to get what they needed—quick turnaround time on orders of aftermarket products. Since dealers could also sell the same products, conflicts between the dealer salespeople and the catalog operation were resolved by limiting distribution of the catalog to users only and by allowing the DEC salespeople to deliver the catalog to their accounts. In this case, since DEC salespeople were not on a commission remuneration system, there was no real conflict between the selling organization and the direct catalog operation.

Virtually all of these multichannel marketer catalog operations function as profit centers and do not have a reporting relationship to the head of an advertising or communications staff division. This is not the case, however, for a great number of catalogs that are essentially buyers' guide booklets or manuals that include product descriptions and photographs. They lack the benefit copy and elaborate illustrations, persuasive sales story, and prices needed for them to be bona fide mail order catalogs. Most are designed for prospect and customer buyers who are familiar with the products represented. Catalogs created and produced with ad-vertising budget dollars consist primarily of sales support material and do not have mail order objectives.

The sales support catalog is an extension of the complete product line sales-promotion catalog that is still used by many firms today as a selling tool for the field salespeople, reps, dealers, and distributors who leave it with customers and prospects when they make calls. Since it is an adjunct to personal selling and not a completely different selling process, it is not classified as a mail order catalog. As with any direct-marketing mail order effort, the catalog itself must perform all the selling functions, including the final step of asking for the order.

Most business-to-business mail order catalogs are designed as booklets to be retained in a file for future reference. They range in size from mini catalogs of

3¾ inches by 5¾ inches, as can be found in business-to-business card decks and package inserts, to the standard pages of 8⅜ inches by 11¾ inches. For example, the Inmac computer equipment and supplies catalog that is published monthly, which has a reputation for being the early standard in the computer supplies field, contains over 200 pages an issue.

GROWTH OF BUSINESS-TO-BUSINESS MAIL ORDER MARKETING

One outstanding strength of mail order catalogs and solo mailings is the convenience provided to the buyer. When business or industrial buyers can eliminate time and effort required to make a needed purchase they will opt for the most efficient and expedient method, providing the price is right. Other factors that contribute to this segment's growth include:

■ An immediate action vehicle in the form of a toll-free number, to some extent the credit card option, and the purchaser's option to review product details and photographs when time permits
■ The fact that business-to-business mail order marketers are in the forefront of innovative marketing, building regional outlets for better and faster service, providing toll-free hot lines, and establishing joint ventures with third-party service organizations
■ The liberal guarantees that mail order marketers promote in their mailings
■ Reasonably dependable products and services

A major reason for the growth of this channel of selling by business firms is the hefty $251 average individual sales call cost, coupled with more affordable computerization capabilities and the business-to-business buyer's improved perception of mail order purchasing. When it takes five sales calls to sell a $1,000 product, there is nothing left for costs of goods, overhead, and profit. In fact, in many business-to-business organizations such costs may preclude the use of salespeople for products under $3,000 or even higher.

Virtually all of the Fortune 500 companies over the past several years have experimented with mail order direct marketing. And many of them are now using it as another channel of distribution. The majority of these direct marketers sell lower-priced products. The fast growing business supplies and business services categories now total $3.7 billion and $4.9 billion in sales respectively. A few marketers talk of bringing in single orders upward of $50,000 via the mail or telephone. It is estimated that sales by mail of office supplies will increase 38 percent in the five-year period from 1984 to 1989, according to the National Office Products Association.

Arnold Fishman, director of research, *Direct Marketing Magazine,* has reported that business and industrial mail-order specialty marketers, those who use mail order as their major selling channel, accounted for an estimated $10 billion in sales in 1985. The industrial mail order category is sluggish with only $1.3 billion in sales.

"Generalized" mail order marketers, those for which mail order is only one selling channel of their marketing mix, account for over $25 billion in mail order

Figure 3-1. Mail order sales: business products and services.

	Mail Order Sales ($MM's)	# Businesses	% Of Mail Order Sales
A. Business Supplies:			
Business Supplies: Data Processing Oriented	750	30	2
Computer Software	940	—	3
Business Supplies Full Line	450	60	1
Business Forms: Full Line	270	20	1
Stationery Specialties: Non-Professional	230	40	1
Office Advertising Specialties/ Executive Gifts	200	50	1
Office Equipment Specialties: Appliance/Machines/Filing	270	50	1
Office Furniture	120	20	*
Business Specialties: Libraries & Schools	80	20	*
Stationery/Equipment Specialties: Professional	180	40	*
Office Specialties: Scheduling/Recordkeeping Systems	90	20	*
Art/Drafting/Printing Supplies	80	180	*
Total	3,660	530	10
B. Business Services:			
Information	1,600	30	6
Communications	1,850	10	5
Trade Publication Subscriptions	320	—	1
Air Freight	730	10	2
Mailing List Services	390	—	1
Total	4,890	50 +	14
C. Industrial			
Industry/Functional Specific	550	170	2
Industrial Maintenance/ Materials Handling	560	40	2
Medical/Pharmaceutical	230	50	1
Total	1,340	260	5
D. Generalized Mail Order Marketers			
(Mail Order as part of the overall selling channel mix of multichannel industrial marketers not specializing in mail order selling)	25,200	—	72
Total Business Products and Services	35,090		100

* less than 1%

Business Products And Services of mail order sector sales consists of sales of Specialty Mail Order marketer segments (28 percent), made up of companies for which mail order is a major selling channel, and of Generalized Mail Order marketers (72 percent), made up of companies for which mail order is part of the overall mix of marketing and selling.

Business Supplies and Services (86%) compared to Industrial Supplies (14%) dominate Specialty Business Marketing.

Source: Arnold Fishman, *Direct Marketing Magazine,* September 1986. Courtesy of *Direct Marketing Magazine,* 224 7th Street, Garden City, NY 11530.

sales. This group of industrial marketers accounted for 72 percent of all mail order sales in 1985. (See summary totals in Figure 3-1 and turn to Appendix 2 for a further breakdown of mail order sales by leading marketers.)

Contributing to the business-to-business mail order growth is the seemingly insatiable demand by businessmen and businesswomen for self-improvement and knowledge-enhancement materials. Leading companies in this segment are McGraw-Hill, Prentice Hall, and the American Management Association. These are marketers who have products and services that appeal to the prospect's desire and need to do a better job for the companies they work for or run. Publishers attempt to meet these needs by promoting their books and services with solo mail order campaigns that rely on direct response media to sell: books; subscriptions to trade publications; training materials such as audio and video cassettes and special seminars and conferences; self-help continuity programs; newsletters; periodic confidential reports that help businesspeople get the inside story on their industry and on the competition; and all sorts of other informational and educational products.

In the area of high-tech products, decision makers feel more confident about buying by mail or telephone because these products do not need as much service as they once did and because there is more in-house technical expertise to take care of minor problems. This growth is confirmed by a 1985 Ogilvy and Mather Direct study of the buying practices of business executives in the United States (see chart on third page of Appendix III). Telephone interviews with 500 executives in the United States revealed that 89 percent had purchased something within the past twelve-month period as a result of a business-to-business mail-order direct-marketing offer. The average purchase was $1,200 with the average purchaser buying products or services from nine or more categories. The following categories were represented:

Product or Service	Percentage of Customers
Business magazines	65%
Business books	54
Seminars, conferences, conventions	54
Office supplies	47
Software	43
PCs	38
Long-distance telephone service	29
Mainframe computers	20
Information systems	18
Vans and trucks	17
Corporate insurance	15
Banking services	13
Real estate and plant locations	6

Interestingly, 25 percent of the executives accounted for 94 percent of all the dollars spent on products promoted by direct marketing. These purchases were for products costing $10,000 or more. Another 23 percent spent up to $10,000 on products and the remainder bought products costing less than $1,000. Results of the complete study are in Appendix 3.

Clearly, the momentum is building in the business-to-business direct-marketing arena. Those who choose to learn the intricacies of the discipline will be rewarded with lower selling costs and higher profits.

SUMMARY

The mail order segment of business-to-business direct marketing is a complete channel of distribution, 75 percent of which is made up of companies where mail order is only one part of the overall mix of marketing and selling. The remainder is made up of business and industrial mail order specialty marketers. Business-to-business mail order is growing because of the convenience of mail and telephone to purchase knowledge-enhancement products, computer and office supplies, business services, and all kinds of industrial products.

4

MARKET SEGMENTATION

The prime goal of any direct marketing program is to reach potential profitable markets. If the right markets aren't reached, the program will fail, regardless of how persuasive the copy or how attractive the product. Unlike mass marketing, which blankets the total market universe, direct marketing relies on market segmentation and targeting to more narrowly define appropriate prospects. Market segmentation divides a market into various distinct groups of customers or prospects, identifying those markets that appear to be most appropriate from the total market universe. Market targeting selects the segments—through segmentation analysis—that will produce the most buyers.

Market segmentation and targeting are what make direct marketing a cost-effective medium. Nowhere is this more apparent than for mail order direct marketers, who must rely totally on printed and phone messages to their audiences in order to make the sale and stay in business. These direct marketers constantly search for cost-effective solutions to the continuing decline in response from mailings to customer lists. They find that targeted mailings to segmented market lists of both customers and prospects prove more productive than mass mailings to vast numbers of businesses in horizontal markets.

Marketers with sales-support direct-marketing objectives also get more cost-effective results when targeting segmented markets. Time and money are not spent on contacting "unqualified" buyers. For instance, a marketer may determine it is better to make a lead generation mailing to a list of more qualified prospects, such as manufacturers of prefab buildings who have 100 employees or more in the Sun Belt states, than to mail to all manufacturers of prefab buildings in the United States.

SEGMENTATION VARIABLES

The marketer's customer base can be segmented into smaller, more homogeneous subgroups by geographic, demographic, and behavioral factors.

Geographics

Geographic factors refer to data about the economic vitality of companies as positioned in regions, states, counties, cities, and metropolitan areas; for some business-to-business marketers, factors such as economic health, nature of the marketer's business, climate, transportation costs, and state tax laws can have an effect on geographic targeting. Most of this information comes from government statistics.

For the most part, the geographic factors are more important in the consumer marketplace than in business-to-business marketing. The exception is mail order direct marketers selling their products or services to businesspeople who purchase for personal use. For these marketers, geographic considerations are very important.

Demographics

Demographics are the factors most commonly used to determine differences between segments since they are the easiest to locate. Demographic factors refer to information about companies, such as the SIC classifications, sales volume, net worth, and number of employees. These are the key elements, but many marketers also examine the year the business started, credit rating, company headquarters, branch or subsidiary location, sales trends, private or public ownership, minority or nonminority ownership, and even the sex of the decision makers. This information can be found in a myriad of published sources, such as directories, reports, surveys, and compilations. The most commonly used source of demographic information for business-to-business marketers is the SIC classifications, discussed later in this chapter.

Behavior

Behavioral factors are more difficult to acquire, but they are essential if segmentation strategy is to be of maximum value. These variables include knowledge of how a company operates, purchasing patterns, special market needs, and the decision maker's personal characteristics. The marketer gathers much of this behavioral information from survey questionnaires, focus group sessions, and salesperson feedback.

Operating Elements

Knowing how a company manufactures its products and whether it is driven by technology, by the market, or by its product provides the kinds of data that help the marketer determine the company's buying needs. These operating elements remain fairly fixed and enable the marketer to get a more precise identification of existing and potential customers within the demographic categories.

Purchasing Patterns

Another useful variable used for segmenting focuses on the customer company's purchasing approach, which is often a neglected method of segmenting industrial markets. It is based on company philosophy and its rules and guidelines on purchasing. Some companies have formal purchasing organizations and functions whereas others are less structured. The size of the purchasing unit and its reporting relationships within the company, divisions, or departments determine how these units are organized.

For instance, the marketer who is successful at selling to those companies with decentralized operations may find it difficult to respond to a centralized buying pattern where individual purchasing units are combined into a single group. Either way, different purchasing approaches usually require different direct marketing strategies.

Some company department heads, for example, can purchase personal computers on their own authority for their own department uses. Yet in other companies all electronic data processing (EDP) equipment, including individual department PCs, is purchased through a centralized management information systems department to ensure its compatibility with a companywide information processing network. Targeting direct mail messages that do not take this difference into account can miss the mark.

Internal management power structures also can have a bearing on purchasing approaches. The financial units in some companies are very price oriented in their purchasing decisions. And the real power structure of the company may lie in this financial department that strongly influences the whole company's purchasing function. So, if the marketer's product can be sold on the basis of a strong return on investment (ROI) message, it may be profitable to segment by companies that have a financial power structure reflected in their purchasing decisions.

Another purchasing pattern centers around the marketer who has preferred supplier status. This marketer should study the purchasing pattern to determine why this status is enjoyed. Knowing whether purchasers buy because of loyalty to the company, to the salesperson, because of price, or for any other reason can help the marketer in the segmentation process.

Special Market Needs

Different product users seek different product benefits that can be targeted with different promotion mixes. This user benefit approach is one more way that successful business-to-business marketers segment their universes. The product application variable, combined with size of company and other company characteristics, can help the marketer determine those who buy because of quality, service, or economy. These three user benefits surface most often in business-to-business buyer surveys. A company may have a continuing need for fast service.

Some marketers have found this urgent need for order fulfillment useful for developing a focused operating and marketing strategy.

Market segment selection can also be based on order frequency and size of orders. Users of a particular product or brand generally have some characteristics in common or at the very least they have a common experience with the product. Volume users especially have similar attributes. All can have a major impact on the purchasing process and thus on the choice of vendor.

Personal Characteristics

Benson P. Shapiro and Thomas V. Bonoma, in their book *Segmenting the Industrial Market* (Lexington Books, 1983), highlighted the buyer's personal characteristics as an important variable in market segmentation. Marketers for industrial products can segment markets according to the personal characteristics of the individuals involved in the purchasing decision. Marketers look at the decision maker's personal management style—his or her level of self-confidence and need for purchase justification. These characteristics determine the amount of risk a buyer will assume when making a purchase.

Some buyers don't like to take risks whereas others like the challenge. The level of risk buyers are willing to assume is related to other personality variables such as personal style and self-confidence. Buyers who don't like to take risks are not good prospects for new products and concepts. They also tend to avoid new supply sources. These buyers are very thorough in their approach to buying. They get several bids and even split their order as a hedge against delivery problems. Others feel safe by continuing to do business with the same vendors.

Business buyers' needs, preferences, and purchasing approaches often are fashioned by these many human factors. Those marketers who are able to establish a routine collection of data on customers and prospects called on by salespeople or telemarketing communicators have the best chance of success in developing highly meaningful segmented marketing strategies and data bases.

Demographic and operating variables can be inadequate when used by themselves in all but the most simple or homogeneous markets because they ignore buying differences among customers. In segmentation development, a review of the geographic/demographic base should come first, followed by behavioral characteristics, including company operating variables as well as personal characteristics of those who buy products and services. These, of course, are the most difficult to get because they are not obvious. However, the marketer should not over-emphasize personal characteristics or the situational factors either, because they can be expensive and time consuming to gather. In the final analysis such data gathering efforts are only justified when there is a return in sales and profit dollars for all segmentation efforts.

Computerization of marketing that is bringing with it increasingly lower-cost data base technology will help more and more business-to-business marketers justify the cost of highly sophisticated and profitable segmentation efforts.

STANDARD INDUSTRIAL CLASSIFICATION SYSTEM

Most business-to-business market segmentation efforts begin with the Standard Industrial Classification (SIC) system developed by the federal government. This serves as the basis for industrial statistical data. In broad use by governments and businesses of all kinds, SIC codes are assigned to about ten million establishments in the United States. A single company may have several establishments. An establishment is defined as an economic unit at a single physical location. It may be a manufacturing plant, a retail store, a doctor's office, or even a warehouse.

The SIC system divides the identified establishments into ten broad industry groups. Each of these groups has characteristics that lend themselves to segmentation analysis. Further segmentation is possible by reviewing the major groups or subdivisions of the broad industry groups, the two-digit SIC codes (see Table 4-1). Further breakdowns into three-digit SIC groups and four-digit SIC-coded industries expand segmentation possibilities even more for the direct marketer.

There are 541,000 establishments within the broad Manufacturing Industry Group 20–39, starting with major group 20, Food and Kindred Products Manufacturers, and ending with group 39, Miscellaneous Manufacturing Industries. The largest major group is SIC 27, Printing, Publishing, and Allied Industries, consisting of about 80,000 firms. Figure 4-1, an excerpt from the 1987 *SIC Manual,* highlights the detail in this major four-digit classification.

Major group 27 has 9 three-digit SIC code subgroups. Under subgroup 273, there is more than one industry. A fourth digit in the SIC code identifies industry segmentations.

However, finer breakdowns are sometimes needed for targeting subsections. List compilers have provided for this need in some cases by assigning a letter suffix to the four-digit number.

The *Standard Industrial Classification Manual* was updated in 1987, the first major revision since 1972. This new edition reflects "technological changes; institutional changes such as deregulation in the banking, communications and transportation industries; and the tremendous expansion in the service sector."

Table 4-1. Broad SIC classifications.

Two-Digit Classification	Industry Group	Number of Establishments
01–09	Agriculture, forestry, and fisheries	125,000
10–14	Mining	23,000
15–17	Construction	923,000
20–39	Manufacturing	541,000
40–49	Transportation, communication, and utilities	270,000
50–51	Wholesale	990,000
52–59	Retail	3,375,000
60–67	Finance, insurance, and real estate	849,000
70–89	Services, business and professional	3,506,000
90–95	Public administration, government offices	120,000

Source: The Standard Industrial Classification Manual, 1987.

Figure 4-1. Major group 27: printing, publishing, and allied industries.

The Major Group as a Whole

This major group includes establishments engaged in printing by one or more common processes, such as letterpress; lithography (including offset), gravure, or screen; and those establishments which perform services for the printing trade, such as bookbinding and plate-making. This major group also includes establishments engaged in publishing newspapers, books, and periodicals, regardless of whether or not they do their own printing. News syndicates are classified in Services, Industry 7383. Establishments primarily engaged in textile printing and finishing fabrics are classified in Major Group 22, and those engaged in printing and stamping on fabric articles are classified in Industry 2396. Establishments manufacturing products that contain incidental printing, such as advertising or instructions, are classified according to the nature of the products—for example, as cartons, bags, plastics film, or paper.

Industry Group No.	Industry No.	
271		NEWSPAPERS: PUBLISHING, OR PUBLISHING AND PRINTING
	2711	Newspapers: Publishing, or Publishing and Printing

Establishments primarily engaged in publishing newspapers, or in publishing and printing newspapers. These establishments carry on the various operations necessary for issuing newspapers, including the gathering of news and the preparation of editorials and advertisements, but may or may not perform their own printing. Commercial printing is frequently carried on by establishments engaged in publishing and printing newspapers, but, even though the commercial printing may be of major importance, such establishments are included in this industry. Establishments not engaged in publishing newspapers, but which print newspapers for publishers, are classified in Industry Group 275. News syndicates are classified in Services, Industry 7383.

Commercial printing and newspaper publishing combined	Newspaper branch offices, editorial and advertising
Job printing and newspaper publishing combined	Newspapers: publishing and printing, or publishing only

272		PERIODICALS: PUBLISHING, OR PUBLISHING AND PRINTING
	2721	Periodicals: Publishing, or Publishing and Printing

Establishments primarily engaged in publishing periodicals, or in publishing and printing periodicals. These establishments carry on the various operations necessary for issuing periodicals, but may or may not perform their own printing. Establishments not engaged in publishing periodicals, but which print periodicals for publishers, are classified in Industry Group 275.

Comic books: publishing and printing, or publishing only	Statistical reports (periodicals), publishing and printing, or publishing only
Magazines: publishing and printing, or publishing only	Television schedules: publishing and printing, or publishing only
Periodicals: publishing and printing, or publishing only	Trade journals, publishing and printing, or publishing only

---

Source: The Standard Industrial Classification Manual, 1987.   *(continues)*

Figure 4-1 (continued)

Industry Group No.	Industry No.	
273		**BOOKS**

2731 Books: Publishing, or Publishing and Printing

Establishments primarily engaged in publishing, or in publishing and printing, books and pamphlets. Establishments primarily engaged in printing or in printing and binding (but not publishing) books and pamphlets are classified in Industry 2732.

Book club publishing and printing, or publishing only
Books: publishing and printing, or publishing only
Music books: publishing and printing, or publishing only

Pamphlets: publishing and printing, or publishing only
Textbooks: publishing and printing, or publishing only

2732 Book Printing

Establishments primarily engaged in printing, or in printing and binding, books and pamphlets, but not engaged in publishing. Establishments primarily engaged in publishing, or in publishing and printing, books and pamphlets are classified in Industry 2731. Establishments engaged in both printing and binding books, but primarily binding books printed elsewhere, are classified in Industry 2789.

Books: printing or printing and binding, not publishing
Music books: printing or printing and binding, not publishing

Pamphlets: printing or printing and binding, not publishing
Textbooks: printing or printing and binding, not publishing

274   **MISCELLANEOUS PUBLISHING**

2741 Miscellaneous Publishing

Establishments primarily engaged in miscellaneous publishing activities, not elsewhere classified, whether or not engaged in printing. Establishments primarily engaged in offering financial, credit, or other business services, and which may publish directories as part of this service, are classified in Division I, Services.

Atlases: publishing and printing, or publishing only
Business service newsletters: publishing and printing, or publishing only
Calendars: publishing and printing, or publishing only
Catalogs: publishing and printing, or publishing only
Directories: publishing and printing, or publishing only
Globe covers (maps): publishing and printing, or publishing only
Guides: publishing and printing, or publishing only
Maps: publishing and printing, or publishing only
Micropublishing
Multimedia educational kits: publishing and printing, or publishing only

Music, sheet: publishing and printing, or publishing only
Patterns, paper, including clothing patterns: publishing and printing, or publishing only
Race track programs: publishing and printing, or publishing only
Racing forms: publishing and printing, or publishing only
Shopping news: publishing and printing, or publishing only
Technical manuals and papers: publishing and printing, or publishing only
Telephone directories: publishing and printing, or publishing only
Yearbooks: publishing and printing, or publishing only

275   **COMMERCIAL PRINTING**

2752 Commercial Printing, Lithographic

Establishments primarily engaged in printing by the lithographic process. The greater part of the work in this industry is performed on a job or custom basis; but in some cases lithographed calendars, maps, posters, decalcomanias,

Changes also were made to improve industry detail, coverage, and definitions. *The Standard Industrial Classification Manual,* 1987, stock number 041-001-00314-2, is available for $24. Send prepayment to Dept. 36-YR, Superintendent of Documents, Washington, DC 20402-9325. (To order with a Visa or MasterCard, call 202-783-3238.)

The Technical Committee on Industrial Classification of the Office of Management and Budget is responsible for the SIC system. This committee is composed of economists, statisticians, and classification specialists representing 18 of the federal agencies that use the SIC. Business-to-business marketers would have found the new SIC revision more valuable if it had included more than four digits to categorize finer breakdowns. Yet, even with its inadequacies, most business-to-business marketers have been able to get by with SIC codes of up to four digits. The SIC system is currently the most cost-effective way to define business classifications of the marketplace for segmentation purposes.

DATA SOURCES

Local, state, and federal governments compile an enormous amount of data that is valuable for segmenting markets, even though the information is general instead of on individual establishments. Most of these data come from the Internal Revenue Service, the Department of Commerce, and the Bureau of Labor Statistics.

For instance, the IRS' statistical reports are valuable reference documents based on tax returns of U.S. businesses. They give the number of businesses by size and by industry and provide overall revenue information. Also, the Department of Commerce publishes census data on major segments of American industry. Included are summary data by SIC code, employee size, and geographic areas.

Some key publications useful for measuring and segmenting markets include the following (all are available from the Government Printing Office, Washington, DC):

> *Bureau of Census Catalog.* Issued quarterly, references all publications issued by the Bureau and lists data files and special tabulations and other unpublished materials.
> *Directory of Federal Statistics for Local Areas.* A guide to sources from the Bureau of Census. Detailed description of social, economic, and technical data including names and addresses of source agencies.
> *Measuring Markets: A Guide to the Use of Federal and State Statistical Data.* From the Bureau of Domestic and International Business Administration. Describes federal and state government publications useful for measuring markets.
> *Statistical Abstract of the United States, Bureau of Census.* Comprehensive annual compendium on the social, economic, and governmental characteristics of the United States.

Census data appear initially in report form as new information becomes available.

They can be ordered from Publications, Subscriber Service Section, Bureau of Census, U.S. Department of Commerce, Washington, DC 20233, or any local field office of the U.S. Department of Commerce.

A good industry source for statistics is *Statistics Sources: A Subject Guide to Data on Industrial, Business, Social, Educational, Financial, and Other Topics for the United States and Selected Foreign Countries.* Gale Research Co., Book Tower, Detroit, MI 48226. Additional sources are listed in Chapter 5, Business Lists.

Mailing lists and other data compilations that are pieces and parts of various information sources can also be used to help a business-to-business marketer determine the profile of the prospect universe. More information can be extracted from surveys and company reports. Of course, all of this data must be pieced together by the individual marketer for every name in the file.

SEGMENTATION STRATEGY

Segmentation Criteria

For direct marketing segmentation strategy to be successful, four standards must be applied. Of course, by definition, the segment has to be a homogeneous group with common attributes. The targeted segment should be marketable, reachable, sizable, and promotable.

- *Marketability:* To be marketable, the targeted segment must have potential sales and profit for the product and selling channel the marketer plans to use. The interest turnover and buying frequency of a product in a given segment may be so slight as to preclude a profitable marketing effort.
- *Reachability:* It must be possible for the marketer to reach and service, cost effectively, by direct mail and telemarketing the firms and organizations within the segment. For instance, viable segments that are not cost effective for selling through personal sales visits may be accessible through the use of the mail order selling channel.
- *Sizability:* The segment must be large enough to be worth pursuing. For example, if a marketer who plans to sell a $30,000 inventory control distribution system finds that only the top 15 percent—those dozen or so customers with revenues of $2 million and above—could afford a system at that price, the segment may be too small to be worthwhile. Markets can be refined to the point where the small size of some segments precludes targeting.
- *Promotability:* The segment selected must have an audience that will respond to direct marketing programs and promotions.

Selection of Segments

Implementation of a segmentation strategy has been a complicated and expensive process for the business-to-business marketer. Many products sold in the business marketplace have more than one application, and many different products can be used for the same application. Also, businesses in the industrial marketplace differ greatly in their methods of doing business.

There is no simple, predetermined way to segment a market. The marketer examines such segmentation factors as geographic location, company customer size, and product end use to find those most common to the entire customer universe. The process of segmentation involves trying different combinations of variables and rating these factors in order of their importance to the marketer.

Of course, any two marketers may weigh the factors differently. For example, in the rating scheme shown in Table 4-2, the marketer—selling through a direct sales force—assigns a value of zero to the factor "mail responsive." A mail order marketer, however, might assign the same factor a value of 50 or more.

When determining the most profitable segment of the market, the marketer also looks at competitive strategy and reach in the same area. This is done through research. Focus groups or questionnaires can be of great help. Armed with results of research, the marketer can formulate a position to combat competition or try to develop a targeted marketplace in a previously untouched segment.

SEGMENTATION ANALYSIS: TARGETING MARKETS

Segmentation analysis in industrial markets is a relatively new development that has been made more viable and affordable by the computer. (Chapter 6 discusses this concept in more detail.) In the past, many companies were successful at using product differences to distinguish their offerings from those of their competitors

Table 4-2. Market segmentation selection rating chart.

Primary Factors	Rating Points
1. Size of business	15
by number of employees	
by annual volume of business	
net worth	
2. Type of business or industry (SIC classification)	15
3. Product end use	20
4. Purchasing interest (special interest category)	10
5. Where and when is the buying done?	10
headquarters, divisions, or subsidiaries	
6. Job function (shows importance as a decision maker or	
influencer)	10
7. Credit rating	15
8. Age of business	5
9. Mail responsive	0
Total rating points	100

in mass markets. Not many businesses in the industrial world today can succeed with that approach.

Overall Strategies

The great bulk of sales in the business-to-business world comes from a very small number of a firm's customers. It is critical for individual marketers to know the ratio in their overall marketplace for their products. Knowing who these customers are is necessary for effective business-to-business direct marketing strategic sales planning. Market segmentation is a key approach in pinpointing sales and profit forecasts more accurately. Some target segments may show promise; others cannot measure up to the bottom line. The marketer may find it necessary to ignore prospects who don't match the good customer profile, targeting only those prospects where the profit is higher.

The marketer may also choose to target several segments and develop different offers for each. The idea, of course, is to appeal to the business-to-business buyer on the basis of the more specific needs of the buyer in the smaller target segments rather than on what the marketer assumes are the more general needs of the larger marketplace. Target marketing with different product offers for different segments usually will produce more total revenue because each targeted segment is marketed to and served more comprehensively. In any one planning cycle, the Fortune 500 marketers, for instance, may target with direct mail and telemarketing as many as one or two dozen or even more market segments.

Multiple costs are incurred when there are many segments. Costs will be higher because more research, planning, production, marketing, and servicing must be customized for each targeted segment. Segmented markets naturally mean smaller lists and smaller media circulation, so the cost will be larger per prospect reached.

Companies that have salespeople covering several targeted segments might have a sales support campaign of multiple direct mailings to move their low potential prospect segments closer to the point of taking buying action. Prospects in the medium potential segments may get a greater quantity of mailings and the higher potential prospect segment may get personalized direct mail materials followed up by telemarketing calls.

In tandem with this type of prospect campaign, the marketer may target high potential customers, regular customers, as well as first-time and former customers through multiple-dimensional and high-impact mailings in combination with an organized telemarketing campaign. Key customers, those who are multiple purchasers or frequent purchasers spending high-dollar amounts, are segments usually targeted for intensive effort.

Targeting small segments can also be a successful strategy. For example, Bernard, a welding equipment supplier, reduced a market down to a segment of 40 power source manufacturers. The objective was to get them to become Original Equipment Manufacturers (OEM) customers of its gun and cable systems. A three-part direct mail campaign that did not ask for a response was sent at two-week intervals. However, a telephone call followed the mailings in an effort to set up a meeting between the supplier and the OEM prospect. This program to such a highly selective segment was very successful at a cost of $212.50 per prospect. The strategy of setting up high-level meetings between OEM prospects and the supplier was accomplished with tactical use of direct mail and telemarketing to the high-potential account segment.

In contrast, a business-to-business mail order marketer may successfully market a range of product supplies through a single catalog mailing to a list of 150,000 businesses. Yet, there may be more profits through market list segmentation. Segmentation analysis may highlight low-risk opportunities to modify the single catalog to incorporate different appeals to match different segments of the list. Loyal buyers can be rewarded for frequent purchases with special incentives. Personalized mailings and telemarketing could be targeted more specifically to higher-interest prospects.

Still another important segment for the sales support marketer is the group of prospects ready to buy from one vendor company or another. They are prospects who salespeople are calling on and who are individually identified only by the salespeople. Reinforced direct mail campaigns should be sent to this most highly qualified prospect segment.

The Market Niche

Another strategy the marketer may choose is to concentrate on one particular segment of a market that does not greatly interest major competitors. Many small companies and small divisions of larger companies are often not able to achieve a major market share, but by occupying smaller market niches they can maintain a very healthy standing in the marketplace. The niche has to be large enough, of course, to justify the marketing costs, and there has to be enough growth and potential sales for the market to be profitable. The marketer must have skills and resources to serve the niche effectively and be able to develop customer loyalty in defense against competitive inroads.

Many marketers who specialize in a niche of a larger segment of the market often do so in one of several ways. They may set their sights on customers of a certain size or type. They may develop the niche in a particular geographic area. They may concentrate on specific products, product lines, or service. A unique end use of the product may be a profitable market niche for a business-to-business direct marketer.

Market Coverage Factors

When the various segments have been identified and evaluated, the marketer can determine the most appropriate target market coverage strategies. The decision of how many and which segments to cover is influenced by several vital factors. Suitability and availability of company resources are the prime considerations. Limited resources almost always dictate a segmentation approach. Homogeneous products such as business forms, office supplies, or steel do not lend themselves to product-differentiated positioning strategies that work best in segmented marketing. Nor does segmentation strategy apply in homogeneous markets where purchasing preferences, order intervals, and order amounts tend to be standard.

Product life cycle also influences market coverage strategy. Many marketers launch a product in a wider marketplace and use segmentation strategies when it is well along in the growth phase. This process applies similarly in catalog launches. For example, a business-to-business marketer begins selling a line of cutting tools by catalog to the universe of tool and die shops. As competitors enter that market with their catalogs—some with sales-force coverage—the market matures and the marketer's catalog begins to lose market share. Segmentation analysis reveals higher volume, and more frequent orders come from specific geographic areas where competitive personal sales coverage is weakest. Also revealed are other segments that can be receptive to solo mail order efforts of specific-purpose tool products. The original single catalog now breaks up into different offerings for different market segments. The cataloger's concentration of marketing efforts on each segment specifically can have a healthier return on investment.

After segmentation analysis a marketer will have some options:

1. To target a market by segmentation, or to not use segmentation at all
2. To concentrate on one or a few segments with one basic product offer
3. To diversify into several market segments with different product offers for each segment

Some marketers prefer to go after bigger shares of market segments with the same product and promotion mix rather than to go after a small share of a large market. As a general rule, when competitors are going after the whole market universe with one general product offer, it can pay a firm that has a product that lends itself to product differentiation to counter with segmentation marketing strategies.

To gain maximum value from market segmentation, the marketer must position the products to relate and appeal to specific needs and wants of the businesses that comprise the segment. The product must fit the segment. If it does not, superficial positioning changes, such as packaging and advertising designed to relate only to how the market perceives the product, may not accomplish this objective in the long term.

SUMMARY

The market segmentation process plays a dominant role in selecting target markets for business-to-business direct marketers who use targeting for sales support or to sell directly by mail or telemarketing.

Segmentation in business-to-business marketing is a relatively new development being made more viable and affordable by the computer as it responds to the industrial marketer's demands for more profitable markets. The segmentation process divides a market into defined groups of current and potential customers.

The customer base can be segmented by three broad groups: geography, demography and behavior. The first two relate to statistical information readily available from many published sources. The Standard Industrial Classification system, revised in 1987, is still the most commonly used demographic factor in segmentation for the business marketer.

Behavioral factors define the way a company operates, its purchasing patterns and special needs, as well as the decision maker's personal characteristics. These factors are important to successful segmentation strategy but are more difficult to assess and more costly to identify.

Direct marketing strategies based on segmentation concentrate on pinpointing the marketing mix directly to the interests of the targeted segments. The marketer's targeted appeal is directed at what the buyer really needs rather than on what the marketer may happen to be selling. The individual marketer specifically selects those segments for targeting that will have the best chance of producing the most buyers. The decision on which segments should be covered by the marketer depends on the suitability and availability of company resources, the degree of homogeneity of the products and the market, the product life cycle stage, and the competitive positioning.

5

BUSINESS LISTS

A business list is a universe or partial universe of names and addresses of establishments. There are many thousands of business lists available, some consisting of all firms within a designated category. But most marketers would not want to mail to a complete universe list because the biggest payoff comes from those prospects who have the highest income potential for the mailer. Business direct marketing strategy aims at the most profitable targeted segments of the large universe lists.

THE BUSINESS MARKETPLACE

As might be expected, the business-to-business marketplace of about 10 million establishments is made up mostly of small firms. In round figures, over 9 million of these firms have fewer than 50 employees, and of these only half have more than 10 employees. This vast marketplace is represented in the 40,000 listings published by Standard Rates and Data Service in *Direct Mail List Rates and Data*. These lists are highly segmented with demographics detailing SIC, number of employees, revenue, and other breakdowns.

The great bulk of business-to-business marketers today are involved in sales support objectives that have prospect markets consisting of perhaps 5,000 to 20,000 establishments. Many small companies and the smaller divisions of large corporations have even more limited marketplaces with as few as 250 or 500 actual prospects. Size, however, does not preclude the use of direct mail and telemarketing in concert with personal sales calls to get productive and profitable sales results.

In contrast to sales support markets business-to-business mail order companies and divisions have vast prospect markets that number in the millions. Products or services that cannot be justifiably sold through personal sales calls can, regardless of market size, be profitably reached through available business lists.

When selecting business lists for either mail order or sales support objectives the ever-changing business marketplace presents a challenge to the marketer. Businessmen and businesswomen get promoted, change jobs, retire, and expire. New people move in to fill vacancies. Also, new companies emerge at a faster rate than those that go out of business.

McGraw-Hill estimates there is some change in the status of 53 percent of company executives every year. This means a personal name business list that has not had anything added to it or deleted from it in a twelve-month period can be 53 percent undeliverable, depending on job function and specific industry or vocation of individuals on the list. Different classifications of businesspeople, of course, have different rates of change. However, many compiled lists do not include personal names. A typical compiled business list without personal names may have up to 25 percent or 30 percent changes in a year.

PERSONAL NAME VS. TITLE LISTS

Although marketers prefer individual names on their business lists, the high mobility of businesspeople makes it difficult and uneconomical to maintain many lists with names. The marketer can, of course, call the company and ask to whom the mail should be addressed. At this same time it may be smart to also get the names of other individuals in the company who are in positions to influence the sale. This tactic produces the sought-after information although it can be costly in terms of time. But when the success of a direct marketing program calls for personal names, the extra effort can be well worth it.

Marketers have more success getting this information themselves directly through the headquarter's office or a custom compiler, rather than to ask the field sales force to come up with the correctly spelled names of the right prospects. Salespeople are not in the business of developing and maintaining mailing lists. They are not good at it and don't have the time for it. Indeed, they should be doing more productive work, like presenting and selling. It costs the company fewer dollars for headquarters marketing support people to handle compiling. Copies of the results of headquarter's efforts should be sent to the salespeople for their information and verification.

Mailing to a title without a personal name is very common in business-to-business mail programs and it is done for several reasons. For some marketplaces there are simply no personal name lists available. For others there may be names but not those wanted by the marketer. As direct marketing professionals have learned from experience, when mailing to business lists a title mailing can, more often than expected, be more cost effective than mailing to a name. Fewer inquiries may result but these will be at a lower unit cost. And even more startling, especially to newcomers in business-to-business direct marketing, is the fact that a title-only mailing will on occasion actually produce more responses than a mailing that includes a personal name on the face of the envelope or mailing piece.

The main reason usually given for the disappointing performance of personally addressed mail centers on the system used to maintain the list. Some personal name lists, such as compilations from directories, are updated annually when the directories are received by the compiler. On date of issue, a directory may be 10 percent out-of-date. Lag time caused by compiling schedules results in some listings being 14 months old or more when the directory is issued.

Some marketers feel title mailings are most successfully used for the more routine type messages that relate directly to the job of the recipient. Functional titles are also used to good effect when potential prospects go by different titles for the same job function in different companies; for example, the executive responsible for business meetings or travel could be the communications director, administrative assistant to the vice-president of marketing, sales manager, or marketing manager.

TYPES OF BUSINESS LISTS

Business lists are classified as three basic types: active customers, qualified prospects, and suspects. Generally, active customers are those who have purchased one or more products within a six- or twelve-month period. Qualified prospects have an affinity for the product and have characteristics of the best customer profile. Suspects are those companies, firms, and organizations that the marketer thinks are likely to have an interest and application for the product but whose characteristics have not yet been determined.

For mail order and inquiry response objectives customer lists as a rule are more valuable than prospect lists. Prospect lists are more valuable than suspect lists. And suspect lists are more valuable than a cold canvass list—the direct marketing equivalent of knocking on doors. A function of marketing and selling is to seek out suspects, develop them into prospects, and then turn them into customers. For any organization to be successful, this selling process must go on without interruption. Segregating and communicating differently and correctly to the various lists of decision makers and response buyers enhance the marketer's success ratio in reaching specific direct marketing objectives. The business-to-business marketer draws on these lists in four general categories: in-house lists, compiled lists, response lists, and business and trade publication lists. Postcard deck lists and marketing data banks are made up of one or more of these categories.

In-House Lists

Customer Lists
The customer base, because of its value, is always kept in-house, under the direct control of the marketer. Recording the customer's name, title, company name, and address is actually the beginning of the marketer's evolutionary data base. The value of the customer list multiplies as the file builds. And to add to

the file some companies are beginning to use focus group research in quest of important customer characteristics and buying behavior patterns.

Customers are the best source of additional business. They are high-level responders to both mail order and sales support lead programs. However, for obvious reasons, most nonpublisher, non-mail order business-to-business marketers protect their customer and inquiry lists and are reluctant to place them on the list rental market.

Prospect Lists

Next in importance to the customer list and counted as a vital part of the business-to-business marketer's in-house file is the prospect list. It consists of several specific segments. One is made up of inquiry names generated from many sources with varying degrees of value. The names come from reader response cards and other inquiries from advertising and press relations efforts, trade show activity, sales call reports, in-house technical service people, engineering reps, activity reports, and company correspondence. Another prospect segment is a compilation of key potential prospects whose characteristics closely match those of the marketer's key customers. Just below this level are the medium- and low-potential prospect groups, all bona fide targets for direct marketing campaigns.

Still another segment includes special names of prospective customers that field salespeople have designated as "tough-to-get-in-to-see" prospects. Custom direct marketing campaigns to each of these special prospect groups are part of the successful marketer's promotion mix.

Some new ad and product managers, fueled by their enthusiasm to develop a direct mail program, will compile their own lists from directories and other sources, only to find that these same lists are already available at low cost on labels, tape, or diskette from a list compiler. The key question the manager must answer is "Do I want to compile and maintain my own prospect lists?" Some unique lists are not available from any source. Also, highly selective prospect profiles in small quantities may not be practical to rent because of the high unit cost. The marketer's commitment to a long-term direct mail program plus the quantity of mailings planned also have a bearing on a decision to build a medium- or low-potential prospect list in-house.

Since an in-house list is unique to an individual company, it cannot cover a complete marketplace nor does it have consistent coverage. Of course, the longer a customer's or inquirer's name has been on the list without a further transaction, the less valuable the name becomes.

Compiled Lists

Before evaluating a compiled or outside rental list the marketer will first want to know if it is simply a collection of names or a list of active responders. Are the responders sales lead inquirers or mail order buyers? This is basic but for the beginner it can be confusing. There is no direct response history in a compiled list unless it is merged or overlaid with a response name data bank. This computerized matching process identifies those firms on the compiled list that have responded to an offer in the past. Reported matches of from 40 percent to 65 percent are not unusual for large business mailers. Most compiled lists contain good selections of demographics from which the marketer's customer profile can be matched. The strong feature of the compiled list is its complete and consistent coverage of an entire universe in a category or line of business.

Keeping compiled lists current is a top priority for the list owner. Unlike mail order response names it doesn't matter how long compiled names have been on the list as long as the list is properly maintained. Compilers protect the list renter by offering postage refunds for undeliverables in excess of a stated guarantee. Typical third-class bulk-mailing guarantees are 93 percent and 95 percent.

Compilers gather data from primary sources by mail and telephone questionnaires, then combine them with more data and statistical information available from hundreds of published sources.

Response Lists

Business response lists are a unique group of names of businesspeople who have acted on a direct marketing offer by either placing an order or asking for more information. These are the lists that catalog, solo mail and phone order marketers, and magazine and card deck publishers find the most profitable for direct marketing campaigns. These lists of purchasers and inquirers are usually selected by the list buyer on

- The basis of the offer that provoked the response
- The amount of the sale or potential sale
- The frequency and recency of purchase
- The geographic selection

The most profitable response lists consist of the marketer's customers. The second most profitable but difficult to come by are the customer lists of competitors. Mail response lists are rented for one-time use only and have very strong pulling power for mail and phone order selling efforts or when the strategy calls for inquiry generation.

Response lists have no SIC selections, nor is coverage consistent or complete. There is no systematic update and, of course, they become less valuable as they get older. However, "hot-line" buyers—the more recent buyers—rent at a premium.

Trade Publication Lists

Trade publications offer business-to-business marketers two distinctly different types of lists. One comes from controlled circulation publications. Here, trade magazines are distributed to individuals in companies at no charge, based on titles and job functions. Recipients must respond to questionnaires to verify the information that qualifies them to get the publication. The second list type comes from paid subscriptions. Controlled circulation names somewhat resemble a compiled list and paid circulation names are more like response lists.

Because controlled lists are based on mandatory verification questionnaires, they have excellent selection criteria in the vertical or horizontal business markets served by the publication. They have characteristics that identify segmentation subgroups within the list. In most cases these lists include personal names. However, there is no direct response history, nor are the lists a measure of a complete universe. Eighty percent coverage of a universe is fairly standard for controlled circulation lists.

The paid subscriber list is made up of those individuals who have demonstrated an interest in receiving the publication by paying for it. This list is usually more responsive to direct response selling by mail or telemarketing than controlled publication lists are. Publishers refer to subscription lists as mail responsive lists, which they are, even though in a limited sphere.

One of the disadvantages of paid subscriber trade publication circulation lists is that they do not cover the entire market. What's more, some magazines will be read by fewer than half of the prospects in the universe of the business category. However, these publications offer demographics that can match a marketer's targeted profile, so their usefulness depends on the marketer's objectives and targets.

On the other hand, business and trade publication subscription names are among the most current personal name lists available, since subscribers keep publishers informed of changes when they occur. This is accented by assurances of publishers like Hitchcock, for instance, who guarantees 99 percent deliverability of its lists, and refunds twice the outgoing postage on undeliverable names (over 1 percent) returned.

In virtually all markets more than one magazine competes for the advertising business. In some, such as the high-tech market, it is difficult to make a selection among the many available. When choosing a publication list for direct mail, marketers study the Business Publications Audit (BPA) *Buyers Guide* very closely, examining the circulation statement to ensure a match of the right mix of SICs and job titles. Most business magazine publishers are heavily involved in the list rental business. The larger ones include McGraw-Hill, Penton/IPC, Chilton, Hitchcock, Cahners, Hayden, and Technical Publishing.

Postcard Response Decks

Postcard response deck lists are selected from various mail order lists, inquiry response lists, and trade magazine publisher's lists. They cover both vertical and horizontal markets. Most response deck circulation lists total 100,000 or less. Some publishers produce decks for their own use that promote their own products or subscriptions. The majority, however, depend on support of outside advertisers for revenue. Many response card deck publishers are also response card deck advertisers using responses from other publisher's decks to augment their own list bases, which in turn they rent to others.

Marketers look for those decks that have advertised offers similar to their own that continue to repeat in successive issues of the deck. However, experienced deck users are aware that most deck advertisers don't try to make a sale on the initial response. In fact, of the three uses of postcard response decks by the business-to-business marketer, the most common is as a first step in a two-step direct response promotion. The card then solicits an inquiry that is followed up by a full-blown solo or catalog mail order or telemarketing effort, which attempts to get a sale without the help of one-on-one sales calls.

A second use—although minor, but on the increase—is to sell directly from the card deck mailing with the card itself presenting the complete sales story. However, one-step mail order selling is confined to fairly low-ticket universal merchandise, usually books and training and educational materials. Marketers with mail order objectives, whether using one-step or multiple-step tactics, test many different decks among the hundreds of decks available, much in the same way they test the more standard response lists. The value of any response card deck lies in its list profile and how it matches the marketer's offer.

Looking for sales leads for a dealer's sales force or the marketer's own sales reps is the third use of postcard response decks. Business-to-business marketers who are after sales support leads focus on response decks addressing the more narrow vertical marketplaces. The jury is still out on the value of the leads produced from card decks. Results indicate the higher the price of the promoted product, the poorer the lead. But the leads are inexpensive on a cost per thousand basis.

Marketing Data Banks

Data banks are a compilation of various combinations of compiled or response files or both merged into one. Now that we have entered the information age, the demand for the data bank's files will continue well into future years. By overlaying one list with another the marketer will have new, enhanced list information in the data bank.

Data banks incorporate the structured data of compiled lists as their core. Overlays of controlled circulation lists add even more structured data. Special-interest categories can be added along with sales information from customer lists and response lists. Recency, frequency, and monetary (RFM) value information as well as purchasing behavior can also be integrated into the data bank.

Today's sophisticated data bank has the comprehensive coverage of compiled lists, the detailed segmentation of controlled circulation lists, and the strong pulling power of response lists with their computerized RFM ratios for all product categories of customer lists. Data banks and data bases are covered in Chapter 6.

BUSINESS LIST SERVICES

Any newcomer to business direct marketing should become knowledgeable about different types of lists, list services, and sources and understand how to use them to maximum advantage. Successful business-to-business marketers learn from business list compilers and brokers who have experience and proven credentials in their markets. They have made studies of current and prospective markets and usually know where the better lists can be found. Experienced list suppliers can provide information not easily available to list users. These suppliers are listed in service directories published by the Direct Marketing Association, in *Catalog Age, Target Marketing,* and in the directory pages of all the direct marketing magazines. One of the best ways a marketer can qualify list suppliers is to talk to firms who have had experience with them.

The professionals in business list services include list brokers, list compilers, list managers, and trade magazine list publishers.

List Managers

The list manager works for the list owner and is paid a commission as the agent responsible for use of the list by others. Some list managers also act as brokers for lists as well as managing them. However, most list managers deal directly with list brokers who in turn service direct marketers. Some large list owners receive enough income from list rentals to pay them to employ their own full-time list managers in-house.

A list manager is similar to a publication space salesperson who represents the publisher and solicits ad agency clients who in turn service the advertiser. But in this case, list brokers are the list manager's clients. List managers normally handle most of the maintenance, marketing, and promotion functions for the list owners. They make sure the list is correctly entered in *Direct Mail List Rates and Data* and other appropriate media. Also, they call on and distribute list information to brokers, and publicize and advertise lists in *Direct Marketing Magazine, DM News, Target Marketing,* and *Catalog Age.*

To manage a list well is not always an easy job. List managers counsel list owners on any emerging opportunities to make further list segmentation available. In addition, they handle the internal paperwork needed to process an order, keep records, provide for list clearance, collect for use of the list by others, and take precautions against theft. For their efforts they get paid a standard 10 percent commission by the list owner. Add to this an additional 20 percent if the list manager also performs the broker function.

List Brokers

The list broker is the person who marketers deal with when they seek list services. Some brokers have been intensely involved with direct marketing programs of clients and have become highly knowledgeable about many direct marketing functions beyond lists and markets. The more experienced and better staffed they are, the more they fill the function of an actual list consultant and the more useful they can be to the marketer.

The list broker's main function is to provide list strategy recommendations and list suggestions for testing, which are usually documented in writing. Marketers can recognize experienced list consultants by the in-depth questions they ask about the direct marketing objectives, programs, strategies, and results expected. The best are very good at not only giving opinions about business mailing list availabilities but also on information about direct marketing personnel and other resources that marketers and agencies need to know to succeed.

List brokers are also good at coordination of details. For compiled lists they provide list counts, arrange delivery, handle the order function, and send bills to clients. For response lists brokers will arrange for receipt of sample mailing pieces, list owner approvals, merge/purge, eliminate dupes, and negotiate with and handle payment to the list manager or owner.

Brokers, as well as compilers, expect many questions to be asked. As part of their function of supplying answers they can become the catalysts to help a marketer move ahead on a customer data base development program—the tool needed to generate a good prospect profile.

Most direct mail agencies and many general ad agencies have set up list brokerage functions. Most letter shops and some service bureaus also include list brokerage responsibilities.

List brokers, as well as compilers and business magazine list publishers, ordinarily will not solicit prospects who have very small target markets (5,000 to 10,000 or less), since they get a commission (15 to 20 percent) based on the number of names. Although they will place list orders for even the smallest list user, the services provided to the marketer will be limited. Because of this, marketers who have relatively small list rental requirements should become proficient enough in understanding their markets and locating the lists available to target those markets.

List Compilers

Marketers who already know their markets can deal directly with compilers and take advantage of the in-depth information that compiler reps have gained from various user experience with their lists. Compilers service the marketer much like a broker does, but only for those lists the compiler represents. However, these lists cover broad categories and individual records number in the millions. Because of the wide coverage of complete market universes, the demographic information large compilers provide can be overlaid onto a marketer's in-house list. In this way compilers can create business lists to profile the marketer's best accounts, design test segments to match marketing objectives, and help the marketer use the proper testing techniques. Also, custom compilations and periodic updates are furnished for marketers who want to own unique lists for special purposes.

Although there are dozens of compilers, the giant in the business field is a consolidation of the three top business list compilers of the past decade—National Business Lists, Market Data Retrieval, and Dun's Marketing Services. This consolidated organization, under the Dun and Bradstreet umbrella, has 8.5 million business establishments and 14 million senior- and middle-management names in its data bank. Dun's compiles lists as a by-product of Dun & Bradstreet's credit data and other information collections. It accumulates an exhaustive amount of data on those U.S. businesses that wish to be included in Dun's credit file. With the acquisition of MDR/NBL, it also compiles from business-to-business telephone Yellow Pages, making its files the largest compilation of business names in the United States.

Trade Publication List Services

Although trade publication business lists are available through list brokers, many marketers deal directly with the publishers. Trade magazine publishers protect the marketer through Business Publications Audit of Circulation (BPA) audits of "controlled circulation" publication lists. In many cases, an individual's job function, name, and title, as well as market coverage of the list, are audited. The audit bureau's reporting procedures ensure that information on subscribers is kept current.

The Audit Bureau of Circulations (ABC) audits circulations of publications that have at least 70 percent paid subscribers. Circulation data for most publications are available from Standard Rate & Data Service, the main source for media buyers. Most publishers prepare media comparability reports that detail the marketplace covered by circulation in specific terms important to the marketer planning target campaigns. These reports also indicate availability of list rental and direct response postcards.

The major publishers have merged circulation of their publications to form massive data bases like Penton/IPC Publishing's 1.5 million unduplicated business names. These lists, by the very nature of their circulation solicitation process, have a great deal of demographic information. This enables a publisher—such as Technical Publications with its 1.2 million names—to offer manufacturers a dealer territory prospect analysis that can result in a direct mail program reaching selected interest categories. Publishers offer list selections by job functions of subscribers, type of business operation, number of employees interested in specific products, and many selections unique to a particular industry. They also offer most recent "hot-line" names representing their reader service inquirers. Trade publication lists traditionally are not rented to marketers for telemarketing uses.

BUSINESS LIST INFORMATION SOURCES

The main source of data for business lists is the *Direct Mail Lists Rates and Data* directory published by Standard Rate & Data Service. Additional information is available from various compilers' catalogs, and trade publication and broker list cards.

Direct Mail Lists Rates and Data

Direct Mail Lists Rates and Data is a combined consumer and business directory with about 550 pages of business listings for list brokers and users. To keep subscribers current there are 24 updates of new listings each year and a completely revised directory is issued 6 times a year.

The lists in this directory are submitted by list owners who are also described as compilers, publishers, mail order companies, and brokers if the broker has an exclusive on the list. These mailing lists controlled by list owners or list managers are made available for rental in an address format and are maintained on various types of addressing systems, mostly magnetic tape.

In this directory, a list as defined by the publisher is "a collection of names derived by a common source and within each list there may be list selections." A list selection is a segment of a list that is also available for rent.

Broad classes of information are found in *Direct Mail Lists Rates and Data* for each list. Reviewing this data can help a potential user determine whether a list or any of its segments is appropriate for further inquiry and action. Figure 5-1 is a representation of one listing, Dun's Decision Makers. This listing is found under the Business Executives classification. A brief review covers the following key categories (many of which are included in Figure 5-1):

1. *Personnel*—names individuals in the selling or service function such as brokers, authorized agents, or list managers.
2. *Description*—spells out characteristics of list selection capability, special features, average unit of sale.
3. *List source*—describes when, where, and how the list was developed or derived and includes source of names, whether from a published source, reference source, or other.
4. *Quantity and rental rates*—gives combination rates, specification selection rates, and minimum order requirement for total list and segments along with price per thousand names.
5. *Commission and credit policy*—gives agency or broker commission, cash discount policy, deposits required, and other credit conditions.
6. *Method of addressing*—gives complete details on addressing methods and availability of magnetic tape lists.
7. *Delivery schedule*—runs 10 days to 3 weeks in most cases.
8. *Restrictions*—gives conditions of availability and reuse and security precautions. For most noncompiled lists, samples are required on all tests and continuations.
9. *Test arrangement*—includes rates, minimum number requirement, premiums, and conditions. Most minimum test requirements are for a 5,000 quantity. However, some test quantities are as low as 3,000.
10. *Lettershop services*—details services performed, mailing instructions, and returned material.
11. *Maintenance*—updates procedures, mail delivery, guarantees, refund conditions, and duplication considerations.

Business List Catalogs

Compilers, business and trade magazine publishers, and brokers publish individual catalogs that spell out specifics on rental lists. These list catalogs are furnished to mailers free of charge. Some catalogs include both consumer and business lists. Others, such as Dun's Marketing Services or American Business Lists, specialize in business lists only. Many of these are promotional in content, but also provide helpful guidance especially to the beginner and smaller marketer who must wear many hats. Order information is included along with bound-in order cards in some catalogs to make it easy to order. Figures 5-2 through 5-6 illustrate the range of information available in list catalogs.

Data Cards

All rental lists are described on data cards, which are maintained by list owners and brokers. The standard data card size is 8½ by 5½ inches; however, larger

Figure 5-1. Direct Mail Lists Rates and Data sample listing.

DUN'S DECISION MAKERS
Media Code 3 045 4648 4.00				Mid 025475-000
Member: D.M.A.
Dun's Marketing Services, a company of The Dun &
Bradstreet Corp.
49 Old Bloomfield Ave., Mountain Lakes, NJ 07046.
  Phone 201-299-7674, Toll free, 800-MAIL NOW.

1. PERSONNEL
Senior Vice-President, Client Services—Thomas
  McCarthy.
Vice-President, Direct Marketing—Gerald Reisberg.
Director/Product Management—Annalisa Wyatt.
Branch Offices
Arizona (Phoenix)—Phone 602-956-9200.
California (Fullerton)—Phone 714-738-0123; (Los
  Angeles)—Phone 213-625-3867; (South San
  Francisco)—Phone 415-871-0930.
Colorado (Aurora)—Phone 303-695-300.
Connecticut (North Haven)—Phone 203-234-0608;
  (Shelton)—Phone 203-926-4800.
Florida (Hollywood)—Phone 305-926-6061;
  (Tampa)—Phone 813-872-0515.
Georgia (Atlanta)—Phone 404-955-0600.
Illinois (Chicago)—Phone 312-263-1623; 312-236-0350;
  (Northfield)—Phone 312-441-8488; (Oakbrook
  Terrace)—Phone 312-574-8310; (Peoria)—Phone 309-
  674-6156.
Indiana (Indianapolis)—Phone 317-251-9729.
Kansas (Shawnee Mission)—Phone 913-262-5520.
Massachusetts (Framingham)—Phone 617-879-3840.
Maryland (Baltimore)—Phone 301-821-1510.
Michigan (Troy)—Phone 313-589-0400.
Minnesota (Bloomington)—Phone 612-885-5621.
Missouri (St. Louis)—Phone 314-997-5353.
New Jersey (Cherry Hill)—Phone 609-662-6633;
  (Rochelle Park)—Phone 201-368-0340.
New York (Albany)—Phone 518-456-1402;
  (Amherst)—Phone 716-839-2063; (Melville)—Phone
  516-293-2230; (New York City)—Phone 212-971-6700;
  (Pittsford)—Phone 716-385-8890.
North Carolina (Charlotte)—Phone 704-535-2270.
Ohio (Cincinnati)—Phone 513-772-1550;
  (Independence)—Phone 216-447-1064.
Oklahoma (Oklahoma City)—Phone 405-843-0944.
Pennsylvania (Pittsburgh)—Phone 412-366-7337.
Rhode Island (East Providence)—Phone 401-433-4600.
South Carolina (Columbia)—Phone 803-731-0132.
Tennessee (Memphis)—Phone 901-761-3090.
Texas (Dallas)—Phone 214-702-9307; (Houston)—Phone
  713-780-0755; (San Antonio)—Phone 512-680-2628;
  (Fort Worth)—Phone 817-429-8319.
Utah (Salt Lake City)—Phone 801-298-8647.
Virginia (McLean)—Phone 800-424-2495.
Washington (Seattle)—Phone206-728-8900.
Wisconsin (Milwaukee)—Phone 414-347-1340.

2. DESCRIPTION
U.S. names and titles of 9 million top and middle
management executives, selected by job function and
company size.

3. LIST SOURCE
Dun's Marketing Services compiled files and direct
investigative procedure.

4. QUANTITY AND RENTAL RATES
Rec'd Aug. 5, 1987.

	Total Number	Price per/M
Total list	9,508,137	*78.00
Executives in companies with 100+ employees	411,619	"
Executives in companies with 20+ employees	1,783,608	"
Chairman	138,343	"
President	2,115,644	"
Owner	1,564,357	"
Partner	1,162,690	"
Principal	81,115	"
Trustee	11,836	"
Vice President-Finance	30,376	"
Treasurer	1,240,797	"
Controller	25,867	"
Vice President	1,077,995	"
Administrator	15,091	"
Superintendent	7,192	"
Manager	89,961	"
VP Research	2,460	"
VP-Data Processing	15,995	"
VP Manufacturing	6,104	"
VP Operations	24,448	"
VP Production	30,187	"
VP Engineering	29,156	"
Secretary	1,324,328	"
Counsel	38,874	"
Clerk	67,781	"
VP Sales	27,014	"
VP Marketing	22,119	"
VP Purchasing	41,349	"
Exec. VP	5,867	"
Sr. VP	12,431	"
Other officers	327,415	"

(*) Quantity discounts and varied addressing capabilities available. Selectors available for all lists; geographic, 2, 3, or 4-digit SIC, size of business (by employment of sales volume), by gender, age, Nth factor;
rank by sales volume or number of employees, year
business started. Minimum order 450.00. Lists also
available on tape or other data processing formats for
annual use.

5. COMMISSION, CREDIT POLICY
Terms are full upon delivery FOB Parsippany, NJ.

6. METHOD OF ADDRESSING
Pressure sensitive labels, labels for Cheshire equipment.
All printed 4-up.

7. DELIVERY SCHEDULE
Normally within 2 weeks after receipt of order.

8. RESTRICTIONS
All labels are furnished on a one-time rental basis only,
and no copies can be made without permission from Dun
& Bradstreet.

11. MAINTENANCE
Cleaned and updated daily. Computerized monthly.

(D-B)

Source: Courtesy of Standard Rate & Data Service, Inc.

sizes carry more information (see Figure 5-7, a reduced version of a larger card).
The card includes standard information such as:

- List source
- Makeup of the list
- Addressing process
- Minimum order quantity
- Selections available
- Restrictions

State counts and other breakdowns are given on the reverse side of some list
cards. Latest list counts appear as of the date on the card. Usually cards are
updated twice a year and there are separate data cards prepared for each major
segment of the list.

(Text continues on page 86.)

Figure 5-2. List catalogs spell out choice of mailing formats.

Prospect Lists

These easy-to-read single line listings are perfect for sales planning, telemarketing, or following up on inquiries. Complete information is provided for each business, including name, address, area code and phone number, and franchise/brand for many lists. Each Prospect List is individually printed on a laser printer for maximum legibility.

Prospect lists may be ordered in 3 different sequences at no additional charge:

(1) BY CITY— This sequence is ordered most often. States are listed alphabetically, with cities alpha within states and business names alpha within cities.

(2) BY COUNTY— Useful if sales territories are set up on a county basis. States listed alphabetically, counties alpha within states, city within county and business names within city.

(3) BY ZIP CODE— This sequence is preferred when ordered along with mailing labels. The matching sequence makes it easier to follow up on the mailing.

We can provide other sequences, depending on your needs. Please specify when you place your order. Additional programming charges may be required.

actual size 8½" x 11"

3X5 Cards

Our 3" x 5" cards are the ideal format for prospect card files or telemarketing "calling cards". Information included is the same as on the Prospect list, and you can order any of the above sequences.

Magnetic Formats

Lists can be provided on magnetic tape or diskettes, allowing unlimited use. This also allows you the flexibility of adding or deleting names and sorting the data in any sequence you may desire.

Tape: Available in ASCII or EBCDIC (IBM) machine languages, 800, 1600, or 6250 BPI. We can provide any blocking factor desired, and any sequence.

Diskettes: are IBM-PC (5¼" & 3½"), IBM-3740 (8"), Apple IIe (5¼"), or Apple Macintosh (3½") compatible. Please check your machine's compatibility before ordering. We also can provide fixed or sequentially delimited files. We also have formatted diskettes which can be used to print one-up labels without any complicated programming. If you are not sure about compatibility, sample diskettes are available at a small charge. See page 62 for diskette charges.

Tape   Diskettes

On-Line Retrieval

On-Line Retrieval - Instant Yellow Page Service

Please See Inside Back Cover
For Complete Details.

American Business Lists Inc., P.O. Box 27347, Omaha, Nebraska 68127   Phone (402) 331-7169   TELEX: 510-101-0855 AMBLIST   FAX: (402) 331-1505

Source: Reproduced with permission of American Business Lists Inc., 5707 South 86th Circle, Omaha 68127.

Selection Options Available

Our database of over 14 million Yellow Page business listings is maintained **online** on our two computer systems. This means that we can offer more selection options than other list companies. We also retrieve more information from the Yellow Pages, so we can provide virtually any combination of selections you may want.
For example:

By Yellow Page Title or SIC Codes...
for the total U.S., by state, county, 3-digit Zip code (SCF), telephone area code, or Metropolitan Statistical Area (MSA). We can also combine any number of titles, and eliminate duplication.

All Businesses ...
for 3-digit or 5-digit Zip code area, county, state, or telephone area code and prefix. (See page 22-23.)

By Ad Size ...
You can select businesses by the size of their Yellow Page ad, such as all "Restaurants" with display ads, regular listing, bold-face listing, or in-column display ad.

By Population Range ...
such as all "Repair Shops" in cities with populations of 50,000 or more.

By Franchise or Brands Sold ...
such as "McDonald's Restaurants", "Chevrolet" car dealers, or "Toro" lawn mower dealers. (See page 46-47.)

New Names Only ...
such as all new businesses who first appeared in 1985 Yellow Pages. (See page 59)

By Professional Specialty ...
such as "Orthodontists" for Dentists or "Cardiologists" for Doctors.

Canadian Business Lists ...
are also available. See page 52-55 for counts and pricing.

We don't have enough space here to describe all the different combinations available. Review this catalog, and let your imagination come up with the best selection options for your specific needs. We can provide the proper selections in most cases.

If you'd like to discuss your list requirements, our customer representatives are ready to help you at any time. Or feel free to call Tom Lingelbach, our Sales Manager, or send a letter outlining your requirements. We'll respond promptly.

List Formats

Mailing Labels

5511A	5511A	5511A	5511A
DON RINGLER CHEVROLET CO 3625 S GENL BRUCE DR ** TEMPLE TX 76501	HARDING LINCOLN-MERCURY 311 E AVE A TEMPLE TX 76501-4398	IRA YOUNG AUTO CO INC 3207 GENERAL BRUCE DR TEMPLE TX 76501	JOHNSON BROS FORD INC 503 N GENERAL BRUCE DR TEMPLE TX 76501-2435
5511A	5511A	5511A	5511A
KUYKENDALL MOTOR CO 15 S 8TH TEMPLE TX 76501-4354	TEMPLE IMPORTS MAZDA 520 N GENERAL BRUCE DR TEMPLE TX 76501-2935	TRANUM-HUNDLEY BUICK 206 E ADAMS TEMPLE TX 76501-4304	FARRIS PONTIAC-GMC INC 4410 S GENRL BRUCE DR * TEMPLE TX 76502
5511A	5511A	5511A	5511A
GARLYN SKELTON IMPORTS 5420 MIDWAY DR TEMPLE TX 76502-1499	T A MOSLEY CHEVROLET CO HWY 95 S BARTLETT TX 76511	GANTENBEIN FORD INC 1 HWY 35 S * BELTON TX 76513	DAVIS SIMMONS CHEVROLET 308 N FANNIN * CAMERON TX 76520-3362
5511A	5511A	5511A	5511A
BILLY YOUNG LINCOLN-MCRY 2823 E HWY 190 * COPPERAS COVE TX 76522-2561	COVE FORD INC 714 E HWY 190 COPPERAS COVE TX 76522-2253	MIKE KILPATRICK PONTIAC 1535 E HWY 190 COPPERAS COVE TX 76522-2343	POWELL CHEVROLET CO INC 507 MAIN * GATESVILLE TX 76528-1316
5511A	5511A	5511A	5511A
SCHWORRENBERG FORD 901 MAIN GATESVILLE TX 76528-1497	SHEPHERD MOTOR CO 819 MAIN GATESVILLE TX 76528-1432	WOMBLE PONTIAC BUICK 2429 MAIN GATESVILLE TX 76528-1899	JOHN EARL GREEN MOTORS 132 E MAIN * HAMILTON TX 76531-1918
5511A	5511A	5511A	5511A
BILLY YOUNG LINCOLN-MERC 903 E HWY 190 KILLEEN TX 76541-7205	CENTROPLEX FORD SUBARU W S YOUNG & RANCIER KILLEEN TX 76541	CONWELL CHEVROLET INC W HWY 190 KILLEEN TX 76541	J & M AUTO SALES 1001 E RANCIER * KILLEEN TX 76541-3847

Standard-size labels are printed four-up, in Zip Code order to facilitate bulk mailings. Other sequences are available upon request. You may order Pressure-Sensitive (peel-off) labels, or ungummed Cheshire labels for mailing house use. Our mailing labels do not include phone numbers. We can print the phone number on the labels, if requested.

Special Mailing Labels: such as one-up labels, clear labels, NCR backed labels are available. Please call for prices and availability.

Carrier Route and 9-Digit Zip Codes: can be provided. In addition, labels can be sorted to meet many bulk rate requirements. Please call our office for prices.

Figure 5-3. Publication list catalogs contain a finer breakdown
of list availabilities than standard compiled directories.

IAN-Instrumentation & Control News

116,980 ACTIVE SUBSCRIBERS @ $70.00/M

STATE COUNTS

IAN-Instrumentation & Control News boasts the largest qualified readership of any magazine serving the instrumentation market, both manufacturer and end user.

Subscribers to *IAN* are design engineers, quality control engineers, production engineers, company and operations managers — all buying influences or producers of industrial instrumentation.

In addition to instrumentation offers, this dynamic list works well for technical and engineering products, scientific books and subscriptions, engineering and design seminars, material handling catalog offers, and more.

Selections: Job Function, SIC Code, Plant Size, Geographic (State/SCF/Zip) @ $5.00/M each; Nth name, NC.

Job Function	Count	%
Product Design Engineers	29,245	25.0
Systems Design Engineers	30,900	26.4
Production Engineers	19,450	16.6
Quality Control Engineers	8,420	7.2
Corporate Management	14,500	12.4
Basic Research	2,370	2.0
Operations & Maintenance	8,130	6.9
Purchasing & Procurement	1,830	1.6
Other Qualified Personnel	2,135	1.9

Business/Industry
SIC

SIC		Count	%
10-14	Mining	1,480	1.3
15-17	Construction	1,700	1.5
20	Food & Kindred Products	2,380	2.0
22	Textile Mill Products	740	0.6
26	Paper & Allied Products	2,995	2.6
28	Chemicals & Allied Products	7,930	6.8
29	Petroleum & Coal Products	1,195	1.0
30	Rubber & Misc. Plastics	3,515	3.0
32	Stone, Clay & Glass Products	1,755	1.5
33	Primary Metals	3,230	2.8
34	Fabricated Metals	5,950	5.1
35	Machinery	18,020	15.4
36	Electric & Electronic Equipment	19,560	16.7
37	Transportation Equipment	5,450	4.7
38	Instrumentation	11,420	9.8
39	Misc. Manufacturing	970	0.8
48-49	Communications/Utilities	7,400	6.3
50-51	Wholesale Trade	1,215	1.0
73	Business Services	4,260	3.6
89	Misc. Services	9,830	8.4
91-97	Public Administration	2,350	2.0
	Other	3,635	3.1

MA	Massachusetts	010-027	5.440
RI	Rhode Island	028-029	570
NH	New Hampshire	030-038	830
ME	Maine	039-049	415
VT	Vermont	050-059	240
CT	Connecticut	060-069	3.190
NJ	New Jersey	070-089	6.210
NY	New York	100-149	8.330
PA	Pennsylvania	150-196	7.850
DE	Delaware	197-199	520
DC	District of Col.	200-205	235
MD	Maryland	206-219	1.800
VA	Virginia	220-246	2.070
WV	West Virginia	247-268	560
NC	North Carolina	270-289	2.260
SC	South Carolina	290-299	1.350
GA	Georgia	300-319	1.680
FL	Florida	320-339	2.830
AL	Alabama	350-369	1.280
TN	Tennessee	370-385	1.650
MS	Mississippi	386-397	450
KY	Kentucky	400-427	955
OH	Ohio	430-458	7.780
IN	Indiana	460-479	2.750
MI	Michigan	480-499	5.180
IA	Iowa	500-528	1.010
WI	Wisconsin	530-549	3.490
MN	Minnesota	550-567	2.700
SD	South Dakota	570-577	110
ND	North Dakota	580-588	120
MT	Montana	590-599	170
IL	Illinois	600-629	7.530
MO	Missouri	630-658	1.995
KS	Kansas	660-679	860
NE	Nebraska	680-693	570
LA	Louisiana	700-714	1.150
AR	Arkansas	716-729	430
OK	Oklahoma	730-749	1.060
TX	Texas	750-799	6.270
CO	Colorado	800-816	1.540
WY	Wyoming	820-831	130
ID	Idaho	832-838	330
UT	Utah	840-847	580
AZ	Arizona	850-865	1.180
NM	New Mexico	870-884	590
NV	Nevada	890-898	270
CA	California	900-961	15.310
HI	Hawaii	967-968	130
OR	Oregon	970-979	1.080
WA	Washington	980-994	1.830
AK	Alaska	995-999	120
TOTAL:			116.980

CALL TOLL-FREE 1-800-345-1214, Ext. 4365
(In Penna., 215-964-4365)

Source: Courtesy of Chilton Direct Marketing and List Management Co., Radnor, PA 19089.

Selections (continued)

Plant Size	Count	%
Under 20 employees	19,660	16.8
20-99	24,370	20.8
100-499	33,795	28.9
500-999	12,810	11.0
1000-2499	13,160	11.2
2500+	12,060	10.3

IAN SUBSCRIBERS BY BUYING INFLUENCE @ $100.00/M

Shown below are counts of *IAN* subscribers who are documented *buyers, specifiers, and on-the-job users* of instrumentation and control products in 21 different categories. With this special selection, industrial marketers can target just those prospects with greatest interest in — and purchase authority for — their product. (*Note:* Duplicate names will be automatically eliminated.)

# of individuals	who buy, recommend, and/or specify:
54,860	Analytical & Scientific Instruments
60,510	Recorders & Plotters
73,350	Sensing Instruments & Sensors
66,930	Test & Calibration Equipment
53,000	Programmable Controllers
46,540	Data Acquisition Equipment
9,900	Large Computers, Main Frame
50,330	Control & Instrumentation Systems
49,880	Mini/Micro Computers
46,020	Computer Peripherals
35,070	Data Convertors, Amplifiers, Interfaces
65,790	Motors & Motor Controls
75,865	Relays, Switches, Timers
67,320	Wire, Cable & Accessories
38,610	Force, Load, Strain & Vibration Instruments
55,460	Valves, Actuators & Positioners
48,240	Pumps, Compressors & Accessories
54,070	Control Panels, Displays & Annunciators
46,720	Controllers, Regulators & Transmitters
39,900	Maintenance/Repair/Operations
49,070	Generators, Power Supplies & Batteries

This List is Especially Recommended for Mailers in These Categories:

All Buying Influence product groups listed, plus:

- Catalogs of Test & Measurement Equipment
- Design/Control Engineering Shows & Seminars
- Employee Motivation
- Computer Support Products
- Continuing Engineering Education
- General Plant Products
- Tools
- Books/Courses/Subscriptions on Quality Control, Bar Code Technology, Preventive Maintenance, Microelectronics, Data Acquisition

Send Orders to:
CHILTON DIRECT MARKETING
1 Chilton Way
Radnor, PA 19089-0350
Attn: Allen Hansen

For Instant Service, FAX to:
1-215-964-4745

Figure 5-4. A major business publisher furnishes classifications by function and title.

Heating/Piping/Air Conditioning subscribers

45,148 Mechanical Systems Engineers—$65/M

Mechanical systems engineering professionals involved in design, product selection, operation and maintenance of non-residential buildings. These responsible professionals can help you determine market potential, develop sales leads and inquiries.

See page 3 for selections and additional costs

Geographical Breakdown

State & Zip Code	Total Qualified
039-049 ME	195
030-038 NH	192
050-059 VT	96
010-027 MA	1,641
028-029 RI	178
060-069 CT	964
New England	**3,266 7.2%**
100-149 NY	4,187
070-089 NJ	2,305
150-196 PA	3,129
Middle Atlantic	**9,621 21.3%**
430-458 OH	2,344
460-479 IN	915
600-629 IL	2,715
480-499 MI	1,601
530-549 WI	1,129
East No. Central	**8,704 19.3%**
550-567 MN	913
500-528 IA	463
630-658 MO	1,174
580-588 ND	76
570-577 SD	88
680-693 NE	354
660-679 KS	351
West No. Central	**3,419 7.6%**
197-199 DE	199
206-219 MD	1,002
200-205 DC	325
220-246 VA	1,193
247-268 WV	194
270-289 NC	924
290-299 SC	612
300-319 GA	790
320-342 FL	1,480
South Atlantic	**6,719 14.9%**
400-427 KY	454
370-385 TN	749
350-369 AL	601
386-397 MS	155
East So. Central	**1,959 4.3%**
716-729 AR	190
700-714 LA	555
730-749 OK	408
750-799 TX	2,452
West So. Central	**3,605 8.0%**
590-599 MT	86
832-838 ID	162
820-831 WY	58
800-816 CO	646
870-884 NM	208
850-865 AZ	417
840-847 UT	240
890-898 NV	123
Mountain	**1,940 4.3%**
995-999 AK	116
980-994 WA	752
970-979 OR	370
900-961 CA	4,012
967-968 HI	196
Pacific	**5,446 12.1%**
United States	**44,679 99.0%**
969 & 006-009 U.S. Territories	162
Canada	144
Foreign	163
TOTALS	**45,148 100.0%**

Classification tables

BUSINESS & INDUSTRY	Engineering Management	Engineering Service for Systems Design	Engineering Service for Systems Installation	Engineering Service for Systems Operation	Other Design Engineering	Other Functions and No Function	TOTAL QUALIFIED COPIES	PERCENT OF TOTAL
Consulting Engineering/Architectural Firms	3,755	8,586	363	294	951	54	14,003	31.0
Engineering/Construction Firms	788	973	367	113	180	12	2,433	5.4
Mechanical Contracting Firms	1,353	1,123	1,903	309	339	7	5,034	11.1
Industrial Manufacturing Firms	4,756	3,153	761	1,421	994	74	11,159	24.7
Commercial/Institutional/Government Firms	4,353	3,161	703	2,535	962	689	12,403	27.5
SUB-TOTAL	15,005	16,996	4,097	4,672	3,426	836	45,032	99.7%
Manufacturer Representatives/Sales Engineers							77	0.2
Wholesaler Distributor of HVAC Products							11	0.1
Others Allied to the Field (Agriculture and Mining)							28	0.1
TOTAL							45,148	100.0%

Primary Mechanical Systems Engineering Function — Classification by Function

CLASSIFICATION BY TITLE	Engineering Management (Owner, Partner, Pres., Dir., Supervisor, Coor., Mgr., Chief Engineer, Vice President) (See Note 1)	Staff Engineering (Design, specification, installation, operation, maintenance, engineer, plant eng., designer and draftsman) (See Note 1)	Company Addressed Copies (Library, Eng. Dept.)
Consulting Engineering/Architectural Firms	7,913	6,036	54
Engineering/Construction Firms	1,613	808	12
Mechanical Contracting Firms	4,250	777	7
Industrial Manufacturing Firms	6,365	4,720	74
Commercial/Institutional/Government Firms	6,823	4,891	689
TOTAL	26,964	17,232	836

Note 1: Engineering Management - Owner, partner, president, director, supervisor, coordinator, manager, chief engineer, vice president. Staff Engineering - Design, specification, installation, operation, maintenance engineer, plant engineer, designer and draftsman.

Source: Courtesy of Penton Lists, Penton/IPC, Cleveland 44114.

Figure 5-5. Helpful information to guide the marketer in planning successful direct marketing campaigns is found in some list catalogs.

A SHORT COURSE IN THE 'HOW-TOS' OF DIRECT MAIL*
By Ed Burnett

RULE #1—is *determine your objective first*—then find out whether direct mail is the best, or the only, or one of a combination of ways to reach that objective.

RULE #2—is *lean on the experts*. You can find out enough in a few phone calls to knowledgeable specialists to tell whether you are equipped to run a direct response operation without the help of a consultant or not. If a lot is involved, buy the best consultant you can locate. If the world doesn't rest on the result of a given test, you may wish, for cost considerations, to wing it for yourself. (But when it involves direct mail, at least *talk* to experts in the list business. They can improve by a significant multiplier, almost any result you can obtain by yourself.)

How to mail

•*Have all lists on labels (cheshire or pressure sensitive) delivered to you, not to your fulfillment shop.* You and you alone must check—for quantity, for spread, for sex, for home versus business address, for keys, for titles, for classification data. Did you get a 5th digit Zip select? Were certain states or SCFs omitted? Is there any discernible duplication? Does the list "feel" right?

•*Mail all of a given list in one drop.* Staggered mailings will produce staggered returns which will destroy any half-life examination.

•*Mail all tests in one drop.* This is the only certain way to remove one variable, timing, from the factors influencing response.

•*Always insist upon a postal receipt verifying the number of pieces placed into the mailstream on a given day.* This does two things—it verifies the quantity of mail delivered on a given day, and the Postal Service date stamp gives the actual date mailed.

When not to mail

•*Do not use direct mail if the order margin is small, irrespective of how great the markup is.* For example, a book to sell at $5 with an order margin of $4 (but a markup of several hundred percent) simply will not fly. The minimum cost in the mail is in the range of $225 to $275 per M. At that cost, the cost of promotion requires sales of some 6 percent . . . which just isn't going to happen.

•*Before starting a direct mail program, ascertain the universe of likely prospects.* If this universe—even if doubled by peripheral concepts or classification—is small, it may be best not to mail at all.

•*Do not mail those lists from a merge/purge where the duplication identified indicates little prospect of success.*

•*Do not mail secondary segments of a list where the primary or ideal segment has not worked.* For example, if current customers of a list have failed, there is no reason to expect older customers from the same list (with the same characteristics) to work. If customers do not work, inquiries unconverted to customer status for the same list certainly will not work.

How to track response

•*Calculate "half-life" on every promotion—for every medium.* "Half-life" is a measuring stick for early calculation of mailing results. Every mailing has a half-life (the time when half the responses that will ultimately come in have been recorded) that occurs within a very brief period after returns start arriving. This half-life is specific and virtually certain.

Just as carbon dating half-life is valuable to the geologist or the paleontologist, the half-life buried in mailing return rates, if used properly, can be valuable to the direct mail practitioner. It is a tool that enables him or her to make (correct) decisions based on only part of the facts.

How to track response and read results

What this means to you is that the success or failure of a given copy, offer, or list test, can, with experience, be predicted within a few days (if first class) or a few weeks (if third class) of receipt of the first responses.

Basically, and historically, and even now during the disruption of what was once a more predictable postal delivery service, the curve of response to a mailing dropped on the same day shows a swiftly rising response at the beginning of the period, followed by a

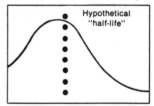

Hypothetical "half-life"

slow descent (per day, week, month), followed by a long, long tail. It is not unusual for a given mailing of some size to produce some responses every week for a series of months. But such responses "on the tail" of the mailing are always sporadic, small, and, overall, rather inconsequential in the mathematics of the offer.

Since this curve is virtually invariable, it stands to reason that *establishing the half-life in number of responses will enable decision-making weeks or months before the receipt of*

*Reprinted from *Folio* Magazine

Source: From data provided by Ed Burnett, Burnett Consultants. Material originally appeared in and is reprinted from *Folio: The Magazine for Magazine Management.* Used by permission.

(continues)

Figure 5-5 (continued)

the final responses.

Now the question is, "How does a mailer determine the half-life on his mailings?"

Determining half-life

To determine the half-life on your mailings, there are a few simple and fairly obvious rules to follow:

•*Drop all mailings on the same day.* If you stagger mailings, you will in effect be laying one curve over another, thus destroying the validity of any given half-life experience.

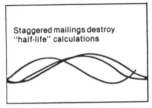

Staggered mailings destroy "half-life" calculations

•*Record responses for each key . . . every day* (Figure 1).

•*Be sure your record keeping includes:*

1. Cumulative responses at end of each day—by key and total. (Cumulative figures can be processed weekly, if desired, once responses begin to dwindle.)

2. Records for each day—even if there is no response for a given key on a given day. Every day is significant . . . even one with no response.

3. Some easy visual means (a pair of ruled lines will do) to identify responses for Tuesdays. (Tuesdays, which usually include responses for Saturday, Sunday and Monday, are normally significantly higher than the other days in the week.) When response on a given Tuesday is lower than the preceding Tuesday, response has undoubtedly "peaked," and the curve of response, in general, will from that point on be downward.

(In years past, Business Reply Envelopes and Business Reply Cards arrived daily, including Mondays. Today, many major post offices hold such mail received over the weekend until Tuesday.)

4. Posting for a given key for a period of three months (six months if the offer shows particular life).

•*On the posting record include the following information:*

1. Mailing description or number.

2. Key number.

3. Description of the variable involved (as list name, or copy test A).

4. Date of drop. (If this varies by key or test, it is important to date each such segment.)

5. Total quantity ordered.

6. Total quantity mailed = Universe (100 percent) against which responses are measured. (Please note that this is hardly ever the same as the total quantity ordered and may differ enough so as to change percentage of response—if measured against the nice neat record "5,000" ordered—by a significant amount.)

7. Estimated or actual cost of the mailing package—in the mail—per thousand.

8. The response rate you require to consider continuing that given test. (This is, in commercial terms, your "breakeven" percentage.) This is your predetermined guide to the number of responses (and/or the number of dollars) you are looking for.

•*Bind into a book, so you cannot easily take it out and lose it,* one copy of each mailing with its number and samples of each variable mailed, plus the daily and cumulative results. You will find this invaluable when the time comes to review mailings, mailing results, and the calculation of "half-life."

•*Track and compare response periods.*

If you have such records for prior mailings, draw a bold red line beneath the day's posting for each key which, cumulatively, includes 50 percent of the total responses.

If your particular offer, package, mailing list and timing follow visual patterns, you will find these red lines,

on a whole series of tests, virtually parallel. If you have mailed first class, such marks are nine days from the date of the first posted response (not from day dropped). Then of 20 such marks, not more than one or two will be outside the range of eight days (9 minus 1) to 10 days (9 plus 1).

If you have mailed third-class bulk (most bets are now off if you have mailed third-class piece-rate due to the vagaries of post office handling), the variation between the marks will be plus or minus half a week. That is, if most such marks are at the end of the third week from the date of the first posted response (not from day dropped), then of 20 such marks, not more than one or two will be outside the range of 2½ weeks (3 weeks minus half a week) to 3½ weeks (3 weeks plus half a week). (For half weeks, combine M-T and W-T-F.)

The data given above relate exclusively to one-time mailings. Series of mailings have their own unique curves which can hardly be measured in the testing stage. The number and frequency of mailings in a series is definitely an art, not a science. Charting half-lives, however, can prove useful in determining the number and frequency of such typical efforts as collection and renewal series.

If you have mailed a catalog, the variation between the marks will tend to center around the fifth or sixth week. But the evidence here clearly indicates that response, particularly length of response, varies by type of merchandise (impulse, for example versus solid "reason why"); class of customer (business houses react slower

A half-life determination

	Key 1	Key 2	Key 3	Key 4	
Daily posting of responses, plus weekly cumulations	X	X	X	X	
	X	X	X	X	
	X	X	X	X	
	X	X	X	X	Plus or minus
	X	X	X	X	24 hours!
	X	X	X		
	X	X	X		
	X	X		X	
	X	X	X		
	X	X			
		X	X	X	
		X			
		X			
	100	140	90	70	

Please note: Do *not* measure from day of drop. What you are measuring here is response rate . . . from the first day of response.

2

	Package A		Package B		
	Offer 1	Offer 2	Offer 1	Offer 2	Total
List AA	X	X	X	X	4X
BB	X	X	X	X	4X
CC	X	X	X	X	4X
DD	X	X	X	X	4X
EE	X	X	X	X	4X
	5X	5X	5X	5X	

10X   10X

10X   10X

and continue to produce long after consumer mailings have "tailed" out); and time of year (a Christmas catalog will at times not just fall off, but simply stop stone cold dead in the marketplace).

An offer involving a sweepstakes or credit can also produce a different pattern of response than one not involving participation or charge privilege.

In addition, half-life on a catalog is usually not as important as half-life on an individual offer. In the case of the catalog, the whole mailing is usually committed, and the half-life simply advises management of where they are now, and likely will be some time later. On an individual product or service offer, the half-life is one of the ways management can proceed with confidence with only part of the facts.

Testing variables simultaneously

If you need to test two or more packages (say a self-mailer versus an enclosed piece, or a computer letter versus a Dear Friend letter) and at the same time test two or more offers over a series of lists, learn to use grid testing (Figure 2).

Let's suppose you require, say, 4,000 names per cell to obtain 30 or 40 responses so that you have reasonable confidence that continuations of that cell will do about as well. To provide enough names in the above grid to test each cell would require 20 cells of 4,000 each—or 80,000 names. This may well be more than the total sum you can allocate to this test.

If you now place 1,000 names (and not 4,000) in each cell and read results from the horizontal and vertical totals only, you will note that each list has 4,000 names (and the same chance for response as all other lists). Package A will have 10,000 in the mail to compare with 10,000 for Package B.

And by combining by offer, Offer 1 will have 10,000 in the mail against 10,000 for Offer 2. Thus, in one grid test, you can find out which package is best, which offer is best, and which lists (if any) are worth continuations. This is the one way that several variables can be tested simultaneously —at reasonable cost.

The next time you hear that only one variable can be tested at a time, bring out your trusty grid. (Caution— you cannot with any safety read results within cells. Your internal response is too small for statistical validity. If you use grid testing, you must record all responses within the grid to be able to read results with any confidence.)

If you would like to receive a copy of the complete 3-part article written by Ed Burnett for FOLIO on THE RULES FOR TESTING LISTS, please send a request on your letterhead to:

Publicity Department
Ed Burnett Consultants, Inc.
99 W. Sheffield Avenue
Englewood, N.J. 07631

Figure 5-6. *Business Week* Subscriber Profile lists industrial
as well as individual demographics and buying habits.

<table>
<tr><td colspan="3" align="center">*Business Week Subscriber Profile*</td></tr>
<tr><td colspan="3">1988 Rate Base: 850,000</td></tr>
<tr><td></td><td align="center">*Number*</td><td align="center">*Percent*</td></tr>
<tr><td>**SEX**</td><td></td><td></td></tr>
<tr><td>Male</td><td>727,600</td><td>85.6</td></tr>
<tr><td>Female</td><td>122,400</td><td>14.4</td></tr>
<tr><td>**AGE**</td><td></td><td></td></tr>
<tr><td>18–24</td><td>30,600</td><td>3.6</td></tr>
<tr><td>25–34</td><td>176,800</td><td>20.8</td></tr>
<tr><td>35–44</td><td>267,750</td><td>31.5</td></tr>
<tr><td>45–54</td><td>193,800</td><td>22.8</td></tr>
<tr><td>55–64</td><td>130,050</td><td>15.3</td></tr>
<tr><td>65+</td><td>51,000</td><td>6.0</td></tr>
<tr><td>25–44</td><td>444,550</td><td>52.3</td></tr>
<tr><td>25–54</td><td>638,350</td><td>75.1</td></tr>
<tr><td>Median Age</td><td align="center">43.1 years</td><td></td></tr>
<tr><td>**EDUCATION**</td><td></td><td></td></tr>
<tr><td>Attended/Graduated College+</td><td>813,450</td><td>95.7</td></tr>
<tr><td>College Graduate+</td><td>675,750</td><td>79.5</td></tr>
<tr><td>**HOUSEHOLD INCOME**</td><td></td><td></td></tr>
<tr><td>Less than $35,000</td><td>91,800</td><td>10.8</td></tr>
<tr><td>$35,000+</td><td>758,200</td><td>89.2</td></tr>
<tr><td>$40,000+</td><td>723,350</td><td>85.1</td></tr>
<tr><td>$50,000+</td><td>635,800</td><td>74.8</td></tr>
<tr><td>$75,000+</td><td>421,600</td><td>49.6</td></tr>
<tr><td>$100,000+</td><td>258,400</td><td>30.4</td></tr>
<tr><td>$200,000+</td><td>70,550</td><td>8.3</td></tr>
<tr><td>$250,000+</td><td>39,950</td><td>4.7</td></tr>
<tr><td>Median</td><td align="center">$74,500</td><td></td></tr>
<tr><td>**PERSONAL INCOME**</td><td></td><td></td></tr>
<tr><td>Less than $35,000</td><td>191,250</td><td>22.5</td></tr>
<tr><td>$35,000+</td><td>659,600</td><td>77.6</td></tr>
<tr><td>$40,000+</td><td>607,750</td><td>71.5</td></tr>
<tr><td>$50,000+</td><td>497,250</td><td>58.5</td></tr>
<tr><td>$75,000+</td><td>293,250</td><td>34.5</td></tr>
<tr><td>$100,000+</td><td>176,800</td><td>20.8</td></tr>
<tr><td>$200,000+</td><td>52,700</td><td>6.2</td></tr>
<tr><td>$250,000+</td><td>32,300</td><td>3.8</td></tr>
<tr><td>Median</td><td align="center">$58,800</td><td></td></tr>
</table>

Source: Courtesy of *Business Week* Research, McGraw-Hill, New York, 1987.

	Number	*Percent*
INDUSTRY		
Agriculture/Forestry/Fishing	4,250	0.5
Mining	6,800	0.8
Construction	18,700	2.2
Manufacturing	264,350	31.1
Transportation/Communication/Utilities	67,150	7.9
Wholesale Trade	40,800	4.8
Retail Trade	45,050	5.3
Finance, Insurance, Real Estate	170,000	20.0
Services	173,400	20.4
Government	22,100	2.6
Other (retired, etc.)	37,400	4.4
OCCUPATION		
Business/Industry/Professions	790,500	93.0
Government	22,100	2.6
Other (retired, etc.)	37,400	4.4
JOB TITLE		
Top Management	366,792	46.4
Chairman/Other Board Member	9,486	1.2
President, CEO	113,042	14.3
Owner/Partner	67,983	8.6
Vice President	120,156	15.2
Financial Officer	13,439	1.7
General Manager	15,020	1.9
Other Officer/Other Top Management	27,668	3.5
Other Management/Professional	342,287	43.3
Total Management	709,079	89.7
COMPANY SIZE—NUMBER OF EMPLOYEES°		
Less than 25	189,720	24.0
Less than 50	233,198	29.5
Less than 100	276,675	35.0
100–999	142,290	18.0
1,000+	370,745	46.9
2,500+	316,200	40.0
5,000+	271,142	34.3
10,000+	199,997	25.3

°Based on those employed in business, industry, professions.

(continues)

Figure 5-6 (continued)

	Number	Percent
SALES VOLUME°		
Less than $1 Billion	566,789	71.7
$1 Billion+	224,502	28.4
$2 Billion+	176,282	22.3
JOB FUNCTION°		
Administration, Management	369,954	46.8
Manufacturing, Production, Operations	113,042	14.3
Engineering, Design, R&D	139,919	17.7
Maintenance, Servicing	97,232	12.3
Distribution	79,841	10.1
Purchasing	150,195	19.0
Advertising, Merchandising, Promotion	144,662	18.3
Transportation, Freight	56,126	7.1
Data Processing, MIS	124,899	15.8
Sales, Marketing	344,658	43.6
Finance	263,237	33.3
Planning, Development	255,332	32.3
Personnel	181,815	23.0
International Operations	60,869	7.7
Training, Teaching	157,310	19.9
All Other	69,564	8.8
INVOLVED IN INTERNATIONAL OPERA-TIONS OF COMPANY°	222,921	28.2
RESPONDENT ON BOARD OF DIRECTORS OF OWN OR OTHER COMPANY°	248,217	31.4
RESPONDENT LOCATION°		
Main Headquarters	508,292	64.3
Branch/Division	282,209	35.7
INVOLVEMENT IN PURCHASE DECISION°		
Chemicals, Chemical Products	90,908	11.5
Petroleum, Petroleum Products	64,821	8.2
Metal, Metal Products	112,251	14.2
Paper	160,472	20.3
Plastics	85,374	10.8
Raw Materials	81,422	10.3
Other Manufacturers' Materials, Supplies	121,737	15.4

	Number	Percent
INVOLVEMENT IN PURCHASE DECISION° (con't.)		
Computer Hardware (Net)	422,127	53.4
Mainframes	112,251	14.2
Minicomputers	237,941	30.1
Microcomputers	303,552	38.4
Peripheral Hardware	240,312	30.4
Computer Software	400,784	50.7
Outside Computer Services	140,709	17.8
Word Processing Equipment	291,695	36.9
Other Office Machines (Copiers, Typewriters, etc.)	291,695	36.9
Office Furniture, Fixtures, Supplies	346,239	43.8
Telecommunications Equipment	313,038	39.6
Telecommunications Services	132,804	16.8
Industrial Automation Equipment	109,089	13.8
Other Industrial Machinery, Fixtures, Accessories	121,737	15.4
Building Materials, Equipment, Fixtures	143,871	18.2
Materials Handling Equipment	116,994	14.8
Auto Purchase, Leasing	232,407	29.4
Trucks, Buses, Trailers	90,908	11.5
Company Airtcraft (Net)	19,763	2.5
Fixed-Wing	17,391	2.2
Helicopters	5,534	0.7
Banking/Financial Services (Net)	318,572	40.3
Banking Services	199,997	25.3
Financial Services (Investment Management, Pension Funds, etc.)	210,273	26.6
Accounting Firms/Auditors	206,321	26.1
Company Insurance (Net)	249,008	31.5
Employee Insurance	226,083	28.6
Casualty, Loss Control, Other Business Insurance	187,349	23.7
Shipping, Delivery (Net)	229,245	29.0
Material, Product, Air Freight	108,299	13.7
Express Delivery Service	198,416	25.1
Advertising, Promotion	216,597	27.4
Meeting Sites, Accommodations	219,759	27.8
Real Estate, Plant/Office Site	143,081	18.1
Consultation Services	222,131	28.1
Travel Arrangements	252,170	31.9
Temporary Help	241,103	30.5

°Based on those employed in business, industry, professions.

(continues)

Figure 5-6 (continued)

	Number	Percent
HOUSEHOLD NET WORTH		
$150,000+	600,100	70.6
$250,000+	447,950	52.7
$500,000+	255,000	30.0
Own Real Estate (in addition to main residence)	414,800	48.8
INVESTMENTS HELD		
Corporate Stock	681,700	80.2
Mutual Funds (other than money market funds)	399,500	47.0
Money Market Funds	546,550	64.3
Bonds (not including savings bonds)	324,700	38.2
INVESTMENT PORTFOLIO VALUE		
$100,000+	364,650	42.9
$250,000+	188,700	22.2
NUMBER OF SECURITY TRANSACTIONS (PAST 12 MONTHS)		
4+	403,750	47.5
7+	248,200	29.2
Household Owns Personal/Home Computer	345,950	40.7
HOUSEHOLD POSSESSIONS		
Video Equipment	638,350	75.1
Car Stereo Equipment	648,550	76.3
35mm SLR Camera	481,950	56.7
Compact Disc Player	96,900	11.4
SUBSCRIBER HOUSEHOLD OWNS WATCHES	838,100	98.6
Number of Watches Owned		
3+	677,185	80.8
5+	352,840	42.1
Spent $500+ on Jewelry in Past 12 Months	294,100	34.6

	Number	Percent
CLUB MEMBERSHIPS		
Country Club	176,800	20.8
Health/Fitness Club	250,750	29.5
ENTERTAIN GUESTS AT HOME IN AVERAGE MONTH		
2+ Times	494,700	58.2
3+ Times	246,500	29.0
Gave Wine or Liquor as Gifts in Past 12 Months	456,450	53.7
MONTHLY EXPENDITURE FOR LIQUOR		
$20+	419,900	49.4
$50+	120,700	14.2
MONTHLY EXPENDITURE FOR WINE		
$20+	403,750	47.5
$50+	103,700	12.2
Bought Liquor or Wine by Case (own use or personal/business gift) in Past 12 Months	227,800	26.8
TRAVEL		
Took U.S. Commercial Airline Trips in the Past 12 Months	719,950	84.7
(Of those who took a domestic air trip)		
Took 4+ Trips	493,886	68.6
Took 6+ Trips	370,774	51.5
Took 10+ Trips	247,663	34.4
Took Foreign Commercial Airline Trips in Past 3 Years	691,050	81.3
(Of those who took a foreign air trip)		
Took 2+ Trips	509,995	73.8
Took 4+ Trips	259,144	37.5
Took 6+ Trips	161,015	23.3

°Based on those employed in business, industry, professions.

(continues)

Figure 5-6 (continued)

	Number	Percent
TRAVEL (con't)		
Number of Nights Spent in Hotel/ Motel in Past 12 Months		
10+ Nights	630,700	74.2
15+ Nights	480,250	56.5
20+ Nights	419,900	49.4
Personally Rented a Car in Past 12 Months	578,000	68.0
(Of those who rented a car)		
3+ Times	407,490	70.5
5+ Times	269,348	46.6
10+ Times	160,684	27.8
AUTOMOTIVE		
Household Has Vehicles for Personal Use	804,100	94.6
(Of households with vehicles)		
Personally Owned	753,442	93.7
Acquired New	742,184	92.3
Domestic	643,280	80.0
Imported	443,059	55.1
Number of Vehicles Household Has		
2+	651,950	76.7
3+	262,650	30.9
Household Member Expects to Purchase		
Vehicle New in the Future	508,300	59.8
Within 12 Months	281,598	55.4

To ensure that brokers stay current, list managers provide them with the latest list card information. Both brokers and list owners present list data cards as suggestions to potential mailers. The handy card format simplifies the list recommendation process. Special promotional use of data cards is reflected in larger size cards and other formats seen in use today that not only contain data card list information but other helpful list use suggestions.

Business List Services

Rental list sources are not difficult to find. List brokers, managers, and compilers are typically listed in the directory sections of the following publications:

Direct Marketing Magazine, 224 Seventh St., Garden City, NY 11530
Target Marketing, 401 N. Broad St., Philadelphia, PA 19108
DM News, 19 W. 23rd St., New York, NY 10010
Catalog Age, 125 Elm St., New Canaan, CT 06840

Figure 5-7. Broker's list card details vital statistics on list availability in concise form.

LEARNING INTERNATIONAL INC. - Unduplicated Master List

	July 1986 K01
(Formerly: Xerox Learning Systems)	A01

210,492 U.S. Buyers/Subscribers (1983-86) @ $70/M	Minimum: 5,000
129,392 U.S. Buyers/Subscribers (1985-86) @ $75/M	

Can Select or Omit by Individual Files @ N/C:

Cheshire/Magtape from:

	Self Improvement	Personnel Development	Working Smart	
(83-86)	122,696	51,559	N/A	Automated Resources
(85-86)	61,797	29,069	44,543	Att: Marge Aquinas

21 Philips Parkway
Montvale, NJ 07645

DATA & PROFILE — An unduplicated Master List combining all three Learning International Inc. Executive Files:

(201) 391-1500

SELF-IMPROVEMENT Buyers have purchased one-shot cassette/workbook programs covering such subjects as Reading & Evaluating Financial Reports, Speed Reading Self Taught, Leading Meetings, Advanced Executive Leadership Skills, Presentation by Objective, Help Yourself Time Management and Negotiating Self Taught. 90% men at business address.

Sample Required on all Tests and Continuations.

Allow 2-3 weeks for delivery.

PERSONNEL DEVELOPMENT Executives who have purchased self-improvement training materials for administrative assistants and/or executive secretaries. 95% men at business address.

SELF-IMPROVEMENT AND PERSONNEL DEVELOPMENT FILES PROFILE 70% of the executies are department heads, general managers, or company officers. 30% have graduate degrees. 49% have a personal computer. Average income is $60,000.

Add $25 for non-returnable magtape.

WORKING SMART is a monthly advisory service developed for executives. It offers executives concise advice to maximize their productivity and their effectiveness in dealing with others. 85% men. 85% are department heads, general managers or company officers. 30% have graduate degrees.

Net Name Arrangement (50,000 minimum): 85% + $5/M run charges

UNIT — PERSONNEL: $129.90. SELF-IMPROVEMENT: Ranges from $79.95 to $190. Average $95. WORKING SMART: $96.

MEDIA — 98% direct mail. No selection by source.

NOTE: Cancellation of order after mail date will require payment of full rental rate.

FILED — Zip sequence / 4-up Cheshire / 9T/1600 Magtape.

SELECTIONS — Nth name @ N/C.
State @ $2.50/M.
SCF or Zip @ $5/M (up to 25 SCF's or Zips). Each additional 25 will be an extra $15 Flat Fee per group.
Pressure Sensitive Labels @ $5/M.

NOTE: These names duplicate lists offered separately on Kleid data cards# 18277, 18315, 18278.

KEYING — @ N/C (up to 6 digits).

DIRECT MAIL THE KLEID COMPANY 200 PARK AVENUE, NEW YORK, NY 10166 (212) 599-4140

Source: Courtesy of The Kleid Company Inc., New York 10166.   *(continues)*

Figure 5-7 (continued)

LIST: LEARNING INT'L INC. – Unduplicated Master List (1983-1986)					
STATE	COUNT	STATE	COUNT	STATE	COUNT
AK	928	KY	1,780	NY	16,830
AL	1,845	LA	2,557	OH	9,255
AR	1,104	MA	6,702	OK	2,263
AZ	2,784	MD	3,995	OR	2,324
CA	28,943	ME	745	PA	9,815
CO	4,280	MI	7,223	RI	788
CT	4,437	MN	4,217	SC	1,976
DC	1,913	MO	4,302	SD	365
DE	689	MS	968	TN	3,239
FL	8,634	MT	532	TX	15,704
GA	4,981	NC	4,109	UT	1,494
HI	1,121	ND	403	VA	4,990
IA	1,757	NE	1,262	VT	439
ID	662	NH	1,052	WA	3,871
IL	11,526	NJ	8,251	WV	818
IN	3,759	NM	1,008	WI	3,841
KS	1,999	NV	818	WY	366

The Direct Marketing Association, 6 East 43rd St., New York, NY 10017, publishes directories that include list service firms. *Direct Mail Lists Rates and Data* directory, published by Standard Rate & Data Service, 3004 Glenview Rd., Wilmette, IL 60091, also contains the names of the list owner, manager, or exclusive broker for each of the 40,000 business listings, as well as a special section of brokers, compilers, and managers.

In addition, currently published response card decks are listed in the business co-op mailings section of SRDS's *Direct Mail Lists Rates and Data* publication and in the direct response advertising media section of *Business Publications Rates and Data.* Response card mailing services are listed in "markets served" classifications and have complete media information (title, representatives, advertising rates, mechanical requirements, issue closing dates, and circulation).

CONSIDERATIONS WHEN RENTING A BUSINESS LIST

After a list rental decision has been made, marketers should get assurances from the list supplier that each aspect of list processing and delivery conforms to the overall direct marketing plan. Even though placing the list order seems simple, it is too important to treat casually. An unanticipated shortfall of list names can mean that unused expensive direct mail materials will go to waste. Also, misunderstandings can generate costly time delays leading to missed mailing dates.

Merge/Purge

When mailers have scheduled the same mailing to customers as will be made to prospects they should discuss the possible need to merge the rented list tape with the customer list to purge the duplicate files. In addition, it may be necessary to suppress certain combinations of files, such as past test samples, selected geographic territories, or poor credit risks.

Coding

Because it is important for the marketer to identify which of several lists used in a mailing program produces inquiries or orders, the list owner must be able to apply a source code on each address label. This coding enables the marketer to distinguish one list from another. Most rental lists are coded for five-digit zip codes and for counties and metro areas as well as major demographic selections.

List owners can key code names for the renter. Key codes, such as letters, numbers, or special markings, enable measurement of comparison tests of copy approaches, offers, list formats, and other elements in preparation for planned test mailings.

List Counts

List suppliers should be provided with a detailed mailing schedule including specific dates that the list will be used and the number of list copies required. This helps the list supplier understand the mailer's real needs. The mailer depends on accurate list counts to prevent costly overruns when scheduling the number of direct mail pieces to be printed.

Time Frame

Although many list brokers ship within ten days, it's wise to allow a three-week turnaround between list ordering and receipt. Date of order begins only after the response list owner approves the sample piece received from the marketer. For compiled lists, sample pieces are not required.

Costs

Base list prices are usually set for a single order of an original set of labels for one-time use. Names are provided in zip code sequence within town, city, and state.

Average list rental rates vary. The minimum charge applies for one-time use for compiled names and can go to $125/M and above for unique response names. Add to this $5/M to $15/M for each special selection within the lists. Lists are sold in quantities of 1/M, and although there are no minimum order quantity restrictions, a charge upward of $150 is usually established as a minimum invoice amount. A duplicate set of list labels or manuscript is charged out at 50 percent of the base list price.

Special rates apply to frequent mailers who take advantage of 12-month list leases for unlimited use. High-volume commitments can save dollars.

Formats

List suppliers can deliver names in a variety of formats to meet any mailer's specific needs. Lists can be Cheshire machine processed, furnished on computer tape or diskette, as well as directly addressed on envelopes or on 33-up labels, regular single labels, or pressure-sensitive single labels. Most orders for lists used for sales support include a manuscript or sheet listing, which is a printout list of approximately 50 lines to a page. A 3-by-5-inch card listing is another popular form used for telemarketing and by the sales force for follow-up.

A typical order might consist of one set of labels for a one-time mailing, one set on 3-by-5-inch cards including telephone numbers for follow-up calls, and a third set for sales manager follow-up activity.

Labels

Cheshire labels This is the most common list format and is run across a sheet of 44 labels to a page on continuous pages. The labels are ungummed, unperforated, and can be cut into label segments and affixed to envelopes or other mailing pieces by a high-speed Cheshire machine. Most rented lists are run off on Cheshire labels. These are 3.44 inches by 1 inch in size and contain up to six lines at 30 characters per line. Lettershop addressing equipment usually dictates that the renter will get four Cheshire labels across a sheet.

Pressure-sensitive labels Self-sticking labels are appropriate for small runs or for use when the prospect is asked to return the label on the reply device. They come on a waxed paper backing, 3.2 inches by .92 inch, and can be affixed either manually or by machine. An additional charge is standard for pressure-sensitive labels.

Gummed perforated, heat-sensitive, and heat transfer labels These are other label varieties offered by most list service firms.

Computer Format

Magnetic tape Lists on tapes are rented for one-time use or unlimited one-year use.

Diskettes Many lists are now available on floppy disk data processing and word processing formats enabling the smaller marketer in particular to integrate the advantages of computerization into the direct marketing program.

Manuscript Listings

Sheet listings Often called sheet or manuscript listings, printouts of compiled names and addresses, telephone numbers, and other information in the file about an individual firm appear as one line on a page, from 30 to 50 lines per page. Ordered along with actual mailing labels, sheet listings are most often used by marketing and sales managers for lead tracking and follow-up.

Index cards The 3-by-5-inch index card is a common format used for lists distributed to dealers or sales offices. It is more versatile than sheet listings but contains the same information for each firm.

List Guarantees

Both human and computer error can cause some very expensive and drastic mistakes. Spot checks of rented lists should be made when received. Another smart control practice is to monitor mailings by asking for a specially coded name and address to be placed on the list.

As a rule, on first-class mail compilers will refund the current first-class postage for any returned mail in excess of 4 percent of the list if received within a specified number of weeks after the list has left the compiler's plant. On third-class return-requested business mail they will refund the current minimum third-class postage rate for any returned mail in excess of 7 percent, or with some list owners, 5 percent, if received within a specified period such as 45 or 60 days.

COMPILING THE IN-HOUSE LIST

To fully appreciate and understand business lists, every marketer should build a track record of experience in compiling, maintaining, and using the company's customer list for direct marketing programs. The marketer will soon learn which segments of the list will work most effectively. A well-developed file that represents a potentially profitable total market can emerge if programmed correctly. The key determinant in deciding the value of in-house list development is the commitment to usage over a long-term period.

Business-to-business sales-support house files, as a rule, are not large. The great bulk are under 20,000 names, although some in the *Fortune 500 Industrials* do have lists in the hundreds of thousands. The company's specific marketing objectives, however, will often target only segments of the total list. This dictates the need for the list to be developed so structured data is readily accessible to satisfy the various requirements of the mailer. Mail order objectives have even greater need for finer breakdowns of the characteristics in the customer list.

List Structure

No matter how small a customer or prospect list is, to be maintained in-house there should be enough identifiable characteristics built into the list for the marketer to be able to profile the company's best prospects for maximum promotion. Small or large mailers, whether for sales support or mail order objectives, seek as much information about their customers and inquirers as they can profitably gather and record. This process is being facilitated by the continuing drop in costs of computerization of data, making sophisticated data base development more affordable to a greater number of marketers (see Chapter 6).

Larger marketers who aggressively implement sales-support lead-development programs compile and maintain unique key prospect lists that profile best customers. Smaller marketers who mail monthly newsletters or other high-frequency campaigns also find it profitable to compile and maintain their own list. For some of the smaller marketers with limited prospect universes, it may be more cost effective to rent the entire universe or segment each time mailings are planned. Still others, who find that an existing compiled list is suitable for prospecting and plan to mail to it frequently, will lease the list for a 12-month period with a 6-month update and unlimited use privileges. In general, however, business-to-business mail order marketers rarely maintain a sizable prospect list beyond the list of their own inquirers. Also, 12-month lease plans for business response names are nonexistent.

The marketer structures the list based on how it is intended to be used. It is very expensive to go back at a later date to add to a list file after the list format has been finalized and the program is up and running. As a minimum, customer and inquiry files for each name in the list should record:

- SIC codes
- Company size
- Date of entry
- Source code
- Date
- Telephone number
- Product or category in which interest was shown or purchase was made

Mail order marketers add to this the proven recency, frequency, monetary value technique to determine potential sales value of past customers (this technique is discussed in Chapter 13).

List File Systems

Card and Plate Systems

The manual 3-by-5-inch card file still performs a useful list maintenance method but only for the small mailer whose lists number in the hundreds. For lists under 5,000 the Scriptomatic addressing system is inexpensive and does not require special personnel. A typist can operate the equipment. Sales lead processing of up to 50,000 units per year can be handled efficiently on this system. Xerox systems effectively handle files of up to 25,000 names. Metal plate systems have been gradually disappearing as plastic cards and computer systems have become more and more cost effective.

Computerization

Virtually all business lists today of any size are computerized. The marketer's target marketing strategies create demand for high degrees of selectivity within marketplaces. Segmentation, to the degree required, can only exist in a computerized list.

Microcomputers can economically handle mini-size house lists especially where personalization is needed. Marketers with smaller lists and limited codings can easily delete files or put new list data on a diskette as information becomes available. Maximum list size is limited only by hardware or disk space. Up to

1,500 records can be stored on a simple diskette. There are various mailing list management software packages at all levels of sophistication, many costing under $200. The best allow for ample sorting capabilities, fill-in letter or report text with any or all elements of the mailing list data, elimination of duplicate names, and list printouts on single or four-up labels or directly on envelopes with or without keycodes.

A list system that operates like a data base offers maximum flexibility for the dollars invested. The marketer who is ready to establish such a business list management system in-house chooses wisely from a menu of software performance tools available from a growing list of software and hardware firms. This software is used to:

- Convert data to and from one format to another—magnetic tape, disks, or punch cards
- Add valuable demographic marketing data to the list
- Perform targeted geographic selections, demographic analyses, match/merge functions
- Eliminate duplicates
- Prepare personalized computer letters
- Handle list rental fulfillment orders competitively
- Capitalize on presort coding for postal savings for big mailers

Business-to-business marketers with sales support objectives mail frequently but in small quantities. For most there is not enough volume of names to justify some of the more sophisticated computer list applications in-house. Where volume does warrant the elimination of duplication between lists, suppression of names or groups from a prior mailing, or enhancement of a list with business demographic overlays, outside service bureaus can be an answer.

Long-term computer format requirements are important. For instance, after three years sales lead production may quadruple. When a list is first computerized, marketers are tempted to format more information than is really needed. Actually, in early stages of development they should capture as much data as possible to help determine format. Then, before formatting, they should examine the data for real needs and discard everything but relevant data.

The development of a computerized file takes into account the value of recording all meaningful industry data. Some of this is available through sophisticated overlay systems that match the marketer's lists with key demographic information from large business data bases. Suppression files and other appropriate data are also matched. These are lists of businesses that the marketer wishes to eliminate from a planned mailing, such as no-pays and poor credit risks.

The steps in the list computerization process itself are relatively simple:

1. It starts by entering a name, title, company address, and other information on magnetic tape or disk where it is stored for subsequent use.
2. For lists kept on tape, updated data are first entered on a storage medium, separate from but in proper sequence with the main file. The additions and deletions are then read and written into what becomes the updated main

file. For lists on disk, the copying step is eliminated. Records can be brought up on a CRT screen to review, verify, or change. In either form the data can be sorted and manipulated in any way the computer program directs.
3. Output can be in the form of printed records and personalized letters, catalogs, and other specialized mailing packages, or the data can remain on the tape or disk to be transferred to another computer in another facility. Since tape rather than disk is most compatible among different computers, and because it is less subject to damage, it is most often used.

The marketer benefits in many ways by having lists on an in-house computer. There is better control over computer scheduling. Short runs and odd-hour runs become affordable. Also, list security increases. On-the-spot access to data enables the marketer to review records, make changes, and take action as necessary. Of course, none of this is possible without the proper personnel and equipment. Employing professional personnel is especially important if the plan includes list rental fulfillment requiring programming talent to handle the computer programs and changes necessary to satisfy the list renters.

Some marketers find it practical to have their own less expensive computer system for some functions and to use the outside computer service bureau for merge/purge and other applications requiring more sophisticated software, hardware, and personnel.

Maintenance of the In-House List

There are actually only three basic things to worry about when maintaining a business list: (1) to put new names on, (2) to take off names that are no longer appropriate, (3) to make changes in existing records such as names, titles, addresses, and telephone numbers. Systems and procedures required to perform these maintenance functions will vary. They will depend on the size of the list, frequency of use, number of list segments required, and list development and maintenance costs.

When a business catalog marketer wants to maintain a house list of 100,000 inquirers and also to rent it to other mailers, the marketer will want to ensure that all new inquirers are systematically added to the list. This can happen only if the list is set up with all the necessary coded selections, enabling its users to implement the most cost-effective targeted campaigns. As inquirers are converted into customers, their names are moved by the marketer's computer program from the inquiry list into a customer file. Inactive inquirers are removed after a specific time period. Undeliverable names will also be removed by employing all necessary list-cleaning techniques.

U.S. Postal Service List Correction Services

First-class mail The postal service will return undeliverable first-class mail along with the reason it was unable to deliver. Although this is a postal service policy, private studies have shown that the mailer cannot expect complete return of undeliverables (known in the industry as nixies). Also, some of those returned to the mailer will have inaccurate information. Ordinarily, mailing quantities of fewer than 2,000 per calendar year are more economically mailed first class because the initial bulk third-class mailing fee of $50 plus the mailer's cost of special preparation of mail (minimum 200 pieces or 50 pounds in each mailing, properly zip coded, packaged, and sacked) offset postage cost savings.

Address correction requested   Undeliverable bulk mail is never forwarded nor is it returned to sender unless "address correction requested" is imprinted on the face of the outgoing envelope or self-mailer. At current rates the cost for address correction service is $.30 per piece.

The cost of getting address changes from the postal service continues to rise to the point where cost-effective use of this correction service is marginal for many lists. All mailers should be alert to the latest postal service releases on this subject. See Appendix 4 for postal service rules for forwarding and return and address correction. Marketers mailing to a rented list would not request such information since they are interested in paying for address changes only for those lists they maintain.

Prospect Update Requests

To solicit list additions, deletions, and changes from those on a list, marketers also include special list-update postage-paid reply cards along with their mailings two or three times a year or they include list correction appeals directly on original direct mail reply cards or outgoing envelopes (see Figure 5-8). Requests are straightforward, asking recipients to verify the name and address and perhaps add other decision-maker names along with any helpful comments. When such name and address update requests are included in sales-prospect inquiry response-

Figure 5-8. Sample list correction appeal printed by Northern Business Information on reverse side of outgoing envelope.

DO WE HAVE YOUR CORRECT ADDRESS?
If your address on the face of this envelope is not correct, please indicate changes on the label, or below:

Name_____Title_____

Company_____

Address_____

City_____State_____Zip_____
☐ **Delete** my name from your list, because
☐ this is a duplicate label   ☐ I have no interest
Return this complete envelope to
Northern Business Information,
157 Chambers Street, New York, NY 10007

Source: Used with the permission of Northern Business Information, New York.

type mailings, higher responses from the original offer will usually come as a result.

Field Sales Update Requests

An ongoing program to encourage field sales force participation is necessary for accurate and consistent file maintenance. However, since salespeople are busy performing their selling functions in the field, most are not geared to fill headquarter's mailing list requests. To minimize this problem many business-to-business marketers, when feasible, will update their lists with newly issued telephone yellow pages, business directories, and other appropriate list sources as they are published.

The field sales organization is then given the opportunity to check over those specially maintained lists, making any changes or additions they may feel are necessary. Some marketers have established procedures for keeping the field sales organization continually updated on all lists maintained for in-house mailing programs. Marketers send manuscripts of customer, inquiry, and special prospect lists that are maintained at headquarters to branch or sales offices for the salesperson's reference file. Salespeople are requested at that time to also make changes as they see fit.

Outside Rentals of the Marketer's Business Lists

Rental of in-house lists of customers and inquirers is not widespread among business-to-business marketers. Customer lists are especially inviolate. Even the custom of catalogers' trading lists—so prevalent in consumer direct marketing—is virtually nonexistent in the business mail order field. The exceptions are several of the larger business mail order firms that operate more like consumer direct marketers in their approach to trading and renting their lists. *Direct Mail List Rates and Data* lists business-to-business mail order firms or subsidiaries of large companies that rent their lists to noncompeting firms.

Many response list owners are not aware that they themselves have a valuable file of customers or inquirers. When such a list numbers 50,000 or more it may be marketable. The dollars generated from list rental can be substantial for some marketers, and represent pure profit. Except for a few giants in the field, most list owners market their lists through the services of a list manager. List owners employ the industry standard direct-marketing package-approval procedure (approving samples, discussed earlier) to prevent any competing programs from being mailed to the list.

Any list on the rental market needs protection against the possibility of theft. Seeding the list with "dummy" names provides the security needed. These are fictitious names and titles inserted permanently in various sections of the lists for control purposes. Because it is difficult to preseed each list segment, especially geographically, some "dummy" names are seeded at the time the list is first processed for rental. The addresses are actual but the names of people or companies are made up in ways that match codes can't confuse with a live record on the list.

Resources for Developing In-house Lists

There is a great deal of information available to marketers that can help them identify their prospect universe. A wealth of statistical information is in the public domain and available from federal offices. Detail on individual establishments can be found in government publications, telephone, business, and industrial directories, and trade and business associations. More and more of the information from these sources is available on magnetic tape as well as in printed form. These sources can be of tremendous help to business-to-business mailers in building an internal prospect list. Public libraries are a fertile source for much of this information.

The following sections list some of the most frequently used resource material for business lists:

Business Directories

Horizontal

Directory of *Fortune* 500 Largest Industrials
Thomas Register of American Manufacturers
Standard and Poor's Register of Corporations, Directors and Executives
MacRae's Blue Book of 50,000 U.S. Manufacturing Firms
Chamber of Commerce directories
Industrial and wholesaling directories (e.g., Dun's Industrial Guides)

Vertical

Directory of manufacturing plants (e.g., Directory of New England Manufacturers)
Department Store Directory
Chain Store Directory
Business services and construction reports
Standard Directory of Advertisers
Professional services directories (e.g., American Medical Directory, National Roster of Realtors)
Schools and libraries directories (e.g., Comparative Guide to American Colleges)
Hospital directories (e.g., hospital phone book)
Financial institutions directories (e.g., American Bank Directory)

Trade Association Membership Directories
Credit Rating Books and Reports (e.g., Dun and Bradstreet Reference Book)

The Gale Research Company, Book Tower, Detroit, MI 48226, publishes the *Directory of Directories,* an annotated guide to approximately 9,600 business and industrial directories, professional and scientific rosters, directory data bases, and other lists and guides of all kinds. Addresses, telephone numbers, and prices of the directories are included with a description of contents. Frederick G. Ruffner, publisher; Cecilia Ann Marlow and Robert C. Thomas, editors.

TESTING

List testing involves trying out a mailing on a portion of a list before mailing to the rest of it (known as a roll-out). When testing one list against others the comparison of results will indicate how much better one list is over another. Those lists that test out well can become the more fertile lists for future mail efforts.

The two keys to successful list testing center around (1) choosing names from a good cross section typical of the entire list and (2) determining the quantity of names in the test. A common method of selecting a sample representative of the entire list is systematic sampling or the Nth name selection. The first name is chosen by random, then every sixth, fourteenth, or other Nth name is used for the test sample.

The formula for computing test sample sizes, law of probability tables, and detailed testing procedures for all aspects of direct marketing all appear in Chapter 12.

Sales Support

Business-to-business marketers who use direct mail for sales support objectives are for the most part dealing with small market segments. Pretesting is not practical for most of these mailers who have 20,000 prospects or fewer. Also, those marketers who have very narrow and limited markets may have very few lists to choose from that haven't already been tested or mailed many times.

List testing, however, is a key tool for those larger multimarket companies using direct mail for lead generation. Trade publication controlled circulation lists are tested against compiled lists. Response lists have also been profitably tested against compiled lists for lead building programs. Marketers with sales support objectives test lists that come from different sources. For example, a mainframe computer manufacturer may want to know which of several available lists—such as circulation lists of several EDP trade publications, Comdex Trade Show attendees, or Dun's Marketing Services' compiled data base of business firms—to use for a continuing lead-generation program.

Lists and list segments with built-in characteristics are also worth testing for many sales support offers. Personal name lists are tested against lists that have a title only. Company size, type of business, and job function can all be determinants in the success of a direct marketing effort and are accessible through list segment testing. Because it does not pay for a marketer to compile and maintain broad base lists of suspects in-house, renting and testing such lists is the practical approach.

Mail Order

The mail order business-to-business marketer thinks about list testing differently than the marketer with sales support objectives. The mail order volume mailer must develop new customers from each new mailing just to remain in business. To maximize this objective not only are new offers and approaches tested, but just as vital, new lists are tested. Continuing list testing is conducted against control lists as new response lists and more defined segments of current lists become available. Successful test results lead to roll-outs of larger quantities, such as from a 5,000 original test quantity to 25,000 for a continuance, and then to 100,000 or more.

Business-to-business mail order marketers test any list that appears to have key characteristics of potential customers. They rarely get a chance to but, of course, they would like to test lists of mail order purchasers of identical products or services in an identical price range from a competitor. If a list surfaces containing the names of businessmen and businesswomen who have purchased a similar product or service by mail—a product of identical price, a product from a similar company, or both—then the list may be considered worth testing.

LIST STRATEGY

Marketers formulate direct mail or telemarketing plans based on their strategic long-range direct marketing objectives. Available list opportunities are then evaluated to determine the best lists to use. The target market should be carefully selected to closely match the identifiable geographic, demographic, and behavioral characteristics of the customer company and decision maker currently buying the product (or research findings if it's a new market).

List size, of course, is especially important in mail order to ensure that the list is large enough to be worth testing. But perhaps more important than size of the list, regardless of the objective, is the makeup of the list segments, which should be in agreement with program strategies. Marketers want to know the SIC breakdown and company size indications such as number of employees or net worth. Titles and job functions are also important as well as personal names that are significant for some campaigns.

A personal name list is especially beneficial if the real decision makers are indeed singled out. Many business lists are promoted as "decision makers," and they may be, but not necessarily for every marketer's product. There is a difference among decision makers, specifiers, and others who are influencers. In any case, for a direct marketing campaign to be effective, its prime targets are those individuals in the prospect's business who actually make the decision. Others who are part of the large company's purchasing structure are usually secondary targets.

Direct marketing business lists are used for various objectives. It will help to look at how list strategy differs depending on the objective.

Sales Support

Business-to-business marketers who support personal selling activities of salespeople most often use their own customer, inquiry, and prospect lists, plus rented compiled lists and business publication controlled circulation lists. In some companies the customer list gets the most action. Other sales support marketers concentrate on direct marketing campaigns directed to their own list of inquirers or prospects. The complete compiled universe list is mailed periodically by some in an effort to furnish new names for the inquiry list they maintain. They also use compiled lists for sales prospecting, market surveys, and sales territory analysis.

Some marketers with sales support objectives prefer the extensive demographic data available on controlled circulation lists. The marketer's direct mail objectives are best accomplished when the editorial material in the magazine plays to an audience that will have an affinity for the marketer's product.

Inquiry Generation

Lead generation by far is the sales support objective most frequently used by the business-to-business marketer. Many potential markets are targeted by direct mail and telemarketing to produce valuable inquiries. One is the customer market. Unfortunately, salespeople don't have time to cover all customers personally to determine when each may be ready to place another order. Direct mail and telemarketing performs this function for them.

Another market is the in-house list of inquirers. These are prospects who have shown some interest in the past but have not been converted into customers. They are no longer being pursued by salespeople but are still worth periodic promotion by mail or telephone.

The third market that the marketer pursues with a lead-building objective is the outside world of compiled and trade publication lists. The tactic here is to apply the profile characteristics of the best customer to these highly structured and segmented rented lists. This key prospect list is then covered by direct mail and telemarketing as frequently as profitable.

In addition, compilations in specialized industries have highly targeted segments needed for successful lead-generating programs. For instance, if marketers are trying to get leads for power conditioning equipment for data processing installations, they may use the International Data Corporation's List of Computer Installations in the United States, where size of installations, makes and types of equipment, and titles and names of purchasers are spelled out in detail.

Prequalified Prospect Penetration

The door-opener objective is aimed at lists of prequalified prospects who are in the "hard-to-see" category. Salespeople know that firms on this list are excellent prospects but for whatever reason they cannot get in to make a personal sales call. These lists are names that salespeople compile specially and send to headquarters for consolidation and direct marketing campaign implementation. The objective of the direct marketing campaign is to arrange specific meetings between decision makers and the marketer's salespeople. These planned door-opener programs usually include dimensionals and high-key breakthrough creative ideas. A door-opener program can run over $100 per name for a complete campaign. Because of the expense involved, this type of program is not practical for a continuing lead-building effort over the long term.

Reinforced Selling

Some of the most successful sales field–office direct-mail programs are initiated and directed by the field, but are organized, created, and mailed by a central headquarters staff. There are two basic objectives involved in these programs.

One aims at helping salespeople close sales quicker on those ten to fifteen or so prospects on which they are currently making calls. The core of such a program usually consists of a series of multipiece direct mail campaigns prepared and put "on the shelf," ready to be mailed from headquarters at the request of the local sales branch manager or the salespeople themselves.

The second objective, reinforcing the selling efforts of the field people, depends on the local sales office personnel to initiate the mailings and also employs centrally prepared direct mail campaigns. However, this objective is to secure leads from suspect marketplaces in the individual sales office territories. Mailing lists compiled from local industry data and club rosters, local business-to-business yellow pages, or local chambers of commerce lists are submitted by the sales offices to headquarters for processing and mailing.

Awareness

To protect and enhance highly valued image and awareness levels among customer and prospect markets, many business-to-business marketers augment ongoing broad advertising and public relations programs with key customer and key prospect awareness direct mail campaigns. These campaigns are usually targeted to a small portion of the customer list, those that bring in the greatest share of profitable business volume. Awareness programs may also go to lists of upper management of new prospect markets scheduled for sales force penetration in the months ahead.

Often because of the high revenue and profit value to the marketer of the firms on some of these lists, elaborate list correction procedures are used to ensure that companies' names and addresses and personal names of customers and prospects are continually updated. Phone calls are made at regular intervals to these firms, ensuring that the status of the files are current. Both key customer and key prospect lists are periodically sent to the field sales offices to inform them of any list changes made by headquarters and to serve as a double check to solicit any changes from the salespeople.

Dealer Support

Dealer support programs center around mailing list data matchings between sales territories and compiled business list data bases, such as those provided by Dun's Marketing Services or other compilers as well as some trade publications. Most direct mail campaigns in a dealer-support program are in a series of three or more mailings. Some run monthly or semimonthly over a 12-month period.

Mail Order

Direct-response mail-order lists in business-to-business are used mainly for marketing two types of products or services. One type includes those that appeal to a single or a few related markets, such as financial institutions, hospitals, or schools. In these vertical markets the lists can be relatively small. The second type of product or service has broad horizontal appeal across all lines of business and includes such items as books, seminars, office products, computer supplies, and writing services.

It has been found that business and trade magazine-paid subscriber lists can work well for some direct response mail order mailers or telemarketers. Experience has also shown, however, that it is not a good idea to mail general merchandise offers to response lists of inquirers since they are not proven buyers. Of course, business mail order marketers, in addition to renting appropriate response lists, also mail heavily to their own customer lists.

The general business-to-business catalog or solo mail order marketer can mail to a massive marketplace of about 7 or 8 million prospect firms or even more. However, for the giant mailers in the business marketplace, there is agreement that this universe of mail order buyers is limited. There just aren't that many large lists available. These marketers must seek other avenues for growth.

Nevertheless, business mail order list owners continue to segment their lists to achieve more profitable results for themselves and more activity from mail order marketers who rent them. The profile of the customer will indicate the specific list characteristics needed to determine which segments should be most effective for the catalog or solo mail order mailing to prospects.

Generally, list characteristics, such as dollar amount of average purchase, types of products or services, and number of units, should have a favorable match with the direct marketing selling proposition. A business publication subscriber paying $20 for 12 issues may not respond to an $89.50 offer of office supplies. Also, the inquirer or buyer for sweepstakes business mail order offers has unique characteristics. The mailer must know what motivates the buyer to action in each case. In any event, marketers do know that lists of new buyers produce sales at a higher rate than lists of less recent buyers.

Catalog Sales

Unlike the solo mail order effort, the mail order catalog is a presentation of a variety of merchandise. Another type is the salesperson's handout catalog, a sales-support catalog that contains product photos and specifications but no prices or order forms and that is not mailed to prospects. Those marketers who try to mail it quickly find out that it doesn't bring in orders profitably by mail or phone.

A planned multimail effort may target a large universe of response buyers in an attempt to sell general business products through a mail order catalog. Or the list may be used in quantities of 3,000 or 5,000 in a dozen initial test mailings in preparation for the launch of a new mail order catalog to selected segments of the business marketplace. According to Direct Media, a large direct-response-list management firm, about 60 percent of a large mail order mailing goes to the marketer's own customer list and the remaining 40 percent goes to an array of rented business response names that have been used successfully in the past or on initial tests and test continuations.

The role of response mailing lists cannot be overemphasized in business catalog planning. Business-to-business catalogs not only sell office supplies, accessories, and general products that can be used in any office or business but some sell specific products for specific lines of business in vertical markets. Catalog mailers generally find it more profitable to prepare special-interest catalogs that appeal to selected audiences. A catalog with a full range of products sent to a broad-based horizontal list may produce profit, but different editions prepared for special target markets can net greater profits.

Solo Mail Order Objective

During the earliest planning stage of any solo mail order effort, if the size of the target audience is determined to be too small to be profitable, then there is no further meeting on the subject. There must be enough potential orders in the universe to make the effort worthwhile. This potential cannot be judged from total list numbers alone. For instance, a total universe list of 500,000 may not be large enough for some products. After testing for the most viable market characteristics, such as type of business and company size, the profitable universe may shrink to 100,000 or 50,000. If order responses can hold up over periodic mailings, and unit product price and profit is high enough, then 50,000 mailing quantities may work. Misjudging the size of the profitable universe is a leading cause of solo mail-order launch failures.

Launching any solo mail order effort, often in concert with new product introductions, can in effect help establish a new channel of distribution for a product or series of related products. It has been proven time and again in business-to-business marketing that higher-priced products can be sold through solo mail order, although most dramatic successes seem to be made during the early launch stages. Before finding a profitable universe, dozens of lists may be tested. Jim Kobs stated that over 300 lists were tested in the highly successful Hewlett-Packard direct marketing campaign of the late seventies.

The process of list testing determines response variance by market segment and lets the marketer know where the buyers are located. SIC breakdowns within the lists differentiate the buyers by types and show who are most apt to buy.

SUMMARY

The audience for the business-to-business marketer is a constantly changing marketplace of over 10 million establishments that includes many millions more of specifiers and influencers within these establishments. Yet, the great bulk of business-to-business marketers have individual markets consisting of fewer than 20,000 firms.

These marketers draw on lists in four general categories: in-house lists, compiled lists, response lists, business and trade publication lists. Postcard response deck lists and marketing data banks are combinations of the four.

Marketers with sales support objectives, such as lead generation, reinforced selling, and awareness, use compiled lists and trade publication controlled circulation lists, as well as their own in-house lists. Mail order marketers concentrate on response lists in quest of direct sales. Various data bank list combinations continue to proliferate in answer to the business marketer's need for more and more market segmentation possibilities.

Professionals in the list business serving business-to-business marketers are list managers, brokers, compilers, and trade magazine publishers. List managers handle the maintenance, marketing, and promotion functions for the list owner. List brokers recommend list rental opportunities for the business mailer's campaigns. List compilers, specializing in the business marketplace, maintain vast data bases of business names for rent or lease. They also custom compile for marketers who have a need to own special lists. Trade magazine publishers rent circulation and inquiry lists to business marketers.

Industry list sources, led by the *Direct Mail List Rates and Data* directory, catalogs, and data cards, are rich in details of list availabilities and list supplier services. The power of the business list is in how it is used to attain the marketer's individual direct marketing objectives. And these objectives range from sales support to direct response mail order.

List availabilities are reflecting the business marketer's need to accomplish specific objectives in selective markets. When renting business lists, costly problems can be avoided by paying attention to important details: merge/purge applications, coding needs, accurate list counts, time frame, costs, formats, and list guarantees.

For the business-to-business marketer, in-house lists consist of customers, inquirers, and prospects. When compiling an in-house list, regardless of size, enough identifiable characteristics should be built into the list to permit the marketer to profile the company's best prospects for maximum direct marketing effectiveness.

List file systems have become computerized and have cleared the way for business marketers to take advantage of list segmentation. A wide range of software performance tools are available today from which the list developer can choose.

Maintenance of the in-house list is a matter of taking old files off, putting new ones on, and correcting those that need updated information. Customers and prospects on the list, the postal service, and the field salespeople become involved in this process of keeping lists current.

Pretesting lists in business-to-business direct marketing is confined to a small group of across-the-board mail-order marketers of generic merchandise and to a very limited number of Fortune 500 companies who use direct mail for massive lead-generation programs. Most other business-to-business marketers, because of their limited markets, test lists as well as other direct mail success determinants as a by-product of making scheduled mailings. Their purpose is to learn which are the best list segments and what the best ways are to approach those market segments with continuing direct marketing efforts.

In the foreseeable future, business-to-business direct marketing activity will focus on those business marketplaces that have been defined by list segmentation methods. The more characteristics that are known about a customer or prospect marketplace, the better the chances are for direct marketing success.

6

THE MARKETING DATA BASE

A valuable new tool has emerged in the eighties to help marketers focus on the problem of selling more productively and on getting new customers from homogeneous segments of prospect markets. The marketing data base, a product of the computer age, enables the marketer to choose the most profitable market segments for the short and long term. It ensures that the audience to be reached is correctly identified and that the message elements of the promotional mix are precisely positioned. The marketing data base also controls operations and can be the key to a profitable program measured on a cost-per-order basis.

The data base management concept has caught on in virtually all Fortune 500 companies. The well-managed marketing data base permits the customer and top prospect lists to be continually enriched by current data. These lists can be further enhanced by overlays with secondary data bases in addition to inputs from research and testing. All this information helps data-based direct marketing identify and establish marketplaces not only for current products but also for new product concepts that must emerge in order for a company to remain competitive.

The term *data base* has become a buzzword in the direct marketing industry as well as elsewhere, and because of this, it now means different things to different people. Some think of a data base as nothing more than a computerized version of the traditional business mailing list of names and addresses. Others reserve the term for giant lists that represent several lists merged into one and that have demographic and geographic elements and can be sorted into zip code strings to simplify list processing. Still others have borrowed the word *data base* from the computer technician to describe and promote their huge merged purged files.

And indeed, as we will see, some of these massive files do resemble data bases in the technical sense of the word.

Richard Courtheoux, an industry consultant based in Chicago, gives a technical definition of a data base as "a comprehensive collection of interrelated data that serves multiple applications and allows timely and accurate retrieval or manipulation of that data." It differs from a file, which is a collection of records of the same type, says Courtheoux, "in that it consists of many files that can be linked together relatively easily and cheaply as needed." *Linked* is the key word (see Figure 6-1).

An existing customer file can include data such as SIC code, company size, decision makers' names, and company credit rating but still not have the file *linked* as in a data base. For example, a marketer could construct best customer profiles from this list, but once the file is linked to similar files containing current transactional data in an on-line system, trends can be predicted that relate to future customer purchases and new selection capabilities can emerge. This is what makes the data base such a powerful marketing management tool.

Simply stated, a marketing data base is a creation of multiple lists or files that are linked and related so that new information results that did not exist on the individual lists beforehand. Technically, a data base is completely interactive, is on-line, and is constantly updated. Practically without exception, the only data bases that meet these criteria are in-house data bases.

The giant lists referred to earlier dominate the commercial list market and started life in the direct marketing industry as *data banks.* Like data bases, they are much more than just mailing lists or files of names and addresses. A data bank is created by combining unduplicated elements from different sources, providing a wealth of demographic information that ends up as one generic entity offering structured data in multitudes of segments for selection by its users. Individual mailing lists of similar types are meshed together to enable a marketer to rent a cross-section or segment of the "superlist" without having to deal with many different list owners. The strengths of each list in the bank are accumulated into one list.

While the advantages of data banks are many, it is important to note the one primary distinction (at least to this author) between data banks and data bases is that data banks are not linked files. You can manipulate and combine the data in a myriad of ways, but you cannot create new information from the data on hand.

As important as this distinction is, it is one that has been essentially lost in the marketplace today. No one in the information industry refers to a data bank; all such computerized files are referred to as data bases, although only a handful may represent linked files. The reason for this lies in the growth of the on-line industry that allows anyone with a computer and a modem to access business (and other) information data banks for a fee. (In some cases an outside information vendor can perform the search function for the marketer.) Referred to as data bases in that industry, the term has carried over to all other areas of business.

The reason for emphasizing the distinction here is not merely semantics. It is important that marketers keep in mind the advantages and limitations of data banks and data bases, particularly when selecting outside data sources or, more important, when creating their own.

Figure 6-1. Difference between a file and a data base.

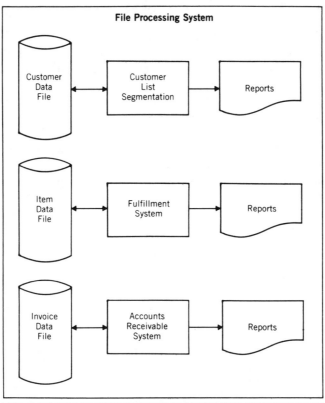

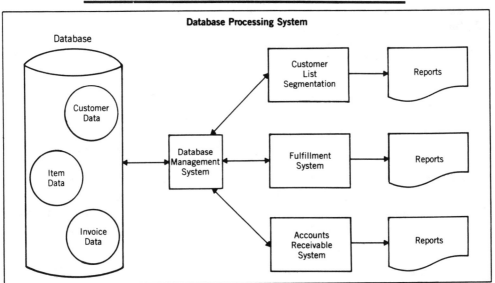

Source: Richard Courtheoux, *Direct Marketing Magazine,* August 1984. Courtesy of *Direct Marketing Magazine,* 224 7th Street, Garden City, New York 11530.

DATA BANKS

Advantages

The direct marketing data bank of business names has emerged since the early 1970s. It was the answer to the business mail order marketer's need to reach more cost-effective target segments. This was done through the use of large business response lists without suffering the high costs and customer complaints associated with duplication of files when mailing to more than one list.

The American Management Association's customized data bank was one of the first attempts to eliminate duplication. In the early 1960s, some seminar prospects would get many duplicate mailings of AMA's seminar offerings since there was no affordable method for eliminating duplicates and most available lists of any size had overlapping names. AMA executives, aware of the need for a solution, arranged with list suppliers to enter their lists into an AMA data bank from which duplicates were purged. With the duplication problem solved, highly segmented files now enable AMA to mail millions of pieces annually without any loss of coverage. Many other organizations have followed AMA's lead and have created their own custom data banks and data bases.

However, there are other advantages than just the elimination of duplication to be gained from the data bank. Many time-consuming tasks once done manually are now facilitated by the computer:

- Handling many lists having different formats and selection criteria
- Arranging names in many lists in zip code sequence to take advantage of postal presort discounts
- Having names cleared, delivered, and shipped to a central point by a firm date
- Billing based on gross names, minimum orders
- Keeping track of many mail dates
- Testing continuations

Specialized or regional business marketers can now have access to substantial numbers of names previously scattered throughout many different files.

Data banks, because of their precise geographic and demographic data, are used as sales territory list sources by marketers who have instituted customized lead-generation programs for their regional dealers or salespeople. Table 6-1 shows an example of the market segments targeted by an insurance company from a data bank's custom selections for a sales territory lead-generation program.

The trend is toward "superlists" and the marketer will see even more advanced selectivity according to Stephen Belth, President of Belth Associates, Inc., New York. This will be fueled by the increased information that business marketers need for better segmentation and target marketing strategy.

Considerations for Using Data Banks

It is important that the marketer be aware of the sources of the lists in a data bank so a proper evaluation can be made of the use of the information. When

Table 6-1. Sales territory lead-generation program.

List Counts for Four Cities at Six Managerial Levels				
Title of Prospect	*New York*	*Boston*	*Chicago*	*Los Angeles*
Top management	78,868	21,235	61,241	50,029
Middle managers	48,697	13,112	37,815	35,831
Finance	29,507	7,945	22,913	21,711
Marketing/sales	19,993	5,367	15,478	14,666
Engineer/technical	52,164	14,046	40,507	38,382
Data processing	18,365	4,945	14,260	13,512
Totals	412,692	111,126	320,471	303,661

An insurance company needed to reach various functional and managerial levels in several different geographic regions. The company was provided with the target numbers for each dealer group. The planning staff was then able to order for several regions at once, making a more cost efficient and thorough lead-generation system than before.

Source: MDA Database, Courtesy of Mal Dunn Associates, Inc.

ready to extract names and titles from a data bank to add to a prospect list, the marketer should inquire about the bank's compilation and maintenance procedures to ensure against getting old names. If updates are made to a personal name data bank only once a year (which is the case when the bank originates from annual directories), a good percentage of names may be incorrect—20 percent or more, depending on the update cycle.

Before using a rented list to augment a list or data base, the marketer may have to make a special arrangement with the list owner. List owners are justifiably reluctant to share their order entry data on proprietary on-line data base systems with other marketers who wish to enhance mailing lists. Of course, any name that comes in as a result of a mailing or phone call automatically becomes a permanent addition to the marketer's lists or data base, regardless of whether it originated from a rented list.

As noted earlier, there are a growing number of on-line business information data banks that are used in much the same way as library reference materials. These provide computer records, statistics, abstracts, and forecasts of a multitude of sources that are valuable for data base development research. Searches can be done by the marketer or by outside information vendors.

Two frequently used on-line data banks or data bases include:

1. *Compustat*—financial statistics on over 6,000 publicly held corporations, produced by Standard & Poor's Compustat Services Inc., 7400 St. Alton Court, Englewood, CO 80112; (800) 525–8640. Distributed by ADP Network Services, Compuserve, and others.
2. *U.S. Central Data Bank*—developed from government and private sources, for example, Bureau of Economic Analysis, Census Bureau, and Federal

Reserve Board. Produced and distributed by Data Resources Inc., Data Products Division Headquarters, 1750 K Street, N.W., Suite 1060, Washington, DC 20006; (202) 862–3760.

Many more are described in publications such as *Directory of On-Line Data Bases, Cuadra Associates' Quarterly Report,* and *The Encyclopedia of Information Systems and Services* (Gale Research Company).

List Enhancement Through Overlays

The more marketers know about their customers, the more successful they will be in profiling the best customers for targeted promotions. This is particularly true for business-to-business mail order marketers whose very business existence depends on the list response to continuing mail order efforts. These marketers in particular constantly seek ways to build more information into their customer list. List-enhancement functions performed through overlays have become important tools for this purpose.

Customer list-enhancement techniques take the guesswork out of "gut feeling" tactics. Enhancement data provide the business list mailer with those characteristics or data elements from which customer profiles are developed. If the marketer has a good customer list to begin with, information from secondary data banks can be added by overlaying information on sales volume, employee size, SIC codes, and other vital information that can have extensive marketing and sales value. When grouped into appropriate ranges, this information can be compared with national data to get an idea of market penetration.

List enhancement enables marketers to choose those specific list characteristics that will help them reach their individual objectives. Those that continue to work well for many business-to-business mail order marketers are the recency, frequency, monetary formula elements. Typical list enhancement selections available from most data banks include:

- Management level
- Job function
- SIC/industry groups
- Home or business address
- Male/female executives
- Company size
- Multiple responders
- Business phone numbers
- Select by individual lists
- State/SCF/5-digit zip
- County select
- Maximum number of names per company (in priority sequence by title)

But before a marketer's list can be enhanced by a data bank, it must be organized into a consistent, fixed computer format compatible with the data bank.

Often a data bank owner or data center has a program that can adapt a marketer's list to the data bank, or can tell the marketer how to format his or her list to be compatible with the data bank. A list-enhancement profile can then be made that indicates the percentage of matches for each data element selected for analysis by the marketer.

Networking

The recent rise of the "superlist" and the rapid advance of computer technology has helped bring about a new concept in the list supplier service business called *networking*. CCX Network, Inc. (Conway, Arkansas), a pioneer in this concept, has brought together huge data banks made available to users through a process called *direct access*. A list user's in-house computer can have access to a list owner's data through a network service bureau. List owners, managers, brokers, and large list users are on-line with the network. This networking concept attempts to fill the need for instant retrieval of segments of lists and the demand for instant updating.

Data Bank Sources

There are several list data banks for the business-to-business marketer. As touched on in Chapter 5, two major files resulted from the merging of Market Data Retrieval and National Business Lists into one organization in 1984, and then that merged into Dun & Bradstreet's Dun's Marketing Services in 1986. This consolidation enabled Dun's Marketing Services to put together a formidable list rental and list-enhancement service for business marketers.

Dun's Marketing Services' Masterfile is the largest compiled file of the U.S. business universe, about 8.5 million establishments. The other, a 14 million executive name active-response file, is a consolidation of 200 different sources. As many as 20 data elements can be selected by a marketer to develop a customer profile from this data bank. Those marketers who use such a data bank for customer list enhancement can typically expect a 40 percent or more customer list match.

Direct Media, a giant in business response list activity, is a direct marketing business list management organization that has matched over 75 response lists to form its 6 million response name Executive Data Bank free of duplications. Another bank, called The Direct Media Business Data Bank, includes over 12 million decision makers pulled mainly from paid subscribers and controlled circulation recipients of many business and trade publications plus business buyer files. Other large data banks include the Masterfile of Business from Contacts Influential and the California Database from Pac-Tel.

Virtually all major trade magazine publishers now have data banks. McGraw-Hill's Business Leaders list, among the early publisher entries, includes just about all of its publications merged and unduplicated. Most publishing groups emphasize their own areas of interest. For instance, another data bank, called Gralla Merged Publications, has over a half million unduplicated names of owners, presidents, and managers that subscribe to one or more of its 14 publications such as *Bank*

Systems and Equipment, Health Care Systems, and *Sporting Goods Business.* This publisher concentrates on the construction, retail, and services marketplaces.

Corporate executives and professionals who read Penton/IPC publications are incorporated into the Penton file, a 1.5 million name data bank heavily weighted toward manufacturing industries. Other leading publishers such as Chilton, Cahners, Hayden, Technical Publishing, C. W. Communications, and Hitchcock also have built sizable data banks from their various publication circulation lists.

Mal Dunn Associates, another business list management organization, has developed a unique file that is a 9 million business executive mail responsive data bank encompassing 24 separate lists including McGraw-Hill's *Business Leaders, Business Week, Kiplinger Washington Editors, Boston Business Journal, Standard and Poor's, United Technical Publications,* and other business publishers and business mail order lists. Of this file, 10 percent are multibuyers.

DATA BASE ADVANTAGES

As noted earlier, most true data bases are in-house entities, created from lists of the company's customers. There are also data bases of prequalified prospects or inquirers that are usually culled from past or current promotional efforts.

A comprehensive data base is viewed today as a major corporate asset. Perhaps its greatest strength is in its capabilities for statistical analysis of the customer's geographic, demographic, and behavioral factors. Because these can be precise and detailed, they enable the marketer to target segments of new customer and prospect universes. Ideally the data base contains a record of every sales and marketing activity related to each customer, and lets the marketer know who responded to different direct marketing promotions, or who did not respond, as well as details about follow-up efforts.

A data base can help the marketer determine who the best customers are and what characteristics they have in common. It provides details on which specific products are purchased, how often an order is placed, and how much a customer is likely to spend. Focusing on the individual customer's value helps the marketer determine the types of customers and prospects to go after and the kind of products and services to offer. It also identifies the most appropriate time frames in the customer's buying behavior cycle for targeting by catalogs, direct mail sales support, telemarketing, or other advertising and promotion programs.

The data base also augments direct mail's effectiveness by providing not only the name and title of customers and prospects but also other personalized data. By having built-in segmentation criteria the database enables marketers to plan and execute direct mail campaigns tailored to the customer's interest in the appropriate targeted segments. This targeting power lets the marketer put more resources into the search for high-quality prospects.

Of course, a well-designed data base helps ensure that money is not spent to send messages to people who are not interested in the product or who cannot afford it, or to people who have no effect on the purchase decision. Some marketers need to be reminded of Pareto's 80 percent–20 percent theory. Most marketers know that few customers provide most of their business. Should the marketer aim 80 percent of the promotion budget at that 20 percent segment? It is a question of the individual marketer's profitability and priorities. The data base can help determine the answer.

Direct marketing efforts are more cost effective because the marketer can fine-tune strategies, techniques, and approaches from the analyses and reporting programs. These tell the marketer how to plan for better sales results. For instance, a data base enables a mail order marketing campaign to be aimed at various levels of inquirers, those who indicated an interest in a product through direct responses in the past six months. Or, in another instance, if the marketer is seeking new business, only those prospects matching the "best customer" profile are targeted.

Sales Support Advantages

A data base will improve the efficiency of direct marketing promotional spending through targeting. In sales support direct marketing the data base helps locate high-interest prospects for salespeople to convert to sales through pinpointed direct mail advertising and telemarketing. This results in a promotion and selling cost per sale that can be measured in ways unaffordable in the past. It tells the marketer which medium or which direct mailing or telemarketing effort pulled best and which promotions generated the most profitable long-term customers. For instance, when the targeted segment is small but with a high sales potential, the marketer may find that custom tailored impact formats will pull best. These highly profiled mailings to best customers keep the dialog going.

Then, too, by using market research in combination with data base information, the marketer can target special personalized offers to competitor's customers. And, as most direct marketers have learned, a personalized mail package with the right offer has an intensity and cost-per-prospect-reached figure seldom matched by other media.

Mail Order Advantages

Not every mail order marketer can cost effectively maintain an on-line data base system. Some business-to-business marketers do maintain profitable mail order operations without such a system. Yet, for those who can afford one, the advantages of a computerized system are numerous and exciting.

For a small but growing number of business-to-business mail order direct marketers the marketing data base is the means to a profitable program measured on a cost per order basis. Key financial reports, such as the complete P&L statement, can be developed by computing operating and promotion costs along with response data by target markets. And this can be determined for complete campaigns as well as for single mailings or can provide up-to-the-minute financial summary data on demand. Having access to a wealth of detailed information on-line, the marketer is in a position to identify problems early enough to take remedial action. Averting inventory shortages is one example.

For telemarketing especially, information retrieval is fast and can cut phone order entry time materially. Quick and easy access of up-to-the-minute data gives the mail order marketer increased productivity and improved customer service. The marketer can give customers and prospects immediate answers via this on-line information resource. And this needed data can be accessed in many different ways.

More than half of business-to-business mail order responses come in by telephone and this is on the increase. It takes a substantial investment in WATS lines and customer service personnel to handle telephone orders. An on-line data-intensive system can increase efficiencies and effect profound savings, providing an important competitive advantage. For instance, when the marketer updates a file, the updated element is automatically corrected in all files in the data base. This saves dollars as well as time.

Although mail order operations improvement and efficiencies are important benefits, they are second to the strategic decision-making capabilities made available by the data base outputs. When marketers have a better picture of their own customers, they will know which segments to mail more often or to target with higher-impact catalogs or solo mailings. They can test the "best customer" portions of the rented lists that previously did not work for them. Also, the data base makes it easier for the mail order marketer to develop an ongoing testing program to measure lists, offers, media, creative approaches, and the profitability of different products.

One unique use of data bases for mail order marketers is to develop the one-time customer into a multibuyer. Each direct marketing effort produces sales, inquiries, leads, or some other measurable response. As a by-product, data from these responses enhance the information in the data base. This continually updated information lets the marketer maximize the advantages of personalization of direct mail and telemarketing promotions. It enables the marketer to tailor a step-by-step direct marketing program designed to turn prospects into first-time customers and then into multibuyers and more frequent buyers and up the scale into the key customer category.

Getting a customer by direct response marketing and keeping that customer is a continuing challenge. Increasing competition and a shortage of business-to-business rental response lists, among other reasons, have reduced the ability of outside lists to pull orders. To make up for this response shortfall, marketers prospecting for new customers are turning toward targeted promotions to various customer segments and are getting more results overall than they have been getting from single promotions to the complete customer list. These segments conform to marketing segmentation criteria, as reviewed in Chapter 4. They are marketability, reachability, sizability, and promotability.

The segments consist of successive levels of customer buying activity. There are four basic steps in meeting customer development program objectives:

1. Move the first-time buyer into a minimum standard purchase on the first order.
2. Build the first-time buyer into a multibuyer.
3. Get the multibuyer to order more frequently.
4. Get the frequent multibuyer to order different products.

Many more audiences can be singled out to receive custom tailored promotions such as:

■ building past customers into current customers
■ locating new buying influences to replace those that no longer have that responsibility in customer companies
■ finding additional buying influences in customer companies including those who buy supplies
■ identifying those customer personnel who are purchase "recommenders"

The marketing data base management system is designed to segment these customers into clusters in a hierarchy of buyer classifications. This view of the entire customer file permits finely tuned communications to build business in ways previously unavailable or unaffordable.

DATA BASE DESIGN CONSIDERATIONS

It takes more than one brainstorming session to identify all the potentially useful information that should be retained in a data base. Critical are future uses of the data and costs of gathering and maintaining it. The more information, the better the segmentation possibilities and the greater the chances are of matching the most profitable markets. This is the key to building an on-target list of customers and prospects for direct mail and telemarketing promotions, combined with personal sales calls if appropriate.

All main marketing and communications managers should be involved in determining the marketing data base requirements to ensure that all marketing needs are considered at the outset. These managers should determine the data they need for supporting short-range tactical programs and activities as well as the data needed for long-range strategies to build new business in new markets.

Marketing data base systems accumulate information from many sources, interrelate it, and render it easily accessible to product and program managers, sales and marketing managers, advertising and communications managers, and all other users. These data come from inside the company or from outside sources.

How data are captured and used constitute the two vital areas of concern in data base development. In the past, most business-to-business direct marketing operations did not gather, track, and evaluate transactional data at a detailed level. However, data base development activity is now moving rapidly as demands for greater depth of business data increase and as data processing costs become more affordable to more marketers.

Data Capture

The data base planner must not only think about what will be useful to the company currently but also two, three, or even five years in the future, and build that capability into the data base. Smart thinking at the design stage is critical since a marketing data base system must have the comprehensive data needed for the development and implementation of strategic target marketing plans. All prospect and customer activity of importance to the business-to-business marketer must be identified and collected, interpreted, analyzed, and integrated into meaningful marketing plans. For the mail order marketer, this also includes order entry, fulfillment, and telephone interaction.

When gathering data, keep in mind that it may be easier to capture data fresh, at the locations where the original transactions occur, than to try to convert existing information from one medium to another. Also, it helps to determine in the design stages whether data can go into the data base directly, that is, on-line.

When designing a data base, often the marketer needs more information than can be captured through normal marketing and operational transactions. Valuable details can be collected by conducting customer surveys by mail, telephone, or personal interviews. Other behavioral-type information of importance can come from sales call reports, tips from field service personnel, conversations with secretaries, loading dock personnel, and other target company employees.

When researching customer, prospect, and suspect marketplaces to enhance and update profiles, the data base planner should be cautious about privacy concerns. Demographic data, such as number of employees, business classification, and annual revenue, are in the public sphere. However, information about kinds and types of behavioral characteristics of individuals who make buying decisions, who influence the decision makers, or who place the orders, can concern those included in the data base. Attention must be given to the need for privacy and confidentiality by the data base planners.

Data Use

There are two basic ways the data base user gets information from the data base: (1) from ad hoc query requests made on demand and (2) from reports and other output formats as originally designed into the system.

For business-to-business mail order or sales support to be most effective, a marketing data base requires a management system that permits different users to enter and track customer questions, get current data or list segment counts, or get extracts for analytical work, all on demand.

Users also need output formats for selecting customer names for mailings or telemarketing and to support managerial decisions. From reports generated by the system, the marketer can get growth and inventory curves, and sales and inquiry data. Trends and events can indicate the need for a change of strategies and tactics. These are all important design considerations that should be taken up with the data base system designers.

The Development Process

Because the design of a marketing data base is a highly technical development process, it requires comprehensive computer-based systems and procedures. These have been detailed by Richard A. Fredrickson, vice-president, Taurus Marketing Inc. and can be found in Appendix 5. A summary of these aspects of the data base development process in business follows.

The process begins by collecting specific records from different departments in the company. Interviews with department heads uncover data not in standard records. Potential system users indicate their information analysis needs. These are then cross-referenced with data already collected. At this point it may be found that additional and new data are needed. From the data accumulated, report patterns begin to develop. Sample reports provide an idea of volume and value for the user.

Master files are then coded, enabling the data base to maintain results of individual marketing efforts on a detailed basis. This file is then matched to incoming orders, inquiries, and other transactions on the basis of promotion and list segments to arrive at percent response, cost per order, and other requested computations. With calculated results and descriptive coding, the reporting data base is sequenced and manipulated as needed.

As a necessary step in maintaining quality standards, processing procedures are established to validate all data. A method of analysis of the master file is developed to provide many varied counts on the file and a quick study of the customer base. A cell-code selection technique speeds up the processing of the detailed results analysis of marketing efforts.

The key factor in data base development is finding out the real needs of the data base users. Fredrickson states it succinctly when he says,

> The principles involved in developing a database are no different than those used in developing a successful marketing program. Proper research of the end user's needs and wants will define the strategy needed to achieve those results for the program to succeed.

THE DATA BASE COMPONENTS

Information to be captured for the data base will depend on the individual business-to-business marketer's needs and objectives. The larger the customer base and prospect marketplace, the more practical it is to capture a maximum number of data elements. However, for the average business-to-business marketer the gross number of customers or prospects in the marketplace is relatively few. Although a data base program may be practical for many smaller marketers, the marketers should minimize the amount of data collected.

The links among the elements in the business-to-business marketing data base are selected by the planner, based on the needs of the users. Richard Courtheoux approaches the construction of a data base by separating data into categories covering business-to-business customer profile elements plus a breakdown of quantifiable functional elements of direct marketing. Those major data elements identified most often in business-to-business data base development programs are listed in Tables 6-2 and 6-3. They are discussed further below.

Business Data Elements

The element in the customer information list component that provides linkage to all functional components is the unique ID that creates the integrated data base

Table 6-2. Business-to-business data elements in the customer information list.

Unique identification
Decision maker's name and title
Company name
Address
Standard Industrial Classification
Telephone number
Source code
	Size of company
	  by number of employees
	  by revenue
	Product demand
	Buying behavior
	Purchase history

Source: Adapted from Richard Courtheoux, "Database Techniques: How to Tap a Key Company Resource," *Direct Marketing,* August 1984.

unit (see Table 6-2). The marketer's use of the various data elements listed is apparent in most cases. However, a summary may be of help to the reader.

- The name and title of the decision maker or those who influence the purchase of a product are needed for promotion.
- Direct mail or phone calls must go to the right people and the field salespeople should know who is being reached by mail or telephone.
- Company name and address indicates the number of buyer locations in one company.
- The SIC code and company size indications are the most basic and prevalently used elements. They are readily available for customer profiling. These elements, plus product demand forecasts, affect promotional strategy.
- The source code is needed to identify customer sources.
- The telephone number is used for outbound telemarketing, salesperson follow-up, and customer service.
- Buying behavior helps determine buying patterns and buyer purchasing motivations.
- Purchase history is needed to show details of business transactions including monetary activity.

Functional Business Elements

In each category of the functional data elements a unique identification is included to connect a current transaction to the enhanced customer file (see Table 6-3).

Order/Inquirer Elements
Order and inquiry data elements such as date and source provide the information needed to analyze the order or inquiry frequency and various marketing response intervals. Methods of order placement and payment as well as details on each item purchased, such as quantity and returns, can give the marketer clues to purchasing behavior. Quality of sales inquiries helps determine types of future promotions and extent of sales force follow-up needed.

Table 6-3. Business-to-business functional data elements.

Order/Inquiry Data Elements	Product Data Elements
Buyer/inquirer ID	Item ID
Date	Price
Source	Product category
Amount	Sales
Placement method	Returns
Payment method	Service problems
Order/inquiry per item	Inventory control information
ID	Media used for selling
quantity	
returns	
out of stock	
dollar sales	
Inquiry quality	
Promotion Data Elements	List Data Elements
Promotion ID	List ID
Cost	Selection codes
Format or offer code	RFM category
Media used	Mailing code
Performance results	Mailing date
orders	List classifications
inquiries	Performance
	orders
	inquiries
	Rental cost

Source: Adapted from Richard Courtheoux, "Database Techniques: How to Tap a Key Company Resource," *Direct Marketing,* August 1984.

Product Elements

Product data elements, such as price and product categories and sales and returns, identify important product characteristics, contribute to customer segmentation, and develop new offers. These elements identify poor products, promotion that misrepresents the product, and inventory problems, as well as indicate the success of a product and evaluate its marketing effort.

Promotion Elements

Promotional activity information includes all the responses to different offers needed by the marketer for analysis and evaluation. These elements help the marketer determine the relative cost effectiveness of direct marketing offers, copy, formats, and other combinations for orders or inquiries.

List Elements

List data elements evaluate list profitability. The recency, frequency, and monetary value information help identify segmentation possibilities. Mailing code, date, and list classification data help the marketer analyze individual list performance.

This list of business-to-business data elements is not necessarily complete. Marketing data base developers will want to include those elements that conform to their own specific direct marketing requirements.

MANAGING THE DATA BASE EFFORT

Staffing

The technological advances in sophisticated data base development have outstripped general management's ability to understand it and put it to use. This has created a need for the marketing data base consultant retained by a company to investigate and recommend an approach to a data base management system and further develop its information requirements. Recommendations may include a start-up that can be implemented by an outside service bureau, an in-house data center, or a combination. The consultant can act as a liaison between company management people and technical personnel to coordinate the start-up.

Most marketers find it is not cost effective to operate all marketing data base functions in-house. These functions include data processing, research and analysis, creative design, production, and fulfillment. The talents and skills of people in each of these disciplines used in direct marketing require a knowledgeable data base professional to head the overall effort.

The Computer

Data base management programs have now become affordable to smaller companies and small departments of larger companies who could not, for whatever reason, have access to the company's corporate computer. However, data base management programs can now be done inexpensively on a personal computer (PC). The PC has become an integral part of just about every business marketing or sales office today. PC technology is moving ahead so rapidly that the marketing data base planner in many cases no longer needs to rely on the company's centralized mainframe organization to get up and running with a data base management system. Computer speed and disk storage capacity have continued to multiply two or three times every few years.

A PC can handle a data base of up to 200,000 names and addresses, provide on-line inquiry and updating, and provide an unlimited number of activity and sales recordings on each record in the file. The marketer can also get multiple addresses for each company and is able to record and select data using defined codes and options.

Brian Buxton, vice-president and product manager with Citibank's corporate cash management division, has had success in using the PC as a data base tool. His approach on how data base planners can use it to obtain vital information on prospects and customers is summarized in Appendix 6. Included are examples of a typical list analysis problem and a sales call tracking problem. Appendix 7 gives complete instructions for file importing, list analysis, and sales call tracking, using DBASE III on a personal computer.

Buxton's advice is most appropriate for the great bulk of sales support direct marketers with files from 10,000 to 20,000 names. The topics are covered from the perspective of companies selling high-ticket items through a sales force that requires many face-to-face sales calls.

Costs

A marketing data base system often originates with the needs of the marketing division or specifically the direct marketing division, but there are many other units in a company that would like to have and should have access to the marketing data base. This is how some marketing managements justify the function and the value of the data base to corporate management to get the funds that are needed to launch the data base.

It is difficult to estimate the total cost of a typical marketing data base management system. Brian Buxton estimates equipment costs for a personal computer data base system can run from $1,500 to $15,000. For instance, for $1,500 a marketer can get a low-end system with 20 megabytes of storage, 640K of RAM, low-speed processor, and dot matrix printer. This can effectively handle a 10,000, 30-character name, address, city, state, and zip code data base. For $15,000 the marketer can get a high-speed processor, a Compaq 386/20, IBM model 80, or top-of-the-line Macintosh, with 5 megabytes of RAM, 150 megabytes of storage, and a laser printer. This data base file could total 250,000.

One-time start-up expenses as well as ongoing maintenance must be considered. Information gathering costs associated with development costs can be substantial.

Personnel and facilities expense to maintain a data base system can be sizable. Some industry experts say development costs are equal to about one year of maintenance costs. These costs are dependent on the size of the system and whether a marketer buys an existing data base package, develops an in-house program, or opts to go with a computer service bureau. The service bureau route gives the marketer the advantage of an on-line data base management system without a substantial up-front investment in the required hardware.

SUMMARY

Database management systems, spawned by advancements in computer technology, have enabled business-to-business direct marketers to effectively use the techniques of market segmentation and targeting to define and choose the most profitable markets for their products and services. A data base is an on-line management system that links existing customer files, enriched by secondary demographic data and files containing current transactional data.

A data bank does not have this linkage but it does combine unduplicated elements from different lists offering rich demographic information in one generic entity. Through a data bank direct marketers can rent a cross section of many lists or enhance their own customer lists with overlays of structured data. Many data banks are accessible through new interactive computer systems that make possible a network of list suppliers and users that exchange data bank information and process list transactions over telephone lines between remote sites.

Segmentation criteria built into the data base helps profile best customers and pinpoints a step-by-step customer development program. The data base management system also enables the marketer to maximize the advantages of personalization as well as to establish ongoing testing programs and build cost efficiencies into operational functions.

The vital areas of data base development include how the data is captured and how it is used. The size of the individual marketer's customer base and prospect marketplace determine the practical limits of data elements to include in the business data base. A unique identification provides the linkage for the data base to function interactively, providing business planning, analysis, and measurement for marketing and operations. These functional data elements can be grouped into order/inquiry, product, promotion, and list components.

Because data base direct marketing encompasses the appropriate meshing of the varied skills of data processing, research and analysis, creative design, production, and fulfillment, a knowledgeable data base coordinator is especially needed for the planning and initial implementation stages. No longer just a tool for the high-volume business-to-business direct marketer, marketing data base management systems are beginning to solve many problems for the smaller-volume direct marketer using the personal computer.

7

THE OFFER

Most experienced business-to-business direct marketing practitioners consider the offer just as important to a successful promotion as the prospect list targeted. Stated simply, a direct response offer is what readers will get when they reply. Most offers are associated with a direct response campaign, which proposes something tangible for the reader, as in both mail order and sales support response generation. But there are also offers that are indirect for campaigns with awareness, reminder, or reinforced selling objectives. For these, the offer is the enhancement the reader gets from being educated, informed, entertained, or motivated by the message in the mailing itself. Whatever is offered in any direct marketing effort, it must have value to the reader.

Because the quantity and/or quality of responses are determined by the offer, it becomes the major implementor of direct marketing strategy. The planner selects the types of offers that could accomplish the mail order or sales support objective and goes with an offer based on the best guess, or various offers are tested and dictated by the magnitude of the risk.

DETERMINING THE OBJECTIVES OF THE OFFER

For business-to-business direct mail programs the planner must determine whether the mailing has an offer that will be direct or indirect. For mail order objectives this is not a problem. But for sales support response objectives, this seemingly simple step in the campaign planning process, when neglected, has probably caused more business-to-business direct mail efforts to produce disappointing results than any other reason. This step defines the direct mail strategy in the context of the overall program objectives. A lack of clear-cut objectives often muddies the focus of the offer in a sales support mailing. This can result in fewer responses. And it does happen especially when the inquiry-generation mailing features the product rather than the offer. Here is an actual case example that featured a test mailing sent to 14,000 bank executives by a manufacturer of bank systems and equipment.

The theme revolved around the idea that an efficient system reduces operating errors and costs. Letter A highlighted the advantages of the system and presented an offer to send a brochure in the closing paragraph. Letter B focused on a descriptive outline of the brochure and presented an offer to send it in an identical closing paragraph. The two letters were on the same stationery and were about equal in length and overall appearance. Letter B was twice as effective in drawing inquiries. Letter A pulled between 2 percent and 3 percent in different markets. Letter B pulled between 4 percent and 6 percent in the same markets with no apparent variation in the quality of responses.

When choosing offer material for response generation objectives the direct mail planner must weigh these basic considerations:

- The composition of the list that ranges from possible prospects to prequalified prospects
- The number of responses that can be expected from a given list with a given offer based on testing and experience
- The cost of getting a response based on the planned offer
- The quality of desired response in the case of sales support direct mail, which takes into account costs of inquiry qualification and sales conversion ratios and costs

Most business-to-business sales support response mailings are directed to non-prequalified lists that can generate anything from raw inquiries to highly qualified leads, depending on the specific offer and the creative emphasis given to the offer in the direct mail package.

A key question that must be answered by the planner at the outset is, Will the offer result in quality responses that can be turned over directly to the salespeople for follow-up, or will there be inquiries that need further qualification by mail or phone?

When mailing to a prequalified list the usual inquiry-generation offers—those designed to identify prospects within a large universe—do not apply since highly qualified prospects have already been identified. The objectives of response mailings to prequalified lists are action steps that move those more highly interested along the prospect-to-customer path. Most of these objectives center around getting the prospect and the marketer together.

Some sales support offers try to get specific kinds of inquiries that warrant more intensive and usually more expensive follow-up; that is, the offer is designed so that those 2 percent or 3 percent who respond out of the broad market can be identified as having certain characteristics. This follow-up is made by additional mail contact, salespeople on the telephone, professional telemarketing communicators, personal face-to-face sales calls, or contact at seminars, trade shows, or other sales events. Face-to-face meetings are the ultimate objective and take place at the prospect's office or the marketer's office, a private seminar location, or a trade show hospitality room.

Tracking sales conversions on various response mailing offers lets the direct mail planner know which offers produce optimum results for specific products in specific markets. Indirect sales support offers do not have any follow-up in this way since they have nonresponse objectives.

OFFERS FOR MAIL ORDER MARKETING

In a business-to-business mail order effort, the product is the basic reason for responding. In the pure sense, the product (and the promise of what it will do for the reader for a stated price) is the offer in mail order direct marketing efforts. Not surprisingly, the marketer often needs to use added inducements to produce enough profitable responses: an offer for the offer, so to speak. Premiums, in their broadest sense, are most commonly used as added incentives to get the reader to respond to a mail order offer. These incentives or inducements also are referred to generally in the mail order field as "offers." It is in this context that they are discussed here.

Business-to-business mail order marketers make first-time sales to two kinds of customers: those who purchase only one time and those who make repeat purchases. To have a profitable ongoing operation, the marketer goes after the maximum number of first-time buyers who will continue to place repeat orders. Often, direct marketers secure these first-time purchasers at a loss. Since they make the bulk of their profits on repeat orders, they choose their selling propositions and offers carefully to avoid bringing in orders from the one-time-only customer. So, mail order marketers look for those offers and inducements that are appropriate for their products and target market at an acceptable cost/revenue ratio, taking into consideration the life value of the purchaser over the long term.

These inducements, or added incentives to buy, have become fixed elements in most selling propositions:

- Pricing
- Payment terms
- Free trial
- Sweepstakes
- Guarantees and endorsements
- Premiums and gifts
- First-step information offers

Pricing

Because the price of a product or service is an integral part of any mail order offer, marketers focus on pricing more than any other offer or inducement. There are many ways to state the same price. In its most simple configuration, the base price can be stated as discounted, as a sale, or as a quantity purchase showing a savings from an established price.

Payment Terms

Business marketers are finding that offering more payment choices for the business buyer has a payoff. Allowing customers to bill to the widely used travel and entertainment cards is an effective inducement to order, especially when smaller companies are targeted (here, executives tend to bill right to their cards rather than following a purchase order procedure as in bigger companies). Higher-priced products are offered on extended payment plans. A payment term such as "bill me later" works well with a free trial offer by helping the prospect make a faster decision. Problems arise, however, when payment terms are too liberal. More orders may result but no-pays will increase.

Free Trial

When the business-to-business marketer has products that lend themselves to trial use, this inducement can be highly effective. Since business buyers tend to be wary or skeptical, especially of new products, they need assurances before they buy. Free trials help overcome objections even though some "free trials" require payment up-front. And these inducements continue to pull high responses even though full return privileges are built into most business-to-business mail order propositions today.

Sweepstakes

Some business-to-business mail order marketers (one example is the National Pen Company) test sweepstakes in their search for breakthrough results from mailings to relatively limited business universes. Sweepstakes have been used successfully by consumer mail order marketers for years but are not profitable for most business-to-business mailers. For a sweepstakes to be practical, the marketplace must be large enough to make the cost per response affordable.

When planning a sweepstakes it is best to involve a sweepstakes or contest management professional in the early phases, since there are many legal restrictions that could involve expensive problems for the marketer if not followed. A sweepstakes cannot be a lottery. Consideration, prize, and chance are the three criteria for a lottery. If the "consideration" is eliminated, then no purchase is required, and therefore it qualifies as a sweepstakes. Having an outside organization handle receipt of entries, drawings, and judging also lends credibility to the effort.

The quality of inquiries generated by a sweepstakes can be a problem to some marketers because it brings in too many responders who are more interested in the prizes than in the marketer's products. It also attracts more than the usual number of people who don't pay for products received, and as a general rule, there will be fewer second-time buyers.

Sweepstakes, however, are exciting to some business prospects and can incite to action some who would not respond to a different offer. Many sweepstakes mailings emphasize the inducement more than the product. They usually include one or a few very big exciting prizes as well as many smaller ones, so most responders feel they have a chance to win something. Sweepstakes can be worth testing for some business-to-business marketers who sell a large volume of general high-use products.

Guarantees and Endorsements

The clearly described guarantee, usually specified for a definite time period, is vital in any mail order proposition because it establishes the marketer's credibility. The guarantee should be spelled out in as much detail as practical. In effect, it promises the buyer that if the product doesn't live up to expectations, all or some of the purchase price will be returned.

Endorsements by industry authority figures and association memberships also make the selling proposition more believable and function much like the guarantee.

Premiums and Gifts

A premium is used as an incentive for a prospect to place an order or to respond to an offer in the first step of a multistep mail order effort. The premium should be perceived by the prospect as having value. The higher the value, the greater the number of orders generated. However, high-value premiums can get the marketer in trouble two ways: first, by getting an order that costs the marketer more than it is worth, and second, by conflicting with the rules some companies have against their employees accepting from vendors such gifts or premiums. Any gift must be in good taste and preferably have use in both the customer's place of business and at home. In most cases it is not necessary for the customer to return the premium or gift if the product is returned.

When premiums and gifts are used in mail order there are usually fewer payers and repeat orders. However, the more a premium relates to the product and its marketplace, the better chance marketers have of getting repeat sales from first-time buyers.

First-step Information Offers

Multistep mail order promotions that eventually lead to a direct sale by mail or phone require a first effort that most often uses an information offer to identify what is usually a relatively small, high-potential market segment for the product. These promotions often involve "big-ticket" products that need elaborate and expensive follow-up by one or a series of mailings and telemarketing campaigns to those who respond to the first effort in an attempt to make the sale.

Most catalog marketers often offer a copy of their catalog as a first-step information offer. Some, especially the smaller entrepreneurs, offer information on selected products from their catalog. Others create special offers that are related to the interests of that particular market segment.

INQUIRY-GENERATION OFFERS

Offers for direct-response sales-support objectives in business-to-business direct marketing are different from those for mail order objectives. For sales support inquiry generation, the offer is not the marketer's product since the objective of the direct marketing campaign is not a direct sale that comes in by mail or telephone. The offer in this case (1) identifies those prospects who show an interest and who may buy later, or (2) brings buyers and salespeople face-to-face. In either case the offers in these direct marketing efforts aim at whetting the reader's appetite to learn more or to take overt action leading to the next step in the selling process.

The main purpose of an inquiry offer is to identify a select number of prospects from the target market who have an interest in a specific subject, as highlighted by the offer. If only the product is pitched, a great many people may be missed who may have a need but aren't aware of it. Once the marketer has the names of the inquirers, planned follow-up by telemarketing, additional direct mail, and face-to-face selling by a salesperson move the qualified prospects along in the customer development process.

Business prospects in any universe at any given time are at specific stages in their buying behavior cycle. Often, prospects lock in their vendor preferences at an early stage for high-tech, complex, and expensive products and systems. For this reason, sales-support direct-marketing planners must identify from the total target market those prospects who are in the part of the cycle most compatible with their sales development strategy. The identification of appropriate prospects is governed by a direct response promotion that includes a choice from a broad range of sales support offers:

- Free information
- Gifts and premiums
- Sweepstakes and contests
- Free trial
- Sample
- Seminar
- Product demonstration
- Sales representative's call
- Free cost estimate
- Free analysis and survey
- Continuity programs

Free Information

The most widely used offer in response-generation programs is free information. And most marketers have a large array to choose from: literature, reports, survey results, and other materials in formats that describe, illustrate, or reference different aspects of their products or systems. Some of these potential offer materials are more elaborate than others. The specific type and the way this offer is described to the prospect determines the quantity/quality response ratio.

The material is usually in the form of booklets and folders. The title given to these offers in the response-generation mailing will determine whether they will be perceived by the prospect as interesting and important. For instance, an offer of a 12-page booklet on "state-of-the-art robotics in assembly operations" will trigger responses only from those prospects who are concerned with this subject. A response-generation mailing should not be designed around an offer of existing literature unless it coincides perfectly with the objectives of the mailing. If not, new offer materials should be created.

A review of information offers, ranging from those of general interest to the more specific, illustrates the wide variety that can be created to help business-to-business direct marketers in sales support attain the desired quantity/quality ratios needed for their response-generation programs.

Information offers fall into the following categories:

- Chapters in a current business book
- Booklets on generic subjects
- Article reprints that are industry generic
- Information packets
- Case history releases
- Industry authority booklets
- Management reports on specific subjects
- Trade and business article reprints
- Basic product/application materials that are product-specific
- Feature/function product folders and brochures
- Company newsletters and magazines
- Catalogs and buying guides
- Technical papers
- Company lab test and survey reports
- Requests to get on a mailing list

There are two classes of informational offer material. The first, industry/product generic, generally produces responses that are of higher quantity but of lesser quality. The second, company/product specific, generates responses that are higher in quality but fewer in quantity.

Generic Information Offers

Generic material has a broader acceptance by business prospects. Since it is written without a vendor's promotional bias, it is perceived as more credible. Generic materials include:

- Chapters in current business books
- Article reprints that do not mention the marketer's name or product
- "Helpful hints" industry booklets

Generally these offers are used to identify prospects from broad suspect lists. They usually pull more responses but resulting inquiry-to-sale ratios are not as good when compared to responses based on company/specific material. They come from inquirers far back in the buying behavior cycle as well as from some not yet in the cycle.

Chapters in current business books Every industry has its share of noted authors. They write about industry developments and new concepts. Their highly regarded opinions are often found in newly published books. The direct mail planner seeking material on generic information offers very often can find excellent selections in various chapters of these books. Once a chapter or two is selected, the marketer can readily get permission from the publisher to reprint the material in booklet or pamphlet form. (Most publishers readily give permission, usually at no charge, since this represents free publicity for their book.) Businessmen and businesswomen never have enough time to read all the current periodicals and books that help them keep up with trends and new ideas. When this specific material is in the reader's interest and is highlighted and offered in a direct mail letter, busy business prospects tend to want copies of these excerpted chapters.

These reprints can pull high response but, of course, the title of the book and the chapter heading must describe the specific subject well enough to draw responses from those readers the marketer wants to identify. For example, a marketer may want to find within a vast retail marketplace those who would be interested in talking to a salesperson about retail theft surveillance systems. Offering a reprint of the chapter, "How to Eliminate Salespeople Pilferage" from a recently published book may be ideal for generating responses from those retailers who have such a problem and need help. Inquiries from this type of offer material usually require further qualification before a salesperson can profitably follow up with a personal call.

Article reprints industry/generic Article reprints that do not mention the marketer's product or company, offered as having an industry/generic emphasis, product a high quantity of responses. But further qualification is most often needed before responses can be labeled "live" sales leads.

Even though business men and women subscribe to trade publications to stay current in their field, many often miss an individual article. Since average readership of a publication is less than ten out of twelve issues, and since readership within an issue is often less than half, there's a good chance individual articles get missed, especially when there are several different trade magazines competing for readers in the same industry.

Marketers usually have no problem getting the publisher's permission to reprint articles for use as direct marketing offers.

Booklets or folders on generic subjects Some companies contribute to the knowledge base in their industry by publishing pamphlets or booklets on generic subjects. Most booklets include a page or two of promotional material about the sponsor company. The more promotion included in such booklets, the less valuable they become to prospects. Yet, without some mention of the sponsor company and its products, such booklets would be in very short supply.

Most reader/prospects who are "just looking" will respond well to offers of materials containing solid and useful general information. Some may be close to taking buying action but as a rule the quality of the average inquiry will be lower than those responses from readers looking for product/specific material. Offers of material on generic subjects do, however, produce inquiries that are useful for identifying large numbers of potential prospects from broad suspect lists as a first step in a multistep inquiry-building strategy. This can be valuable to some marketers because there is much evidence to indicate that larger numbers of less-qualified inquiries can produce more sales conversions overall than smaller quantities of highly qualified inquiries.

Industry authority booklets Each industry has its own gurus—outspoken authorities who are often quoted on important industry issues. These people are frequently found on the platform at state and national trade shows and conventions. Many are consultants in the industry. They are information purveyors and are often involved in research.

A marketer may contract with one of these industry figures to write an article, with the author's byline, on an agreed upon topic for the sole purpose of being used as an offer piece. The intent of the article may be to highlight a specific subject that would be of special interest to a segment of the audience the marketer wishes to identify. This document becomes, in effect, a third-party endorsement of a concept or point of view that coincides with that of the marketer's. Readers benefit by learning something from an independent authority about a particular subject. Quantity and quality of inquiries produced from this offer depend on the title and subject matter chosen.

Company–Product/Specific Offers

Prospects responding to offers for information that is definitely from the marketer's point of view get specific company and product promotional material. The offer in direct mail packages in this instance is often generalized by the wording, "Send for more information" and is described briefly so the prospect does not know exactly what kind of information will be sent. Marketers who do this have the built-in option of choosing, after the response is generated, specifically what they will send an inquirer from their bank of available printed materials. However, the number of responses generated will be more qualified if the offer is described more specifically.

Information packets The information packet, often called a fact kit, is an array of printed materials containing specifics about a product or system. It is usually offered when the products, systems, or services promoted require detailed and complex explanations. Marketers new to a marketplace also include in the packet company information that presents a positive image. The packet may include several pieces of promotional literature in an envelope or a folio with pockets that hold the material. It attempts to tell a more complete product or system story than can be provided in only one piece of literature. When practical, the packet includes product samples.

Because a packet can be expensive to produce, it is usually not offered to marginal prospect lists. It can appear attractive as an offer because the reader perceives it to be more valuable than a brochure or a folder.

The information packet often generates higher quantities of inquiries than most other company–product/specific offers. For example, Jim Kobs, chairman of Kobs & Brady, tested three offers in a search for leads that would most profitably convert to sales of telephone systems: an offer of more information, an offer of a free demonstration, and an offer of a systems information kit. The more information offer was least productive. The demonstration offer pulled the most qualified inquiries in terms of the ratio of conversion to sales when compared to the systems information kit offer, which pulled a greater quantity of inquiries. However, the systems information kit won since the number of sales conversions in total was much larger.

Case history releases Just about all marketers have among their most valuable assets proud customers who are enthusiastic about the products they have purchased. Very often, these satisfied users are more than willing to provide the marketer with testimonial statements that form the basis of a case history of their experience with a product or system. Because the statements are highly positive, the case history offer in a direct marketing effort has advantages similar to a typical trade publication article highlighting an ideal application of a product. Most satisfied customer companies approached by a vendor marketer for a testimonial know that a case history, promoted and publicized by the markeer, gives the customer company the chance to publicly enhance its image.

Case histories range from a brief one-page summary to elaborate multipage booklets. A brief story of the user is spelled out and comparisons are made between the new and old product or system. Case histories are most effective as offers when product applications are in the same line of business targeted for the direct marketing effort. When prospects request this information, they identify themselves as having a product application and need similar to the one described in the offer. For instance, a marketer's offer of a case history detailing a credit union's use of a computer network, when used as an offer in a mailing to manufacturers, will not pull well at all. When used as an offer in a mailing to commercial banks, it will produce more inquiries. But, it would be most effective if it were offered to credit unions.

Case histories as offer material are popular in business-to-business direct mail. They tend to bring in large numbers of responses from appropriate vocational lists—lists of firms in similar areas of business. Further qualification of these inquiries is usually required before passing them on to salespeople for personal follow-up.

Management reports Perceived by prospects as valuable information, the management report is one of the more popular formats in the marketer's hierarchy of offers. Management reports have a personalized one-on-one appearance as though prepared for a select few. And many are. The prospect thinks of them as special, unique, and somewhat personal.

The typical report is 8½ by 11 inches, often consisting of a dozen or more nonillustrated pages in typewriter type. This sheaf is usually affixed to a plain cover that has minimum company identification. Often a die-cut rectangle on the cover permits the title of the report to show through from the first page. The inexpensive format of a management report eliminates the marketer's risk of stocking large quantities of elaborate printed materials that may never get used, or stocking too few that may necessitate an expensive small quantity reprint. Management reports can be produced practically overnight, affordably, in quantities of 50 or 100 at a time.

The reports can be written or edited by direct mail writers as part of the response-generation direct-mail campaign. Technical literature, management speeches, and engineering and lab reports provide the basis for the reports. Higher response results from offers of management reports described in an inquiry-building mailing as new information that includes breakthrough thinking and updated product concepts. To get maximum quantity response from any management report offer, the mail planner should avoid report titles and descriptions that make this offer appear like an advertisement.

Trade and business publication article reprints Some business-to-business marketers send product publicity releases to the trade press with a view toward using a reprint of the published article as offer material in direct-response campaigns. The prospect tends to find the article reprint more credible than if the information was in a printed folder produced by the marketer, since such articles carry the endorsement of an authority in the industry—the publisher.

Product/specific article reprints usually will not generate the high number of responses associated with industry/generic article reprints. However, those article reprints that contain case histories, testimonials, or announcements relating to the marketer's products produce more qualified inquiries precisely because they identify the serious prospects, those closer to taking buying action. It is only logical that the closer prospects get to making a buying decision, the more they seek specific product information.

Basic product application material Basic product application material describes in paragraph form the user advantages of the product features. It consists of factual data about a product, system, or group of related products, and does not contain elaborate graphics but does include product photographs. Content for this type of material comes from the systems engineers and sales-oriented product developers. Like the case history, this literature offer presents the product in one type of application only. This makes it more selective in identifying qualified prospects since inquiries come from prospects seeking specific product application information.

Yet such offer material, if described correctly in an inquiry-building direct-marketing effort, can appeal to those prospects who are still in the early stages of learning about the product. This offer should take prospects from the developing interest stage to the next step where, through additional information and offers from direct mail, a telephone call or a salesperson's visit will be requested by the prospect. Basic product application offer material should give prospects insights into what the product can do for them. The marketer must make sure that this offer material performs that function if it is to succeed in directing the prospect to the next step in the prospect-to-customer development process.

Product feature/function material Specific product facts that apply to any application are spelled out in product feature/function folders or booklets. It is a fairly complete, although not technical, explanation of a product or system and how it functions generally.

When a marketer releases a new product or wants to expand product distribution into new markets, product feature/function folders or booklets are often used as offers. The offer singles out from a broad array of SIC classifications specifically those businesses interested in the product highlighted in the mailing. These identified prospects could be the most profitable for future targeting. This is a form of research, but the offer can also produce valuable inquiries as a by-product of this research objective.

The offer can also identify prospects in the marketer's present marketplace who are ready to study product details and therefore may be close to wanting to talk to a salesperson about those details. Whether this product feature/function offer is used for research or strictly for getting more business, the responses are fairly well qualified.

Company newsletters or magazines Company newsletters are one of the most frequently used contacts between business-to-business marketers and their customers. However, newsletters and magazines written as internal house organs are of little value to the prospect and therefore are of no use as offer material in direct marketing. The marketer's employees may like these publications but prospects are not all that interested in what is going on in the vendor's company.

The most helpful newsletters contain valuable generic product and industry information. Because of their periodical format they commit the marketer to a program of continuing communication. When written in the interest of the reader, and promoted as a direct marketing offer, the free newsletter can pull healthy quantities of responses.

Newsletter content should be 90 percent generic and not overly promotional to be of value to the prospect. Some purported newsletters are little more than promotional brochures with a newsletter masthead. If such an offer has been oversold in the response-generation promotion, those who receive it will be disappointed not only once but each time a new issue arrives, producing a long-range negative effect.

How an offer of a newsletter is described in a direct marketing promotion will determine how many prospects will want to get on the list to receive it. Those who respond will have a higher interest in the marketer's products than those who do not respond. Responses to this offer are of low quality and will have a low ratio of conversion to sales. But this higher-interested, semiqualified group can be very valuable as a next step in a prospect development program.

NCR's *EFT Digest* is an example of a newsletter in which less than 10 percent of the content is product/specific. In the early stages of the banking industry's formulation of the electronic fund transfer (EFT) concept, NCR established a four- to six-page monthly newsletter. A business clipping service provided copies of all articles that appeared in U.S. publications on that subject. NCR then selected the most timely and important articles, edited them for quick reading, and produced a well-read and respected newsletter that reflected the company's interest in the industry's development of that EFT concept. Because the publication was unique, and had high perceived value to readers, it became well known in the industry. It therefore received high response when offered in direct mail and business publication direct response efforts.

Buying guide catalogs Business-to-business marketers, especially those who sell staple products in their industries, maintain buying guide catalogs that include product specifics. Those catalogs that get revised more frequently contain prices whereas others include separate price sheets. Purchasing agents and other industrial and business buyers often purchase directly from these catalogs even though the vendor company's salesperson routinely calls on the buyer. Third-party sellers, influencers, consultants, and dealers also use buying guide catalogs.

These guides are of value to those prospects who have a need or feel they will have a need to purchase products represented in the guide from that company. These can be effective direct mail offers when the strategy calls for developing a list of serious inquirers who can, with further mail and telephone contacts, turn into good customers.

Technical papers Marketers in some industries have employees who have written technical papers. Their contribution to the general knowledge within an industry is encouraged and recognized by associations, publishers, learning institutions, and the government. These academic, nonpromotional treatises make good offers when the appeal is to the technically oriented prospect. Technical papers are also ideal offers that generate inquiries from prequalified lists, especially when used in mailings to influencers and approvers in larger companies where decision making is a joint process.

Company product performance tests, lab tests, and competitive comparisons Factual data about a company's product presented as a test report can have great credibility with the prospect because it implies nonpromotional objectivity. Information for the report comes from test or research results and is usually described in a management report format but with heavy emphasis on charts, graphs, and diagrams. For some products the reports can be highly technical.

As offer material in business-to-business direct marketing, test reports interest prospects who are looking for ways to justify a purchase to themselves and others in the approval line who need hard facts to be convinced. Quality responses come from serious prospects interested in analytical comparison.

Virtually any survey or test report circulated by a company shows its products in a superior light. And there are times when the marketer will design a performance test or a competitive comparison survey with the specific idea of using the results as offer material to identify specific groups of qualified prospects. In most industries these survey reports are well accepted and make good offers.

Getting on a mailing list Offers to place the reader on the company's mailing list to receive new and valuable information as it becomes available are rarely used as the only offers in a business-to-business inquiry-building mailing. Yet, such offers single out a specific category of interested prospects. These offers identify, aside from competitors, those who show an interest in getting more informational mailings. These prospects are more likely to respond to specific offers in future mailings or telemarketing efforts.

Gifts and Premiums

The role of the gift or premium in inquiry-generation promotions is a secondary offer or inducement to get the prospect to act on a primary offer, such as a free product demonstration, a free analysis and survey, a free seminar, or a salesperson's call.

If the gift or premium is perceived as having high value, responses will increase—especially those from nonprospects. In this case, the use of gifts and premiums as an adjunct to a primary inquiry-building offer may not be affordable if mailing to marginal prospect lists. However, when the premium is deemphasized by being buried in the message, those who respond to the premium offer will be better qualified prospects. This technique could make the promotion pay off. When mailing to lists of prequalified prospects, the gift or premium cost per sale will be lower. Here the same gift or premium can have a better chance of cost effectively maximizing response, since everyone on the list is prequalified and is a potential buyer.

In any event it is not the cost of the premium that decides the response, but rather the interest a prospect may have in a particular premium. A marketer can spend $100 on a premium and get poor results in terms of conversion whereas a $10 premium may have gotten the job done. Gifts or premiums that relate to the message, the product, and its user benefits generate more qualified responses. Also, if the gift or premium is unique, new, and exciting, even more responses will be generated.

Because the integrity of the marketer's company is at stake, items selected for these inducements should not in any way be interpreted by the prospects as bribes. This is why the gift or premium should relate to the business environment.

Sweepstakes and Contests

A secondary offer or inducement that has been known to hype response for inquiry-building campaigns is a sweepstakes or a contest. However, because most business-to-business marketers have small target markets and cannot cost justify the effort, the use of these inducements is rare.

Sweepstakes can also be put to work in awareness, reinforced selling, and reminder sales support campaigns in an effort to build prospect involvement. Because these mailings have indirect response objectives and are sent to highly qualified prospect and customer lists, usually no attempt is made to follow up those who send in contest or sweepstakes entries.

Free Trials

In inquiry-building direct mail the offer of a free trial generates one of the highest-quality responses of any business-to-business offer. The free trial of a product or system is a powerful prospect incentive because it immediately establishes value and the marketer's credibility. Unfortunately, it is not practical for most high-cost industrial products.

The free trial offer for sales support objectives differs from the free trial offer in mail order because the products involved are more complex, more technical, and of a higher unit price. Most industrial products require high levels of explanation and installation procedures can be complex. Often the personal efforts of salespeople are required to arrange shipment as well as installation. Once a product or system is installed for the trial, marketing, and engineering personnel if needed, follow-up with the prospect should be made to assure that the product's performance will be successful. This ensures a very high close ratio.

The free trial offer is often used to introduce new products or to clear inventory. For certain products such an offer may not be cost effective. But some marketers, who want to quickly build a base of users with longer-term profits as a goal, promote the free trial offer when introducing new products even though they may incur a loss from the trial installation.

Samples

Not every company markets products that lend themselves to offers of samples. But where they are applicable and affordable, the free sample offer almost always gets good response. The relatively high costs of samples limits their use as offers to narrowly defined target markets.

The quantity/quality response mix is related to the application of the sample to personal or business use. Generally, if the sample does not have functional value to the user, those who do request it will be better qualified. For instance, an offer of free personal stationery as a sample from a manufacturer of specialty papers for business may produce high-quantity, low-quality inquiries. But an offer of a sample valve fitting from a machinery manufacturer could generate low-quantity, high-quality responses. Sample offers are effective partially because of the sense of obligation felt by those prospects who respond to the offer.

Some awareness campaigns are built around offers of samples. But the sample in this case is designed into the awareness mailing itself with an objective of getting greater prospect mind-share, leading to buying action at a later date. An excellent example comes from Champion promoting its new Pageantry text and cover stock (see Figure 7-1). The sample note pad has functional value to the prospect while also demonstrating the qualities of the product.

Seminars

Businesspeople continually seek information that relates to the roles they play in carrying out their specific business responsibilities. They are always interested in opportunities to learn more about advanced systems, procedures, and methods in their industry. This is why professional seminars run by associations, universities, and consultants on business subjects of all kinds are well attended.

This predisposition can work to the advantage of marketers who learn how to use the seminar offer in their sales support response programs. And this is the

Figure 7-1. Product samples build awareness and encourage new product trials.

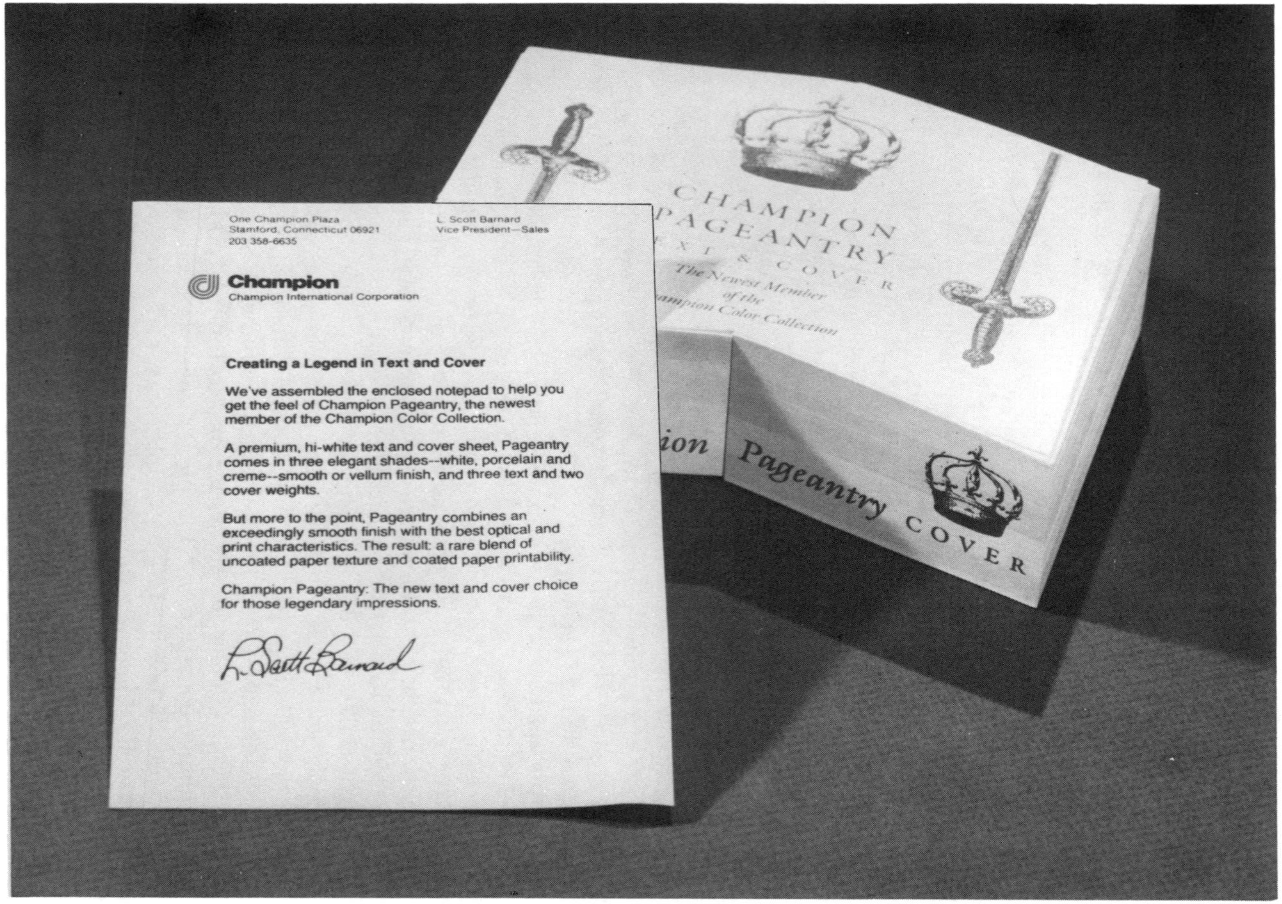

Source: Courtesy of Champion International Corporation, Stamford, CT 06921.

reason that company-sponsored seminars can be successful in spite of the natural reluctance of the businessman or businesswoman to interrupt a busy schedule to attend a vendor marketer's seminar. Offers of seminars are perceived to be helpful when the subject matter is relevant to the target audience and is persuasively spelled out in the response-building promotional material.

Companies well known in their industries, those that come up with leading-edge products, usually have no problem attracting prospects to a new product demonstration billed as a seminar. There is nothing wrong with this kind of promotion as long as prospects are informed beforehand and they get what was promised in the description of the offer. Very few businesses can afford to sponsor industry educational seminars without some self-promotion. However, an offer of an educational seminar that turns out to be strictly a sales promotion event can turn off some good prospects who may have attended. Seminars sponsored by companies and promoted as educational in content should have at least 75 percent of generic information.

The quality of response from a seminar offer is usually dictated by:

1. The emphasis given in the promotion about how much information will be generic and how much will be about the marketer's products
2. The degree to which the target list used for the mailing is prequalified

The objective is to seek out the maximum number of the right kind of prospects. One approach is to mail or phone a seminar offer only to lists of prequalified prospects. This is not practical for many marketers because such lists may be too small to produce adequate seminar attendance. Another way is to rent a list of a sufficient number of potential prospects from within the marketer's universe, choosing those who would appear to have the geographic and demographic characteristics that would reflect a positive interest in the subject and location of the seminar. Since response rates for seminar offers to broad universe lists are historically low, unless the offer is directed at highly qualified segments, fairly large blocks of names are needed for the mailing to result in an acceptable number of attendees.

For instance, for a high-ticket computer systems software marketer, a mailing to 3,500 prospects in a broad universe may produce 80 acceptances. Only 55 of these may actually attend. Qualification questionnaires, filled out at the seminar by those who attend, might single out about 20 highly qualified prospects who should be followed up by salespeople.

The fact that a marketer offers a seminar implies to the prospect that the marketer has substantial industry product knowledge. This helps the marketer establish authority in the field.

Product or System Demonstrations

Some products cannot be sold without a product demonstration, especially if the product is new or the marketer is not well known. Many marketers are using videos or film to demonstrate their product, especially when the product or system is difficult to transport.

A demonstration is usually held either at the prospect's or the marketer's place of business or at the location of one of the marketer's satisfied customers. It may be a multiprospect demonstration or simply a one-on-one interface between the prospect and the demonstrator. When several prospects are involved in the demonstration the individual prospect feels less obligated to buy.

A demonstration offer can be made to low-, medium-, or high-potential prospects, because those who respond to that type offer will most likely be high-quality prospects. Very few businesspeople will sit through a product demonstration unless they are serious about making a purchase. Highly complex and technical products— such as computer software, computers and business equipment, heavy machinery, and electrical systems—lend themselves to a demonstration offer. Secondary offers of a premium or gift help some marketers get more prospects to respond to a demonstration offer. However, overall quality of response falls off as the perceived value of the premium increases.

Sales Representative Calls

Businessmen and businesswomen who check a box on a direct mail business reply card or direct response ad coupon that requests a salesperson to call are serious about buying. This offer is usually used in tandem with an offer of information but it may also be the primary and only offer in a response-building campaign. Some marketers who use this as the sole offer are disappointed at the low response rate. There is well-established evidence that a general information offer will outpull a sales call offer 15 to 1 when both are used in the same mailing to a broad universe list. An offer of a "request for salesperson to call" should allow space for the prospect to indicate the best time to call.

Free Cost Estimates

When prospects can get a free estimate of a planned purchase without obligating themselves to a sales representative, they are tempted to respond. Cost estimates can make good offers for those marketers who have new products or systems to introduce and for those whose selling strategy requires close contact with and detailed knowledge of a prospective customer's needs. When marketers can get into the prospect's place of business to assemble information on which to base the estimate, they have a better chance of making a sale. When used as a primary offer, responses will be few, but highly qualified. Also, it can be a solid secondary offer when paired with a free information offer.

Free Analyses and Surveys

Marketers use the free analysis and survey offer as a device to get their salespeople in to see qualified prospects at an early stage in the prospect's buying behavior cycle. It permits the sales representative to be involved with the prospect on a continuing basis over a preset span of time. The representative is then exposed to the prospect's real needs. With this information the salesperson can recommend the best product configuration possible.

In many sales organizations this offer is actually extended by the sales representatives themselves as a step in the personal selling process. This offer, in a
direct mailing or telemarketing effort, enables the marketer to identify those
prospects among a larger group who are ready to take the next step. Generally
prospects responding to this offer feel they have a weakness in an operational
system, method, or procedure, and are ready to learn more about how at least
one vendor company would attack the problem. Their hope is that without cost
they may learn something they do not already know. Keep in mind that prospects
who accept such an offer are opening their doors to the marketer, often divulging
proprietary information. The prospect will usually not do this for an unfamiliar
vendor.

Analysis and survey offers can be costly for the marketer but they generate
excellent responses, since in the analysis process the prospect becomes a highly
defined sales target for the marketer. The prospect gains from the survey results
factual documentation and justification for a major purchase. The sales close rate
on inquiries that develop from this offer is very high.

HIERARCHY OF OFFERS

Table 7-1 lists a hierarchy of business-to-business sales support offers that generate
a range of responses from low to high quality.

For most sales organizations chances are that the sales-support response-building
offers in the upper portion of the table can be classified as generators of raw
inquiries that need further qualification before they can be categorized as bona
fide leads. Some sales managers of higher-priced products give these raw inquiries
directly to salespeople, asking them to perform the qualifying function. These
managers believe this stimulates more prospecting and sales call activity by the
salespeople. However, in the more successful sales organizations today, these
prospecting and prospect-qualification functions are handled by direct mail, telemarketing, and other promotional efforts. This can be ten times less expensive
and, of equal importance, it saves the salesperson's time for the more cost-effective
field functions of presenting and selling.

The offer hierarchy begins with the classic high-quantity/low-quality offer of
free information of a generic nature. Moving down the list, each offer tends to
be less general and more specific. These more specific offers generate higher-
quality responses that have a greater chance of being converted into a sale by a
salesperson.

Business-to-business marketers who plan to use direct mail and telemarketing
for response-building objectives should establish their own list of offers. If the
planner has direct mail experience to begin with, so much the better. As more
and more mailings are made, it will become easier to choose the right offer for
a desired objective. All the different offers will earn their places on the hierarchy
depending on the direct marketing objective and the quality of the list.

Establishing a wide range of offers to choose from is especially critical at the
early stages of planning, since use of various offers facilitates the fine-tuning
necessary to get optimum quantity/quality results.

Table 7-1. Hierarchy of business-to-business sales-support
inquiry-generation offers.

Quantity/Quality Ratios Range from High to Low

---

1. Gifts and premiums
2. Sweepstakes and contests
3. Chapters in current business books
4. Printed materials on generic subjects germane to product
5. Article reprints industry/specific
6. Information packets
7. Case history releases
8. Industry authority booklets
9. Management reports on specific subjects
10. Reprints of product/specific business magazine articles
11. Basic product application brochures
12. Feature/function product brochures
13. Company newsletters or magazines
14. Prospect's name on mailing list
15. Catalog buying guides
16. Technical or scientific papers
17. Reports on laboratory tests, product performance, and surveys
18. Free trial
19. Samples
20. Seminars
21. Product demonstration
22. Sales representative call
23. Free cost estimate
24. Free analysis and survey
25. Continuity programs

OFFERS FOR SALES SUPPORT INDIRECT RESPONSE

Indirect response mailings are usually referred to as direct mail advertising. In indirect response direct mail, the response that is sought is attitude or opinion modification. With this type of promotion no overt action is required of the reader.

When the sales support objective calls for an indirect response program, such as awareness, reinforced selling, or reminder direct mail, the message becomes the offer. The offer in this sense is the reward readers will get as a result of reading the mailing package. That reward is immediate: more knowledge, understanding, or information about a subject in their interest. The creative task must be approached with the idea that every sentence must pull its own weight in enhancing a reader's knowledge, understanding, and appreciation of a product, company, or issue. This challenges the creative writer/planner to come up with the most appealing approach and helps eliminate the common problem of ineffective brag-and-boast messages.

With some indirect response objectives, a simple letter may get the message across. For others, more elaborate enclosures may be added to the package. For instance, a marketer may be interested in building customer loyalty by letting customers know about some solid commitments made in product development as described and illustrated in a new booklet. An 8½-by-11-inch semipersonalized letter from the marketer accompanying such a booklet may be mailed to a list of key customers. The function of the letter would be to set the stage for getting the readers interested in the message and to direct their attention to the enclosed booklet, to assimilate its contents, and to enhance their understanding of the message.

A marketer who plans to release a product in a new market one year from now may choose to design a direct mail campaign series of 12 soft-sell mailings—an indirect action program aimed at building a cadre of believers in that marketplace who will be receptive to the new product when it is released.

The Champion Company's continuing awareness direct mail program to decision makers and influencers who are involved with the purchase of commercial paper is a classic example of providing a reward for reading. This company often provides a tangible item of value to the reader as an integral part of a mailing.

Materials that can be used as enclosures to enhance the offer/messages of indirect-response sales-support direct-mail packages consist of the same or similar information offered in direct response programs, such as article reprints, booklets on subjects germane to the product, company newsletters or magazines, case histories, management reports, product feature/function materials, product application brochures, technical papers, product performance tests, survey reports, industry authority articles, and dimensionals and premiums.

OTHER TYPES OF OFFERS

Breakthrough Offers

Another offer that can be used by the individual marketer is the breakthrough offer, which implies something unique and perhaps never done before. Breakthrough offers are often needed for new product launches to provide greater impact to counter a competitive surge, to enter a new market, or simply to give sales a needed boost.

Ideas for breakthrough offers do not come easily. Specific reasons for their need, relative to the product and market characteristics, guide the development of the creative effort. They are custom created around individual situations in targeted markets, and usually result from new combinations of old ideas generated by the free-association techniques of group thinking, such as brainstorming and its several variations.

Direct marketing planners who stretch their thinking beyond the normal range of affordable offers do not always have good cost/revenue ratios in the short term, but breakthrough offers, on the average, attract long-term customers, making them highly cost effective. An example is an offer made by a developer of a new software product to provide use for six months of a portable personal computer with the purchase of the new software package.

Continuity Programs

Airlines, car rental firms, and hotels are the main business-to-business users of continuity offers. These industries promote club membership programs on a continuing use basis by providing free services and special discounts as incentives to the businessperson. Sophisticated sales-promotional uses of direct marketing are also designed to appeal to the self-importance of the prospect and the need for businesspeople to be members of a group.

The objective of the continuity offer in a response-generation effort is to sign up new members. Once signed, prospects are encouraged to use the service on a continuing basis. Subsequent mailings in the continuity series are reminder and awareness packages that aim at making the prospects more frequent purchasers. Few marketers can use continuity program offers, but, when applicable, these programs are known to have high-profit potential.

Combination Offers

Some marketers make the common mistake of including many offers in one mailing. Their thinking is based on a belief that the more offers there are, the better the chances of interesting the reader in at least one. But in the great bulk of cases, just the opposite is true. The rule to follow is: the fewer offers in a mailing, the better. Mailings should have one primary offer to prevent reader confusion.

When several offers are combined it usually means a marketer wants to minimize the expense and maximize the value of a mailing while accomplishing several sales support objectives. For example, a laundry list of offers attempting to identify specific groups of prospects, set up meetings, and arrange for sales call appointments might include three different software product brochures, a computer hardware booklet, an article reprint, a product demonstration, and a calculator wallet as a gift for attending the demonstration, plus an offer to have a salesperson call the prospect. With so many choices, it may be easier for the reader not to make any choice at all.

In this example, the real problem lies in the marketer's trying to do too many things at the same time in one mailing. If, for instance, an objective is to identify prospects from a broad universe list who have an interest in a specialized software package, the offer of a software information brochure should be the main focus of the inquiry-building mailing. If three brochures are involved, they should be discussed and offered as a set of three, not offered individually.

If an objective is to identify those who want to attend a product demonstration, the entire mailing should be designed around the benefits of a product demonstration for the reader.

Some marketers attempt to justify combination offers in a single mailing as a way of getting inquirers identified by varying degrees of interest. The problem with this strategy is that the copy, graphics, and format emphasis are rendered ineffective when they are spread over several offers. The inquiry mailing may not be read beyond the letter headline or the first sentence because it is too difficult to promote several offers appropriately in one mailing. The more pinpointed the proposition, the easier it is for prospects to relate what they are reading to their specific needs. When there is a combination of offers, fewer responses result, which can make this a costly method for setting up future targets.

There are some combination offers that do not have conflicting objectives. These can actually increase overall response. An example of this is the direct mailing that is designed for the primary purpose of generating inquiries by using an information offer of a booklet on a specific subject. Yet a secondary offer on the reply card in that mailing could provide an option to have a sales representative call. This will identify those prospects closer to taking buying action. However, responses from this subordinate offer, although valuable, should be secondary in importance when establishing a measure of effectiveness for the mailing.

SUMMARY

The business-to-business offer is what prospects get when they reply to a direct response effort. For mail order the offer is basically the product and what it will do for the reader at a price. Inducements such as price terms and premiums are added incentives often necessary to increase response to these promotions.

Offers used to get responses for sales support objectives identify prospects who show an interest and may buy later or bring buyers and salespeople together face-to-face. Both mail order and sales-support direct-response offers propose something tangible that require fulfillment by the marketer. Basic considerations when choosing an offer include the composition of the list, predictions of response, and costs.

The quantity/quality ratio of response to a direct-marketing sales-support effort is determined by the offer selected. Most direct response promotions offer free information. These materials fall into two classes: industry–product/generic and company–product/specific. Other sales-support response-program offers that have a place in business-to-business programs include gifts and premiums, sweepstakes and contests, free trials for products, samples, seminars, product demonstrations, sales representative calls, free estimates, free analyses and surveys, and continuity programs for the few business-to-business marketers who find them applicable.

The direct response planner who has an ongoing sales-support direct-mail program should establish a hierarchy of offers from which to choose, which will facilitate the quantity/quality fine-tuning needed for best results.

The business-to-business offer is also defined as increased knowledge, an enhancement prospects get as they read awareness, reinforced selling, reminder, and other forms of indirect-response direct-mail advertising. Some indirect response programs have, as an integral part of the package, enclosures that use the same or similar information materials offered in direct response efforts.

To maximize effective response, any single mailing should focus all creative aspects on only one primary offer.

8

CREATIVE CONSIDERATIONS

According to a widely held belief among direct marketing practitioners, the relative value of the mailing list, offer, and creative aspects to the total mailing effort is 40 percent, 40 percent, and 20 percent, respectively. While all three areas are vital for direct marketing objectives, mistakes in choosing the right target markets and selecting the right offer/product can be more devastating than a poor creative approach, especially in mail order. However, the creative approach should not be minimized because it often spells the difference between a winning effort and a losing one.

This is even truer for sales support direct mail, since many of the direct mail objectives—such as increased awareness, reinforced selling, goodwill building, and certain types of lead-building efforts—seek indirect response. As such, the *offer* in these campaigns is whatever learning experience or enhanced knowledge the readers get as they continue to read the mailing. If the message is obscured, or if the wrong creative approach is used, the direct mail campaign will lose its effectiveness.

CREATIVE DEVELOPMENT

Before a concept is developed or a single word is written, the direct marketing creative staff must be satisfied that it has at its disposal organized research results of the marketer's products and markets as well as an analysis of competitors' efforts. Additional input is also needed in these areas:

- Campaign objectives
- Markets to be targeted
- Decision makers to be reached
- Direct mail creative budget
- Time frame
- Makeup of approval chain

Each of these elements can have a profound effect on the final outcome.

Knowing the Objective

The creative planner must understand the main objective to be addressed even though there may be other subordinate purposes that can be built into the mailing. Determining the specific objective of a direct mail campaign seems so elementary that it is hardly worth discussion. This is especially true for mail order. Yet most failures in business-to-business sales support direct mail stem from fuzzy objectives. Lead-generation direct mail campaigns get confused with awareness campaigns. As noted in Chapter 7, all too often the thinking that comes down the line in a company's marketing unit is that one mailing can accomplish several tasks. Too many choices dilute the impact of the real objective of the mailing.

Knowing the Market

To make an impact on prospects the creative planner must specifically address the needs and interest of the market in the language of the marketplace. Yet all business markets are not the same. The more common characteristics of the customer and prospect list identified in the target group, such as line of business, size of company, and product end use, provide clues on what the approach should be for the creative strategy.

The creative planner gets to know the marketplace by getting into the life-space of the typical prospect. This is made easier if segmentation studies are available. Even if these are not available, guesswork is a poor substitute. The planner can still get insights about the audience by talking to the salespeople who sell to that market or by communicating with past purchasers of the product. Questionnaires that request prospects' opinions on topics in such a way as to expose interests and needs also provide good copy research for the copywriter.

Knowing the Decision Maker

The individual businessperson is not usually affected by the complex graphics and emotion-building techniques that work so successfully to generate impulse responses from consumers in the home. Of course, we know consumers and businesspeople are one and the same, but we also know they react differently to the same stimulus, depending on the role they are playing at the time.

Businessmen and businesswomen are continually aware of the responsibilities and obligations of their jobs, when on the job. The way businesspeople react to direct marketing is important to the creative planner. And depending on the specific jobs, reactions will vary. For instance, the president of a large company has a different set of responsibilities and will be driven by different needs than the production control manager or the individual entrepreneur who runs a small firm.

Middle managers of large firms need to feel more secure in the decisions they make, since they must often justify their decisions to others in the company. Because of this, most of their business purchases tend to be thought out well. Emotional factors are not used to great effect in business-to-business direct marketing promotions. They do come into play, however, when competing products in the marketplace are very similar.

The creative planner must attempt not only to understand the common attitudinal characteristics of business decision makers in the targeted market but the behavioral factors as well. It is helpful to know how businesspeople go through their business day. For instance, most scan their mail quickly and attack it positively. They are more interested in mail they get as businesspeople than they are about mail they get as consumers, because business mail is pinpointed to their specific interests.

The decision maker reads business mail to be informed, not to be entertained. The creative planner must realize that business prospects are busy, and they do not spend any time with mail that is not in their interest. Business prospects search their mail to learn something new, looking for propositions that offer opportunities that can help them do their jobs better.

Decision makers are also more interested in reading facts than reading the marketer's opinion. They want proof of claims, and the claims have more credibility when they come from third-party endorsements. Specific facts help the business buyers to feel more secure as they make up their own minds about the marketer's proposal.

Knowing the Budget

Creative costs are especially critical in business-to-business mail order marketing operations. They are an important part of the promotion budget and are based on estimates detailed in pro forma profit and loss statements. Any overspending on promotion will automatically affect the business unit's profit center by showing higher expenses than estimated and less profit. Creative costs for sales support direct mail should be, but are not, as critical as in a mail order profit center because sales support mail costs are less easily discerned. They are usually only one aspect of a much larger advertising, communications, or marketing budget.

If enough homework is done by the sales-support direct-marketing planner during the development of the annual marketing financial plan, sufficient funds will be allocated for individual sales-support direct-mail programs. The budget must be large enough to create and produce a campaign that will have a good chance of accomplishing the results expected. But that is not always the case in many companies. When the results do not measure up, the fault may lie in a creative budget that is too lean.

The dynamics of the business marketplace often generate changes in marketing plans that affect budgets. Some organizations habitually pull back approved budget dollars when revenue or profit shortfalls occur, causing direct mail or telemarketing programs to be halted or even abandoned before completion. Because of this the planner must anticipate at the concept stage any potential budget problems that could cause a direct mail project to be abandoned, perhaps wasting those dollars already spent on creative preproduction. This risk can be minimized at the outset by planning alternative approaches that use the creative package. For instance, less pieces could be produced if fewer were mailed to smaller segments of the original target market.

The creative planner first needs a working estimate of the dollars it will take to create the direct mail package. The package may consist of an inexpensive two-color letter and one-color reply card in a plain number 10 envelope. Or the package may be a four-color, 16-page brochure with a personalized two-page letter on a four-color letterhead with matching four-color outsized reply card in a 9-by-12-inch display window envelope. Either way, the package is reviewed in terms of its priority in the program budget to determine its affordability. If the budget is a limiting factor with stringent parameters, then the package is scaled back to fit the budget.

Cutting essentials in the package can put the entire effort in jeopardy because the right format and graphics can be critical to meeting the objective. Attempting to hold down direct mail creative costs by skimping on the professional effort may solve an immediate problem of getting out a mailing but can lose big when the results are in. Rather than mail an inferior package to a complete target market, it may be better to mail to only a segment of the market up to the limit of the budget.

If creative costs are exceedingly high in proportion to the printing and mailing costs due to a small mailing list size, the cost per thousand pieces may exceed the ability of the mailing to produce a cost-effective response. For example, a $7,500 creative cost added to a $700/M printing and mailing cost to a list of 2,000 prospects would total $4.45 per prospect reached. Whether this is an acceptable cost depends on the objectives. Typical direct marketing mailing costs average around $350/M to $450/M.

Knowing the Time Frame

The direct marketing planner has a need to know, at least generally, how long it will take a writer and artist to put together a letter and reply card inquiry-building mailing or a complete mail order package. If too little time is allotted, the hoped-for results of the mailing can suffer. When determining the time frame for creating and writing direct mail campaigns and putting together telemarketing scripts, three key factors are taken into account:

1. The scope of the assignment
2. The speed of the individual creative people
3. The deadline

Before starting, the creative planner will have agreed to a due date. The research and idea development phase usually take more time than the actual writing and design. The critical concern is that sufficient time be built into the project so a quality campaign can be created. The mail order solo mailing, with its multiplicity of elements that perform the entire sales function in one package, takes the most time to create. And obviously, those programs requiring research into new products and new markets need extra time to complete.

Scope

The scope of a mail order campaign is fairly self-evident. However, for sales support, the creative planner must keep in mind that direct mail is an integral part of the marketing mix of most business-to-business firms, and strategies and tactics must coincide with the larger marketing effort. This may include trade show activity, product publicity releases, trade publication advertising, sales literature, audio visual programs, field seminars, and other promotions. Since most of these efforts require different skilled personnel, it takes large blocks of coordinating time for the planner to work in concert with these other professionals.

Speed of the Creative Team

One creative team may take two weeks to complete a campaign, another three weeks, still another one week. When estimating creative time, the direct mail planner should always allow for slower than average writing and designing speed, even when he or she knows a specific individual's speed with words or graphics. Some creative people turn out quality work rapidly whereas others do so slowly. The inspired and motivated writer or designer often beats deadlines. Of course, planners must guard against letting creative time extend to where it is no longer cost effective.

Deadlines

The dynamics of marketing in the competitive marketplace frequently force changes in sales and promotion plans, requiring new and more critical drop-dead dates. Experienced business-to-business direct mail creative people have learned to adjust to changes in time frames in the business environment.

Some copywriters and artists turn out their best work under pressure, whereas others fall apart. If the business-to-business creative person is fortunate enough to work with product managers, ad managers, or marketing managers who have scheduled mailings three to six months in advance, there will be fewer problems with deadlines. But because managers can cause bottlenecks in the approval routine, creative planners must allocate enough time in the approval stage for unexpected delays. Proper scheduling eliminates backups that cause deadlines to be missed.

Knowing the Approval Routine

Professional copywriters and artists do not like to have their efforts changed or rewritten. Of course, the fewer the number of people in the approval routine, the better. Some creative people can afford a "take it or leave it" stance, but most are continually frustrated by the approval routine.

Creative people should know who the approvers are in the chain, the specific reason they have an approval function, and how much each of them will be involved. Some approvers, such as marketing specialists and engineers, review for technical accuracy. Company attorneys examine the effort for indications of mis-representation or other causes for litigation. Marketing, product, or ad managers look at it to ensure that the theme is in accord with other related marketing communications.

As a by-product of the approval process, a latent interest in artistic critiquing often surfaces, possibly causing the creative effort to suffer. Such critiques are unwarranted and unwanted. Direct marketing creative people certainly should have an open mind and always be on the alert for good ideas. But they should also resist opinions about the creative aspects that come from those who are supposed to approve technical accuracy, legal aspects, and so forth.

Legitimate opinions about the creative aspects of direct mail usually come from the copy supervisor, the creative director, the ad manager, and others who are equipped by training and experience to pass on the creative efforts of others. The more writers and artists know about how the approvers think, the less intimidated they will be and the easier it will be to get over the roadblocks caused by unwarranted opinions.

Copywriters and artists who work in a direct marketing agency, advertising agency, or internal staff of a large industrial company need to justify their creative campaign efforts only to their immediate supervisors, usually the copy supervisor, senior art director, or creative director. These efforts are usually presented as part of the overall program by the supervisor to those in the approval chain. Then changes, rejections, or additions come back once removed from the source. This can make it difficult for the writer or artist to respond positively. In smaller companies, ad managers, product managers, or marketing managers often create and write their own sales support direct mail. Here, the approval chain may consist of only one person—the division head or president.

Writers and artists who can create quality direct mail copy and graphics that successfully run through the approval routine with the least resistance have learned to minimize the roadblocks by keeping in perspective what and where they are.

Needless to say, high standards should always be maintained for copy and graphics. With that in mind, it is time to look more closely at these cornerstones of any direct mail campaign.

COPY

Any direct mail communication should be written so the targeted business audience will quickly understand it wherever and however they read their mail. Business mail is more formal than consumer mail, yet it should not be stiff. It can be warm and friendly as long as it is businesslike. The creative planner wants the reader to perceive the proposition or offer in the mailing as a positive influence and react to it accordingly.

Dozens of books on writing advertising copy have been published. There are about a dozen specifically on writing direct mail copy; however, virtually all of these focus on the skills and techniques of consumer mail order copy. Yet there is much to be learned from consumer mail order copy principles as well as from general advertising copy concepts.

Many of the most meaningful general copy points that are most relevant to the business-to-business direct marketing writer, whether for mail order or sales support, are imbedded in nine or ten basic formulas on how to write copy. Professional direct mail copywriters have their own favorite formulas and for the most part have committed them to memory. Following the steps has become automatic. Highly talented copywriters who "play it by ear" find formulas get in the way of creativity. Regardless of how any writer thinks about formulas, some method, guideline, or checklist is needed to ensure that all the elements of effective writing are covered.

Five basic elements run through all advice for writing good copy. Four of these elements make up the most popular and most often quoted AIDA formula: Attention, Interest, Desire, and Action. The missing element needed to complete a direct mail package is conviction. The job for the copywriter then is to keep these elements in mind along with four important areas of creative direct mail copy: approach, content, style, and choice of words.

Determining the Copy Approach

If direct mail is to do its job it must first be interesting enough to get read and persuasive enough to influence the reader's behavior in some way, directly or indirectly. Effective direct mail employs the proper combination of writing style and selling principles. Direct mail writers, as writers of persuasive copy, need great skill in assembling words and phrases to get ideas across. They must be masters of expression and understand business decision-making behavior. Without adequate research to gain insights into the specific needs, wants, motivations, and attitudes of buyers in the market, copy can miss the mark even though it may be well written. Its aim must be to the interest of the audience.

The main idea for the mailing comes from the writer's estimate, based on the program objectives, of the most powerful appeal the offer or product will have to the decision maker. Unless the writer knows the decision maker's real motives for buying, the job of creating and developing the basic idea becomes a high-risk effort. The copy framework is constructed with convincing "reason-why" arguments persuading the reader to think or act in a way that the writer suggests. The actual reasons why decision makers place orders are built into that approach.

The more successful direct mail writers prepare for the writing task with highly organized research findings, listing all possible appeals for the market to be addressed and possible product benefits in order of their value to the buyer. Every product feature should be backed up with facts, examples, and testimonials. The campaign objective determines the detail involved. This is the starting point for the concept of the package. Seven or eight ideas may surface. The writer may develop one or two and try them out on a few friendly prospects, or better yet, on a couple of focus groups to get a reaction before proceeding further. The bigger the proposed mailing and the more sizable the potential profit to the marketer, the greater the need to research creative concepts and approaches first, even before testing the package in the mail.

Some writers identify major interests by testing different copy approaches in lead-building mailings to a good representative sample of the target market (known as Nth name list selection). Any number of different creative approaches may be used, depending on the magnitude of the overall marketing effort. The different approaches used for this type of testing must appear only in the headline, first sentence, or paragraph of the direct mail letter, which is the initial statement the reader sees in a mailing package. It is not unusual for the difference between the best and worst approach in terms of response to be as much as 200 percent or 300 percent. Because it is not easy to guess the best creative approach, dollars spent in the early stages of direct marketing program development can pay off. Without testing or research, it may take more time than the marketer has, to eventually find the most cost-effective creative approach.

A direct mail writer who also has personal selling experience in a specific market has a decided edge in knowing how to approach that market. But such a writer is rare. Regardless of how much sales experience an individual writer or artist may have had, creative skills are the key to effective direct mail communication. However, the entire creative effort must be based on sound sales strategy.

Content

The fundamental job of all direct mail copy is to convey the offer to the target market in terms that ensure maximum response and effect. Developing the content always begins by determining the main selling point, sometimes called the "unique selling proposition," or "the big idea." And the direct mail writer always tries to spell it out as something of news value to the reader, or something dramatic, different, and interesting. Separate enclosures should be used where highly complex and technical products require extensive details.

Style

Writing style depends on the attitude the writer wants the reader to adopt. This depends on the objective and is aided by the format. Since one of direct mail's main built-in strengths is personalization, a polite, pleasant, and even conversational tone is most appropriate, as long as it is completely businesslike.

The writing style also reflects a marketer's personality, so copying a competitor's style can be counterproductive. To create the right impression it is important that the use of the same style continues throughout the package. Thoughts should flow in a logical sequence. All excursions and side issues should be eliminated to help keep the flow on track.

Communicating through words would be chaotic without rules of grammar. However, common usage of language has rendered some of the rules too rigid for use in advertising and direct marketing copywriting. Splitting infinitives and ending sentences with a preposition are acceptable. Actually, sacrificing the natural flow of language to strict rules of grammar can hamper readership.

Choice of Words

Copy communicates better with the reader when it is written in plain and simple language. Copy that does its job best does not attempt to be clever, coy, or pompous. The best business-to-business direct mail writing is lean, straightforward, sensible, clear, and understandable while being believable and exciting. Words alone, for the most part, must fulfill the objective in direct mail, especially for sales support objectives, whereas in conversation, words have the support of gestures and inflections. What may be a friendly quip verbally can be interpreted as sarcasm in direct mail copy.

The lazy writer won't take time to dig out the specific facts that address the prospect's interest. For example, the following phrases taken from direct mail business-to-business letters could be improved by being made more detailed and precise:

- ". . . with proven reliability you would expect from . . ." (Saying it is "reliable" doesn't make it so. The writer must give the reasons.)
- ". . . you need special knowledge and special skills . . ." (Words like "special" are overused and are not specific enough to retain an impression.)
- ". . . the enclosed facts speak for themselves . . ." (This is a worn-out expression that passes up the opportunity to restate one or more memorable key facts.)
- ". . . you are sure to get the highest quality available . . ." (Hollow expressions such as this need quantification to make them credible.)

General words such as "highest" should be avoided. "Many" and "most," "more" or "less," "bigger" and "better" are also in this category. Adjectives and adverbs, such as "very" and "extremely," should be kept to a minimum. They tend to lose their punch. Words that give specific details are more believable. They paint pictures that are memorable.

Too much use of the words "we," "us," and "our company" are the result of well-meaning and enthusiastic marketing and sales personnel attempting to tell prospects in brag-and-boast words how great the company and product features are. Readers are more interested in what the company and its products can do for them. Reader benefits are spelled out more convincingly when using "you" and "your" words. They express the message best.

Strong action verbs convey urgency, excitement, and forward movement and propel the direct mail letter reader along to the next thought. Such words are found in phrases like these:

- ". . . all rush to capitalize on . . ."
- ". . . alerts you to key factors . . ."
- ". . . slash the high cost of . . ."
- ". . . you'll grab their attention . . ."

Use of the present tense puts the readers in the action where they can relate to the activity or events described. For instance, "You're geared up for full production" is better than "You'll be geared up for full production."

Trite expressions should be avoided. They adversely affect the prospect's judgment of the company. Also, yesterday's buzzwords can be today's cliches. Words should be legitimate, precise, correct, and consistent with the tone of the copy message.

Some words are received negatively whereas others convey positive thoughts. Descriptive words make it easier for the reader to visualize the benefits of the proposition. But if overdone, they can lead to hyperbole or lack of credibility, which destroys reader confidence.

The writer edits out jargon—words that have narrow usage and meaning to the marketer. They may not be understood by the reader. On the other hand, the writer should understand and use the particular terminology characteristic of the marketplace addressed. Every word written should have one intention—to make the reader want to continue to read.

GRAPHICS

All components of direct mail packages should include a graphic designer's input. Professional design is needed to lay out the elements of the direct mail letter in the most effective configuration. Graphics are needed to illustrate what cannot be explained with words alone. Graphics are often needed to emphasize an offer or important parts of the message. Mail-order direct-mail packages require, by virtue of the selling job to be done by a mailing alone, hard working, very specific graphics. Yet graphics can cause more than communications problems if misused or overemphasized. For instance, four-color costs can be a burden too heavy to handle.

In business-to-business direct marketing, graphics are downplayed compared to consumer direct mail where photographs and illustrations support more emotional appeals. The design should focus on only one dominant element augmenting the basic idea. Graphics should not detract from the copy. Captions should be written before photographs or illustrations are selected. Also, white space is important because it makes other elements in the message stand out. Consider the one-sentence paragraph that reads more easily because it stands alone.

THE DIRECT MAIL COPYWRITER

Those who write copy for business-to-business direct marketing come from different areas of experience. Many have been writers of newspaper articles, speeches, house organs, press releases, contests, technical and sales literature, and publication advertising. There are very few who have a solid background of direct mail copywriting experience. However, regardless of earlier experience, there are those who have acquired a fair degree of expertise in business-to-business direct mail copywriting, either in sales support or mail order and in some cases, both. In fact, many business-to-business mail order writers are also proficient in sales-support direct-mail applications. On the other hand, most who write sales-support direct-mail materials have not necessarily mastered the mail order writing techniques.

Direct mail writers fall into two groups: (1) those who create and write direct mail packages and campaigns on a professional level, full-time; and (2) those who write copy, as well as perform many other responsibilities in the normal course of doing their jobs.

Full-time Writers

Most of the best professional direct mail writers are found in direct marketing agencies, advertising agencies, and small free-lance writer-consultant firms. A professional writer may also be part of the direct marketing staff. The bulk of sales-support direct-mail copywriters have advertising or sales promotion experience and have either learned or are learning how to measure the results of their direct mail efforts.

The full-time direct mail writer may not necessarily contribute to the planning aspects of the direct mail campaign. The specific sales objective, direct marketing strategy, target marketplace, budget, and even the offer are often determined before the writer gets involved. It depends on how the organization is structured. For instance, in some organizations the direct mail planner, creative director, copy chief, and writer may all wear the same hat.

Part-time Writers

The larger group of writers of business-to-business direct mail have other functions in addition to their writing responsibilities. These multifunction management personnel are usually found in the small- or medium-size companies or in smaller divisions of larger companies. They have many different titles—advertising manager, account manager, consultant, marketing director, project manager, sales manager, product director, direct marketing coordinator, communications vice-president. Some of these part-time writers know how to develop a direct mail creative strategy and the copy to go with it at a professional level, but they are few. However, increased numbers of college courses, seminars, book sales, and other training materials on direct marketing creative development make it evident that more and more businessmen and businesswomen are interested in learning the art.

Brilliant copywriting requires special talent. When the mastery of the direct mail writing craft is combined with innate creative talent and selling ability, blockbuster direct mail packages are created. This kind of talent is rare. Yet, fortunately, most fairly well educated men and women oriented in business marketing can become adequate at writing acceptable direct mail copy for just about any objective. For the average writer it takes dedication, discipline, and perseverance to master the basic rules, principles, and proven creative techniques. In addition, the writer needs a heavy load of writing assignments. Critiques by professional direct mail writers can be invaluable for the beginner. And since direct mail is a results-oriented medium, attention should also be paid to the measurement of effectiveness of the writing efforts, whether for readership, inquiry response, or awareness level change.

Those ultimately responsible for reviewing and approving the copy of others also must learn how to tell the difference between good and bad direct mail writing. And they should be able to spell out the reasons why, for each of the different direct mail objectives. They must know what constitutes a good reinforced-selling campaign, a good lead-generation letter, and a good telemarketing script. Only by knowing why direct marketing succeeds or fails can those responsible for the finished effort improve results. In the final analysis, professional-quality creativity plays a significant role.

Direct Mail vs. the Print Ad

Since many business-to-business sales-support direct-mail creative people are print ad oriented, it is worth reviewing the differences between the two.

Creative personnel, in both business-to-business advertising agencies and company advertising departments, have been and are involved heavily in print advertising. This is not unusual since trade advertising often gets a three times greater share of the budget than direct mail. Those professionals who have written both kinds of advertising know there is a vast difference between direct mail copy and print ad copy.

One main difference relates to the way each is read. As readers thumb through a business publication looking for editorial material to read, they are occasionally stopped by an ad headline or illustration that gets their attention and provokes them to read the ad. The reader sees the entire message at a glance. When this happens, it is an interruption, and competes with the time the reader has to spend with the editorial material. Noticing or even reading the ad is incidental to the reader's purpose in picking up the publication. The ad must be creatively compelling to get noticed and read because it competes with ads on many other pages in the same issue of the magazine.

Also, the reader knows that the magazine has many other readers and obviously each ad's message speaks to the entire audience in the circulation. Therefore, even though the reader may be addressed as "you" in an ad, the magazine format precludes "one-on-one" communication. What's more, in a print ad, the format and number of words of copy are limited.

In addition, the print ad delivers the message to a market or submarket chosen by the publisher through controlled or paid subscriptions, so a marketer may have a problem targeting a specific segment of a marketplace cost effectively. The publication and not the marketer defines the audience. Having to address the publication's overall circulation base tends to make the copy in an ad more general.

Direct mail, on the other hand, reaches its audience with a communication that does not compete directly with any other communication when it is in the hands of the reader. It gets the individual attention of the prospect. It is a piece of business mail that is picked up, perhaps read, acted upon, and then filed, passed on to associates, or disposed of.

The direct mail piece goes into an environment where the prospect thinks positively about reading business mail. The contents of the letter become the "editorial," allowing greater opportunity for better readership.

A review of the time-tested Starch readership scores in business publications reveals that a "read most" score of 10 percent would be above average for an ad in a business publication. A projection of the results of such studies indicates that 10 percent of the circulation would have read at least half of the ad. On the other hand, according to an industrial direct mail readership survey designed by a large business-to-business manufacturer, professionally created and produced business-to-business direct mail is read by well over 60 percent of those who receive it.

Although direct mail readers do not know how many others have received the same direct mail pieces, they do know they were on the list to receive it and this somehow makes them special. Since list availabilities for direct mail are much more highly selective than the circulation of a business publication, the creative planner has more opportunities to appeal and relate to more finely targeted market segments. Direct mail can include multiple illustrations, photographs, testimonials, and as much descriptive copy as needed. The copy message can be more specifically detailed and pertinent to the reader's interest, reflecting a higher degree of personalness. Also, direct mail, with its many action reply formats to choose from, has a greater potential for making it easier for the reader to respond.

SUMMARY

Creative considerations in business-to-business direct marketing can spell the difference between winning and losing. While there are a few full-time professional copywriters dedicated to writing business-to-business sales support direct mail, most write mail order copy. Also, the great bulk of direct mail copywriting for sales support is written by those who also perform other job functions.

A writer may in addition be the direct marketing planner or sales planner, depending on the size of the marketer's organization. An understanding of the objectives, markets, business decision makers, budgets, approvers, and timetable all have a critical effect on the approach to the creative effort. Direct mail writers must know how to separate the many objectives that get assigned to a campaign by those in marketing into one major attainable objective. Approaching the writing task involves a study of the marketplace and research into the buying behavior of the business decision maker as it relates to the product being promoted. And the business-to-business writer must be aware of the difference between business and consumer reaction to direct mail. Writers also need to know how the business person receives, handles, and reads direct mail.

Budget planning must be as precise in sales-support direct-mail campaign planning as it is for mail order or catalog mailings. Scaling back a mailing to reach only a segment of the market may be preferable to reducing the creative quality of the mailing package to fit a tight budget. The time frame allocated to create direct mail campaigns is related to the scope of the individual assignment and the speed of the writer. The writer's understanding of the approver's functions minimizes roadblocks caused by unwarranted opinions.

The five universal elements found in virtually all copywriting formulas are attention, interest, desire, conviction, and action. The job of the direct mail writer is to incorporate these into the content of the campaign with appropriate style and choice of words that make the reader want to continue reading.

When print ad copywriters switch to writing direct mail they must consider the main advantages of direct mail in effecting readership and response: less competition for attention, a more personalized writing style with more space for the message, a more selective market segment for targeting, and greater format flexibility to make it easy to respond.

9

CREATING THE SALES-SUPPORT
DIRECT-MAIL PACKAGE

Before determining the specific creative approach for any particular use of direct mail the planner needs to know what works generally for business-to-business marketers. Some creative techniques have been proven to be more effective in most cases than others. These provide guidelines that may help many marketers minimize the risk of coming up with unsuccessful mailings. They also provide a framework for developing appropriate creative approaches for the various types of sales support campaigns.

THE DIRECT MAIL LETTER

The basic element most widely used in direct mail is the letter. Because letters are the main communication vehicle in intercompany business correspondence, they carry authority and are perceived as having a special importance. Most businessmen and businesswomen are experienced at writing business letters but not, however, a direct mail letter. Very few nonprofessional writers know how to write an effective direct mail letter because its broad circulation in the marketplace demands that it be uniquely written. It is the most personal communication the marketer can have with the customer and prospect next to a personal sales visit or telephone call.

A direct mail letter has maximum impact only when it is written in ways that capitalize on its one-on-one format. This does not presuppose that every letter should be a personal letter, yet the approach should be that each reader is an individual.

Formats

Reader eye-movement studies of standard letter layouts reveal that attention is first very briefly focused on the salutation. For nonpersonalized letters this is the area reserved for the headline. The typical reader then scans the signature, the P.S., and finally looks back up at the salutation area again and begins reading the lead paragraph. Although postscripts are not standard procedure on a business letter, they do get early and prime readership in the direct mail letter.

The closer the direct mail letter format resembles a typed business letter, the more effective it will be. But there are exceptions to this guideline. One exception is the elimination of the date on the letter. A date rarely appears on a letter used for volume direct mail applications and it is not missed by the reader. When dates are used, scheduling difficulties in production can cause a letter to appear to arrive too late.

Another exception concerns personalization. Some managers and salespeople in business are under the assumption that direct mail letters, to be effective, must be personalized with the prospect's name and address on the letter. Yet, this is far from the truth. In many business-to-business direct mail applications personalization of the letter is not necessary or cost effective. When the letter is not personalized it is preferable to form the headline into a two-, three-, or four-line block of copy simulating a name and address business letter format.

Still another exception is the letter that extends to multiple pages. Normally in a business letter each page is produced on a separate sheet of paper. The two-page letter on both sides of one sheet now is becoming more common in business-to-business direct mail and is getting more readership than in the past. Its use is not unrelated to cost effectiveness. However, many business-to-business direct mail practitioners still prefer separate sheets for letters of more than one page, especially to higher-level executives.

Fairly wide margins (1¼ inches) are preferable. Above all, the letter should look businesslike and be easy to read. A 1½-inch margin should remain at the bottom of the page. Justified right margins are not recommended.

Paragraphs should be relatively short with no more than six lines of varied lengths to avoid monotony. Four or five paragraphs per page are usually sufficient in a sales support letter.

Although multiple page letters may require some emphasis devices such as underlining of words, capitalization, a second color, indentions, and bullets, they should be minimized or not used at all, especially in sales-support one-page letters. The one-page letter does not need typographic devices to bring the reader from the salutation to the closing. Also, such devices, when employed to excess in multipage efforts, cause the words, phrases, and paragraphs to have so much emphasis that there is no emphasis at all.

Format Mistakes to Avoid

A quick review of business direct mail may reveal several common format mistakes that direct mail creative planners should avoid.

- One occurs on multipage letters where the first page ends at the conclusion of a sentence or paragraph. To help ensure that the reader will continue to read on, the break should be made in the middle of a sentence.
- Another mistake is failure to put a signature on what appears to be a letter or memo format. The reader perceives this as carelessness and lack of attention to detail, which can lessen the reader's esteem of the company.
- Still another error that reduces effectiveness is when the right- and left-hand margins are reduced to ¾ inch or less, crowding in all the "golden" words. This letter layout appears to be too heavy and too difficult to read. And it is obvious that the letter was not typed by a professional secretary or approved by a discerning boss.
- When letter copy is set in a nontypewriter typeface, the reader gets the impression that the message has been "printed" and distributed to many others, thus reducing its perceived value as a one-on-one communication.

One misused format that continues to show up in business-to-business direct mail is the typewritten 8½-by-11-inch sheet that is written like a letter but does not have a heading, closing, or signature. It may be viewed as a bulletin, news release, newsletter, or advertisement. But more often, it appears to be a little of each. The business reader has, by experience, learned how to read a bulletin, news release, newsletter, advertisement, and direct mail letter, but when they all appear to be combined, the result is a confused reader who does not have the time to interpret the communication.

Copy

A direct mail letter should be written in a natural style in contemporary English. Whether personalized or nonpersonalized, the letter should be written from one businessperson to another. Even when nonpersonalized, it should sound personal and informal yet sincere.

Simple declarative sentences, few "ing" words, few "thats," short words, and short sentences make the writing more crisp and concise. Teaser headlines, coined words, empty promises, rhymes, double meanings, superlatives, jargon, and generalities are out. News to the point, reader benefits, descriptive salutations such as Dear Wholesaler or Dear Subscriber, and relevant and startling statements of fact are in.

Contractions, personal references, and conversational and diplomatic phrases make the writing seem friendly. The letter should not be stiff or stuffy nor should it sound like advertising. Emphasis on the active voice rather than the passive voice gives letter copy vitality and interest. Reading the finished letter aloud to see if it sounds good to the ear is a way to judge whether it will hold the reader's attention.

The Heading and Salutation

As in other forms of advertising writing, but particularly in direct mail letters, the writer must always appeal to the self-interest of the business-to-business reader: "What's in it for me and my company?" And this appeal begins with the letter headline or, if the letter is personalized, with the lead sentence. The effective letter reaches out and grabs the prospect with a vital and pertinent statement. The immediate goal is to overcome the natural inertia of the reader.

When a personalized letter is planned, it is preferable to use a full four- or five-line company name and address above the salutation, especially when targeting higher levels of executives. However, a one-line personal salutation such as Dear Mrs. Stewart, without a company name and address, is generally sufficient for middle- and lower-level management. When personalized letters are used, the lead sentence of the first paragraph becomes the most critical portion of the entire letter.

The nonpersonalized letter employs headline techniques. Some writers use two headlines in one letter. One headline runs across the top of the letter. Another may be placed below it. This becomes a subhead and is positioned flush left on the page, one to four lines in block form. From a layout standpoint this block simulates an inside address in a personalized letter.

Most marketers use the block headline only and not the headline across the top of the letter. This is preferable because it more closely resembles the format of a business letter. The combination of a block headline followed by a salutation, such as Dear Executive or Dear Hospital Administrator, works well for many business-to-business marketers. Short headlines are preferred, although not at the expense of clarity.

The Body

Since the businessperson has limited reading time, the copywriter must get to the point quickly. If the letter begins with an irrelevant story, attention will be cut short. The first sentence in the first paragraph of the letter should expand on the promise made to the reader in the headline. The promise implies that the reader will learn more by continuing to read. This elaboration process continues throughout the letter. Without question, the headline or the first sentence is the most important part of the letter, since readers will take less than five seconds before deciding whether to read further. Provoking attention and interest at that point is critical and is where most letters fail.

Letter copy must be sensitive to the reader's interest. Every word must give evidence to readers that the marketer understands their business and their problems. This can be done by establishing a common ground with the readers. The pitfall here is to tell the readers too much of what they may already know. Prospects are more interested in learning something new. The proposition should be written in logical steps similar to the way a business prospect might expect to hear it discussed in person.

As the message continues to unfold, one sentence should lead to another without interruption. The seasoned writer knows the reader will move to the next sentence in the letter only because the previous sentences continued to hold the reader's interest. Each paragraph should be connected to the preceding paragraph to achieve sales story flow. The following is a list of paragraph connectors taken from an assortment of successful business-to-business direct mail letters:

- "In the meantime, if you have any questions . . ."
- "Is it any wonder, then . . ."
- "But meeting that challenge . . ."
- "But if you find . . ."
- "And all it takes is . . ."
- "While there are many others . . ."
- "What's more . . ."
- "First of all . . ."
- "Now let's take a look at . . ."
- "Of course, that's just the beginning . . ."
- "Now there's a way . . ."
- "Because you depend on . . ."

The letter will be persuasive, informative, or explanatory, depending on the best way to accomplish the objective. The appeal for response may be laced throughout the body of the letter. However, the last paragraph is usually reserved for the final call to action, even if that action is indirect as in certain types of awareness and goodwill mailings.

When the writer has moved the reader as far as the last paragraph in the letter, the final challenge is to make it appear simple for the reader to pick up the business reply card or order form, fill it out, mail it, or pick up the telephone and call the toll-free 800 number. The writer has to make the offer easier for the reader to act on than to pass up.

The Closing
"Yours truly" as a letter closing in direct mail is archaic and has been replaced by the warmer, ingenuous, more unaffected expression, "Sincerely." But the friendlier "Cordially" and "Best regards" are reserved for use with those who are personal business acquaintances of the signer of the letter. Winding up a business direct mail letter with expressions such as "Have a nice day," and "Yours for more business" are not recommended by professional business-to-business direct marketing practitioners.

The Signature
Blue remains the preferable signature color. Just about any color except black has a personalized effect on a letter. Some mailers, to effect economies, prefer to use the same ink color for the signature as that used on their two-color letterhead. This can save a print charge for extra costs needed to get a blue signature.

Most business firms use actual names. A title for the letter signer should reflect credibly on the subject discussed in the letter. The word "sales" in a title could have a negative connotation to a reader. It indicates a solicitation or an attempt to "sell" the reader on something. The plain title "vice-president" always works well.

The P.S.

Copy tests have proven that a P.S. in business-to-business direct mail letters can improve results. The P.S. that does best is the one that restates the offer and action necessary for the reader to get the offer. Simply stating or restating a product benefit in the P.S. seems to do little to effect response. A double P.S. (or P.P.S.) is not recommended.

Graphics

The use of graphics in sales-support direct-mail letters should be approached with caution. Whether a letterhead design, photograph, or illustration of the product or offer, the wrong graphic can reduce the letter's effectiveness. Tests have shown that the plain direct mail letter will outpull the illustrated version by as much as three to one for sales support objectives. Businesspeople seem to feel that graphics imply advertising rather than an urgent business communication.

The Letterhead

The letterhead tells the reader that the marketer is stodgy and unimaginative, or aggressive and innovative, or anything in between. The marketer who wants to be perceived as a forward-moving organization will employ a well-designed letterhead. Letterhead designs used for direct mail campaigns should be contemporary and free of printed advertising copy and photographs of buildings or offices. Also, letterheads should not include names of company personnel, except the name of the person who signs the letter.

There are times when it may not be appropriate to include the address or telephone number of the sender on the printed letterhead. For instance, a company headquarter's sales support mailing may have as its objective the generation of reply card inquiries to be returned directly by prospects to a local sales office. A generic company letterhead designed without a headquarter's address or telephone number can cause less confusion in letting readers know where they should respond.

Most companies have corporate identity programs designed around a symbol or logo that represents the company name or a product name. The standard company letterhead may or may not be adequate for a direct mail campaign. A redesign may be necessary. A letterhead design may appear best on the bottom of a page or on the bottom of the second page if it is a two-page letter. The direct mail planner needs freedom to create a variety of effects and is not normally restricted to the use of the corporation's standard letterhead design.

The Typeface

The criterion for typeface use is to have the letter perceived as a personalized business letter coming from one businessperson to another. The typeface should closely resemble what a business reader perceives as words in a letter that has been typewritten rather than typeset. A typewriter face with a serif looks more personalized than a nonserif face, which is usually associated with printed materials. The use of standard typefaces is best for direct mail letters. Elite is standard and generally acceptable. As the word processor, minicomputer, and desktop printer replace the typewriter, reader perceptions of "personal" typewritten styles will, no doubt, change dramatically.

The Paper Stock

When mailing to top company officials, direct mail letter stock does not have to be 100 percent rag content bond. However, water-marked stationery is still popular when a marketer wants to reach top executives. Paper quality can be a factor in readership. A poor grade of stock has an old washed-out look that feels limp and wrinkles easily. Since white remains the preferred color for corporate stationery, it is the preferred color for direct mail letters. However, off-white, light grays, and tans, and light greens and blues on a calendarized stock have become quite acceptable.

THE ENCLOSURE

Generally, the enclosure is not as critical to a sales-support direct-mail campaign as it is to mail order, where it is the campaign so to speak. However, it is often a valuable element of the mailing.

Catalogs, flyers, broadsides, newsletters, house magazines, spec sheets, and other formats are all a form of literature, used either as part of a direct mail package or as a self-contained mailing piece. When used as enclosures, brochures, broadsides, and even booklets are read less like a book (page by page from beginning to end) and more in random fashion with viewers searching for a heading, illustration, or photograph that will grab their attention. Some readers scan this material in seconds and move on to something else. Others stop at a segment that interests them. If the copy is persuasive and fuels their interest, the entire piece may get read. Since this is the creative objective of the enclosure piece, it must be written and designed not only to highlight various important statements and strategically place them in the piece but also to tie these statements or segments together into a cohesive whole that tells a complete story.

The creation of any brochure or other enclosure naturally starts with an approved concept. If it is a highly visual one, design considerations probably come next. However, since copy provides the direction and organization for most brochures, it normally comes first.

Working With the Graphics Designer

The best creative work usually results when the direct mail enclosure project is a joint effort between writer and artist, from the discussion of copy to graphic emphasis. Focusing the best of these two complementary creative talents on an individual project at the same time is the goal of most creative directors. However, problems can arise between the two talents. The chemistry must be right.

In those cases when writers must work without an artist the finished copy is usually accompanied by a writer's rough layout, which is a sketchy placement of various general elements within a predetermined rough format. The writer must also provide the copy lead for the sales letter, brochure heads, subheads, response card, and outer envelope.

Creative Strategies for Direct Mail Enclosures

There is no substitute for good judgment and an ability to communicate effectively. But any effort can be made better regardless of the objectives when supported by a healthy helping of proven creative techniques. In fact, the listing that follows consists of more than techniques. It is a list of powerful creative strategies applied to direct mail enclosures.

1. Include more of what is novel and pertinent, excluding what is commonplace.
2. Create arresting and interesting copy and graphics with attention to style as well as content.
3. Use facts, figures, and specific statements to build credibility.
4. Repeat main points several times in different ways to aid message retention.
5. Use industry terminology to tag the marketer as knowledgeable and understanding. Eliminate jargon and cliches because they conjure up an old and tired label.
6. Design only one major headline on a page or spread to encourage readership.
7. Use bullet copy sparingly with no more than six on one page.
8. Use contemporary graphics and layout to have a positive impact on how the company is perceived by the reader.
9. Use headings, sidebars, callouts, captions, and footnotes, and enclose photos and illustrations, to get high readership.
10. Include powerful tools such as charts, tables, and graphs to convey complex (or simple) information.
11. Combine all visual elements: heads, subheads, photos, illustrations, and body text in size, shape, color, and contrast to lead the reader from one element in the layout to another.
12. Include photographs and captions to lend credibility and readership to the message.
13. Show products in use with happy "unposed" people doing real things.
14. Avoid mixing typefaces in a single printed piece.
15. Write and design printed materials in ways to make readers perceive them as worth keeping because they have a continuing value.
16. Use a layout that calls attention to the message rather than to the layout itself.
17. Blend graphic devices, colors, rules, photographs, and illustrations together for visual continuity that leads the reader through the story.

Since the cover of a direct mail enclosure gets examined, at least momentarily, by all who open the mail package, it should immediately tell readers what is inside and entice them to want to read further. A single photo or illustration on the cover is more effective than a few smaller ones.

ACTION REPLY FORMS

Direct mail reply vehicles are designed to make it easy and trouble-free for readers to identify themselves to the marketer as casual inquirers, interested prospects, or customers. The reply form directs the reader to take a predominant course of action. Those that do the best job in pulling responses restate the offer expressed in the mailing package, highlight the main reader benefit, and provide ample room for readers to write in the name and address. Even when the prospect's name and address are placed on the reply form by direct imprint or label, a space should be provided for the respondent to include his or her name and telephone number. This tends to further commit a reader to the offer, as well as encouraging persons other than the one named in the mailing address to respond.

The specific copy and format of the reply vehicle is determined by the overall mailing objective and format. Action reply forms range from the simple 3½-by-5-inch standard business reply card of .006 minimum thickness with sparse copy to elaborate reply forms accompanied by a 6-by-9-inch business reply envelope.

Most business reply cards in use today are 3½ inches by 5½ inches or 3½ inches by 8½ inches in size. A label or imprint on the former is designed to double as the mailing address by showing through a window in the outgoing envelope. The use of a perforated stub on the card increases the overall size to about 3½ inches by 8½ inches and ensures that the address portion can still be viewed through the window, eliminating any shifting of the card in the number 10 envelope. The stub also has value as additional space for promotional copy.

Computerized direct mail printing systems are available for marketers who want multiple and duplicate name personalization. The reply form is personalized at the same time as the letter. In this case, since the reply form is normally cut from the same sheet as the standard letter, it may not meet minimum weight standards. Therefore, a business reply envelope will be required.

Reply cards are used most in inquiry-generation campaigns. For sales-support direct-mail objectives a reply card that does not match the color of the rest of the package can increase response. Many busy prospects actually read response cards before other components in the package to get the gist of the offer. Writers often approach the creative task with that in mind.

ENVELOPES

The direct mail creative planner wants to ensure that any copy or graphics on the outgoing mailing envelope does not give prospective readers an opportunity to prejudge the contents unfavorably. A good number of business executives in the larger companies, as well as the many millions who work in small firms, open their own mail. Some industries operate with leaner secretarial staffs than others, causing many managers who share a secretary to open their own mail. Private secretaries of top managers usually screen and open mail addressed to their bosses. How the envelope is handled affects orders.

Therefore, creative planners have a need to know who opens the mail. "Appearance" is a key word when making decisions about business mail envelopes.

As a general rule, obvious advertising mail gets fewer openings when sent to executives who have secretaries who open their mail. Mail volume is greater in this higher managerial group. Secretaries, either by the boss's edict or on their own authority, screen much of what appears to be advertising, self-mailers, and envelopes laden with printing and graphics. Middle- and lower-level managers and professionals who open their own mail also perceive advertising mail differently than they do business mail.

Many business-to-business mailers have found that the best standard copy rule for envelopes is the no-copy rule. For the most part, copy only detracts from the businesslike approach. If the envelope does not look like a mail order mailing, and does not contain advertising copy, there is a greater chance that it will be opened.

There are many ways to create the "right" envelope. In some cases, the return address should be minimized. The logo can be sufficient identification if the company is large enough. A few business marketers actually claim higher responses by putting their return addresses on the back flap of the envelope. Official-looking envelopes, such as brown kraft, get more openings and more response. Where a specific function is handled by different people in different companies, and the marketer does not have the prospect's name, using functional titles actually printed on the envelope close to the address gets good results.

The standard letter and envelope size most prevalent in business use is 8½ inches by 11 inches in a number 10 envelope. When it fits the creative objective it is helpful at times to make the envelope appear different from other mail. This is why some business-to-business marketers will occasionally use less common envelope sizes. But when an odd size is used there should be a good reason. To avoid expensive problems, a review of postal regulations governing the use of nonstandard mailing envelopes can be helpful.

Any copy important enough to be used on an envelope should attract the reader's attention without being insulting. If a promise is made on the envelope, there should be a follow-through on the inside. "Personal" and "confidential" are grossly misused. They may get more openings and orders, but they are eroding credibility for all direct mail. The same is true of "free gift inside" when the reader finds the "free gift" is very conditional. If the copy on the envelope is misleading, the reader questions the integrity of the marketer.

Some business-to-business marketers use window envelopes with the address label from the reply card displayed through the window. Another benefit of a window envelope is that it allows coding on the label, which tells the marketer the list source.

CREATIVE INQUIRY-GENERATION OBJECTIVES

The creative approach for inquiry-generation direct mail is quite different from that of the mail order objective. There, the creative approach must perform all the selling functions. In an inquiry-generation mailing the offer is more important than the product. It governs the quantity and quality of inquiries generated by the mailing. But it is not the only factor for generating inquiry response. The number of inquiries and their quality for any given offer can be controlled by the degree of creative emphasis given to the offer and the options in the response portion of the inquiry-mailing package.

There are two basic types of inquiry-generation programs. The first is a highly structured program designed to continually generate inquiries on a scheduled weekly or monthly basis for salesperson follow-up. As an integral part of the annual marketing plan, this program usually consists of many different direct mail campaign packages depending on the number of products and markets involved. For any individual product the same inquiry-generation package may be sent two, three, or even four times to the same list over the plan period, as long as the response results meet the planned objectives. New "beat the best" creative packages are often tested during the course of the program to ensure maximum results.

The second type of inquiry program is the short-range, noncontinuous mailing campaign. A marketer may need inquiries for individual territories in specific time periods to boost sales activity. Each mailing is usually custom created for a highly definitive purpose. It may employ one direct mail package as a one-shot effort or it may consist of a series of packages in a campaign, mailed at two- or three-week intervals. A series of several mailings designed to accomplish one inquiry-building objective is more effective when each mailing in the series uses a different approach within the series-family theme. Each mailing has the same offer but highlights a different benefit the reader will get in response to the offer.

When a company or product is new to the marketplace, the selling process is particularly complex, or the product is very technical, the creative approach most often consists of a series of mailings. With this approach the campaign makes use of all but the last mailing in the series to be informational and provocative, setting the stage for a persuasive appeal to the reader to respond to an offer in the final mailing.

Copy Approach

In creating inquiry-generation direct mail the copywriter's job is to find out who among those on the mailing list are interested in a particular offer. The writer wants to say only enough about that offer to get the maximum number of readers to respond. Giving too much information to the reader in the inquiry-building direct-mail package will result in fewer responses. By telling a more complete story, most of the prospect's questions will be answered. Many would-be prospects learn enough from the material in the mailing to preclude the need to send for more information. So the marketer may never know who those prospects are. This is why inquiry-generation objectives for the most part call for short copy.

Some effective direct-mail inquiry-building packages consist of no more than four paragraphs of copy in a letter plus a reply card that includes two check-boxes, one for the offer and another for a salesperson to call. Of course, companies selling complex products or new companies in some markets may need more than a letter and a business reply card to get enough of their story across to provoke a response.

The strategies and techniques used to help the creative planner fine-tune an inquiry-generation program are explained in Chapter 7. But the creative writer is also involved in this fine-tuning process. The writer needs to identify individuals who are at a specific stage in the purchasing behavior cycle. The writer must also know the quality of the inquiry that is expected because it has a bearing on the copy approach. For instance, if the marketer wants softer leads, the copy will be very brief. It attempts only to sell the booklet, literature, or other offer material.

The Letter

When personalization is used, the opening sentence or lead line of the body becomes, in many respects, the focal point of the letter and the key to whether the reader will continue to read. When nonpersonalized letters are used, headlines fill this function of capturing immediate reader interest. The more closely the copy writer can focus on a current interest and concern of the target audience, the more successful he or she will be in building readership. Some of the best inquiry-mailing results are recorded when writers mention the offer in the headline of the letter or, if the letter is personalized, in the first sentence. The headline or lead line is then expanded on throughout the remainder of the letter.

Figure 9-1 shows examples of headlines and salutations that reach for readers who have specific interests. These are examples of solid business-to-business approaches.

For many business-to-business marketers, the plain, unillustrated letter works best as the standard inquiry-building format. Graphics, aside from letterhead design, tend to reduce response. Few offers are powerful enough to be depicted graphically in a letter. However, there are exceptions. Depending on the offer, a photograph or illustration of the specific offer can pull more responses than a plain letter. Figure 9-2 illustrates such a letter from the 3M company. Because the smaller executive-size letter was used with an illustration, the writer felt two pages were needed to deliver the message. Unused white space on the second page indicates the copywriter was not lured into saying more than was necessary for the quality of inquiry wanted.

Because the letter in Figure 9-2 ran over to the second side of the sheet, the designer was able to move the letterhead information to that side, allowing the offer illustration to be placed on the front side. The letter does not talk about details of the company's approach to better communications. What it does promise is some very "solid information"—learning to be more effective in group meetings and making business presentations.

The 3M letter (Figure 9-2) also has a good example of effective use of a P.S. to enhance the offer. Other examples of what should be highlighted in postscripts are shown in Figure 9-3.

Action Response Card

The inquiry-generation response format consists of business reply cards mostly because there is little required of the interested prospect other than a simple

Figure 9-1. Sample letter headlines from successful inquiry-building campaigns.

```
Here's some help
if you're getting
ready for scanning.

A limited opportunity
for NCR Century System users only.
Dear NCR Century System user:

This Pennsylvania contractor
has a "success story" about
cost management that you
should read!

You can be totally informed about
this new management approach developed exclusively
for wholesale distributors.
The facts and complete details are in the free
booklet I'm offering you.

Here's how one Savings & Loan
resolved the branch reporting headache
and earned extra dividends in the process.

The Morris County Savings Bank
saved time and money
with an efficient forms system.
Our free booklet explains how.

If you give credit
and aren't a financial genius
I've got the booklet for you.

And it won't cost you a cent!
Dear Doctor:

This computer system
has applied programs
designed especially
for manufacturers!

Two competitive terminals
can almost do the job of one
NCR 2950 Remittance Control Terminal.

A free booklet with the inside
facts on minicomputer processing
for moving and storage companies.
Return the enclosed card.  I'll send
you a copy right away.
```

Source: Used by permission of NCR Corporation.

Figure 9-2. Model inquiry mailing with perfect linkage of offer, copy, graphics, and format.

Source: Reprinted by permission of 3M, Audio Visual Division, St. Paul 1987.

checkmark or two and perhaps the writing of a name, address, and telephone number. Because there are no bank checks or "private" information involved, a business reply envelope is not needed.

In effect, the reply card summarizes in a sentence or two the gist of the offer. If the offer is information in the form of a booklet or other literature, the title of the offer material should be mentioned, such as, "Send me a copy of your booklet on 'Capturing Financial Markets with New Leading Edge Network Banking Systems' " rather than "Send me more information," which is too general. Specifying the title of the booklet or the specific type of information will produce more selective inquiries.

Enclosures

The standard direct mail package has often been referred to as a letter, reply card, and enclosure. This is the case in most mail order packages. However, tests have shown that an enclosure can actually reduce response when sent as part of an inquiry-generation mailing. The key to optimum response lies in the writer's ability to say what is needed to be said in the letter. It is much more difficult to write a powerful, short letter that excites and persuades than it is to write an illustrated brochure.

Enclosures are used in inquiry-building mailings only if additional explanatory information or illustrative material is needed because the letter copy alone cannot provide the complete message. This occurs when the product or service is highly complex, or the concept is extremely technical. This is also true for new products or systems or if the company is not well known. Those marketers who do not

Figure 9-3. Examples of effective use of the P.S. to enhance the offer in inquiry-generation letters.

P.S.   Send back your card today. The booklet is yours without cost or obligation.

P.S.   Illustrations of the reports provided as part of the STARCOM accounts-payable application are included in your special brochure.

P.S.   The free brochure offered includes illustrations of the reports offered by IIDS.

P.S.   Remember, our 2125 booklet is yours without cost or obligation. Why not send for yours today?

P.S.   You'll especially appreciate the audit trail provided by the NCR 7750 as described in detail in the 20-page brochure.

P.S.   Examples of the valuable reports you can receive from this system are shown in your free report.

have a presence in the marketplace may need more than one enclosure simply to establish credibility. In every instance, when enclosures are warranted, they should lead the reader directly to the reply card.

Some marketers incorrectly create inquiry-generation mailings without letters, using only printed enclosures and duplicated typewritten sheets. These lack the personalization needed in order to get good readership. Enclosing ad reprints, corporate and product information booklets and brochures, price lists, spec sheets, announcements and notices, bulletins, newsletters, and other promotional literature that may be on hand is not acceptable in inquiry-generation direct mail programs.

The Self-Mailer

Most users of business-to-business inquiry-response mail agree that the self-mailer when compared with inquiry-response formats in envelopes pulls less response. Except for a few specialized computer formats, self-mailers are not able to capitalize on one of the outstanding strengths of direct mail—its personalized aspect. A self-mailer is perceived by the business reader as printed literature or advertising material and, as such, does not get the readership or the response that a more personalized envelope-enclosed mailing generates.

The Envelope

For getting envelopes opened there are not many envelope-enhancement devices that are any better than the plain business envelope, personally addressed directly on the envelope, with first-class postage. That is the way business mail is sent to other businesspeople. However, any envelope will get opened if the recipient perceives that it may contain worthwhile information. That should be the criterion with which to determine the value of any element utilized for enhancing openings.

Although the plain number 10 or executive-size business envelope has the best chance of getting opened, other unique formats that give away the contents on the envelope can do well if the product is new, innovative, or highlights advanced technology in business. Window envelopes can outpull a nonwindow mailing for inquiry-generation mailings. The main reason for the greater response is that the preprinted name and address on the reply card (which shows through the window) makes it easier for the recipient to respond.

Many business-to-business marketers find third-class bulk postage and label addressing the most cost effective for inquiry-generation mailings. There may be fewer envelopes that get opened and fewer responses, but cost per inquiry and cost per order in the long run may be more affordable.

So-called "teaser copy" or any copy or illustrations on envelopes is not recommended for inquiry-generation mailings. More often than not it just alerts the recipient to the fact that advertising material is enclosed. Also, the return address on the envelope can deter openings if the business recipient perceives that it comes from a company sending out mailings of no interest.

CREATIVE PREQUALIFIED PROSPECT PENETRATION OBJECTIVES

The creative approach for a prequalified prospect penetration direct mail campaign begins with a different premise than the standard inquiry-generation campaign— the prospect is already qualified. Roughly 90 percent of these door-opener campaigns include a premium offer. The objective of this type of campaign may be that the marketer wants the prospect to meet with a salesperson or an official of the marketer's company, to come to a company-sponsored seminar, to visit the sales office for a demonstration or to a VIP session at a trade show, or to respond to one of a dozen other events. The copywriter must come up with some powerfully persuasive words to get the message across and emphasize the identified benefits correctly.

Overall, the writer's goal is to make the reader feel that time spent in the visit will be more valuable than time spent any other way. Rarely is this accomplished by talking about the company and its history. The benefit often highlighted in this type of campaign is the positive learning experience the prospect will gain by keeping up with the latest products and technology in the industry.

Getting prospects to return a reply card requesting an information booklet is much easier than convincing them to arrange an appointment to attend a meeting or agree to meet with a vendor company official. The commitment for a meeting places the prospect somewhat at risk, whereas simply asking for more information does not. Getting this commitment takes personalization and usually more than one page of copy to move a prospect to action. The more successful prequalified prospect programs employ a series of multiple-piece mailing campaigns, many of which are dimensionals (three dimensional). Usually the higher the unit of sale, the more the marketer can spend for especially creative and unique inquiry-generation high-impact enclosures. The planner's creativity is especially challenged to come up with appropriate concepts for these programs.

Some prequalified prospect mailing program offers are actually invitations but consist of more than one contact with the prospect. The first mailing provides details about the event and is usually mailed four to six weeks in advance. Subsequent mailings are made with a final reminder mailing about a week before the event. Telephone call follow-ups can increase acceptances substantially.

The format chosen depends on the type of activity suggested and the relationship the marketer has with key prospects. The personal invitation can take the form of formal printed invitations with RSVP cards in return matching envelopes; less formal but businesslike letters, preferably executive size; and response cards and envelopes. RSVP cards are recommended regardless of format.

A special premium offer is very often needed to get the reader's attention and to be a strong motivator to get the reader to make the commitment. For instance, a Xerox Corporation mailing offered a "Free executive's change kit" to the prospect and to the secretary in exchange for sitting in on a dealer demonstration of the Xerox Memorywriter. Grays 1 Software offered a "Free silver letter opener" to prospects ready for a free trial or benchmark test. A communications company giant sent a Mont Blanc Diplomat fountain pen to a highly select list of prequalified prospects along with an invitation to attend a one-on-one sales presentation at the marketer's place of business. When a premium is used to increase response, the creative emphasis is shifted to the premium.

Chances are that creative approaches and offers normally used for inquiry-generation mailings to general prospect lists will not be effective if used for prequalified prospect lead objectives. These mailings take more than specialized, persuasive writing skills. If the prospect has been qualified, but has not yet been sold, there may be hidden roadblocks. The writer must be made aware of the roadblocks and build the campaign approach that eliminates them or circumvents them. Because average writers have difficulty coming up with this highly defined creative approach, marketers should lean on only the most experienced professional direct mail writers for this assignment.

CREATIVE AWARENESS OBJECTIVES

Awareness objectives using the direct mail medium are, in most respects, similar to awareness objectives of the more encompassing advertising media. Both attempt to influence attitudes and beliefs of prospects and customers. However, awareness publication advertising in business and trade magazines speaks to broader marketplace segments, and within more restrictive creative parameters than does direct mail awareness advertising. (The differences between direct mail and a publication ad are discussed in Chapter 8.)

Awareness direct mail advertising campaigns usually have very specific objectives directed toward narrow target markets. The writer must know exactly what the marketer wants the campaign to accomplish, such as:

■ Causing specific products to be talked about
■ Creating a greater awareness of a new line of products
■ Building an identity as preferred supplier among selected dealers targeted for signing up within the plan year

Causing prospects to think the way the marketer wants them to usually means modifying the prospect's opinions. And the best way to find out if an awareness campaign accomplishes this objective is to measure specific opinions before and after the campaign is mailed and then compare survey results. Before starting the writing, the copywriter and planner must agree on the specific questions to be used in the survey. The survey questions are built around the campaign objectives. The writer emphasizes those points, issues, or ideas that will influence the prospect.

The same basic copywriting principles apply in awareness direct mail campaigns as in other types of direct mail programs. However, the action required of the prospect is different. The writer is after indirect action or share of mind in specific ways that will eventually lead to direct action and a sale. Awareness and inquiry-building objectives are often combined into one campaign *series* to launch complex products or help lesser-known companies enter a marketplace. It works only when the two objectives are not combined in a single mailing. The first several mailings inform and persuade a reader toward a definite point of view. The last mailing in the series ties the campaign mailings together with a very brief summary message while having inquiry-generation as its main objective. This last mailing requests specific direct action from the reader. A series of campaign mailings combining awareness and inquiry-building objectives is most successful when telemarketing calls follow the final mailing.

Any single mailing in the series should be based on only one main objective implemented with one basic idea. This prevents reader confusion and poor message retention, which are problems many business-to-business marketers encounter in their direct mail efforts. For instance, in an attempt to become better known in the marketplace, a marketer may mail out a brochure or a folder that resembles a full-line sales catalog. Unless one basic memorable idea is presented, the mailing may be remembered only briefly, if looked at, or not at all.

There may be many specific product benefits highlighted in an awareness campaign and, indeed, each can be the focus of an individual mailing in the campaign series. But there should be one basic unifying theme in all the mailings.

Awareness copy can be either short or long, but from a readership standpoint, the shorter the better. Yet to modify a reader's opinion, awareness copy must relate enough information to create an impression on the reader. Also, since the marketer is not offering anything tangible, the prospect needs compelling reasons or rationalizations for reading. The copy should offer, in and of itself, reader enhancement by informing, educating, or entertaining, and at the same time provide the reader with positive perceptions about the company.

There is often much to tell about a product, but to reach the awareness objective, it must be told over and over. This is why awareness direct mail almost always consists of a series mailed at periodic intervals. The creative planner must ensure that each mailing is viewed differently from those that preceded it. And to instill initial and continuing interest in the campaign, personalized techniques are often used.

Arresting formats run the gamut, from simple executive-size letters on tinted stock with matching envelopes, to a series of multipiece dimensional packages, "lumpy" or outsized envelopes, mailing tubes, boxes, burlap bags, or other unique formats. Using dimensionals and showmanship graphics is not a substitute for great creative writing. However, when used in combination, the result can be extremely rewarding.

Figure 9-4 is a good example of showmanship and prospect involvement created in a mailing from a Champion International Corporation awareness campaign series.

CREATIVE REMINDER OBJECTIVES

Reminder direct mail fills still another objective of the business-to-business marketer. This creative platform is one of cordial contact. It is different from awareness direct mail in that it keeps the company or product name in front of qualified prospects, so the marketer will have an edge over competition when purchase

Figure 9-4. Champion International showmanship awareness series mailing.

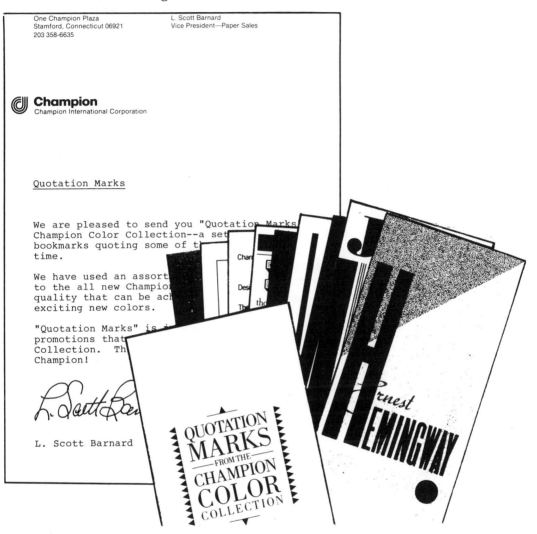

One Champion Plaza
Stamford, Connecticut 06921
203 358-6635

L. Scott Barnard
Vice President—Paper Sales

Champion
Champion International Corporation

Quotation Marks

We are pleased to send you "Quotation Marks
Champion Color Collection--a set
bookmarks quoting some of t
time.

We have used an assort
to the all new Champio
quality that can be ac
exciting new colors.

"Quotation Marks" is
promotions that
Collection. Th
Champion!

L. Scott Barnard

QUOTATION MARKS FROM THE CHAMPION COLOR COLLECTION

Source: Courtesy of Champion International Corporation, Stamford, CT 06921.

decisions are ready to be made. Reminder mailings are sent on a regular basis to identified prospects to get them to switch vendors or to customers to keep them sold.

Effective reminder direct mail copy is simple and brief and does not detail the company's product benefits. Rather, it simply attempts to register in the mind of the prospect the company's name and product designations positively. Each mailing should leave the prospect with the impression that the company is contemporary, progressive, and thinks highly of the prospect.

Because these mailings are not aggressive, they do not go after immediate response. They become a form of advertising. Often the marketer will include a standard business reply card in a reminder mailing to make it easier for the reader to contact the marketer just in case the reader is ready to take action.

Since reminder mailings must have impact for lasting impressions to be made, few creative limitations are placed on formats, length of copy, or use of graphics. Some of the best reminder mail is about 90 percent format and 10 percent copy. The creative planner takes advantage of attention-getting devices and useful or interesting information to target the needs, emotions, and mind-set of the reader/ prospect. Although creative letters in a series are used by some marketers, dimensionals are used more often to entertain or provide functional value. The format can be as simple as a few words on a memo pad or monthly calendar, or periodic ad preprints, or copies of prereleased press releases. Reminder mail may be in the form of a gift of nominal value that works best when it is directly related to the marketer's product.

External company newsletters and house magazines fall into the reminder direct mail category. Those that get highest prospect and customer readership provide mostly helpful generic nonpromotional product or industry information. Some reminder-type newsletters have been received in the marketplace so favorably that the prospects actually pay for issues on a subscription basis. Even though the marketer's cost of publishing such a newsletter is often greater than the subscription income, at least the reminder objectives are accomplished at low cost. A disadvantage for the marketers who charge for a newsletter is that they cannot control the scope of the targeted market.

CREATIVE REINFORCED SELLING OBJECTIVES

The creative objective for reinforced selling campaigns is to help salespeople increase their productivity by providing messages that communicate the same things the marketer's salespeople talk about to the twenty or so most qualified prospects they currently call on. The direct mail copy specifically reinforces the salesperson's personal selling messages.

Reinforced selling programs are always created as a series of multiple mailings. Three-piece and five-piece direct mail campaigns are most often used, but sometimes more are used, since it can take at least six to twelve months for a sale to be finalized.

Copy for reinforced selling campaigns has some distinct features. It can be as detailed as necessary without concern for length and still get good readership, because the prospect is already in the ready-to-buy cycle when the need to know is greatest. As a rule, reader benefits and product or system features of specific product applications are spelled out in a single series. Because the copywriter of a reinforced selling campaign is writing to a qualified prospect—one who already knows a great deal about the product—it is easier to build on the interest that has already been established by the salesperson. A headline or lead line such as, "Here is more information on the bank teller terminal system you are considering" speaks directly to a prospect's identified need.

Each mailing in a reinforced selling campaign series should not only look different but actually be different from what prospects have reviewed before. Reinforced campaign mailings usually have an abundance of illustrated material, showing the product in use, charts, graphs, and factual pictorial representations of competitive comparisons or benefits for the buyer. For maximum effect, mailing pieces should resemble or carry the same graphic theme as used in ads and sales literature.

Printed personal notes are often used to transmit detailed, reinforced-selling direct-mail materials. It is not necessary to enclose reply cards in this type of mailing, but some marketers do enclose reply cards, just in case.

SALES PROMOTION LITERATURE AS ENCLOSURES

Literature used for direct mail should emphasize a need for the reader to take the next action step:

- A call to an 800 number or non-800 number
- The return of a reply card that may be an integral part of the literature
- A visit to a sales office
- A suggestion to pass the literature on to others in the organization
- A suggestion to place the material in the file with a reminder to have it come up for review later

Sales promotion literature takes the form of brochures, booklets, pamphlets, pocket folders, one-page flyers, and other formats produced in everything from black and white to four-color, on very expensive or inexpensive paper. In small- and medium-size businesses and in advertising agencies, writers of sales promotional material usually also write direct mail. Some are communications professionals who know the techniques of both. Others tend to make the rather common mistake of writing direct mail letters that read like product feature manuals, or self-mailers that resemble folders or ad reprints. A review of the professional copywriter's approach to the objectives of the more common sales promotional literature can be helpful especially to the beginning direct mail copywriter (see Chapter 8).

Considerations for Sales Literature Use

Focus
Since printed sales literature has many different uses, problems can arise when a piece of literature is used to serve several sales purposes, including direct mail, without regard to its original intent. A promotion piece must have the kind of message that fits a given objective. For example, if a folder that describes and illustrates a specific product or system is sent as an enclosure in an inquiry mailing, it will fit the product message objective and no doubt could help a prospect learn more about the product or system being promoted. But it will miss the direct mail use objective because it may tell the reader too much, with the result of far fewer inquiries than if the piece were not included. This piece of literature does not fit the direct mail use strategy, yet if it were positioned as the offer piece, it would be used correctly.

Obviously, the custom creation of sales-support inquiry-generation direct mail offer pieces, and enclosures for reinforced selling, awareness, and other direct mail campaigns, is ideal. But all too often, cost constraints and immediate availability of existing materials convince the direct mail planner to opt for the direct mail use of sales literature material presently in stock but originally prepared for other purposes. If sales literature used as an enclosure for a reinforced selling campaign, as an example, does not tie in well enough with the objective of the accompanying direct mail letter, then it may not only miss the message objective but also leave a bad impression on prospects.

With some copy modification, existing literature can become a custom direct mail enclosure or an offer piece. In such cases, the marketer must proceed cautiously when selecting this literature to be part of a direct mail package. Since the title and contents of an offer piece become the key points of discussion in an inquiry-generation campaign, they also determine the quality as well as quantity of inquiries. The creative planner, therefore, must be sure that the offer piece selected conforms to the kind of inquiry the marketer wishes to generate. If the title of the available sales promotion piece is not applicable to the objective, but the contents are acceptable, the creative planner may retitle or simply ignore the original title and instead highlight the contents in the direct mail letter. Retitling should not be done in any way to mislead the reader but only to describe the contents more in the context of the direct mail objective. This, of course, saves the cost of reprinting the entire piece.

Copy

Copy must relate to the different objectives based on each specific use category of the various types of sales literature. Most literature is picked up and read because the reader/prospect has shown interest in wanting the product or one like it, now or in the future. For instance, the letter in a direct mail package builds the reader's interest to the point where the details and explanations in the supporting literature enclosed get read. Or the prospect has requested the literature to find out more about the product.

Copy in promotional literature should not be informal as in a letter nor should it be as tight as in an ad. The copy's role in getting attention is not as significant as it is in a direct mail letter and literature has more room for details. Literature should concentrate on advancing the prospect's interest, strengthening desire, and establishing credibility for the marketer's product, system, or service.

Most effective sales literature does not contain superlatives or jargon, nor does it lean on hyperbole for excitement. On the other hand, it should not read like it was written by an engineer and rewritten by the legal department. It should have good selling copy with headlines or main headings and subordinate elements under that, if necessary. The printed piece should not include simple listings of elements opposite bullets, except as summary material. And it should all be tied together in a unified message.

Sales literature used for direct mail purposes provides details, answers questions, emphasizes features and functions, anticipates objections, and responds to these. All basic copy principles apply to the writing of literature. It must be well organized, have a story flow, be clear and factual, appeal to the self-interest of the reader, be enthusiastic, and, as in other forms of promotional writing, name the benefits to the reader. The copy should avoid statements that lack credibility, unsupported claims, and overstatement.

The theme supported by active graphics should relate to the business interests of the reader. Ample space allows photographs and illustrations to demonstrate products and systems and highlight third-party endorsements. Facts are better than generalities. They are needed to convince the business buyer who does not want to take risks when making capital expenditures.

Graphics

The writer and graphic artist must work as one to represent the subject matter convincingly and in an easy-to-read format. Spreads should be used to advantage and copy and graphics assembled into cohesive units.

Individual company graphic design formats are necessary for a company or division to be perceived in the marketplace as a well-coordinated, unified organization. Many companies have established corporate identity guidelines to ensure that all materials have the corporate look. Considerable time and expense can be saved through the use of a standard matrix that gives the writer and artist specific layout direction for every printed piece. But even though standardization reduces creative costs and makes the creative process more efficient, too strict an adherence to a matrix strategy stifles the creativity needed, especially when a new product is released or other objectives call for exciting new impact layouts.

Types of Printed Sales Promotion Materials

There are eight basic types of sales promotion literature:

1. Basic product application material
2. Product feature/function material
3. Case histories
4. Corporate image brochures
5. Approach material
6. Technical product or system summaries
7. Specification sheets
8. Feature and application proposal material

Of these, the first four types can be integrated most effectively into direct mail programs since they do not need a salesperson to further explain the contents.

Basic Product Application Material

Basic product application material is a type of printed promotion most often used by salespeople as a logical follow-up to approach pieces. The writer's job in this case is to help build the interest aroused on the initial sales call by providing a more detailed description of the product or system. Literature in this group highlights the purpose, features, and function of each product application or series of applications. These are results-oriented pieces illustrating key benefits to be gained from purchase of the product. The writer helps convince the prospect that the expressed benefits are, in fact, applicable to the reader's business.

Although written and produced for salespeople to use during a sales presentation, this product application material usually can stand on its own. It can be very effectively used in reinforced direct mail selling campaigns when mailed together with direct mail letters that restate one or a few of the key points covered in the brochure or folder. Or when the specific application described is appropriate, this material can serve as an offer for an inquiry-generation campaign.

Product Feature/Function Material

This group of printed pieces usually employs the format of a brochure or a sizable booklet. Feature materials for industry-oriented products contain action pictures and photographs of the product in use in its intended environment. Such pictures lend authenticity to the product and immediately help the reader to identify with its purpose.

The writer describes all product features, functions, and value but includes only salient specifications because other publications include the more technical data. Salespeople do not use feature/function-oriented brochures with prospects until they have determined which product or group of products they will recommend. Then they use the particular brochure that supports their presentation of specific product features. This class of material, which is similar to product application material, makes good reinforced selling direct mail when accompanied by a letter or note. It can also serve as direct mail offer material for inquiry building.

Case History

Case histories of successful products in use are a favorite tool of the field sales organization. The writer helps the salesperson tell the prospect the story of the satisfied customer in a brief mini-format or larger folder or booklet format—and all the better if it is in the particular prospect's line of business. The promotion writer uses the case history technique to help salespeople convince the prospects they call on that their sales message is indeed credible.

In this publication the writer usually presents a short history of the user, explains the business, and describes one or several functions handled or processed by the products purchased. Where applicable, a comparison is made with previous products or systems used. The writer usually visits the customer who has agreed to the testimonial, to gather all needed data and to take photographs at the customer's site.

The salesperson uses the case history publication on the initial sales call to arouse interest, or on recalls, or as an effective component of a proposal. The publication lets the prospects sell themselves as they read about time, money, and information benefits claimed by a peer.

Case histories make excellent direct mail inquiry-generating offer material. They are effective as reinforced selling direct mail pieces when used with a letter or other personalized transmittal piece. When produced in series, especially in mini-format, case histories can be successful enclosures in awareness and reminder direct mail campaigns.

Corporate Image Brochures

As the name implies, corporate image material aims at enhancing the marketer's image in the marketplace. It may be a publication that is generic in subject matter and renders a service to the industry such as "Data Processing Terminology," or "Techniques to Curtail Theft in Retail Stores." The goal here is to produce a tastefully written publication that will cover subjects truly in the industry's interest and leave the reader with a favorable impression of the company. Generic corporate image literature can make good offer material for direct mail campaigns targeted to prequalified prospects.

Corporate image brochures written and designed to describe a specific company, its products and operations, do not generate many responses when used as offer material in inquiry direct mail campaigns directed to nonqualified markets. They are appropriate, however, in some reinforced selling direct mail campaigns.

Approach Material

This type of sales promotion material often takes the form of brochures and is written to help salespeople arouse the prospect's interest in a product application or the general features of a system that may involve many products.

It is normally used on initial sales calls, providing basic information about the product or a complete system. Approach material is written and designed to help salespeople identify strong points of interest by generating questions from prospects as they review the brochure together page by page. Customer benefits of the product are emphasized. Any reference to product details is minimal. Because of this, it is not particularly useful as an offer piece in a direct mail program or as an enclosure in a direct mail package.

Technical Product or System Summaries

This literature group is highly technical and often prepared by technical writers rather than promotional writers. The writer provides product application detail for operational management in a prospect or customer organization. This type of material also provides a source of information for engineers, contractors, CPAs, consultants, and other third parties.

Because of the length and technical nature of these summaries, illustrations are generally restricted to systems and program flow diagrams, charts, and test results. From this information the prospect's operational management picks up facts about the product and learns how product application results are achieved. The writer emphasizes technical details of each product component, capacities, options, specifications, restrictions, and all pertinent information needed for understanding the product and how it operates.

Salespeople usually rely on this black-and-white printed material initially for self-education since it provides them with the basic information they need to discuss the product or system intelligently with the prospect.

This document is the informational source about the product or system. Technical literature is not considered a prime component in direct mail programs.

Specification Sheet

One- or two-page "catalog" sheets are the most commonly used types of printed sales promotion by the business-to-business sales force. For many products they consist of not much more than a photograph of the product on one side of a sheet and a list of product specifications on the other. They are usually printed in one, two, or four colors. Because of the expense, four-color printing often depends on the product and whether the company has four-color printing negatives on hand from some previous use.

Salespeople use specification sheets along with feature brochures in their custom proposals to prospective customers. This type of sales promotion piece, which is completely devoid of selling copy or explanatory copy, should only be sent to people with prior product knowledge and perhaps to those who have had a product demonstration. These specification sheets have little further value in professional direct mail programs.

Feature and Application Proposal Material

There is yet another group of folders and single pages on the business-to-business marketer's literature shelf, also written by the promotional writer—standard proposal material. The writer includes descriptions and photographs of the basic product, its features, and where applicable, salient specifications. Salespeople use each set of proposal materials as is, or tailor them for individual prospects. Proposal material is rarely suitable for use in direct mail campaigns.

SUMMARY

The most widely used basic element in sales support direct mail is the letter. The headline or lead sentence is the most important part of a direct mail letter. Body copy and the P.S. that lead the reader to the action reply piece are a continuing elaboration of the promise made to the reader in the headline. Enclosures elaborate on the key ideas and facts indicated elsewhere in the mailing package. The creative strategies for enclosures enhance readership and message retention. Direct mail reply vehicles make it easy and trouble-free for readers to identify themselves.

The direct mail planner's choice of creative strategy in envelope usage determines the number of direct mail packages that get opened. Envelopes should look more like business correspondence and less like advertising.

Business-to-business inquiry-building direct mail programs are mostly sales support campaigns whose objective is to sell the offer, not the product. Thus, the degree of creative emphasis given to the offer in the mailing material affects results.

Most inquiry campaigns consist of letters and response cards. Enclosures are usually not needed. Nor is it necessary for inquiry-building letters to be personalized to get read. However, letters should include as many personalized features as practical. The nonillustrated letter, depending on the offer, often pulls more responses.

The creative approach to prequalified prospects demands special persuasive copy and graphic techniques. To produce dimensionals and other high-impact formats, the most experienced creative talent is required.

Direct mail for awareness objectives attempts to modify or build very specific attitudes. Often a business-to-business marketer will use the first several mailings in a campaign for awareness objectives with a final mailing requesting reader action.

Reminder direct mail keeps the marketer's name in front of prospects with brief copy messages and attention-getting devices that involve the reader.

Reinforced direct mail copy stresses the same sales points that salespeople cover when calling on prospects in person. The creative effort builds on the already established interest. Enclosures add to message reinforcement.

Printed promotion pieces designed as sales literature for salespeople to integrate into their selling activity can have some value as components of direct mail programs. For use in a direct mail campaign the copy message of available literature must relate to the direct mail objective. Sales promotion material most adaptable to direct mail objectives include basic application material, product feature/function material, case histories, and corporate image brochures.

10

CREATING THE MAIL ORDER PACKAGE

CREATIVE MAIL ORDER OBJECTIVES

More disciplined writing and design skills are required for direct marketing mail order than for other direct marketing objectives. There are two reasons: First, the entire range of selling functions must be performed by the writer and artist in order to make the sale; second, the measurement of the objective is finite. The job of the mail order copywriter is to move the prospect along the successive steps of the sale by having the mail order package perform the selling functions. These follow the basic formula described in Chapter 7—get attention, build interest, create desire, instill conviction, and provoke action.

These are the same selling functions performed by salespeople when they call on the prospect in person. To accommodate a smooth transition in the creative process of bringing the reader from the attention stage through the final action stage, mail order copy must have all the virtues of effective direct mail copy, but then it must go beyond those. This is done by repeating, persuasively and convincingly, the main selling points as much as a dozen times or more in the contents of the mailing package. The writer must envision all the steps the mailing will go through once it is delivered by the postal service—how it is received, handled and opened, read, acted on, and disposed. Methodical planning of the entire mail order package will ensure that it includes copy and graphics that address all the selling functions.

The mail order objective is to have the businessperson personally justify the purchase, get the necessary approvals to generate a purchase requisition as may be necessary, and spend the company's money, all without the help of a salesperson. It is assumed there is a match between the decision maker's needs and the product's capabilities.

Since mail order copy must tell the complete sales story in writing, and tell it convincingly and quickly, the writer needs extensive product and market research to back up the first packages created for test mailings. The main motivations of the business reader are studied in relation to the product, its features, and benefits. "What is in it for me and my company?" asks the prospect.

In most cases, prospects are more receptive to written information than they are to a salesperson making a sales call. Generally, businesspeople will not see a salesperson except by appointment. They do not want someone to "sell" them something; they want to "buy"—and this goes for mail order as well. Aware of this attitude, the business-to-business mail order writer and designer must concentrate on providing enough specific and precise information to make it easy for the prospect to make the buy decision—not concentrate on empty hard-sell copy. Businesspeople are comfortable dealing with product claims backed up with figures, specifications, and facts. The writer must be highly sensitive to the explicit interests of the targeted marketplace. Some marketers try to reach a market so broad that the creative appeal and copy approach cannot be pinpointed enough to convince the prospect to buy.

In some business-to-business companies, to make a mail order purchase, the recommender in the prospect organization may need two or three levels of approvals before filling out the order. For example, a production control manager may be a decision maker who reports to a plant manager, who in turn reports to a vice-president of operations. It all depends on company size, specific industries targeted, and particular positions targeted. The writer must ensure that the selling arguments the reader/recommender will need to influence the approvers are included in the mailing package. In large corporations where many may be involved in the purchasing decision process, the person who will have the most apparent need for and motivation to buy the product should be "sold" first, even though others in the corporation influence the sale. In the smaller company, often this person is the decision maker and approver, all in one.

Some products and services, especially those that are complex and technical, require highly elaborate mail packages to tell the story completely enough for the prospect to have the information needed to make a purchase decision. In this case, a two-step mail order campaign may be more cost effective than the usual one-step method. Rather than mail an expensive package to the complete market targeted, an inexpensive inquiry-generation mailing is created and mailed with the objective of prequalifying the prospects who will receive the hard-sell mail order package. Mail order telemarketing is also used as a second step or a third step to follow up the second mailing.

THE MAIL ORDER PACKAGE

A business-to-business mail order package, often called a solo mailing, promotes one product or a group of related products. The components have become fairly standard. Although there are variations, the basics consist of an outer envelope, a multipage letter, a brochure or other enclosures, an order card or form, and a business reply card or business reply envelope.

The Letter

The Headline or Lead Line

Of all the items in the mail order package, the letter almost invariably gets looked at first. And, as in sales-support direct-mail letters, if it is personalized, the first sentence is the spark that ignites the reader's interest. If nonpersonalized, the headline becomes the spark. The lead headline has about five seconds to heighten that interest into desire to read further. This is the most critical point.

Following are the four most effective ways the headline or lead line can reach out and capture specific readers who have an interest in the product:

1. *By having news value that ties in directly or indirectly with the product.* A good example is this headline from a business-to-business publisher soliciting subscriptions to its newsletter: "6 New Ways to Tackle the Feb. 17 Increase and Speed Delivery."
2. *By referring to the reader favorably.* This appeal to the businessperson's ego is done well in this lead line used as a first paragraph: "Quite frankly, the American Express Card is not for everyone. And not everyone who applies for Cardmembership is approved."
3. *By piquing the reader's curiosity in a way relevant to the offer and message that follow.* A subscription solicitation letter from *Business Week* is a fine example of this approach: "I know something very important about you." The lead sentence then refers to the reader favorably while it follows through on the headline claim: "Although I've never met you, I know you're on a career path that can lead to limitless rewards."
4. *By mentioning products favorably in relation to how the reader benefits from purchasing the product.* An example of this "here's-the-product-and-here's-how-it-can-help-you" type of headline appears in a newsletter publisher's nonpersonalized solicitation letter: "Announcing . . . an insider's report to help you increase direct-to-customer sales of your publications in multinational markets—whether they be in 2 or 100 countries."

When mailing to a list that has been finely targeted, the use of a unique headline request promotes reader involvement. A learning system company has used this technique to advantage in the following headline that immediately precedes "Dear fellow executive" in a nonpersonalized, four-page letter: "Would you please be kind enough to acknowledge receipt of this letter. Simply check the appropriate box on the enclosed blue reply form and return it at once in the postage-paid envelope provided. Thank you."

The First Paragraph

Once the headline has been created, the writer grabs the serious prospects up front by telling the gist of the story in the first paragraph. That way, the interest of the maximum number of potential buyers is secured from the very start. The copy must be exciting yet believable to make the readers want to read further. Readers will continue to read the next sentences only if they have expectations of learning more.

The writer cannot let the readers rest until they think positively about the offer. The main selling theme is driven home again and again by detailing the advantages and benefits for the prospect. Negative consequences that can be avoided by buying can be demonstrated. Product characteristics unique from those of competition and superior service can be shown. Product and company credibility is created in the mind of the reader by:

- Showing who uses the product
- Highlighting the company's reputation in the industry
- Providing testimonials
- Backing up benefit statements with facts and proof
- Offering a money-back guarantee

Above all, the complete sales story must be told, and any objections that can be anticipated should be answered. This is why virtually all mail order letters need four pages or more to tell the sales story.

The use of illustrations and photographs in business-to-business mail order letters should be considered cautiously. Since the businessperson perceives the business letter as a familiar, credible, and serious communication, the mail order letter should appear that way also. Even though graphics are used in all the elements in the rest of the package, the designer should minimize them on the mail order letter portion of the mailing package.

Enclosures

The opening and closing guns in business-to-business mail order packages are the selling letter and response vehicle respectively. Yet most products sold by mail need something in between—the printed enclosure. Often it is a restatement of many of the points made elsewhere in the package. It provides needed emphasis while it helps the sales story to be perceived as believable.

Some enclosures are created only as support materials that supplement and enhance points or issues raised in the main selling vehicle—the letter. Each element in the mail order package has its own purpose. While the letter sells the product, premium, or other offer, the brochure's job may be to describe the product. An additional flier may describe the premium even further. Although there should be persuasive "sell" in enclosures, with some products they should be more explanatory and detailed. In any event, enclosures should never be simply a rework of the letter.

This material is usually loaded with illustrations that bring the product to life and includes product functions and feature benefits not appropriate in the sales letter. Regardless of whether the broadside, brochure, circular, or other enclosure is big or small, or printed in one, two, or four colors, it has a massive job to do. In most cases it performs all the steps of the sale visually as well as in the copy.

Supporting enclosures often take the form of testimonials printed on the endorser's letterhead or they can be separate printed fliers filled with photographs and third-party endorsements to lend credibility to the sales proposal. An article reprint from the trade press, substantiating why the purchase of a specific product is a wise decision, can carry the prestige of the publication.

Validating Enclosures

Lift letters, notes, and other validating enclosures, although worth mentioning, have not proved very effective nor are they used often in business-to-business mail order. However, when they are used, copy is very brief. They are printed on odd-size slips of colored paper and are signed by someone of higher authority than the person signing the regular letter. The small memo size of the lift letter, usually folded, stands out, making it quick and easy to spot and read. This letter or note gives additional reasons why the reader should act favorably on the offer. These enclosures are meant to add to the package one more convincing selling argument.

Action Response Vehicle

Action response copy usually appears at the end of each component in the mail order package directing the reader to the response card or form. The mail order marketer asks for the order confidently and tactfully only when all decision maker's and influencer's anticipated doubts and questions have been adequately covered in the mailing.

The action response vehicle is designed and written so it can virtually stand alone as a mailing piece. It restates the offer and outlines the main benefits while succinctly convincing the prospect of the offer's credibility. There is great emphasis placed on the guarantee, which is usually close to the reader's signature line or final reader commitment check-box. The response form is designed to appear urgent and valuable.

The experienced creative planner accommodates many of these key elements in the action response vehicle:

- Name and address label preaffixed
- Sufficient space to print or type the name of the respondent, title, company name, address, and telephone number
- Prominent display of toll-free number
- Offer or offers spelled out in detail
- Photo of product
- Premium for purchasing
- Premium for placing order early
- Statement of money-back guarantee
- Complete costs, including shipping and handling
- Payment options, cash with order, company purchase order number, "Bill me," mention of acceptance of bank cards and space for the bank card number
- Business reply envelope

Asking customers to expose their bank card numbers on business reply cards is a practice known to decrease response. Yet, apparently it is cost effective for some mail order marketers who continue to request bank card numbers on business reply cards rather than on order forms in business reply envelopes.

Most business-to-business mail order marketers use prepaid business reply cards or envelopes.

Outgoing Envelopes

The envelope is definitely not an afterthought when planning the mail order package. The creative decision here obviously affects the number of packages that get opened. A wrong decision negates an otherwise brilliant creative effort inside. Plain envelopes without teaser copy that appear to the businessperson to mean *business* have the edge. It is a normal reaction. But there are many exceptions. Some mail order offers are so powerful that a mention of them on the envelope will actually get more openings. A good rule to follow in business-to-business mail order is that plain envelopes get more openings than envelopes with poor copy or envelopes heralding average offers.

Most business-to-business direct marketers do not use the same envelope devices that are successful for many consumer direct marketers, such as outsized envelopes, multiple windows, dramatic graphics, and copy. They either do not use copy or graphics or minimize them on the face of the envelope. The number 10 and the 9½-by-4-inch envelopes are the most commonly used for mail order selling of low-priced products and services such as books, training materials, self-help programs, newsletters, and magazine subscriptions.

High-priced or more complex offers usually require more elaborate mail order direct mail materials that go best in 6-by-9-inch and 9-by-12-inch envelopes. Larger envelopes very often contain offers unique enough to justify creative approaches. If the 9-by-12-inch envelope contents are not in themselves substantial enough to prevent bending and wrinkling in the mail, then envelope stiffening should be used.

Most mail order marketers test various envelopes to determine what works best in the specific market targeted. Some marketers are succeeding using envelopes without copy, some with the corner card on the back flap, some with printing, using only the logo as a corner card, and others with no printing whatsoever.

The appeal of the understated envelope that does not show a return address on the face is curiosity. However, it more often than not does about as well in business-to-business mail order as the plain corner card envelope. Brown kraft number 10 envelopes that resemble important government materials get high interest especially when the corner card is identified with a generic name such as "Verification Division" or the name of a person rather than a company. But design strategy must stop short of deliberately misleading the reader, which would also create a negative reaction from prospects toward future offers.

Those business-to-business mail order marketers who have unique, new, and especially timely products usually use product illustrations or photos on the envelope to maximum advantage. Figure 10-1 is an example of a powerful product offer to its market in a mailing from Newstrack Inc. that uses over 50 percent of the face of the envelope to illustrate a series of audio cassettes. It then highlights the contents of the cassettes by listing some of the top names in advertising. The powerful envelope graphic capitalizes on the main benefit of the offer, which is to make the reader's ad programs more effective. It leads the reader to the premium inside the package, a free wall poster, and a promise of information in the envelope, aside from the order form.

Most business products sold through the mail do not lend themselves to this kind of highly specific appeal. In this particular case, the promise of an exciting personal benefit in the audio area is built into the product. The illustration on the envelope plays to the more emotional self-help motives of the reader.

A copywriter can arouse the reader by stirring the emotions. But this is difficult to do with most industrial products or services. If the marketer uses a highly graphic envelope to inspire and it misses the mark it will be relegated to a pile of printed material to be reviewed later. Perhaps.

Here is a listing of teaser copy taken from mail order envelopes. The first three are a deterrent to getting envelopes opened in the business-to-business market-place. The last three have promise.

1. "Save on the most important tool for the worldwide television, cable and related industries."
2. "With Better Data/You'll/make better decisions. Quick! Rip this open!" . . . And see our special discount offer.
3. "Don't let your stories die young."
4. "Why are some executives more successful than others? Is *Working Smarter* the answer?"
5. "The best business books of 1985–86. How many have you read? Now you can read them all—in just 15 minutes each! How? See inside."
6. "The 7 biggest mistakes personal computer marketers are making right now. These deadly strategic errors have already generated multimillion dollar losses for scores of companies. How many are *you* committing? Check your score inside and discover an easy way to avoid *all* of them."

CREATIVE CONSIDERATIONS FOR MAIL ORDER CATALOGS

There is a big difference between writing promotional copy for the standard business-to-business product catalog used by the salesperson when calling on the prospect and the mail order sales catalog that attempts to sell products without the aid of salespeople. Writers of the former normally have difficulty in adapting their writing skills to mail order selling because it requires a different set of techniques. The salesperson's catalog that simply describes and illustrates the product line just won't pull its weight as a mail order vehicle when mailed to prospects.

The mail order catalog, along with a telephone sales service, has been an effective channel of selling for a long time for many business-to-business companies that sell staple products, equipment, and parts in common use in specific industries. These catalogs provide a delineation of product features, black and white pho-tographs, prices, and order blanks. And they are still working for some of the

Figure 10-1. Powerful offer from Newstrack Inc.

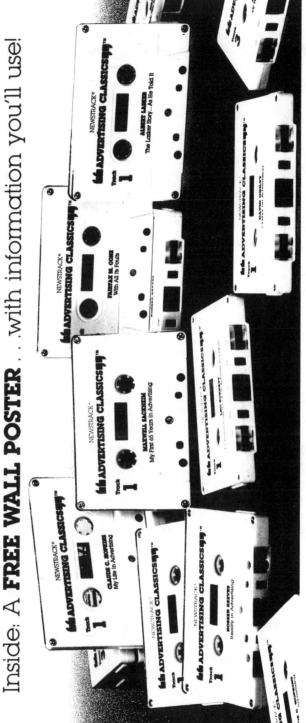

ROSSER REEVES, MAXWELL SACKHEIM, ALVIN EICOFF, CLAUDE C. HOPKINS, LEO BURNETT, FAIRFAX CONE, ALBERT LASKER and **DAVID OGILVY** will make your advertising and marketing more effective. Listen to their words on audiocassettes in your car, wherever you go.

Inside: A **FREE WALL POSTER** . . .with information you'll use!

Bulk Rate
U.S. Postage
PAID
Newstrack, Inc.
Englewood, CO

Source: Courtesy of Davison Associates Inc., Denver.

well-known old-line companies who either have monopolies or safe niches. But in the competitive marketplace the mail order catalog requires sophisticated creative selling techniques such as those used by Inmac, Globe, Drawing Board, Moore, and IBM.

Copy

Many business-to-business catalog copywriters are taking a page from consumer catalogs. Copy is more reader-benefit oriented. Even though the mail-order copywriter must perform the complete selling job, it has been made easier for mail order marketers because the process of market segmentation has permitted them to find target markets, which allows the writer to pinpoint the audience. By knowing more buyer characteristics, the writer can better understand the buyer's rationale for purchasing the product. Therefore, catalog copy can talk directly to the needs and interests of a specific audience and speak its language. Catalog readers look for good reasons to buy from one catalog marketer rather than another. The writer must provide those reasons with persuasive copy that actually sells, and not just describes, the products in the catalog.

The more successful catalogs make it easy for readers to understand what each product will do for them. While any nonproduct copy adds to catalog overhead, hard-sell editorial copy can have a payoff, as long as it does not come off as editorial puffery.

Reader benefits always come first followed by features and functions for each product. Headlines are used to tell the benefits of one product or a group of related products on a whole page or spread. Readership studies show the main headline is viewed first along with the main illustration that supports the headline. The reader then looks at the specific product picture, price, and text, in that order.

Copy style should match the image of the company. If the company has dramatic prices, copy as well as all other elements—such as graphics, and paper stock in the catalog—should reflect that image. The writer should convince the reader that doing business with that catalog marketer is fast, easy, and risk-free. Some do this by eliminating all footnotes and "continued on page . . ." instructions. Also, the 800 number should be repeated many times throughout the catalog. Repeating the guarantee several places in the catalog, as well as on the order form, helps build credibility. Keeping the shipping chart simple, or eliminating it altogether, and offering special inducements to buy make it easy to order.

Reader involvement techniques are being used with success by many catalog marketers. Figure 10-2 is an example of an aggressive promotion by Inmac, a high-volume business-to-business catalog marketer, to build prospect and customer interest and orders with a unique " 'big 10' birthday game."

Graphics

Experienced business-to-business catalogers maximize the value of prime readership pages with high-volume, high-profit items. These include the front cover, the

Figure 10-2. Inmac, a top mail order marketer, builds customer participation and loyalty with involvement techniques.

Source: Courtesy of Inmac Corp., Santa Clara, CA.

inside front cover, the first right-hand page facing the inside cover, the back and front of the back cover, the page facing the order form, and the centerfold.

More and more business-to-business catalogers have learned to take advantage of the attention-getting value of photography and graphics. Most often photographs are preferable to art work since they leave no doubt in the reader's mind as to what the product looks like. However, artwork should be used when the marketer's product line has many similar items or when it is difficult to photograph the products in ways that present them in their best image. Using artwork and photographs in combination is a practical solution for some catalog offerings. Also, type should be large enough for easy reading—eight point, at least. Reverse type should be avoided.

The Inmac catalog design is also a good example of a graphic concept applied to the entire catalog. Figure 10-3 shows how individual photographs of products are grouped by customer use, how layout is varied to fit the product, and how price and other specifications are kept in designated areas of product layout.

RESPONSE CARD DECKS

Except for mail order sales of low-priced items, business-to-business marketers use response card decks mostly for inquiry generation as the first step in a two-part mail order campaign.

In just about all direct mail situations, the creative concept determines the copy approach and the format. But in response decks, the 3½-by-5½-inch business reply card format is a limiting factor for the copywriter. This places a heavy work load on the headline and graphic that must clearly state the offer in no uncertain terms. The writer must also keep in mind the fact that busy business readers will not spend much time fanning through an average 50-card deck—60 seconds perhaps.

Since the great bulk of cards are designed horizontally the business reader reviews the deck that way. A card with a vertical layout must be unique to get attention. Response deck cards must aim for a specific reader need with split-second accuracy since they must attract potential prospects quickly during the 60-second deck review. The writer's concern is to first have the reader identify the product category and then the product being promoted.

Copy

Response deck cards have a better chance of succeeding when they conform to these four essentials:

1. *Descriptive/benefit headline.* The headline that identifies the product or product category and presents a reader benefit in a few words is best, especially if it implies new. A good example is "Self-Stick Notes Now in Cubes." The role of a subhead is to expand on the headline description and benefit with a key offer, dramatic price, free sample, or free booklet.
   Some marketers simply use the headline and graphic to spell out the

Figure 10-3. Leading edge business-to-business catalog graphics concept.

Cleaning Products

Save $16 with a Master Clean Kit!

Our Master Kit combines the best of our other cleaning kits into one low-cost package—a $55 value for just $39.

It has *everything* you need to clean your tape and floppy drives, printer and CRT.

Here's what you get:

- Head cleaning disk to prevent oxide buildup. Good for 20 weekly cleanings.
- Tape and floppy drive cleaning solution.
- 50 lint-free cleaning wipes.
- 10 dual-ended cleaning wands.
- CRT screen cleaning fluid. Antistatic ingredient prevents dust build-up.
- CRT screen wipes for lint-free cleaning.
- Type-font brush to remove ink.
- Antistatic spray to protect equipment and data from electrical charges.

Order this kit and save $10 on *your* mini and micro's cleaning costs.

A $55 value for only $39, our Clean Cycle Master Kit helps keep your mini or microsystem in tip-top shape.

Clean Cycle™ Master Kit for systems with 8" flexible disk drives.

Price each	Qty 1	2-5	6-10
No. 7190	**$39.95**	**$35.95**	**$34.95**

Clean Cycle™ Master Kit for systems with 5¼" flexible disk drives.

Price each	Qty 1	2-5	6-10
No. 7191	**$39.95**	**$35.95**	**$34.95**

Cleaning kit keeps your mag tape heads working perfectly!

Read/write errors are often caused by something as simple as a dirty tape drive. But you can make sure your drive works properly by keeping your tape heads, guides and capstans clean with our Clean Cycle Kit.

Bend the Kit's dual-ended wands to remove dirt from those hard-to-reach areas.

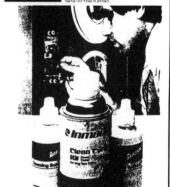

Make sure your tape heads read and write properly—keep them clean with the solution, power duster, wands and wipes in our Clean Cycle Kit.

The *cleaning solution* removes even microscopic oil, smoke particles, oxide debris, dust and dirt. It dries in seconds without leaving a residue.

The *cleaning wands* are dual-ended ... one end can be used as a scrubber and the other as a buffer.

And the lint-free *wipes* are so soft, you'll never have to worry about scratching delicate equipment.

Call us and your Clean Cycle Kit will be on its way to you this afternoon.

Clean Cycle Kit. For all instrumentation and computer magnetic tape systems. Includes two 4 oz. bottles of cleaning solution, 100 lint-free cloths, 30 dual-ended wands, one 12 oz. can of power duster and instructions. Wt. 3 lbs.

Price each	Qty 1	2-5	6-10
No. 7150	**$29.95**	**$26.95**	**$25.55**

Screen cleaning kit banishes CRT smudges!

Our Clean Cycle™ Screen Cleaning Kit quickly and safely eliminates smudges and dust from your CRT screen.

Just apply the no-streak cleaning solution to your screen, then wipe away grime with our lint-free cloths.

Add a kit to your next order and see what a difference a clean screen makes.

Clean Cycle Kit for CRT Screens. Two 4-oz. bottles of cleaning solution, 50 wipes.

No. 7199

Qty 1	2-5
$12.95	**$11.95**

End CRT grime with our no-streak, OSHA-approved solution and lint-free wipes.

Helpful Hints

Carelessness could cost you weeks of work.

Prevent disasters! Avoid these common floppy disk dangers.

Good habits pay-off! Simply taking basic precautions in caring for disks could save you megabytes of unexpected, frustrating and costly data loss.

- **Don't bend or fold:** creases can cause permanent disfiguration.
- **Don't expose to strong sunlight** or heat.
- **Don't expose to magnetic fields.** Telephones, radios, and even paperclip holders can cause minor or major data erasures.
- **Don't put pressure on the disk.** Writing on a label with a ballpoint pen, or even the weight of an empty soda can, might cripple disk performance.
- **Always protect your disks by storing them properly** in vinyl envelopes, binders, library cases, or specially designed cabinets. Vertical storage is recommended.

Source: Courtesy of Inmac Corp., Santa Clara, CA.

product category or product in words and pictures, such as "Modular Displays," "Ad Reprint Frames," "1000 4-Color Presentation Folders," and "80 Frosted Write-on Slides." Better results are possible, however, when the writer can also squeeze a prospect benefit into the headline without losing the at-a-glance reader, with headlines such as "The Can't-Jam Printer Stand," "Maxell Quality at Fuji Prices," and "Trade Commodities With a Professional Before Investing a Dime."

2. *Headline and graphic in concert.* A graphic, unless tied directly to a headline, can confuse the reader. A photograph or illustration that enhances the pertinent interest-getting aspect of the headline should be placed in close proximity or integrated into the headline. The headline and graphic in combination should be strong enough to make the offer immediately understandable to the reader.

3. *Easy to respond.* The toll-free 800 number tells the reader that the marketer is interested in making response trouble-free. A coupon with a large enough space to write on is also a help. Some coupons are so small they are an insult to the reader. Payment options simplify ordering for buyers. Prepaying the postage gets more cards back.

4. *Special reason to respond.* Many products are undifferentiated and readers need reasons why they should respond to one individual marketer rather than another.

Focusing the headline and graphic only on potential customers from the card deck audience can get high readership among the targeted group because they speak directly to that segment, as in this example: "Heath/Zenith Users—Get the Information You Need from the Magazine Exclusively for Your System!" The narrower and more exclusive the segment addressed, the more effective the creative effort can be. But the size of the targeted segment must be large enough to be cost effective.

Cards without graphics need a powerful bold headline to compete with graphics on other cards. And in any response deck there is no room for teaser copy, clever copy, or copy that provokes curiosity in the headline. Response deck copy can consist of listings of product features or reader benefits in telegraphic style, it can be written in the narrative style, or it can be a combination. Of course, only the most relevant facts are mentioned. With scant space, copy has to be succinct and tight, but there can be more "sell" in copy that speaks in the narrative. Generally, 100 words or less should suffice along with a professional illustration and design.

Graphics

The fact that prospects receive from 25 to 100 response deck cards, plus perhaps a mini-catalog or two, in a polybag containing many offers from many companies severely limits the advantage of direct mail's personal aspect. In some respects a card competes for the reader's attention much like a space ad in a trade publication.

Because of limited space, some copy and even the coupon occasionally are squeezed onto the address side of the card. Cards are usually on white stock and printed by the publisher from the advertiser's camera-ready copy. The best cards provide enough writing space to fill in name, address, and phone number legibly. Some marketers ask the prospects to tape their business cards to the business reply card before mailing.

The illustration on a card should show what the prospect will get. If a photograph will not reproduce well enough in a typical card deck print-run, when reduced, a graphic illustration can be used or the marketer can print the cards and send them to the deck publisher.

The Inquiry-Generation Response Card

Mail order products represented by response card decks seeking inquiries only are usually higher priced or involve a more complex purchase that requires a sales call follow-up by telephone or another mailing with more elaborate explanatory selling materials.

When the objective is to get inquiries as a first step in a two-step mail order effort, the response card uses headline and graphic strategy similar to the one-step mail order card. But it differs because the message emphasis is on the offer and the benefit of the offer rather than on the product as such. Figure 10-4 shows good examples of cards with headlines that sell the offer.

The Mail Order Response Card

The headline and graphics in the mail order response card seek out the interested prospects only. Words and card space are not wasted on those not in the market for the product. A benefit headline that also identifies the product has the best chance of reaching potential buyers. The marketer's product may be so generally recognized in the market reached by the response deck that a simple main headline description of the product category with supporting graphics lets the reader know immediately what the marketer is selling.

A subhead should state the fact that the product offer is indeed a good buy. It often does this by mentioning a key user benefit. The copy goes on to state the reason the prospect should buy from that particular marketer. Over 50 percent of the cards in many decks ask for an order. The great bulk of these mail order response cards are from publishers.

SUMMARY

The creative objective for mail order direct mail is to cover the entire range of selling functions. Copy and graphics pinpoint the proper decision maker.

A typical business-to-business mail order package consists of an outer envelope, a multipage letter that details the complete sales story, one or more brochures or other illustrated enclosures that enhance the points raised in the letter, and an order form designed to appear urgent and valuable.

Mail order marketers test the outgoing envelope to determine what works best in a specific market. When copy is used on envelopes it should not read like

Figure 10-4. Response deck cards that seek inquiries stress offer benefit.

Source: Quill card used by permission of Quill Corporation; Datapro card used by permission of Datapro.

advertising. Some products lend themselves to a two-step mail order marketing method—an inquiry-generation first mailing followed by a more elaborate mail order package and telemarketing to inquirers.

The mail order catalog writer groups photographs and illustrations of related products under headlines and subheads, spelling out reader benefits along with explanatory copy. Graphics should present the best image of the product.

The creative effort on a response card deck is limited by its standard card format. Response card decks have a better chance of success when they conform to these four essentials: a descriptive/benefit headline, a graphic in concert with the headline, an ease of reader response, and a special reason to respond.

11

TELEMARKETING AND OTHER
DIRECT MARKETING MEDIA

In the near future only those products that are very technical or complex, or that have a large profit built into their already high price, will warrant personal selling methods. The business-to-business marketer who once sold only through a sales force today has other options—among them, telemarketing, print, and electronic media. The bottom line is based on economic necessity. Marketers will use whatever media is most cost effective for their sales objectives.

It has now become affordable for even the smallest marketer to take advantage of the computer's efficiencies for direct marketing applications. The integration of telemarketing and other electronic media into sales and marketing plans plus the higher and higher costs of face-to-face selling are two key forces rapidly changing the way business-to-business firms market their products.

Even though applications for telemarketing are indicated throughout the various sections of this book, additional discussion of this fast-growing direct marketing tool can be helpful. In fact, telemarketing has evolved into a direct marketing specialty profession. Its interaction with other direct response media, especially direct mail, mandates that the business-to-business marketer develop an appreciation of its characteristics, its functions for inbound and outbound calls, and how other marketers perceive its value.

GROWTH OF TELEMARKETING

Business-to-business telemarketing got its real start in the early 1970s when sales call costs began their rapid rise. In 1980, sales attributable to both business-to-business and consumer use of telemarketing were about $3 billion. In 1987, according to business-to-business telemarketing consultant Eugene Kordahl, that figure was $142.2 billion with anticipated growth of 15 percent to 25 percent per year through the decade. Kordahl says, "Telemarketing is the planned use of the telephone in conjunction with traditional marketing methods and techniques."

The most dramatic growth area in the telemarketing industry is business-to-business, which in 1987 had 81 percent of total telemarketing activity. Other figures are equally revealing. The value of the average business-to-business telemarketing sale has jumped from $230 in 1980 to $1,500 in 1986, and the number of telemarketing service bureaus (in existence for at least two years) went from 15 to 78 in the same period. Inbound telemarketing in business-to-business may account for 14 percent of the overall sales of goods and services in 1987. Of the 78 telemarketing service bureaus referred to, 11 are inbound only; the rest are for both inbound and outbound operations.

HOW BUSINESSES APPROACH TELEMARKETING

Statistics on the numbers of telephone programs in business-to-business companies are only part of the story. There is a marked difference in a casual use of the telephone and the use of sophisticated telemarketing procedures. This fact was highlighted in a 1983 study of telemarketing usage by 4,000 business product manufacturers.

The study—conducted jointly by Bob Donath, editor, *Business Marketing* and Murray Roman, president of Communication Corporation Inc., New York—employed both a mail questionnaire and telephone interviews. Results indicated that two out of three companies use the telephone for sales support lead generation or as a selling channel. However, only about 20 percent of them use the key telemarketing control and accountability procedures—recordkeeping, training, comparison of results, monitoring, scripting—in a professional way. About half of the survey respondents used at least one of the five control procedures. Here is how they scored:

■ Seventy-nine percent of those using at least one control keep records.
■ Sixty-one percent train telephone personnel.
■ Thirty-six percent compare results to objectives.
■ Twenty-nine percent monitor calls.
■ Twenty-six percent use pretested scripts.

Analysis of results of this business-to-business survey indicated that:

■ Professional telemarketers tend to have fewer years' experience using the telephone than other marketers.
■ Older marketing people are less sophisticated in the use of newer telemarketing techniques and procedures.
■ Most companies using the telephone support fewer than ten products.
■ About 70 percent of business-to-business marketers who use the telephone

use it for both inbound and outbound calls. Twenty-eight percent claimed to have outbound programs only.
- Eighty-eight percent receive orders by telephone including the routine customer reorders.

USES OF TELEMARKETING

The business-to-business direct marketer uses the telephone in two distinct ways. One is to handle inbound orders and service calls that emanate from the customer or the prospect. The other is mainly for marketing products and services.

Inbound Telemarketing

Increased use by business-to-business marketers of the toll-free 800 number on advertisements, sales literature, direct mail, trade show materials, customer newsletters, house organs, annual reports, and fulfillment packages has helped to change business buyers' methods of ordering. Over 50 percent of business-to-business responses are coming in on the telephone when there is a choice between it and business reply mail, even though a small minority claim it does not help them to use the 800 number. Increased use of this service for sales in addition to customer service needs is paying off for those marketers who have the products and markets where telephone ordering has been at least somewhat of an accepted practice in the past.

According to John Wyman, an AT&T vice-president, total response to a direct marketing program can be 20 percent greater if an 800 number is included in addition to a business reply card. He has found that the sale closure rate is four times greater for those who inquire by telephone than those who do so by direct mail. Also, each incoming call is an opportunity for the telemarketer not only to receive and solidify an order but also to:

- Upgrade incoming orders, thank the customer for the order, and ask if the customer wants to purchase something else
- Sell during service calls
- Further qualify inquiries before passing them on to salespeople
- Get more information for the data base
- Immediately handle problems that arise

Some marketers are putting 800 numbers in product publicity releases as a service to the reader. Inquiries that result can open the door for the inbound telephone representative to help move the inquiry along the path to a sale or to pass it on to an outbound caller whose personality, experience, and training is better suited for marketing and selling.

Outbound Telemarketing

Outbound telemarketing programs for business-to-business marketers also have multiple objectives, some similar to inbound objectives. Outbound telemarketing is used as a selling channel. It is used to qualify inquiries generated by other media, direct mail, trade shows, seminar attendees, reader service cards, and other selected sources. And it tracks these through to the sale or no-sale decision.

These inquiries can provide opportunities for telephone sales for some marketers, especially in the direct selling of low-end products to accounts where face-to-face sales calls would be unprofitable. Among customers who have recently purchased, buying activity can be increased through cross-selling, upgrading the sale, or selling other products in the line.

Also, structured outbound telemarketing programs develop information for the data base, determine which inquiry sources are best, verify accuracy of names and addresses for special mailings, help make sure leads to the field are followed up, and research the effectiveness of publication advertising messages.

Trained telesales communicators know how to gain new accounts from among highly segmented prequalified targets and they know how to sell customers who have not purchased recently. These outbound communicators are experienced in the use of telephone interview techniques and can perform all the steps of the sale. They know how to test an offer, approach, or list, and get feedback quickly. They know how to follow up a scheduled mailing. They can take customer complaints from inbound communicators and attempt to turn them into sales. Also, they know how to promote customer loyalty among key accounts, and in so doing, move them along the selling process.

A good outbound telephone communicator can make 30 to 40 completed calls a day on the telephone. This amounts to 7,200 to 9,600 decision makers in 240 working days. A communicator can dial 1.8 people and get one call through to a decision maker, reaching 5.2 decision makers in an hour. Incoming calls are handled at a rate of 7.8 per hour because they are easier to handle and usually do not require the telemarketing communicator to seek a response.

It is not cost effective to use the telephone to prospect for sales or inquiries among cold lists of suspects. But it can be highly profitable—and is, for many business-to-business marketers—to use telemarketing techniques to convert pre-selected groups of prospects into customers or qualified leads for salespeople to follow up. These select groups are characterized by their degree of affinity with the marketer's company and products. They are those market universe segments most likely to respond—current and past customers, prospects who have inquired over the past two years, and prospects who match the profile of the marketer's best customers.

Telemarketing goes hand-in-hand with direct mail inquiry-generation programs. This is its greatest strength for business-to-business marketers. Telemarketing is often used before and after direct mail is scheduled to be sent to highly selected segments of customer and prospect marketplaces. Identifying qualified leads for the salespeople can be a profitable function for telemarketing only if the list called is predisposed toward the proposition in some way.

A high-quality lead secured through telemarketing for a salesperson's follow-through should include not only a company name, address, and telephone number but also information on the key decision makers, budget size, product application, competition involved, purchasing behavior, and other details that can be gathered best from a two-way communication.

A continuingly expanding need for personal contact in the business-to-business arena between marketers and their customers and prospects fuels the need for experienced telecommunicators. The lack of qualified people in this area has led to the growth of computer telemarketing procedures that increase the communicator's productivity. Barry Wagar, sales vice-president of AT&T, stated in *Direct Marketing*, July 1986, that computer-assisted telemarketing can increase telemarketing productivity by 20 to 50 percent and is growing even though only 9 percent of the 85,000 organizations using telemarketing are now automated. In fact, 39 percent are still fully manual.

Creative Considerations for Telemarketing: Scripts

Telemarketing script writing is an entirely different technique from writing for direct mail. Scripting for telemarketing inbound and outbound calls is a necessity, since most telephone communicators are not seasoned salespeople with personal sales experience who also happen to have telephone selling aptitudes. Professional telephone communicators who can work effectively without a script are in short supply. Scripting has many advantages: Problems of telephone communicator personnel turnover are minimized, newer personnel are trained quicker, and the marketer is assured that all calls are handled uniformly, rather than with relatively undisciplined approaches.

Standardized scripting is used at two levels. The most common is the simplest and consists of pages in a binder or folder arranged for convenient use by the telephone communicator. Those questions, answers, and comments usually involved in each telemarketing program are reduced to script form, making it easy for the communicator to get the key points across and, most important, to know what to say next. Even though the business-to-business marketer's field salespeople have always used the telephone when performing their selling functions, the well-designed telemarketing script, written for the specific use of the salespeople, has opened up new approaches for them, especially in lead building and lead qualification.

A second level of standardized scripting employs, when volume permits, a more sophisticated system that programs the script into a computer, so the appropriate sections of the telephone communicator's dialogue and responses can be accessed through a desktop CRT by the communicator.

To be effective the script writer must learn basic selling and listening skills to understand the strengths and weaknesses of the communicator/prospect interaction. The well-written script projects a positive self-assured salesperson/communicator, one who is an enthusiastic conversationalist.

The script writer anticipates beforehand the main objections a prospect may have in response to comments made by the communicator. For most standard telemarketing applications, outbound calls are made to possible prospects to prequalify them for personal sales calls. The script then moves the communicator along the steps leading to prospect qualification.

The script begins with an introduction of the communicator, then quickly helps disqualify the obvious nonprospects to prevent expensive time from being spent with the wrong people. The writer develops the reason for the call and indicates the proposition and its importance to the prospect, while not yet focusing on selling the product.

As the script moves forward, it attempts to establish a mutual positive feeling between communicator and prospect. Then to build interest, the advantages of the proposition are stated. Prospect involvement is encouraged by the communicator who asks questions about what already has been discussed. This also gets a fix on the prospect's level of understanding. The script then spells out product benefits and the advantages of the offer in detail. At a specific point an offer is made. Here is where answers to objections are inserted into the script. There should be answers prepared for specific objections to avoid confusion by the telephone communicator. Additional questions by the communicator at this stage attempt to provoke a specific commitment, such as setting up an appointment for a personal sales call, or attending the marketer's sales seminar on a specified date. Last, the communicator reconfirms the prospect's commitment.

The essential difference in script writing for mail order telephone selling and telemarketing for lead qualification is the emphasis in the script given to the selling functions: in building interest, creating desire, instilling conviction, and impelling action. Once a script is developed it is tested on several calls and revised to include any new objections that may surface before using it as a final script for all communicators.

Unlike other types of written communication, telemarketing scriptwriting is a specialty in itself. Experienced professionals in telemarketing organizations teach this script copywriting technique. Copywriters who write direct mail packages are often adept at writing script outlines of standard approaches for experienced telecommunicators to use as guidelines. These outlines usually follow the same theme and approach used in the mail program.

CONSIDERATIONS FOR CHOOSING PRINT PUBLICATIONS

Some business-to-business marketers who cannot locate lists large enough for prospecting may find print advertising a viable alternative because it can reach many people. Direct response space advertising can cost ten times less than direct mail per exposure. However, historically, direct response space has been productive for only a limited range of business-to-business products and offers. For selling new products, for developing markets, and for generating inquiries as a first step in a two-step mail order effort, publication response advertising can be cost effective.

When looking for the right business magazines for a direct response offer, the seasoned business-to-business marketer first reaches for publications that are complementary to the product. The editorial content should draw the kind of readers who would be interested in the products generally advertised in that publication. This affinity should be pronounced. On close examination, the editorial environment usually reveals whether the magazine audience will be right for the product or offer.

Demographics and psychographics have to match as nearly as the direct response planner can tell from a study of past issues of the magazine, the ABC statement, and special audience surveys. One additional factor of importance to direct response marketers is mail responsiveness. The marketer should examine a publication's reader response history. Also, magazines that are paid for by subscribers have some measure of mail responsiveness.

Marketers who place their direct response ads in vertical trade publications usually do not have this measure since most vertical publications have nonpaying controlled circulation. Reader service cards found in these publications offer the reader an additional opportunity to get more information. Inquiries from these cards when received by the publisher are then sent to the appropriate advertiser for fulfillment or other action.

Types of Publications

Business magazines can be separated into two groups based on market coverage. The vertical category is directed to a single industry, vocation, or line of business, attempting to reach many decision makers in the management hierarchy of each firm. This group falls into the category of trade publications such as *American Banker, The Wholesaler,* and *Supermarket News. Consulting Engineer* and *Family Practice News* are similar publications for professionals.

A second group is directed to a specific function or activity within many different industries, thus the designation, horizontal publication. For example, *Inc.* is edited for entrepreneurs and *Purchasing Magazine* is edited for purchasing agents regardless of their industry. General business publications such as *Business Week* and *Forbes* also fall into the horizontal category.

Marketers unfamiliar with publications available for their particular needs can choose from among 3,200 listed and described in the Standard Rate & Data *Business Publications Service* directory. It provides the marketer with vital information about the publication and its editorial content. Rates, discounts, split-runs, ad dimensions, personnel, mechanical requirements, bleed specifications, printing specifications, and issue and closing dates are all listed, making it easy for the marketer to make comparisons between the various possibilities. Part III of the directory, *Direct Response Advertising Media,* lists direct response advertising media arranged by market classification and alphabetical sequence within classifications.

Creative Considerations for Print

The pages that are considered prime for advertising are the front inside right-hand page, cover, and inside back cover. Also, right-hand pages are considered better than left ones. Premium positions may command an additional 15 percent. If the direct marketer wants a response ad to appear at the top of a right-hand page next to editorial material, along one vertical side, the cost may increase 30 percent.

Early placement of ads helps prevent being placed in the back of the book (not the special direct response section). Since four-color ads are very expensive no matter what size, black and white ads are more cost effective for the average business-to-business direct marketer. These also have an advantage in that they can be placed anywhere.

Many publications have a special section, usually in the back, for small ad placement by direct marketing advertisers. Some publishers offer regular volume discounts, but the most highly reduced rates come from space that remains unsold or from canceled orders close to publication date. These remnant buy discounts can be sizable. However, remnant space is like bargain merchandise—it is not always there when it's needed. Advance scheduling is impossible. For remnant buys to work for the business-to-business direct marketer, the media buyer must be given complete authority to accept or reject a media opportunity on the spot as it becomes available.

This kind of discount can be very inviting to the marketer who is testing a marketplace or a product. But remnant buys aren't always best buys because placement may not always be where there will be high readership. Some publications have regional editions that can be a better buy, especially for testing. There is less risk with these even though they cost more per thousand readers reached. An ad in a regional allows the marketer to analyze results before making the roll-out.

Similar to any general advertising, direct response print ads should show the marketer's company in its best light and reflect its marketing philosophy. But that is where the similarity ends. Because a direct response mail order ad must pay its own way, it must do the complete selling job. However, a large ad isn't necessarily the most productive in terms of reaching an objective. Mail order marketers often test different sizes, always measuring the response rate against the cost of the ad. Once the most effective size has been determined, that size should be used as the control.

Testing Procedures

The advantages of direct mail testing apply equally to print ads. Print ad response should be monitored and analyzed just as seriously as any other medium used for direct marketing. In addition to testing for the most responsive publications for placement of ads, marketers often test different offers, approaches, and products.

A service offered by some publications appeals especially to the direct marketer who has a need to test publication ads. It is called the split-run and is constructed to produce valid results when tests of two or more response ads are printed in alternate copies of a given press run. These are equally divided runs in which the advertiser can place different ads. By comparing responses the marketer can assess the relative strengths of the different ads in a given issue of the publication. SRDS lists those publications that offer split-run testing. A marketer needs a very large marketplace to make use of A-B split runs. They are usually higher-circulation horizontals rather than limited-circulation verticals.

RIDE-ALONGS OR OUTSERTS

In late 1968, a new medium appeared on the scene called the ride-along. This took the form of a full-size catalog or other advertising piece included as a separate insert along with a magazine, both wrapped together in plastic wrap. A new postal regulation, enacted to facilitate the handling of publications through the mail, allowed *Inc.* magazine in November 1986 (which was testing a new market) to include a catalog for Global Computer Supplies in a polybag. Both were sent to a cross-section of *Inc.* and *Global* subscribers at their business addresses.

The postal regulation allowed third-class inserts to go at the second-class rate, as long as they both were included in the polybag. Not only did this save dollars on lists and lettershop services and mailing costs for the direct marketer, but second-class mail could be delivered faster. Effective December 1988 a new ruling by the postal authorities eliminates independent published material as ride-alongs. Supplements directly relating to the main publication, however, may still be enclosed.

ELECTRONIC MEDIA

Broadcast, TV, and Cable

Electronic media have not been used by even the largest business-to-business marketers because they reach mass audiences. However, there are some direct marketers who are testing direct response ads on cable networks that provide financial and business news and programming. There are also all-news radio stations that solicit advertisers who have a need for inquiry generation.

To be cost effective, the audiences from these media have to be highly defined and targeted. Some of the cable stations permit business buyers to have more than 60-second or 120-second spots for their commercials. Seminars or half-hour shows of a commercial nature are being scheduled on some cable stations. This flexibility can make electronic media very tempting for some business-to-business marketers who have high-profit products that can be sold by this type of medium. However, production costs for direct response TV can quickly escalate if commercials get too sophisticated. Using professional actors and special effects can add considerable expense to the budget.

Direct response marketers could not make a profit if they had to buy time at the same rates as paid by conventional advertisers so they buy preemptive availabilities. This is TV time bought on a standby basis at a very low rate. However, if a general advertiser wants that spot at the full rate, the direct marketer is preempted. Much like the print buyer looking for remnant space and discounted rates, the TV-time buyer must make decisions on the spot to increase schedules or cancel them. Unless very high-profit/high-price products are being promoted, the average business-to-business direct marketer will find electronic media a very costly way to generate inquiries or orders.

Videotex

A promising medium called videotex allows business user–subscribers to view frames of written material, with or without illustrations. These are transmitted from a computer network over telephone or cable line and displayed on TV or computer terminal screens right in the customers' offices. Since videotex is an interactive electronic information system, viewers can buy products directly using their computer keyboard and a telephone or cable hookup. Whole frames or just lines within a frame are bought by advertisers who use the medium as another way to get information about their company, products, or services to interested business prospects and buyers.

This kind of low-overhead medium has the potential of reaching a broad audience efficiently, and since this is a direct transaction to a highly targeted audience, it can be personalized. Interactive video systems are in use as electronic catalogs by business-to-business direct marketers, especially those who sell products to distributors.

Videotex has many sophisticated options that are making the medium especially attractive to the business marketer. It is being used to display brochures as well as catalogs complete with color graphics and an order form. Some videotex services even offer animation. Direct response business-to-business marketers can produce response ads with complete buying information and an 800 number to make ordering easy for those customers not hooked up to the host computer network. Another attractive option is that videotex is flexible enough to accommodate the direct marketer's need for testing.

New videotex services provide research for the business marketer by creating questionnaires. When customers' answers are matched with preselected offers, a direct marketer can determine customer needs and wants. Capabilities also include analysis of response and nonresponse attitudes (see Figure 11-1).

One interesting use of business-to-business videotex comes from Videotex Information Corporation with its Videolog. Videolog makes component makers' product information available to electronic engineers. It offers a directory of all manufacturers of electronic components, equipment, and services. With this service, users are able to select appropriate components from manufacturer's data

Figure 11-1. A diagram of the videotex system.

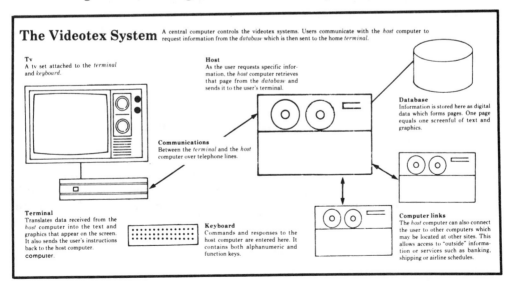

bases and place orders for information or specific products directly with the manufacturer. The system also supplies industry news interspersed with advertiser information including pictorial displays of products, specifications, and new product announcements. Videolog also provides a national "bulletin board" where users can post notices for parts needed, help wanted, or other requests.

The potential advantages of videotex for the business-to-business direct marketer are exciting. Customers and prospects can easily retrieve comprehensive product information and product application documentation. Customers have access to manufacturing and shipping reports and can be kept informed with electronically published newsletters.

The medium allows marketers to have direct contact with buyers without additional staff. Also, videotex provides for immediate ordering capabilities between a company and its suppliers. Another key advantage is that marketers can cross-reference other products that satisfied customers may want to buy from them. Also marketers can easily modify product availability and price with the on-line database.

Electronic Mail

Electronic mail is a sophisticated enhancement and advancement of Western Union telegrams developed in 1844. By using microwaves and satellites, messages can be sent anywhere in the country instantly to an infinite number of addresses.

There are two kinds of electronic mail. One is called priority messages. These are the best known and are delivered either by the United States Postal Service or by direct mail firms. Since priority messages are placed in distinctive envelopes, it is hoped they will get opened before ordinary mail.

The other kind of electronic mail message is delivered by a computer to another computer where it must be accessed by the recipient. With a private password and a personal computer or other device that is able to communicate over the telephone, one businessperson can transmit messages electronically to one prospect, one customer, or thousands. And the message can be sent instantly to others who have receiving equipment. For those who do not, the transmitted message is delivered as regular mail in a day or two. Systems with paper delivery are of greatest interest to the business direct marketer because they are more similar to the traditional mail delivery system.

For the business-to-business direct marketer, electronic mail is frequently used to reinforce earlier contacts with prospects and customers and to encourage additional purchases of other products or services. Electronic mail can also be personalized with the sender's signature and letterhead.

Because of its impact and speed, electronic mail is an especially good prospect qualification tool that weeds out from lists of raw inquirers those who are not interested. The business-to-business direct marketer also puts electronic mail to use by generating inquiries from selected target lists, promoting a product line enhancement, transmitting bid and price quotations, gathering information through surveys, announcing price changes, sales promotions, and direct mail promotions, announcing meetings, inviting customers to special events, and informing customers of shipping delays and order confirmation.

Electronic mail is often paired with telemarketing to selectively canvass the marketplace. Telemarketers use it mostly for research and to let customers know they will be receiving a call. Electronic mail can improve a telemarketer's productivity. Reports of telemarketing results can be computed and sent to clients, agencies, fulfillment centers, or any other interested parties. Information and order can be moved in seconds. Marketer's reports can be prepared and transmitted, warehouse and suppliers can be communicated with instantly, leads can be sorted by zip codes and printed out at a branch, or they can be batched and transmitted after midnight to save dollars.

SUMMARY

Other media are available for direct marketing objectives for those business-to-business marketers who have suitable products and markets.

Telemarketing has evolved into a direct marketing specialty profession. With business-to-business telemarketing accounting for 81 percent of total telemarketing activity, growth continues in both inbound and outbound applications.

Telephone script writing requires an understanding of basic selling and listening skills to guide the telephone communicator through the steps of the sale or through the process of prequalifying the prospect for personal sales calls. Highly structured scripts, which also can be programmed into a desktop computer, maximize the value of telemarketing for the marketer.

Print media for these marketers consist for the most part of trade and business publications. Editorial content and reader response history help determine attractiveness of a magazine for an individual offer.

Special mail order sections, remnant space discounts, regional editions, and split-run issues for testing ad variables offered by some publications are enticements that make print advertising alluring for the direct marketing advertiser.

Cable TV, with its financial and business news programming, commercial length flexibility, and standby basis availability, can interest some business-to-business marketers searching for new markets, but for the most part it is not cost effective at this time.

Videotex, an interactive information system, holds promise for business-to-business marketers as a way to provide information about their companies and products over cable lines directly to interested customers and prospects as an electronic catalog. Electronic mail delivers priority mail as a letter in an envelope or as accessed from a computer by the recipient. Its speed of transmission encourages its use for many business-to-business transactions.

PART II

Managing the Direct Marketing Effort

12

TESTING AND EFFECTIVENESS MEASUREMENT

The purpose of testing in business-to-business direct marketing is to reduce risk. Mail order marketers who use direct mail in volume must attain preset sales goals from their mail or publication media direct response efforts or go bust. Pretesting complete direct mail packages or specific elements within those packages identifies best approaches.

In sales support direct mail pretesting is usually not practical because target markets are too small. But posttesting package elements or complete packages as a byproduct of a scheduled mailing can be very valuable in determining the best list segments, offers, or creative approaches to use in future mailings. Pretesting direct response advertisements in representative regional issues of magazines, or posttesting in full-run issues using split-runs, also enables marketers to project better future efforts.

Testing is an ongoing function in business-to-business direct marketing. The mail order marketer tests every new direct response effort. When a winner emerges, it is called the control and is used until further testing proves that another effort beats the control. The sales support marketer continually tests to determine the best approaches to communicating effectively with new and current markets.

WHO TESTS?

High-volume business-to-business mail order marketers, such as catalogers and magazine, newsletter, and book publishers, are among those who use pretesting techniques—the same techniques employed so effectively by consumer mail order marketers—most often. They rely on test results to survive and grow, prospecting rented lists to seek new customers. List testing and resultant roll-outs, then, become a large part of their direct marketing plan.

On the other hand, while most business-to-business marketers have direct-response sales-support objectives, they make little use of testing. A survey performed by Dun's Marketing Services and the Direct Marketing Association's Business/Industrial Council reveals how testing continues to elude the direct mail planner (see Table 12-1). Of 169 responses from marketers recorded in the survey, 65 percent never test mailings to business prospects and 20 percent do so rarely. This parallels the results of an earlier study from the Center for Marketing Communications, Princeton, New Jersey, that reported: "Out of 527 business marketer respondents, 85% are inclined to use only judgment in appraising the business direct mail they use; 10% show an interest in alternatives for testing; and only 5% pretest mailings" (see Table 12-2).

There are underlying reasons why those marketers who use direct mail do not do more testing of their mailings to prospects. Some believe that because their market universes are small, the need for testing isn't as vital as it is in mail order direct marketing. Others do not have in-house research expertise. They are unsure of the correct way to set up a program for testing or are intimidated by the laws of probability and statistical formulas involved in testing. Some marketers would like to test but do not because it is too far down on their list of priorities. Others fail to plan for testing at budget approval time and consequently cannot come up with the dollars when a need for testing becomes apparent.

Pretesting may indeed be unfeasible for many of these non-mail order marketers because most of their markets are too small. For instance, for a list of 10,000 names, testing matched samples of 3,000 each will leave virtually nothing to roll out to. Yet comparative testing of offers, creative approaches, entire packages, or prospect lists is feasible and can be conducted as a by-product of making a scheduled mailing. This falls into the category of posttesting. Because most business-to-business products and marketplaces remain relatively stable, what marketers learn from one direct marketing effort can be applied when mailing again to that same marketplace.

Table 12-1. Business/Industrial Council
research survey.

Do you test mailings to business prospects?	
Always	2.5%
Frequently	12.3%
Rarely	20.2%
Never	65.0%

Source: Direct Marketing Association, 1980. Used by permission.

**Table 12-2. Business marketers' use
of pretest mailings.**

Frequency of Pretest Mailings by Business Marketers

Number of Responses	527

Done frequently	3%
Done once in a while	12%
Done rarely	24%
Never done	61%

*Business Marketers' Relative Interest in Three
Areas of Measurement*

Number of Responses	465

First Choice	
Appraising results	85%
Selecting alternatives	10%
Pretest mailings	5%

Source: From Report #14 of the Center for Marketing Communications.

WHY TEST?

Those business-to-business direct marketers who have well-established ongoing programs using direct mail can afford to base some of their judgments on their accumulated experience when choosing lists, offers, or creative approaches. In fact, many of their decisions could be the same as if they had been based on test results. Nevertheless, a testing program can produce much valuable information that enhances experienced direct marketing judgment.

New Start-ups

Sales Support Programs

When introducing direct mail as a new marketing tool for sales support objectives, at least 20 percent of the direct marketing budget should be allocated for "finding out how to do it right." The line item in the budget might read, "Testing for Direct Mail Effectiveness." Testing helps ensure that the program gets on track and stays there. Marketers cannot rely on other marketers' test results, because all markets are not alike and each marketplace reacts differently to different product offerings.

Newcomers to direct marketing need to learn which elements of a mailing effort are most important to the success or failure of a campaign. Business-to-business marketers in the early stages of implementing a direct marketing program should test some aspect of the program in every mailing. Making a mailing and counting the responses tell the marketer only that the package worked or didn't work, without the reasons why. A failure could perhaps have been a success if a different offer was used, if a different creative approach was used, or if the mailing was sent to a different list segment. Successful mailings can be even more productive when direct mail planners know which specific elements of the mailing package decision makers react to, and what will produce the most responses for each product and each market.

The best direct mail programs run on a continuing basis. An ongoing testing program is the insurance that helps keep the mailings effective. New offers, creative elements, and lists should be sought and tested, and past tests should be repeated periodically to see if the successful direct marketing techniques continue to be profitable.

Mail Order Programs

Most marketers are seldom totally successful in their initial attempts to sell products by mail. Mail order marketing is an evolving process, one that initially involves a major testing and research program to determine if there will be enough potential business in the suspect universes for a profitable program long term. To succeed, mail order marketers must identify those businesses that will purchase their products by mail or phone. They then assess the common geographic, demographic, and behavioral characteristics of these customers in order to build a profile for further list testing. In addition, they need to know which mail order techniques work best in their markets and how often they can profitably solicit those markets.

In order to get all of this information, the launch of a product sold by mail must be preceded by a series of tests of lists, offers, complete package variations, and specific package components. These tests are made in multiple phases, each attempting to refine, verify, and expand on the findings of the previous phase. The first phase usually tests those aspects having the greatest impact on results. Testing in the second and third phases pursues the most effective combinations of the lists, offers, and creative approaches.

Keeping Abreast of Changes

Computerization is changing the way business is conducted and how businesspeople communicate with each other. Testing helps the marketer stay abreast of these changes. For example, in some business applications electronic mail can be more profitable than the standard direct mail package, and telemarketing lead-generation in some cases can be more cost effective than mail lead-generation.

Successful direct marketing planners periodically test the innovations that are being gradually accepted as a way of doing business. They can do this by actually implementing a telemarketing, electronic mail, or other program to a small list sample.

WHAT TO TEST

Direct mail planners use testing for essentially two purposes: (1) to test direct mail packages or their components and (2) to test product acceptance. Sales support and mail order marketers use the first type of testing, but product acceptance is most prevalent in mail order marketing (some sales support marketers do use it for researching a new product in the marketplace).

In addition to testing price and the complete mailing package, the elements that should be tested early on are those that have the potential of making the greatest change in response. Most marketers will test elements from this basic list:

- Offers
- Creative approach
- Lists
- Timing
- Frequency
- Postage
- One-step or two-step mailings

With regard to product acceptance, focus groups and market surveys often precede actual direct mail testing. But the only sure way to determine if a particular product will sell by mail is to pretest it in the marketplace.

One of the cardinal sins in direct marketing testing is to spend dollars testing the wrong components—those that, at best, can make little difference in the outcome of a mailing. Not every element is important enough to justify the expense of testing.

For instance, it is wasteful to test one specific color signature against other colors. Testing to determine which day of the week the direct mail package should arrive is futile. There is evidence that responses are lighter on Monday and Friday and also on the day before and after a holiday, but there is no cost-effective way to guarantee the day of delivery of a direct mailing. Printed postal indicia, colored envelopes and paper stock, underscoring of words in the headline, and two-color versus three-color reply cards are other test components that may reveal only minor differences. There are times when minor differences can fool the experienced consistent mailer, but not often.

Offers

Sales Support

Since the offer is the main reason the prospect will read a direct mail piece, a change in the offer can make a big difference in the end result of an inquiry-building mailing. The marketer chooses the offer on the basis of the campaign objective. If large quantities of raw inquiries are wanted for further qualification by telemarketing, a generic information offer may be tested. If inquiries with a high sales conversion ratio are needed, the marketer may test an article reprint on an industry/specific subject against an offer for a feature/function brochure of a company's product.

Each marketer must test different offers because markets, products, and sales conversion ratios vary. The 25 inquiry response-building offers listed in Chapter

7 (see Fig. 7-1) can be tested by marketers. They range from a very general information offer of a chapter reprint in a recently published business book to a highly specific offer of a free analysis and survey. Marketers will find many of these appropriate for their individual market.

Testing combination offers can be enlightening. The marketer will find that many offers in one mailing will restrict response. However, in some marketplaces, putting "Have a salesperson call" along with an information offer on the reply card can actually increase the number of responses.

Mail Order

Testing the offer in a mail order marketing campaign can be a tricky business. Since the creative aspects of a mail order package are designed to promote the offer, testing offers that are vastly different most often result in many creative changes. When this happens—if the variables changed extend to creative elements as well—the test essentially becomes a package test, not an offer test. For example, when testing a premium offer against a price offer, the envelope copy may be different. The entire package emphasis may change. Copy, graphics, and format may highlight the premium in one test package and the product in the other.

There is, of course, nothing wrong with testing the package, as long as that's what the marketer set out to do. (This concept is discussed later in this chapter under Approaches to Testing.) The typical mail order offers that can be tested include:

- Pricing
- Payment terms
- Free trials
- Sweepstakes
- Guarantees
- Premiums and gifts
- First-step information offers

Creativity

In both mail order and inquiry-building packages, copy, graphics, and format spell out the offer in terms of the specific marketplace to be reached. Of the many ways to express and emphasize the offer or the product, letter headlines and lead sentences are the key creative elements that can effect a major change in response.

The typical elements tested in inquiry-generation packages also include:

- Letter vs. self-mailer
- Plain letter vs. illustrated letter
- Personalization vs. nonpersonalization
- Enclosure vs. no enclosure
- Plain envelope vs. copy on envelope
- P.S. vs. no P.S.
- Burying the offer vs. highlighting the offer
- Preaddressed business reply card with window envelope vs. non-preaddressed reply card with nonwindow envelope

Lists

More and more business-to-business marketers who have historically relied on their sales forces to make the sales are now turning to mail order marketing. These marketers are testing lists of small limited markets or of large but limited business response list universes.

Mail order marketers who run mature operations are familiar with all appropriate list availabilities and do test any reasonable new list that comes on the market. But, because new business lists are scarce, their testing is confined essentially to marginal lists and lists they have tried before. These marketers look for ways to make business response lists more productive by testing narrower selections such as most recent buyers, specific business classifications, company size, and other list characteristics that most closely match the key customer profile.

Typical tests include geographic and demographic list selections. For example, some marketers sell more profitably in urban areas, others in rural. Most marketers specialize in specific vocations. A test of 88 SIC codes may indicate 18 vocational classifications are winners, 10 are marginal, and the rest are not worth a continuation.

The new business-to-business solo mail order or catalog mailer tests the product or catalog concept in many different list universes. These new entrants in the mail order arena soon run out of lists to test in their quest for new customers. The most appropriate lists to test are those of competitors. However, these are not available except on a list exchange basis and a new mail order marketer does not have anything to exchange.

Testing in the start-up, then, usually involves testing lists that have only the most promising characteristics for maximum response. This reduces the financial risk in the event that the product or catalog concept is unsuccessful, but it also limits the scope of the roll-out possibilities if successful. Testing too few lists in too small sample sizes often will not allow the marketers to develop a large enough universe for mailing. Often it takes a great deal of list testing to establish a sizable bank of target prospect names that can be mailed to profitably.

Timing

Some months are better for mailing than others, especially for mail order. For instance, mailings to schools are more successful when made before school-year budgets are finalized. Also, generally, the three weeks before Christmas are poor response mail months for business-to-business marketers. Making a 12-month study as a by-product of scheduled mailings will provide the marketer with timing information unobtainable in any other way. However, if mail order marketers test in July but cannot project continuations (the results from mailing to a larger sample or the rest of the list) until February, for instance, results may be way off.

Frequency

Frequency of mailings is also related to timing. How often the same offer can be made to the same list depends on the interest turnover and buying frequency of the product in the targeted marketplace. These factors can be determined by mailing the identical package at varying intervals to different test samples of the same list.

For instance, Test List Sample A may get the package mailed monthly for six months. Test List Sample B may get the same package mailed every other month for six months. Test List Sample C may get the same package mailed the first month and the sixth month. Results of the test let the marketer know the cost of an order or inquiry on a high-, medium-, and low-frequency mailing basis. An analysis of the responses will reveal buying frequency and interest turnover of the product in the market represented by the list, thus indicating optimum mailing intervals.

Chances are that responses received from these direct mail packages mailed at different time intervals will not have a material effect on the back-end aspects, such as returns, bad pays, and customer longevity for mail order or on sales conversion ratios for the non–mail order marketer. As long as there is nothing different in the package that is mailed in any of the time intervals, the inquiries or orders should all be of the same back-end quality.

Postage

It may be worthwhile to test first-class postage against other types. Many business-to-business mailers have found that third-class bulk postage on the outgoing envelope will produce the same percentage response as first class. However, in many marketplaces, the use of first-class postage is necessary to reach top executives (and some marketers feel commemorative postage stamps work best for selected appeals).

One-Step vs. Two-Step Mailings

For some new, unique, or complex products or systems to be sold successfully by mail, elaborate direct mail packages are needed to develop and explain the selling story and to persuade and convince the reader to make a purchase. Where this applies, a two-step mailing may be tested against a single mailing.

A two-step mailing consists of an inexpensive first mailing to prequalify the prospects who will receive a much more detailed selling package when they respond to the first mailing. A typical first mailing may consist of a letter, possibly an enclosure, and a reply card. Those who respond usually receive an elaborate package consisting of a personalized letter, a four-color folder or broadside, a sales presentation booklet, special information on payment options, perhaps a lift letter, an order form, and a return envelope.

This strategy has an objective of bringing in more qualified inquiries at low cost, using heavier budget dollars to provide a more powerful selling package targeted to the limited list of inquirers. The test compares this two-step method with a less elaborate single mailing of a more moderately priced selling package to the entire original list universe.

BASICS OF TESTING

Methods

Testing makes use of sampling analysis whereby a projection of a relatively small number of responses can be attributed to the complete universe. Testing employs mathematical statistical methods to make comparisons, to choose representative samples, and to determine the correct sample size. Whether pretesting direct mail, testing as a by-product of making a scheduled mailing, or placing A and B split ads in a publication, the same testing guidelines and techniques that deal with the laws of probability must be used to ensure that the tests will be valid and produce definitive results. In each method the marketer compares two or more alternatives.

Pretesting

Since the pretesting approach assumes a sizable target universe list (generally 50,000 and over), it is used mostly by the mail order marketer. Before making a scheduled mailing, a pretest using paired representative samples taken from the target universe determines from various alternatives which has the best chance of succeeding in a continuation. Mailing results that show a significant difference when compared dictate the elements that will be used when making the roll-out.

Testing as a By-product

Since most business-to-business marketers who use direct mail as a sales support tool deal with small markets, their testing opportunities conducted as a by-product of a scheduled mailing consist mostly of comparisons of offers, lists, and package elements. The procedure is simple. The mailing list may be split in half. For example, in a list of 20,000, half the prospects on the list (every other name) will receive one package and half will receive the alternate package.

Another test option is to pull a representative minimum sample, say 2,000, from the list of prospects who would receive the alternative package. The remaining 18,000 would receive the preferred package. This 2M/18M split is used when the direct mail planner has more confidence that the preferred package will do better.

An uneven comparison test sample is also used when one package is much more costly than the other or when the preferred package is the control package that has pulled well in the past and the planner is trying to "beat the best." Another reason for uneven sample sizes is that they minimize the problems of "selling" the test mailings to sales management and merchandising them to salespeople.

Because precise measures of determining significant differences between two or more test results require complex statistical methods, some direct marketers use a rough shortcut method translated into a very simple equation:

If the numerical difference in the responses of two test mailings is greater than the square root of the total number of responses, then the difference is statistically significant.

If, for instance, a marketer of educational materials wants to test a plain versus an illustrated letter in an inquiry-building mailing to sixth-grade school teachers, two matched samples of 2,000 may be chosen for the test based on an anticipated return of 3 percent. If test A, the plain letter, gets 52 responses and test B, the illustrated letter, pulls 69 responses, the total number of responses is 121. The difference in response between the two test samples is 17, which is greater than 11, the square root of 121. If test B had generated only 58 responses, the difference would probably not be significant. The difference between a response of 52 for test A and a response of 58 for test B is 6, which is less than 10, the square root of the total responses of the two test samples.

The A/B Split-run

Publications such as trade and business magazines, business and executive demographic editions of newsweeklies, and related publications are used by business-to-business marketers looking for direct orders or inquiries. Some of these publications offer advertisers the opportunity to test their advertisements through a split-run. A/B splits offer the marketer a chance to determine the relative power of two versions of an advertisement. The advertisements are printed in alternate copies of a given press run to be distributed evenly throughout the magazine's target area.

For example, two different offers may be tested. The offer that pulls the most cost-effective responses may then be used in a full media schedule in a national campaign. The advertisement in an issue with offer A may be found in the first, third, fifth, and so forth copies in a newsstand. The advertisement with offer B turns up in the second, fourth, sixth, and so forth copies. Such distribution provides representative coverage, making results completely comparable. A/B splits usually command a premium price.

When a publication cannot provide an A/B split, it may offer a 50/50 split where one-half of the circulation carries advertisement offer A and the other half carries advertisement offer B. However, severe bias in either half can throw off results considerably. Marketers should use this kind of split-run with caution.

A third type is the geographic split or regional edition of a publication. Testing offers and copy approaches in limited geographical areas can be valid if a representative number of regions is scheduled for the test.

APPROACHES TO TESTING

Test One Thing at a Time

Under pressure to learn quickly, some marketers test several elements concurrently. The often-heard admonition to test only one thing at a time means that only one variable should be tested within a pair of test sample cells in a given mailing. For instance, if the marketer wants to test one copy approach against another, each of the two-test mailings should be made to a minimum representative sample of the complete universe list. All other variables in the two-mailing packages to be tested must be identical. When one variable is tested against another the quantities of each sample do not have to be equal as long as the lesser quantity meets the proper sample size required for a valid test.

Several variables can be tested at one time in one mail drop, as long as there are enough acceptable minimum-size sample cells for each component to be tested. When marketers want to test several variables they select several pairs of samples, but in each pair they change only one variable. Figure 12-1 shows an example of how several variables can be tested in sample cells of 3,000 each for a total mailing quantity of 24,000.

In the example, two offers are tested in quantities of four matched samples of 3,000 each. Two copy approaches are tested in four matched samples of 3,000 each and two letter formats are tested in four matched samples of 3,000 each. Pyramiding test cells in this way enables the marketer to analyze combinations as listed in Table 12-3 to determine which offer, copy approach, and letter format will be most effective in a continuation. The marketer, however, must resist the temptation to total the results of the four illustrated letter test cells and compare them with the total results of the four plain letter test cells. They are not comparable because there is more than one variable in each of the packages. Only *matched* cells representing one variable can be compared.

A similar test matrix but one that includes list variables is shown in Table 12-4. In this example the mailing quantity of 24,000 is again broken down into sample cells of 3,000 each, sufficient to test two different offers over four different lists, providing different combinations from which to choose.

A complete package test does not attempt to single out the pulling power of any one variable in the package. For a valid comparison test of one package against another, only the acceptable minimum sample size is needed as shown in Table 12-5.

Even though testing variables can be expensive, testing costs for the business-to-business marketer are investments in more effective future mailings.

Beat the Best

A beat-the-best strategy is used in solo mail order marketing as well as in continuous inquiry-response sales support programs. Once a direct response package has been proven a winner, it is mailed continually at various time intervals as long as it pulls profitable orders and inquiries. A beat-the-best strategy is simply a continuing effort to improve a mailing package that is currently generating profitable responses. It is rare that one offer, one approach, or one package can perform equally well, month after month, year after year. Fresh ideas must be tested, often resulting in complete new package testing or package element testing in an effort to pull more profitable responses than the current control mailing.

Breakthrough changes come from tests of complete package changes. These tests usually occur when projections of responses from the current mailing package show diminishing results and past element testing efforts have not proved to be the answer.

Figure 12-1. Testing of variables (sample matrix).

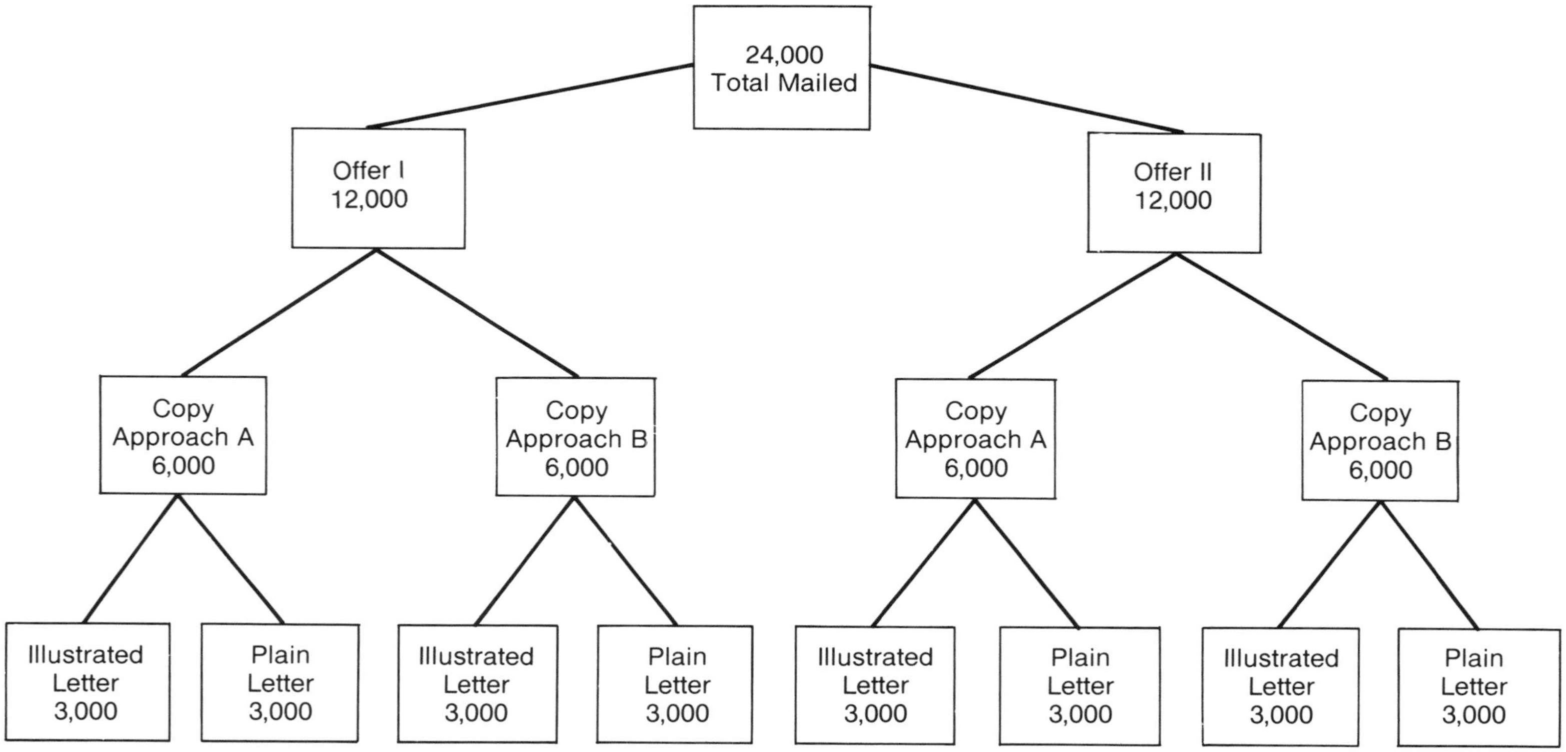

Table 12-3. Test combinations.

Offer Combinations

| Offer I | Copy Approach A | Illustrated Letter |
| Offer II | Copy Approach A | Illustrated Letter |

| Offer I | Copy Approach A | Plain Letter |
| Offer II | Copy Approach A | Plain Letter |

| Offer I | Copy Approach B | Illustrated Letter |
| Offer II | Copy Approach B | Illustrated Letter |

| Offer I | Copy Approach B | Plain Letter |
| Offer II | Copy Approach B | Plain Letter |

Copy Approach Combinations

| Offer I | Copy Approach A | Illustrated Letter |
| Offer I | Copy Approach B | Illustrated Letter |

| Offer I | Copy Approach A | Plain Letter |
| Offer I | Copy Approach B | Plain Letter |

| Offer II | Copy Approach A | Illustrated Letter |
| Offer II | Copy Approach B | Illustrated Letter |

| Offer II | Copy Approach A | Plain Letter |
| Offer II | Copy Approach B | Plain Letter |

Letter Format Combinations

| Offer I | Copy Approach A | Illustrated Letter |
| Offer I | Copy Approach A | Plain Letter |

| Offer I | Copy Approach B | Illustrated Letter |
| Offer I | Copy Approach B | Plain Letter |

| Offer II | Copy Approach A | Illustrated Letter |
| Offer II | Copy Approach A | Plain Letter |

| Offer II | Copy Approach B | Illustrated Letter |
| Offer II | Copy Approach B | Plain Letter |

Table 12-4. Sample list testing matrix.

	Offer I	*Offer II*	*Total*
List 1	3,000	3,000	6,000
List 2	3,000	3,000	6,000
List 3	3,000	3,000	6,000
List 4	3,000	3,000	6,000
Total Mailed	12,000	12,000	24,000

Test Combinations

List Test Combinations	*Offer Test Combinations*
List 1 Offer I	List 1 Offer I
List 2 Offer I	List 1 Offer II
List 3 Offer I	List 2 Offer I
List 4 Offer I	List 2 Offer II
List 1 Offer II	List 3 Offer I
List 2 Offer II	List 3 Offer II
List 3 Offer II	List 4 Offer I
List 4 Offer II	List 4 Offer II

TESTING TECHNIQUES

Representative Sample Selection

The principle of sampling is based on the logic that a group of names selected at random from a much larger group of names will exhibit the same characteristics as the universe group. A representative random sample of a business list that matches as closely as possible the attributes and structure of the entire list is necessary if the projections are to be meaningful. The more that the important characteristics of the sample match the universe, the more representative the sample will be.

An Nth name selection is the preferred procedure of choosing a representative sample for direct marketing testing. The first name in the universe list is picked at random; succeeding names are then selected based on predetermined intervals.

For instance, if a marketer wants a test list size of 2,000 from a universe list of 12,000 names, every sixth name would be selected. If the second name on the list is chosen at random as the first, then the eighth, fourteenth, twentieth, twenty-sixth names—and so on in intervals of six—would provide a test list total of 2,000. To get a matched sample of the same list of similar quality, the marketer starts with another name on the file. If the fifth name were selected as the first, then the eleventh, seventeenth, twenty-third, twenty-ninth, and every sixth name thereafter throughout the list would provide the required sample size.

Table 12-5. Complete package test.

Variables	Test A (scheduled or control package)	Test B
Offer	Offer I	Offer II
Creative	Copy approach I	Approach II
Letter Format	Illustrated letter	Plain letter
	3,000	3,000

Since most mailing lists today are computerized and can provide random samples geographically and demographically, it is relatively easy to select every Nth name. Another technique selects samples at random from those parts of the list that are representative of the entire list. There are computer programs that are able to skip list test segments when further roll-outs are warranted. However, fairly sophisticated programs are needed to be able to furnish these Nth name selections that are not duplicated on a continuation.

Size of Sample

The size of the test mailing, not the size of the list on which the test is being made, governs the reliability of the test results. The proper test mailing quantity is determined by the percentage of responses predicted and the amount of accuracy needed to minimize the risk.

The minimum test quantity for the volume business-to-business mail order marketer is usually 5,000. On the other hand, a minimum quantity of only 2,000 may produce a statistically valid test for inquiry-generation direct mail because, as a rule, these pull more responses than mail order mailings.

Responses, sample variance, and confidence level are the three factors that determine whether a sample size is large enough to produce statistically significant results for direct mail testing.

Response

The most important factor in determining the size of a test mailing is the response the direct mail planner expects to get from the proposed mailing. As a rule, for a test result to be valid there should be a minimum of 40 or 50 responses per test. But, of course, the higher the response rate anticipated from a test mailing, the smaller the test quantity required. A mail order marketer who expects a 0.8 percent response to a newsletter subscription offer needs a test quantity of 5,000 to reach a minimum goal of 40 responses. An inquiry-building test mailing, however, may have a response assumption of 2 percent. This means only 2,000 names are required to produce 40 responses.

Some mailers have past experience with lists and offers on which to base this important estimate. But even the most experienced marketers are seldom consistently accurate in predicting the response figure, since responses vary dramatically according to the vagaries of offers, lists, and creative efforts in various markets.

A general response figure of 1.5 percent can be used as a reference point by sales support marketers who are inexperienced at direct mail and are mailing for the first time. This estimate may be appropriate for a specifically stated offer of information on an existing product in a third-class bulk mailing to a middle-level management title in a medium-size manufacturing organization. If the new planner feels the offer for his or her marketplace is narrower and more specific, then a lower response should be expected.

An average response rate in direct mail is often quoted at around 2 percent but that is misleading. Depending on the product, the offer and inducements for any objective rates of response can run the gamut from one-tenth of a percent upward to even 25 percent for some catalog and premium offers to highly select lists. Of course, promotion cost per sale is the real leveler.

Sample Variance

When determining the size of the test sample, mail planners choose the amount of sampling error they feel they can afford. This error is the variation that could occur by chance alone. It is strictly a mathematical probability based on sample size. The more closely the sample size resembles the size of the entire mailing universe, the smaller the sample variance. What is important to the planner is what will be at risk if the roll-out generates responses only at the lowest limit of the variance. A response from the test less than this limit will convince the mailer not to make the roll-out.

Mail order planners by virtue of their profit center mind-set must be more on target in anticipating response than inquiry-response sales-support planners since they have more at risk. When marketers know their product or market, they can take more risks by accepting a larger variance and a smaller-size sample. When launching a new product, however, a smaller variance is required. A second test may also be in order in this case.

Confidence Level

The third factor in determining the size of the sample is the planner's confidence level. This is simply the degree of certainty the mailer has that the response will not be less than the lower limit of the sample variance.

Probability tables have been prepared by statisticians and are reprinted in various forms in direct marketing books and learning materials. These tables are pure mathematical probabilities and reflect expected results from larger mailings of packages identical to the test mailing.

The marketer can determine the sample size for a test either by probability tables or an equation. These tables are discussed next in this chapter, but learning how to use the statistical equation for determining sample size can be an advantage to many business-to-business direct marketing practitioners. Pierre Passavant eliminates the statistical jargon in demonstrating how to do this in Figure 12-2.

In this example an assumption is made that a 90 percent confidence level is acceptable. This indicated chances are 90 times out of 100 that the predicted response will fall within the error limits. In the formula it is expressed in terms

Figure 12-2. Sample-size formula.

The formula for determining sample size written in plain English (rather than the usual statistical notation) is:

$$\text{Sample} = \frac{(\text{Confidence})^2 \times (\text{Response}) \times (1 - \text{Response})}{(\text{Error})^2}$$

Substituting the assumed values (.02 response, .003 variance, 1.64 confidence) in this equation, the resulting sample size is calculated as follows:

$$= \frac{(1.64)^2 \times (.02) \times (.98)}{(.003)^2}$$

$$= \frac{.05272}{.000009}$$

$$= 5,856$$

Thus, the correct sample, given the three conditions assumed, is 5,856. Most mailers would probably round that number up to 6,000. Note that the sample size resulting from the above calculation is correct only for the three specific variables assumed. The sample size would change if different assumptions were made as demonstrated below.

Variations Around Above Examples:

Assumed Response	Allowable Error		Desired Confidence	Sample Required
2%	.3%	(±15%)	90% (1.64)	5,856
2%	.3%	(±15%)	95% (1.96)	8,366
2%	.2%	(±10%)	90% (1.64)	13,179
2%	.2%	(±10%)	95% (1.96)	18,824
1.5%	.225%	(±15%)	90% (1.64)	7,948
2.5%	.375%	(±15%)	90% (1.64)	4,683

Source: Direct Marketing Association, 1982.

of the number of standard deviations. A standard deviation is a measure of dispersion in a frequency distribution. Standard deviations at 90 percent and 95 percent levels are 1.64 and 1.96 respectively.

In the example, a 2 percent response is expected and 0.3 percent is assumed as the allowable error or variance. This means that response will fall between 1.7 percent and 2.3 percent. The formula for computing the error limit may be used by a marketer who made the assumptions in Figure 12-2. If the result of the mailing of 5,856 pieces was only 1.5 percent instead of the 2 percent predicted, and the marketer still wishes to make a continuation projected from this test based on this 1.5 percent response, the following formula can be used:

$$E = \sqrt{\frac{(R)\ 1 - RO}{N}} \times C$$

where E is the error limit, R is the response, N is the number of pieces to be mailed, and C is the standard deviation (of 90 percent confidence level). The calculation would appear as follows:

$$E = \sqrt{\frac{(.015)\ (.985)}{5,856}} \times 1.64$$

$$= \sqrt{\frac{(.014775)}{5,856}} \times 1.64$$

$$= \quad .00158 \times 1.64$$

$$= \quad .00259 \text{ or } .259 \text{ percent error limit}$$

Probability Tables

Some probability tables are more complete than others but most are simple to use. Figure 12-3 illustrates an array of sample sizes at various levels of response. These figures are based on a 95 percent confidence level. Here is an example of how this table is used.

A sales-support direct-mail planner assumes a test mailing response will be 3 percent. Column three of the figure tells the marketer a test mailing size of 1,000 could be used with a 95 percent confidence level if the planner can accept a low limit of a 1.92 percent response from the test. However, if the low limit is 2.24 percent response for a profitable promotion, the size of the test mailing must be 2,000. With a 5,000 sample size it can be assumed that in 95 chances out of 100 the response on the identical mailing to the whole list will be between 2.52 percent and 3.48 percent.

This chart can also be helpful to business-to-business marketers who track inquiry-to-sale conversions by salespeople. They can get an early indication of the final conversion ratio by using early lead conversions as a sample to be projected. For example, for a sample of 500 inquiries at an estimated 20 percent sales conversion, the probability chart tells the marketer that in 95 chances out of 100 the overall conversion will range between 16.42 percent and 23.58 percent.

A probability table prepared by the Allen Drey Company presents a more detailed calculation on yet a more narrow range of responses, 0.1 percent to 4.0 percent. It is reproduced in Appendix 8. This kind of detail lends itself especially to the fine-tuning needed in business-to-business mail order. Yet it is also used for finding test sizes for inquiry response-generation direct-marketing efforts. Response percentages appear in the first column at intervals of one-tenth of 1.0 percent. Error limits are stated in percentage points ranging from 0.02 to 0.70. Sample quantities have been computed for each combination of response and

Figure 12-3. Law of probability as applied to evaluation of the results of test mailings.

LAW OF PROBABILITY AS APPLIED TO EVALUATION OF THE RESULTS OF TEST MAILINGS					
If — the size of the test mailing is:	and — the return on the test mailing is:	then 95 chances out of 100, the return on the identical mailing to the whole list will be between:	If — the size of the test mailing is:	and — the return on the test mailing is:	then 95 chances out of 100, the return on the identical mailing to the whole list will be between:
100	1%	0 & 2.99%	250	1%	0 & 2.26%
100	2%	0 & 4.80%	250	2%	.23% & 3.77%
100	3%	0 & 6.41%	250	3%	.84% & 5.16%
100	4%	.08% & 7.92%	250	4%	1.52% & 6.48%
100	5%	.64% & 9.36%	250	5%	2.24% & 7.76%
100	10%	4.00% & 16.00%	250	10%	6.20% & 13.80%
100	20%	12.00% & 28.00%	250	20%	14.94% & 25.00%
500	1%	.11% & 1.89%	1,000	1%	.37% & 1.63%
500	2%	.75% & 3.25%	1,000	2%	1.12% & 2.88%
500	3%	1.48% & 4.52%	1,000	3%	1.92% & 4.08%
500	4%	2.25% & 5.75%	1,000	4%	2.76% & 5.24%
500	5%	3.05% & 6.95%	1,000	5%	3.62% & 6.38%
500	10%	7.32% & 12.68%	1,000	10%	8.10% & 11.90%
500	20%	16.42% & 23.58%	1,000	20%	17.48% & 22.52%
2,000	1%	.55% & 1.45%	5,000	1%	.72% & 1.28%
2,000	2%	1.37% & 2.63%	5,000	2%	1.60% & 2.40%
2,000	3%	2.24% & 3.76%	5,000	3%	2.52% & 3.48%
2,000	4%	3.12% & 4.88%	5,000	4%	3.45% & 4.55%
2,000	5%	4.03% & 5.97%	5,000	5%	4.38% & 5.62%
2,000	10%	8.66% & 11.34%	5,000	10%	9.15% & 10.85%
2,000	20%	18.21% & 21.79%	5,000	20%	18.87% & 21.13%
10,000	1%	.80% & 1.20%	100,000	1%	.94% & 1.06%
10,000	2%	1.72% & 2.28%	100,000	2%	1.91% & 2.09%
10,000	3%	2.66% & 3.34%	100,000	3%	2.89% & 3.11%
10,000	4%	3.61% & 4.39%	100,000	4%	3.88% & 4.12%
10,000	5%	4.56% & 5.44%	100,000	5%	4.86% & 5.14%
10,000	10%	9.40% & 10.60%	100,000	10%	9.81% & 10.19%
10,000	20%	19.20% & 20.80%	100.000	20%	19.75% & 20.25%

Note: The size of the test mailing, not the size of the list being tested, governs the reliability of the test results.

Source: Direct Marketing Association, 1967.

error limit. This table helps the planner find the mathematical error limit and the minimum sample size that will produce a statistically significant result.

Figure 12-4 is a version of a portion of the probability table in Appendix 8, computed with the 95 percent confidence level. Using this chart to determine the error limits on a test mailing already made, the planner begins by reading down the first column to find the response percentage, then moves horizontally across until a sample-size figure is found closest to the sample used. The heading of the column in which this figure appears is the limit of error expressed as a percentage point. For example, the chart indicates that a 1 percent response from a mailing of 6,000 pieces comes closest to the actual figure of 6,084 found in the column heading of 0.25 percent. This indicates that a test mailing that pulled

Figure 12-4. Excerpt from 95 percent confidence level probability table.

R Response	Limits of Error (as percentage points) 0.16	0.18	0.20	0.25	0.30
.1	1,499	1,184	958	614	426
.2	2,994	2,366	1,917	1,226	852
.3	4,467	3,546	2,872	1,838	1,276
.4	5,977	4,723	3,826	2,448	1,700
.5	7,464	5,897	4,777	3,057	2,123
.6	8,948	7,070	5,727	3,665	2,545
.7	10,429	8,240	6,675	4,272	2,966
.8	11,907	9,408	7,621	4,877	3,387
.9	13,382	10,573	8,564	5,481	3,806
1.0	14,854	11,736	9,506	6,084	4,225
1.1	16,322	12,897	10,446	6,686	4,643
1.2	17,788	14,055	11,385	7,286	5,060

Source: Courtesy of Alan Drey Company Inc., Chicago 60601.

a 1 percent response will pull between 0.75 percent and 1.25 percent response 95 times out of a 100 when mailed to the larger universe.

Another set of tables of value to business-to-business mail order marketers are those found in the Direct Marketing Association's Manual Release 610.1, *Decision Rules and Sample Size Selection for Direct Mail Testing,* by Professor Robert C. Blattberg. This publication details the complex formulas that include break-even values and provides the tables needed to determine sample test sizes for package element comparison tests and list testing.

MEASUREMENT OF EFFECTIVENESS

Unlike most other business-to-business promotions, response direct mail has built-in accountability. The number of inquiries that come in by mail or phone, as well as actual orders, goes a long way in measuring the value of the direct marketing campaign. Awareness, reminder direct mail, and other types of indirect response obviously don't have this built-in measurement. However, they do use readership surveys and before-and-after attitude change surveys as indicators of effectiveness.

Awareness

Direct marketing awareness measurement, often referred to as "before and after" research, is most often used to help evaluate the effectiveness of awareness direct mail advertising programs. It is a relatively simple procedure. Before the mailings begin, a representative sample of prospects who will receive the direct mail campaign is pulled from the mailing list. Although these prospects have not yet received the mailings, they are asked questions that relate to the selling points that are spelled out in the direct mail campaign mailings. After the complete campaign has been mailed, these same questions are then asked of a different representative sample taken from the list. If all other marketing variables are relatively constant during the direct mail campaign period, significant differences in the test results can indicate the degree of effectiveness of the campaign.

Here is an example of how direct mail was used to help increase prospect awareness of a product in the financial marketplace for NCR. NCR's system—a central information file (CIF) computer system linking together all of an individual's financial transactions in the one bank—was tailormade for banks in the medium-size range in the United States, a market of some 7,000 financial institutions.

The direct mail campaign consisted of seven mailings spaced at even intervals over a four-month period. The main objective of the messages in the mailings was to make bankers more aware of central information file processing and to have them associate it with NCR. To measure the effectiveness of the campaign, an outside marketing research firm surveyed random samples of 847 bank presidents before and after the four-month program period. The questionnaire and covering letter did not disclose NCR's role in the survey. "After" replies indicated that the presidents' familiarity with CIF as a concept was vastly improved.

Table 12-6 presents the highlights of the survey results. Answers to the first question showed that 58 percent were very or moderately familiar with the CIF concept before the seven-piece direct-mail series was mailed. This jumped significantly to 77 percent in the "after" survey. When the prospect was asked to name the leading CIF manufacturer, the "before" and "after" opinions changed drastically, from 30 percent to 52 percent for NCR.

And the results also revealed an interesting phenomenon familiar to research professionals. When asked a question for which an audience may not have a solid answer, it may guess at the answer. In this case, many guessed in the "before" survey that the computer industry giant, IBM, must be the leader in CIF processing. Obviously, the seven mailings during that four-month awareness campaign period made many recipients change their minds, since the "before" and "after" opinions for IBM also changed dramatically in the opposite direction, from 51 percent to 30 percent.

After the campaign was completed, answers to the third question revealed that about twice as many respondents noticed CIF advertising as before. And when asked where they noticed CIF advertising, direct mail was cited over three times as much in the "after" survey. Significantly, the audience associated the direct mail advertising with this awareness increase.

Reminder

Since the objective of reminder campaigns is to keep the name of the company and its products prominent in the minds of prospective purchasers, the more detailed probing of specific issues or selling points reflected in "before" and "after" surveys is not appropriate.

Table 12-6. Awareness direct mail campaign results measurement "before" and "after" test.

How familiar are you with Central Information File?

Before	After	
13%	21%	Very familiar
45%	56%	Moderately familiar
42%	23%	Not familiar

In your opinion, which manufacturer is the leader in providing Central Information File Processing?

Before	After	
18%	18%	Burroughs
51%	30%	IBM
30%	52%	NCR
1%	0%	Xerox

In the past month have you noticed any advertising for Central Information File?

Before	After	
31%	61%	Yes
69%	35%	No

Where have you noticed CIF advertising?

Before	After	
78%	58%	Magazines
20%	66%	Direct mail
8%	4%	Newspapers
16%	8%	Seminars

To measure the effectiveness of reminder mailings, the marketer can simply take two matched representative samples from the mailing list, holding back all mailings to the names on the first sample for a period of four, six, or nine months. Reminder mailings are then made to those names in the second sample. The testing period is usually determined by the interval of time between prospect identification and the sale. Sales from companies in the second test sample are compared to sales from the control sample to determine if there is a significant difference. However, changes in other variables during such a test period—such as number of salespeople, amount of advertising, special promotions, product price changes, unusual publicity or trade show events—can affect the result and negate the test.

Direct Mail Readership

Business-to-business marketers who plan to use direct mail can gain valuable insights that can lead to better direct mail campaign planning by studying the patterns of direct mail readership in their specific markets. A sample telephone survey of direct mail readership that can be adapted for use by any business-to-business mailer to determine readership for specific mailings can be found in Appendix 9.

Typical business-to-business non-mail order marketers have limited but relatively stable marketplaces they contact on a continuing basis. Communication is accomplished through ads and product publicity releases in the trade press and business magazines, trade shows, personal sales visits, and direct mail. Because of this, some of these marketers go beyond a review and analysis of the responses and look at the 98 percent or so of those who do not reply to an inquiry-response direct mailing.

There are two important reasons for reviewing this prospect group: the first is for the extra readership bonus, which direct mail consultant John Yeck has often identified for his business-to-business clients. Even though a mailing may be designed for a response-generation objective, direct mail readership below 45 percent is rare, and is often as high as 85 percent or 90 percent. If, as a by-product of making a response-objective mailing, a positive impression is left on all those who read it, there can be a latent payoff in increased awareness, understanding, and interest that can lead to future sales from this group.

A second reason to examine the nonresponder group is that it gives the marketer a chance to study the characteristics of those who are least likely to become customers. An effort can then be made to segment out of future direct mailings those undesired nonprospects. However, since it is often difficult to eliminate these segments when rented lists are used, a marketer can create a mailing having an offer not only designed to appeal to good prospects but also one that is specifically not in the interest of the nonprospect.

TEST RECORDS

Keeping good test records sounds simple but this is where breakdowns often occur, especially in the smaller organizations. Gathering test data and maintaining records are often left to untrained clerical assistants and go unchecked. An incorrect count of the number of pieces mailed or number of responses received can result in costly mistakes triggering wrong decisions. Therefore, the direct mail planner should visit the service bureau or lettershop when the tests are being run to ensure that instructions are followed correctly and that mailing pieces are delivered to the post office in the specified quantity.

SOURCE CODING

Direct marketers must have a system for tracking sales from both mail order and face-to-face selling by the sales force to determine the value of various promotions.

The system focuses on the key code or source code. These codes permit tracking to be done through a special designated number that is imprinted on direct mail reply cards, order forms, labels, or print ad coupons. Numbers with few digits are best.

Different key numbers are required for each list cell when more than one list is being tested for a single promotion. The coding can be done by the list house when the list is being run. Orders and inquiries that come in to the marketer by telephone should also have a source code assigned for the promotion piece or ad that prompted the call. The telecommunicator should always ask the caller for that key number or the source. It is easier for the caller to find the number or designation when it is placed on the mailing label so it does not conflict with the match code number. (Match codes are used for matching records contained in another file.)

Using a department number within the mailer's address on the promotion piece as source code provides a familiar place for the caller to look when the communicator asks. This reduces the typical 30-second caller search time to locate the code.

Key numbers have become synonymous with computerization in direct marketing. But for the small mailer, coding can be done by other means. Reply cards and various reply envelope stocks, as well as different colored inks on reply forms, are often used. Also, special department numbers in the mailer's address or unique spelling of the mailer's company name can serve as an unobtrusive code.

One simple method of color coding small quantities of business reply cards manually continues in use today because it costs next to nothing and it works. Before inserting and mailing, the mailer takes printed business reply cards, separates them into stacks for easy handling, and rifles through each stack so about 1/32 of an inch of the edge of each card picks up the coding color of a felt tip pen that is run quickly down the slightly fanned edge of the stack. In about 60 seconds a thousand cards can be color coded.

SUMMARY

Business-to-business mail order marketers rely on testing programs to survive and grow, but marketers who use direct marketing as sales support, for the most part, substitute judgment rather than a testing program. A lack of the use of testing techniques is attributed to insufficient expertise, poor planning, and the general belief that business-to-business mailing universes are too small. Pretesting may not be feasible for most sales-support direct-marketing programs, but comparison testing as a by-product of making a scheduled mailing can have a big payoff in more effective future promotions.

Testing programs are needed to enhance experienced direct marketing judgment and for beginners to learn which direct mail elements work better than others. Mail order direct marketing start-ups consist mostly of testing products, pricing, offers, creative elements, and lists. Newcomers to sales support direct marketing should allocate at least 20 percent of their budget for a testing program. Continuing to test helps marketers stay abreast of changes in their marketplaces.

Only one variable should be tested within a pair of test samples in any given mailing with all other components identical. Quantities of the test samples do not have to be the same as long as the lesser quantity meets the minimum size requirement for a valid test.

Pyramiding test samples allows several component combinations to be tested in one mailing, but only matched cells representing a single variable can be compared. Beat-the-best strategies attempt to improve mailing packages currently generating profitable responses.

The main testing objective in a business-to-business direct marketing effort is to find significant differences between two or more offers, lists, or mailing components.

Sampling analysis and mathematical statistical methods select representative samples and determine correct sample size. The most important sample-size determinant is the direct marketing planner's estimate of responses expected from the proposed mailing. The sample variance is the amount of sampling error marketers feel they can afford. The confidence level is the degree of certainty planners have that the response will fall within the expected variance.

Probability tables help planners produce statistically significant test results by specifying proper sample size, error limit, and confidence level for each test mailing planned or to determine error limits on tests already completed.

"Before" and "after" measurements, readership measurements, and actual sales results provide the marketer with valuable awareness, reminder, and other non-response direct mail advertising effectiveness evaluation data that can have a positive effect on future mailings to the same market.

When poor gathering and maintainance of test records are left to untrained personnel, poor decisions can follow.

13

MANAGING RESOURCES

Managing a direct marketing business function requires highly honed management skills: short- and long-term planning, organization, direction, and control and measurement of the work effort to ensure that the objectives get accomplished. What the business-to-business marketer should know about selecting, evaluating, organizing and, in effect, managing the internal and external direct marketing resources is reviewed in detail in this chapter.

SALES SUPPORT VS. MAIL ORDER MANAGEMENT

Sales-Support Direct-Marketing Management

The management of sales support direct marketing, which uses direct mail and telemarketing to reach its objectives, normally comes under the responsibility of a sales support staff department such as advertising, marketing services, or marketing communications. The manager may have a title of direct marketing manager, direct mail coordinator, or manager. Or the direct marketing responsibility may be handled by an advertising manager who wears many hats.

Since managers of direct marketing have the responsibility of using it cost effectively, they must be well versed in its principles, applications, techniques, and procedures in both the creative and administrative aspects. These managers must have a firm understanding of the marketplace, how to use customer, prospect, and inquiry lists, and how to determine if a long-range lead-generation program is feasible for the sales force.

Managers of sales support direct marketing must plan and work in concert with those who manage other functions in the marketing mix, since advertising, sales promotion, trade shows, product publicity, public relations, and literature programs, as well as direct mail and telemarketing, all have basically common sales goals. These managers must also have sufficient knowledge of the concept of the data base and sales information systems to know how to use them or get them proposed and implemented in ways that improve sales performance.

Mail-Order Direct-Marketing Management

Business-to-business marketers using mail order in a multichannel company assign this direct marketing responsibility to a marketing manager, usually with the title of manager of direct marketing. In essence, mail order marketing managers run individual business units. Yet, the problems and opportunities they have in managing their profit centers are very similar to those of a CEO of an independent business-to-business specialty mail order company. Managing a mail order profit center requires a sense and knowledge of financial planning tools, such as profit and loss statements, contribution to selling and profit figures, and customer life value analyses. These managers are responsible for bottom-line profits, short and long term.

An in-house telemarketing operation, because it can more readily support a catalog or solo direct marketing program, often becomes a separate function under the umbrella of direct marketing management. However, many of these in-house telemarketing operations sell their services to sales support groups within the same company.

Mail order direct marketing management's effectiveness is in direct proportion to the depth and sophistication of its information resources. The onrush of the information age has opened up many new marketing opportunities. Successful mail order managers must use this information more efficiently to track competition, predict trends, set objectives, and allocate budget dollars.

The strategic plan for any direct marketing mail order operation must focus on building and maintaining the organization's most important asset—the data base. The data base is so fundamental to this selling channel that mail order direct marketing is referred to by some practitioners as data-base marketing.

The mail order direct marketing manager is concerned with an analysis of potential markets, products, and competitive activities not only at the outset of the venture but on a continuing basis. Finding out qualitatively how decision makers perceive a product offering is a very critical aspect of this. Researching the marketplace by asking the right questions means finding out what influences decision makers, what determines the strengths and weaknesses of the product, and who the potential customers are. Focusing on buying behavior of the decision makers will help make a correct analysis of best prospects.

For the most part, direct marketing managers have not made the best use of the traditional tools of marketing. For example, Professor Philip Kotler of North-western University believes it is much more cost effective for direct marketers to pay for focus group research and a survey instead of gathering all the necessary marketing information through test mailings. One or a series of focus group sessions, each consisting of a dozen or so business decision makers, can turn up ideas on products, market segments, or other aspects. The results can be confirmed with mail questionnaires or other quantitative surveys, thus reducing the number of actual direct response tests needed.

Experienced direct marketers know that making a direct marketing plan for a universe or whole market can be wasteful and ineffective. Management's job is to make sure the right segments are targeted. Learning where customers may be heading in the future, communicating with them, and getting feedback on products and services will provide valuable insights. And since the objective of the mail order business is to get repeat orders from multibuyers and avoid the one-time customer, improved products and new products must be continuously researched and tested.

MANAGING FINANCIAL RESOURCES

Financial planning for direct marketing objectives must be long-range because making a one-time sale, whether or not it is made with the help of a salesperson, is not a profitable marketing strategy for most marketers. Financial resources for any type of direct marketing must also be organized and managed so as to make the best use of the various service functions needed to meet individual objectives. How these financial resources are managed tests the mettle of those who control them.

Financial Planning for Mail Order Direct Marketing

Business-to-business mail order marketers have precise numbers to look at when analyzing whether a promotional strategy has paid off or whether a particular product, price, or market is desirable. It is easy to track the number of prospects contacted, the number of responses, and the exact cost of the promotion. By evaluating costs and results, the financial planner is able to determine a promotion's profitability and the break-even point. Achieving break-even or various levels of profitability is dependent chiefly on response, which is contingent on the offer and how it is presented and promoted as well as other factors.

The marketer must know the number of orders needed to break even on any promotion. Adding up the costs of getting and filling an order is a first step. By preparing a pro forma profit and loss statement, the financial planner assembles a detailed record of costs and sales, and calculates the response needed to break even at various levels of profitability for each promotion and for each product.

To measure the profitability of a mail-order direct-marketing program, the manager needs to know the contribution to promotion costs and profit. The total costs of the product, including an overhead allocation, are subtracted from the average selling price to get the contribution to selling cost and profit. And this is usually calculated for each unit sold or for average order handled. Then by taking the total cost of the mailing package, and dividing that by the contribution, the required number of orders to break even is determined. As costs fluctuate, so will break-even. If the program sells only enough products to break even, of course, there is no profit.

Development costs will vary and should be budgeted separately from standard costs that determine break-even. Some of the fixed costs of creating response advertisements include copy, graphics, photography, typesetting, color separations, and plate making. These fixed costs stay the same regardless of the size of the mailings. However, the more mailings go out or the more ads are placed, the more these fixed costs get amortized. Variable costs, such as printing, postage, and list rental, change in proportion to the volume of pieces mailed.

Direct marketers have to pay more for short runs or low volumes, so a response ad for a new product placed in regional editions rather than national editions for one time only—a typical testing method—will command a higher rate. Therefore, direct marketers should evaluate results of test efforts on the basis of projected lower costs when the program is rolled out. Then standard costs can be established and budgeted for each mailing or response advertisement based on quantities typical of ongoing programs.

Financial performance of a mail order product varies with response for every mailing. And since variation in response can cause big differences in profit, response must be evaluated. Experienced direct marketers base their projections on the standard error of response, especially when testing or when small mailings are made. This statistical range gives the error limits in which a marketer can expect response to fall when making a mailing. (Chapter 12 reviews this margin of error concept.)

Mail order direct marketers continuously test promotions designed to produce new buyers who will become profitable future customers. The direct marketing manager may have some lists that in the past have produced orders only at the break-even point or near it. If the response falls within the statistical error limits, these lists can be tried again in small test quantities. But the manager should remember that the more mailings there are with a response rate close to the break-even, the greater the risk of having an unprofitable program. The financial plan of a campaign should strive for response rates that will be greater than the break-even level.

Some lists will not always produce good enough response rates or large enough orders. So profit, as well as the break-even figure, may be different for each product and for each list. A direct marketer selling through a catalog must compute the break-even for all the products, pages, or fractional units in the catalog and also calculate the probability that response will fall within the response limits. Business-to-business mail-order direct-marketing managers can evaluate their proposed campaigns more easily and quickly when using a computerized program.

One of the better examples of a calculation of break-even and profitability has been developed for the Direct Marketing Association by Pierre Passavant, senior vice-president of marketing, Wunderman, Ricotta and Kline. This instructive guideline begins by developing the pro forma profit and loss statement.

Details of step-by-step calculations that can be used by mail order marketers to evaluate the potential profitability of a direct marketing effort are found in

Appendix 10. This guideline demonstrates the link between cost per thousand (CPM), cost per order (CPO), and response rates for both one-step and two-step mail order efforts. Specific examples of break-even calculations, back-end analysis, and return-on-promotion investment analysis are also given. Even though the analysis is based on a solo mailing, the same principles apply to catalogs.

Computing the Recency, Frequency, Monetary Ratio

Since no mail order marketer will place the same potential sales value on all customers in the file, the simple recency, frequency, monetary (RFM) value ratio in one form or another has come to be the preferred method of evaluation. With this technique each customer is evaluated on *when* the last order was placed (recency), *how often* orders are placed (frequency), and the *monetary value* of the orders (monetary). A weight is assigned by the marketer for each of the three factors. This can vary widely among different marketers.

Some consumer mail order marketers feel recency is the most relevant factor and rate it equal to the other two combined (recency 50 percent, frequency 30 percent, monetary value 20 percent). These ratios will differ in business-to-business mail order buying because, as a rule, these marketers receive more dollars per order, have fewer merchandise returns, and are subject to the particular business buying patterns of the product sold.

A company will assign recency rating points, for example, for an order received within the past three-month period and then a lesser rating for each preceding period. A frequency rating can be assigned on the basis of number of orders received each quarter on a value scale similar to that used on the recency rating. Another method of establishing the frequency rating is to assign a point value to be multiplied by the number of orders received during the measured time frame. Monetary value is usually based on a value scale—the larger the order, the higher the points assigned. Another method is to award a point value equal to a given percentage of dollar orders. In each method a maximum value is built in.

An example of how the RFM formula can help the marketer maximize the value of the customer list is illustrated in Table 13-1. The maximum rating points established by the marketer for the recency factor is 26. Frequency is 15 and the monetary value is 9. A sampling of three customers from the list shows customer A getting 26 recency points because of placing an order within the most recent quarter. (Recency point scale: 26 points, first quarter; 22 points, second quarter; 17 points, third quarter; 12 points, fourth quarter; 6 points, fifth and sixth quarters.) Customer B ordered in the third quarter and customer C in the fifth quarter. Customer A ordered three times within the measured time period. The frequency was given an assigned point value of 3 by the marketer, which, when multiplied by the number of separate orders, gave a rating of 9. Customer B ordered one time for a 3 rating and customer C ordered three times for a 9 rating. In the example, a point value of 1 is assigned for every $500 of sales; $2,500 in orders is received from customer A during the measured time period for 5 points. Customers B and C spent $4,000 and $1,000 respectively. Point values of the totals determine the direct marketing activity each will receive in the future. Prime buyers who continue to place substantial orders often will get the highest ratings and the most attention from the marketer. Those who cannot meet the predetermined minimum rating points are eliminated from the file.

Using current information and future projections, good estimates of future revenues from each customer can give an indication of future profits. These profits, discounted back to the present, indicate the lifetime value of the customer. One medium will produce buyers who may have characteristics that are quite different from those of another medium. Any new group of customers must have their lifetime value calculated. As new groups of customers are acquired, their performance can be matched with the control group.

Budgeting for Sales Support Direct Marketing

The non–mail order business-to-business direct marketing budget is almost always a subset of a much larger advertising or promotion budget dedicated to promote a product or service, and in some cases, a corporate objective. Since sales support direct marketing has the same or similar sales and marketing objectives as other advertising and promotion activities, the planner competes for the available dollars.

When direct marketing is one element in a larger budget, it is often treated as being as efficient, no more or less, than the other items in the budget. This becomes apparent when the advertising budget gets increased or decreased. Just about all elements end up with a similar percentage change. This assumes all are equal producers and all elements have equal spending levels. Yet direct marketing may return 50 cents on the dollar, compared to 25 cents for trade publication advertising, or 30 cents for trade shows.

Higher spending levels should be appropriate for those elements in the mix that can justify the greater potential contribution to the objectives. Direct marketing planners must prove, however, that the programs planned for in the next budget period have greater value when compared to others. This can usually be achieved because the results of lead-generation and prequalified prospect penetration programs can be measured by return on investment. This built-in accountability gives direct marketing a better chance of proving its value than the other elements in the communication mix.

Approaches to Budgeting

Sales Maintenance

Many advertising budgets use the sales maintenance approach. Typically, the marketer calculates the average advertising to sales ratio for all firms in the industry or all products or product categories. Then the previous year's sales or next year's estimated sales are multiplied by this ratio to determine the size of the budget. This method of budgeting is popular because it can be defended by the advertising manager or the agency when getting marketing management's approval. The rationale is that by matching the competition, sales will be maintained. If sales decline, the budget can easily be scaled back. But if sales go up, management can be assured that increased revenues will offset any sales-support direct-marketing budget increases.

Table 13-1. Recency, frequency, monetary value customer analysis.

	Maximum Assigned Rating Points	Customers		
		A	B	C
Recency	26	26	17	6
Frequency	15	9	3	9
Monetary value	9	5	8	2
	50	40	28	17

This is the safe approach and sales-support direct-marketing expense will never be excessive. But it is obvious that this approach will not maximize the financial return from the direct marketing investment. A superior method is the management by objectives approach where the budget is matched to potential gross profit rather than sales.

"Top Down"

Another method used by many companies today employs the arbitrary budget guideline handed down from the division or executive office that says the advertising or direct marketing planner can budget for a given percentage increase over the past plan period if it can be justified. Anything beyond that figure requires extra special justification. Under this system, too many managers of staff departments play it safe. They have become so intimidated by the constant pressure from financial planning and accounting staffers, and by upper management's steel grip on the dollars, that they have become timid about proposing great new promotional ideas that include more than the allowable guideline budget increase. Obviously, this approach discourages new high-impact approaches.

When planners think only as far as the allowable guideline, they and their companies never get to identify all that may be needed, much less assess direct marketing's value to the company. Yet management should be encouraged to think big about proposing new programs or expanding successful current programs. If managers believe more dollars for a lead-building effort or a reinforced-selling direct-mail campaign will increase the company's market share, they should build a case and go for it. In fact, if they don't, someone upstairs may be wondering why not.

Task Method

The task method of budgeting is the purest approach. The direct marketing planner links sales and advertising objectives to the optimum incremental revenues that can be realized from the various sales-support direct-marketing strategies and tactics. Assessment of all the opportunities to use the sales-support direct-marketing discipline makes the task budgeting approach valuable. And, of course, this is true even though a percentage ceiling may be and usually is arbitrarily imposed. The task method is important because it lets upper management budget approvers know what the direct marketing specialist says it will take to get the job done and conversely what programs will be missing in their marketing plan if the dollars are cut back or cut out.

No company today can live precisely within a calendarized budget projection over a 12-month period or even a 6-month period because business thrives in a dynamic marketplace. It is continuously in flux. Marketers must react to opportunities as they occur. If a new prequalified prospect-penetration mail campaign is needed to help attain a new objective within the plan period, the planner should go for the discretionary dollars for a well-thought-out program.

Budget Planning Process

There are three basic steps in the task budget planning process:

1. Determine the direct marketing tasks that can cost effectively support marketing, sales, and advertising objectives.
2. Cost out programs based on the tasks to be accomplished.
3. Back up a budget plan with well-documented details, convincing proposals, and recommendations that spell out how the dollars will be invested and what the company will get back in return.

This bottom-up top-down approach recognizes the fact that every profit center has a cap on sales support expenditures put there by the head risk taker. The job of the manager responsible for sales support direct marketing is to recommend plans that have a high likelihood of success that can be measured. The more specific the details of the plan, and the more quantified the objective, the better the chances of getting the budget approved. For instance, the planner may come up with a proposed program to mail six packages bimonthly during the plan period to 5,000 bank presidents with an objective of pulling a 1 percent response from each mailing to get 300 inquiries. Telemarketing can qualify 150 of those as sales leads. Salespeople in turn will convert 50 of these leads, generating a total of $6.5 million in sales.

If the planner requests a sizable increase in a direct marketing budget, as a one-line entry in a preliminary budget plan with the idea of filling in the details later, chances are it may get cut before the final budget session three or four months later. Budget planning should begin with a presentation of a formal plan, including details and quantitative objectives, very early in the budgetary process, well before the formal budget sessions begin. Six or nine months may not be too early. In this way the marketing or product manager will have had time to consider the proposal, and later when the one-line entry in the preliminary budget is seen, there will be a better chance that it will get approved.

How well sales-support direct-marketing budgets are planned and implemented is a reflection of how well the planners handle one of their most important functions—fiscal responsibility. Four basic cautions keep planners on track.

1. Never overspend the approved budget. Additional spending requires an authorized overrun.
2. Never promise anything that cannot be delivered within the approved budget limit.
3. Never overbudget or request more dollars than cannot be backed up with successful accomplishments at year-end.
4. Never underspend the approved budget without "reason-why" hard-copy back-up.

The balance of this chapter addresses the issues managers must grapple with when considering in-house or outside resources.

IN-HOUSE OR OUTSIDE RESOURCES

As direct marketing has developed over time, it has become a succession of specialized but integrated functions. And business-to-business marketers who run comprehensive direct marketing programs use all these basic functions: plans and strategies, concepts, copy, graphics, testing and research, printing, data base development and maintenance, computer services, mailing services, response handling, fulfillment, and telemarketing.

Some marketers get the complete range of needed services through direct marketing agencies or advertising agencies. The majority of marketers, however, choose to handle some functions in-house. But it is rare indeed that a business-to-business marketer has all the functions together in-house under direct control. The marketer's objective is to strike a balance that works best. The perennial question, then, is which functions, if any, should be established in-house and which should come from outside resources.

First the marketer needs to examine the make or buy issues that surface regardless of the specific functions involved. Individual marketers will place a value on those specific issues that focus on where the services can be performed for them at less cost, more creatively, and more effectively. Then marketers can examine the specific functions that are most in demand: creative services, telemarketing, lettershops/mailing services, computer service bureaus, and response-handling services.

Make or Buy Issues

Costs
Advocates of in-house operations point to several reasons why their costs can be lower than those of the independents:

■ There is quicker turnaround time and no overhead costs.
■ Accounting audits of outside service organizations and other duplicate efforts are eliminated.
■ In-house people claim more comprehensive cost control with the elimination

of elaborate client presentations, entertainment, and other "window dress-ing."

■ Corporate cash flow can be more easily controlled in-house.

Business-to-business marketers say that when running the in-house operation as a profit center, management is provided with a more realistic measure of its productivity and value, and in so doing, demonstrates the cost savings most dramatically by simply adding up the profit. This profit goes directly to the corporate financial statement.

Outside services people claim that the in-house operation becomes "an expensive tenant," committing to long-term costs of equipment and maintenance. When adding up true costs companies don't always remember to include overhead, benefit programs, and expense accounts. Direct salaries, they assert, represent only one-half or less of the total cost of maintaining an employee.

Independents emphasize that productivity is often higher in their outside re-source firms because keen competition forces them into the most efficient and cost-effective methods and systems. They believe that the marketer's return on investment could well be higher when using outside resources.

Creativity

Proponents for in-house creative services say they know how to turn out winning plans because direct marketing creative talent is not restricted to outside direct marketing agencies only. Moreover, having continuing contact with the decision makers in the company lets an in-house creative staff dig out in-depth information as may be needed to focus on the real selling proposition. This interaction fosters client confidence in the validity of the proposed creative plans.

In-house people contend that this direct communication without any intervening layers is an advantage that permits more on-target programs. The integration of direct marketing into the company organizationally guarantees that everyone speaks the same language. This means that all company information, sensitive or not, can be shared.

In addition, insiders suggest turnover of creative professionals is healthy. Hiring talented people who continue to grow in their careers and then wishing them well as they move into other positions is a way to continually have bright talent that keeps the operation sharp and contemporary. Also, to stay competitive creatively, in-house managers say they employ free-lance and "a la carte" creative services occasionally to compare quality.

Outside service firms claim they are the leaders in direct marketing and its individual functions. They feel they are better at recognizing a really creative professional and therefore can hire superior creative talent. They say talent is in short supply, and is most productive when in the stimulating environment of the outside agency and firm whose business is idea creation and implementation. Outside groups maintain that in-house services can't hold the creative talent nor can they find replacements easily.

The agencies and service firms that specialize in direct marketing claim they not only have more creative people to choose from but they provide the opportunity for their employees to make career moves without leaving the direct marketing business.

Another issue raised by the in-house advocates regards evaluation of programs. In an outside firm, independents say there is a built-in evaluation by the firm's associates.

Objectivity

Outside resource firms accuse in-house people of being intimidated by pressure of company management, thus preventing objectivity. Since outside people are shielded from client management, they are more apt to make an unbiased "call." Because they deal with many clients who have various goals and problems, outside service firms contend they can be more objective in the way they approach a problem. They have a broader perspective than the insiders who focus only on their company's products and markets. And that's not all. In many cases, the user of the service in the company is the same person who controls the service. This places the manager in a position of approving his or her own work.

In-house staffers imply that just because they are directly associated with the company's strategies and programs, it doesn't necessarily mean they are not objective. However, to prevent any lack of objectivity, they feel the occasional use of outside consultants for opinions on inside work minimizes any problem of in-house bias.

Standards of Performance

In-house managers claim they have the same discipline and dedication to the individual service function as is found in its outside counterpart. Standards of performance are high when measured by copy and concept testing, readership studies, awareness scores, and detailed daily time sheets.

Outside service firms indicate their performance standards are usually higher because they have learned from many thousands of hours of experience how to operate efficiently and effectively. In competition with many other firms, they have to keep their standards high to stay in business and make a profit.

Convenience

Insiders say that getting the job done in-house can actually minimize reaction time because lines of communication are shorter. Questions get answered sooner and problems get resolved quicker. Increased efficiency in creating and approving work ends up in significant time savings and therefore it becomes easier to do business. Business-to-business marketers get what they want when controlling the service.

Independent resources point to the flexibility the business-to-business marketer has when using outside services. With relative quickness the outside resource can be turned on or off as business conditions dictate. A campaign can easily be curtailed, a program cut off in midstream, or a resource put on hold or replaced when budgets are reduced. Putting an in-house staff on hold can be much more of a problem if not an impossibility.

Specific Function

When examining the specific functions that they require most, direct marketers are faced with a more clear-cut choice. Here the question is less of a debate and more simply a matter of "Where will I get the most effectiveness for my direct marketing dollar in the long term?" The answer comes from a careful analysis of the marketer's needs. Some key considerations are identified below for the functions most in demand by marketers.

Creative Services

Having an in-house creative director is an advantage, since the more knowledgeable the creative head is about product benefits and market needs, the greater the chance that creative concepts will be on target. This also applies to sales support copywriters and, perhaps more so, to mail order copywriters who must have numerous questions answered before the complete mail order package is written.

The more creative business-to-business mail order catalogs and solo mail packages are done by outside direct marketing firms and usually include all production elements as well as creative elements.

An in-house graphics person may not be warranted, especially for the smaller company or division of a larger company. But, if there is a need, the first graphics person hired for the staff should be the graphics designer. Since there are more graphics professionals than copywriters available in the marketplace, compensation is lower and they are easier to locate and hire. Like direct marketing copywriters, creative graphics artists are stimulated by creative input and need to be continually challenged and rewarded.

Telemarketing Services

Depending on the volume, types, and consistency of calls, going in-house with a telemarketing operation can have a payoff in dollars for business-to-business marketers. Since a telemarketing facility involves a large initial outlay in ergonomically designed facilities, phone lines, CRTs, staffing, and training, this investment, in effect, institutionalizes the function. Of course, the more sophisticated the computer-generated scripts and record systems, the higher the cost to develop and maintain.

Marketers who have a first-time need for a telemarketing program, but who cannot justify the initial cost or the time to start up an in-house telemarketing center, often run their new program with an outside service as a test. If the test is a winner, they then establish it in-house.

Lettershop/Mailing Services

Both large and small business-to-business direct marketers need lettershop services. The level of sophistication of the equipment and expertise called for is determined by the size and volume of the program.

The high unit cost of the high-speed equipment that best performs lettershop services discourages the formation of in-house lettershops by all but those marketers who have long-term commitments of large volume mailings on a continuing basis.

However, there are those marketers who use direct mail in unique ways and find it advantageous to bring the lettershop inside where everything is under direct supervision and control. For instance, some programs include high-frequency multimarket special-purpose mailings. In these complex cases, the process of transmitting complete and accurate information and selective lists on a timely basis to an outside lettershop can invite serious mistakes. With the lettershop inside, communications can be more direct, thus reducing errors. What's more, it's also easier for the in-house lettershop manager to change schedules to accommodate rush mailings.

Once a sizable investment in staff equipment and facilities is made, the pressure is on to cost effectively use the in-house lettershop support center. Many marketers opt to minimize their risk by choosing an outside lettershop. (Chapter 15 discusses lettershops in more detail.)

Computer Service Bureaus

Computer service bureaus have also become prime resources for many direct marketers. Many business-to-business marketers have corporate computer centers within their companies. Use of this computer center for timely information processing and accessing requirements for direct marketing demands a much higher priority than it usually gets from the corporate data center. There may also be a lack of internal technical programming expertise that is necessary to design a state-of-the-art direct marketing system. This often forces the marketer to go to an outside service bureau or establish a dedicated system in-house within a division of the company.

However, to get an in-house computer support center running takes time, capital, and a professional staff. Assembling the necessary expertise, equipment, and facilities can take many months. The more complex the system, the higher the level of supervision and staff needed. Larger operations have full- or part-time computer analysts and programmers to help them set up and run a fully automated system. Routine functions are handled by clerical staff with the computer doing most of the work. The first focus should be on those applications most important to the direct marketing program. It may be personalized printing, mailing list maintenance, data base development, inquiry processing, response analysis, or other high-priority applications.

Business-to-business marketers with sales-support direct-marketing objectives use a computer system mostly for list maintenance, computer letter processing, and inquiry handling. They can get rapid and accurate statistical analyses and highly targeted personalized mailings, which are an integral part of most programs. Business-to-business mail order marketers use computerization for list rentals, order and lead processing, fulfillment, and other specialized applications. Speed and accuracy produce better data that aid in keeping fast-moving inventory at sufficient levels. The timely information produced also enables mail order marketers to make better decisions because they can immediately react to various marketing efforts.

For some business-to-business marketers, signing up with an outside service bureau is a way to learn more about how the computer can enhance their productivity and value of their individual direct marketing applications. It at least gets them into computer processing and gives them experience and knowledge needed to objectively assess any advantages of going in-house at a future date. When computerized in-house, outside processing costs and list security concerns are eliminated. Special runs are hassle-free since they are done by the marketer. And instant data retrieval permits the marketer to modify records and check for bad debts.

When comparing present costs with estimated costs of computerized applications, the marketer may find on a dollar for dollar basis that computerization may not produce a savings on any one application. But a savings may be apparent when computerized costs are allocated over several applications. The ROI on the overall program is key to the action plan.

If service is needed for a one-time-only effort, selecting the right computer service bureau surely is not too critical. But, when seeking a more permanent arrangement that may involve maintenance of valued customer and inquiry files, for example, finding a bureau that can be trusted is vital. The choice of a service bureau is crucial because having to switch later can be expensive and difficult.

Most important in making a selection is the experience the service bureau has in the business-to-business marketer's individual applications. The firm should be financially sound in controlling most of its own hardware. A visit helps size up the professionalism of those who run the computer system by getting a good reading on the skills, talents, and credentials of the personnel.

Some companies have joint arrangements where they handle some direct marketing functions in-house and others outside with a service bureau. For instance, in-house they may input inquiry responses onto magnetic tape, resulting in output reports for fulfillment letters, statistics, and other needed documents. The service bureau may be responsible for list rental, duplicate elimination, fulfillment, and address label production.

Response Handling Systems

Response handling systems are unique among these functions in that how inquiries are handled is of critical importance to a marketer's program. The in-house or outside service decision involves many more issues than can be discussed here. Chapter 14 discusses these systems in depth.

CONSIDERATIONS WHEN MAKING A RESOURCE CHOICE

The decision to bring one or more direct marketing services in-house will depend on the following considerations:

- Company philosophy and style
- Type of business
- Existing capabilities of staff
- Volume and consistency of services to be performed
- Dominance of the direct marketing discipline in the company's objectives
- Type of product

By reviewing these considerations the marketer can make more intelligent choices.

Company Policies and Management Style

Companies that are centrally organized lend themselves more naturally to in-house support center functions. These operations most often have "captive" clients and are more inclined to generate the in-house volume needed to fund the necessary expertise, facilities, and equipment.

Decentralized companies are structured as commercialized entities: business units, subsidiaries, and autonomous divisions. For the most part, these companies do not maintain large internal staff departments. However, in-house direct-marketing support centers can succeed in this environment especially when chartered as profit center line operations. Mailing, creative, and telemarketing services, as well as fulfillment, computer centers, or any other key direct marketing functions can actually thrive in-house in a decentralized company.

A decentralized policy usually allows divisions or business units the prerogative of choosing their own resources. Under this policy, the in-house support center cannot expect to have all the company's direct marketing business. Fast-track, independent company divisions and business units take advantage of their freedom by looking outside the company for many different resources. But in spite of this aspect, it also works as a built-in motivator, challenging the in-house operation to excel.

The problem caused by use of outside services can be offset by a management policy that allows an in-house operation to solicit business from outside clients. It not only helps balance the work flow but more important, it establishes the necessary free-wheeling commercialization that the in-house enterprise needs to compete with its outside counterparts.

Better than average talent is needed to run a successful in-house service. When good people leave an in-house operation, replacing them may be difficult. Not only are experienced, talented business-to-business direct marketing people scarce, but they command higher salaries from outside direct marketing specialist firms. The salary increases needed to keep good people can be more than corporate salary-management policy guidelines will allow. However, if in-house operations are functioning as profit centers and are soliciting work from outside clients, they may have less trouble getting such salary approvals.

Type and Size of Business

Multiproduct and multimarket industrial companies are the ones that usually generate enough volume and activity to economically support in-house direct marketing operations. Companies with highly seasonal products—unless balanced with products for alternate seasons—have difficulty maintaining full-time in-house functions.

Small companies, which make up the great bulk of business-to-business marketing, often lack resources and expertise to have an effective in-house direct marketing operation. And some of these companies don't have a large enough volume of work to justify doing it in-house. In addition, these companies and small divisions of large companies often don't have the budgets that attract outside

direct marketing service firms. This forces many marketers to do the work themselves without the necessary expertise, all too often producing less than satisfactory
results.

They could improve results by using the small but professional independent
direct marketing services available in most cities today. (The yellow pages have
listings.) The categories of services needed for direct marketing operations are
listed at the end of this chapter.

Staff

Manager

The manager of an in-house support center should have highly respectable
direct marketing managerial credentials. There is a temptation in many companies
to slide a promotable but unqualified employee into an in-house manager's slot.
Managers who have previous experience with in-house direct marketing programs
in other companies know what it takes to succeed. They know how to sell their
ideas and services to others. They know how to motivate people and they know
how to handle volume work flow. In addition to demonstrating fiscal responsibility,
they may also know how to run a cost center, or better yet, a profit center.

Support Personnel

When transferring company staff into line operations of an in-house support
center, the manager has to make sure these people make the adjustment. It is
much more difficult to conform to the stricter rules of the in-house profit center
than to the less stringent operating environment of a department budget center.
Yet, if company staffers can become competent in appropriate direct marketing
functions with a minimum of training, and can adapt to new direction, hiring
problems can be resolved.

Hiring of outside professionals is not easy either, since much of the available
direct marketing talent is steeped in the consumer side of the discipline rather
than the business-to-business side. In fact, after determining the length of the
learning curve required to train a qualified staffer to run the function, or the
time it takes to locate and hire an experienced direct marketing manager from
outside, the marketer may decide to postpone or abandon the decision to bring
the operation in-house altogether.

Justifiable Volume of Work

To perform any of the major direct marketing functions in-house requires high
fixed costs of facilities, equipment, and staffing. Volume of work governs investment
risk—usually the more volume, the less risk. But volume alone is not enough.
Consistency of work flow is critical for a cost-effective operation. If a 90 percent
or greater use of the resources can be projected over a 24-month period, chances
are it can pass at least one part of the ROI test.

Outside resources respond to peaks and valleys efficiently because their work
is spread over a larger client base. The business-to-business marketer pays for

this in overall fees. But for many marketers it is worth the extra dollars since erratic work flow can play havoc with productivity ratios and can cost an in-house operation heavily.

Dominance

When the direct marketing function plays an important role in the company's long-range strategic plan, there is more of a commitment to direct marketing programs.

This is true for a relatively small number of business-to-business direct marketers who generate huge quantities of mailings on a fairly consistent schedule. These are the catalog and solo mail order marketers whose products have universal appeal that crosses all businesses horizontally. For the most part, their very existence depends on the results of direct response mail and telemarketing efforts.

But, even though direct marketing is their dominant method of selling, the temptation to go in-house with all of the direct marketing service functions is tempered by the cost of high technology, specialized processes, and high-volume equipment. For instance, it is not unusual for a business-to-business mail order company to process its own orders, maintain inventory, and run accounting records, sales analyses, and reports in its own in-house computer center. However, the list maintenance function, because of its need for more sophisticated software and hardware, may be contracted outside. The payback on any large in-house investment calls for a consistency of use normally outside the range of an individual business-to-business direct marketer.

Technically Complex Products and Operations

One reason business-to-business companies or their divisions go in-house with direct marketing functions, particularly plans and creative ideas, is because their products or operations are extremely complex and difficult for outside direct marketing service firms to readily understand. The problem is compounded by the high turnover rate of outside resource service employees, which results in the expenditure of extra company time and dollars to continually orient and educate the replacements who service the account.

In-house staff turnover not only decreases, but educating and training the staff are easier because those functions become by-products of the daily job. These staffers have easy access to the information bases surrounding the products being promoted. They speak the language of the engineers and product managers, and are on the spot where all the marketing interaction takes place.

Companies with sensitive operations need the security implicit in a tightly controlled environment. Others with highly technical products tightly control what is said about their products as well as how their graphic identity is used. Many of these business-to-business marketers have in-house support centers because they feel outside creative groups usually have problems conforming to their stringent corporate guidelines. Also since specialized copywriters work within the company, they are in a better position to use the terminology peculiar to specific products.

KEYS TO EFFECTIVE IN-HOUSE OPERATIONS

For an in-house direct marketing support center to succeed, aside from adequate capitalization, it must have the key elements that comprise effective in-house operation:

- Staff talent and skill
- Managerial competence
- Motivation to succeed
- Freedom of action
- Selling know-how

How well this mix of abilities, incentives, and policies is formulated will determine the degree of success of the effort.

Staff Talent and Skill

The range of talents and skills in use today in business-to-business direct marketing is enormous. Some individual talents are in great demand by both in-house and independent direct marketing services—planners, strategists, and creative idea people top this list. Even though most direct marketing professionals lean toward working in independent direct marketing firms and agencies, a sizable number in just about every direct marketing category will opt for the relative job security of the business-to-business marketer's organization.

Effective functioning of an in-house direct marketing operation centers around talent and it begins at the top. The right manager in that spot knows how to hire talented, skilled, and motivated staff members. The professional most in demand for any marketing position has the right mix of experience, education, talent, personality, supervisory skills, and energy. However, direct marketing also requires sophisticated training, state-of-the-art knowledge, and commitment.

Recruiting top talent takes time. Forecasting the need well in advance improves the hit rate. If the decision is to go in-house with a direct marketing function, it is vital to get state-of-the-art talent and skill.

Managerial Competence

Even though an in-house operation may not be chartered as a profit center, it should be managed like one. If it is to succeed in the long term, it must be able to compete on the basis of value with its counterpart in the open market. In-house operations have a tendency eventually to either disband or grow into profit centers. So the in-house manager, if not already operating the unit as a profit center, should be prepared to expand the operation's financial parameters to include profit and loss statements, balance sheets, contribution to promotion and profit analyses, and other key financial documents.

The in-house manager must be able to calculate and compare the estimates with the actual costs of each completed job. All work effort must be pinpointed precisely not only to ensure a proper cost accounting system but also to learn who is good at a particular task for future assignments. Managers can compete better with independents by keeping track of the productivity of each employee with daily time sheets.

Actual costs of each completed job as listed in monthly computer reports can be a shock to managers who are getting this information for the first time. The manager now becomes aware of the cost effectiveness or shortcomings of each staff member. It is difficult when the manager finds out that some of the present staff members are not productive. Managers who work for large companies seem to wait too long before moving out the unproductive employees. Most large companies try to relocate these people into other jobs in the company. If unproductive people are unable to be removed, obviously the in-house operation won't succeed for very long.

On the other hand, the manager may find a need for more personnel to handle increased demand of in-house services. Ordinarily, hiring additional people may not be a problem. But, for instance, if the company has a temporary ban on new hires, the manager is challenged to come up with another solution. Overcoming this and other road blocks creatively is a necessity for in-house management effectiveness, especially in larger corporations. In this case, the solution could involve use of temporary help, employee overtime, or use of free-lance or contract workers. Although this may seem to cost more, a short-term solution can be more prudent over time.

Motivation to Succeed

More and more company managements are beginning to understand and appreciate that salary alone is rarely enough motivation for an in-house manager to succeed. The reason is simple. The manager competes with independent businessmen and businesswomen in direct marketing service firms who have a different and powerful motivation—personal profit. The in-house manager may be motivated for only two or three months until the effects of the latest salary incentive wears off. Therefore, special bonuses, profit sharing, and other rewards tied to the results achieved from the in-house operation are necessary.

Freedom of Action

Company guidelines and policies inhibit the in-house manager's decision-making ability and activities. Restrictions on overtime, hiring and firing, pay scales, and use of facilities and equipment stifle the freedom that the in-house manager needs to compete with outside resources. The more that an in-house support center resembles a profit center, the more freedom the in-house manager is allowed to get the job done.

Selling Know-How

Managing an effective in-house support center also includes competence in selling services to others and selling a point of view on occasion. Since outside firms survive or fail on their ability to sell their services, those who remain have mastered the techniques of selling. In the same way, by understanding and effectively using these skills, the in-house manager will not have difficulty getting and keeping clients.

CREATING AN IN-HOUSE SERVICE

Business Plan

A well-formulated business plan precedes the start-up of any in-house direct marketing function, whether or not it is a profit center. Of course, the underlying reason for a plan is its help in gaining financial support if the operation is a profit center. Other reasons for the plan are:

- It forces the direct marketing planner to think through the basic aspects in a businesslike way.
- It makes the marketer more disciplined and decisive by committing in writing to an action plan for achieving well-defined objectives.
- It spells out the mission and becomes a track to run on as implementation of the in-house plans move forward.
- It sets parameters for measuring operating results and allows the planner to maximize strengths and lessen potential problems.

A useful preliminary to the development of the business plan is visitation with in-house managers who run the same or similar direct marketing functions in other companies. Such meetings produce valuable advice that can help form ideas and expose pitfalls.

The written plan will list potential clients and a calendarized forecast of services that these clients will require from the new in-house support center. If the forecast is too low, the in-house operation will be understaffed and underequipped, damaging its reputation and causing problems in meeting clients' needs. If too high, many fixed costs and considerable overhead expense can result in higher client charges or a loss to the operation. Either way, the operation can lose. However, having a forecasted work load gives the marketer a target to shoot at and a basis for action when off the mark.

Beyond this, many questions need to be answered in the writing of the business plan. Among them are:

1. What can be done better in the new in-house operation compared to an outside independent service?
2. What are the short- and long-term objectives for the operation?
3. Specifically, how will it be organized?
4. What special strengths will the operation have that should be emphasized in the selling plan to clients?
5. What are marketing plans and schedules?
6. Will charges to clients reflect competitive pricing?
7. Are performance objectives high enough?

8. Do direct marketing service descriptions adequately cover in-house capabilities?
9. Is there substantiating research back-up for the plan?
10. Will original capitalization cover start-up expenses?
11. What can cause the plan to change in the next 12 months and what is at risk?
12. What is growth potential?

A pro forma profit and loss statement and balance sheet should be prepared for the marketer's own benefit, even if it may be a break-even operation. This exercise in fiscal responsibility can only help it become more cost effective. A return on investment analysis is mandatory in any case.

The marketer will have a detailed blueprint to follow when the in-house support center business plan is approved. Next, major action items need to be implemented early:

- Charter development
- Organization of personnel
- Facilities and equipment
- Budgets and financial plans
- 12-month timetable

The Charter

Although a charter for an in-house service function may not consist of more than two typewritten pages, its importance should not be underestimated. In it the scope, functions, and authority of the in-house service are spelled out for all in the company to see. In effect, it becomes a legal document or a tie breaker in those cases when interdivisional disagreements occur. The charter typically includes the extent of the company's commitment to the in-house direct marketing service, if it is established as a profit center or a cost center, and the degree of autonomy and authority the operation has. Also included is a statement indicating whether the policy is to allow the in-house group to solicit outside business and whether all divisions of the company would be "captive" or be permitted to choose their own services.

Personnel

It is not really difficult to attract talent. Although in-house salaries are not comparable to those of outside independents, there are some talented direct marketing people who are interested in the benefit package that the larger business-to-business companies offer. Long-term benefits and better job stability are the most prevalent reasons why in-house operations can attract these experienced professionals.

members. However, in an effort to promote from within, sometimes companies justify putting the wrong person in the slot. Managerial knowledge and experience in an in-house direct marketing function is mandatory. The more successful in-house direct marketing start-ups are run by managers who have entrepreneurial qualities.

More and more corporate cultures today allow entrepreneurial spirit to thrive. The entrepreneurial style is to make decisions quickly, and act on them fast. It can uncover failures quicker, establish successes quicker, and show a keen desire to focus intensely on goals. Joan Irish, a consultant on entrepreneurial management, lists seven major qualities of an entrepreneur:

- Low need for support
- High need for achievement
- High need for independence
- Leadership ability
- High level of energy
- Integrity
- Good judgment

Facilities

Ideally, the in-house facility should be centrally located and on a ground-floor location to facilitate movement of printed mailing materials. Because operational facilities are continually at a premium in most companies, in-house support centers often have difficulty getting the space they need. Skimpy allocations by the company limit the activities of the operation, severely so in many cases. Highly aggressive managers fare better in getting adequate facilities.

On the other hand, in-house profit centers usually don't have difficulty in getting what they need. However, some in-house profit centers have exorbitantly high overhead allocation charges imposed on them by their companies. Since cost of facilities varies significantly, it pays to know comparable local real estate rates. Often, corporate real estate and financial people are open to negotiation when excessive allocations can be proven.

Equipment

Deciding on the proper direct marketing equipment for in-house telemarketing, computer center, or lettershop is a challenge because the choices are extensive. Electronic data processing equipment, computer-controlled automatic equipment, along with highly sophisticated software systems that change rapidly, are understood by relatively few.

Talking to equipment salespeople can be informative, and sitting through vendor sales demonstrations can be educational, but viewing the equipment in operation in another user's place of business is the best learning experience. Also, independent EDP consultants, experienced in direct marketing, are invaluable in helping marketers make the equipment analysis.

Budgets and Finances

Only after having fully explored staff, facilities, and equipment needs can a realistic calendarized budget be prepared. Start-ups can generate sizable expenditures well before the in-house operation receives client income or allocations. Consequently, a firm understanding of the financial commitment and knowledge of how the in-house support center will be capitalized during this period helps establish implementation plan priorities. This knowledge could help avoid roadblocks caused by an unexpected event, such as management change or a company profit shortfall, that may prevent the full planned funding from moving forward on schedule. But aside from any funding problems, it is typical for an in-house operation not to break even the first year or two.

Soliciting the interest and guidance of financial and accounting management, and thoroughly acquainting them with the direct marketing goals, strategies, and programs, benefits the operation and the company. Most corporate financial people are not well informed in the direct marketing discipline and they welcome the orientation. Chances are that the more they understand the business plan and charter, the more conversant they will be in direct marketing, and the more they will support the operation.

Timetable

A well-constructed timetable can eliminate some of the confusion, time delays, and extra costs. Programming a detailed network of events and action items can lead to an up-and-running in-house support center. The timetable delineates a plan for accomplishing the projects in the precise order needed to optimize time and dollars.

After identifying the interaction that occurs among the various facets of the project, an estimate is made of the "best case/worst case" time frames for each step in the progression of events. From this a time schedule is established that alerts the manager early enough to take remedial action when a crucial date may be missed.

EVALUATION OF ONGOING IN-HOUSE SERVICES

The most objective evaluation of services handled in-house should come from clients: division marketing managers, sales managers, program managers, and others whose budgets and profit centers get charged for the in-house work performed for them. The in-house manager who may also happen to be the sole client for the services of the in-house support center must rely on the bottom-line profitability figure as a measure. If the operation is not a profit center, the manager will have to pay for an outside objective opinion. However, either way, any in-house group should operate under the assumption that it is competing with the best of the independents.

In-house service managers should periodically ask clients, "How are we doing?" questions. Of course, the questions will relate to the types of direct marketing services performed. But there are some basic qualification and performance criteria that apply in most situations. Questions about charges, quality, and timeliness of the service usually lead the list.

Getting the clients involved in the evaluation starts with a questionnaire in typewritten form. This is sent to clients followed by a personal review session between the in-house manager and each client. In this way performance analyses can be made for each criterion being measured. In addition, the relative importance of each criterion is taken into account and weights assigned accordingly by the in-house manager.

When all clients have made their comments in response to the specific questions, an overall rating of the in-house services is compiled. A quantitative view of the value of each criterion is derived by employing a rating guide. By comparing the clients' comments, the importance of each criterion on a comparative scale can be assessed.

To accomplish this, each criterion is given a rating of 1 to 10 (10 is excellent), and a composite rating is determined from the analysis of client's answers. After all the composite ratings have been determined for each criterion, an overall weighted rating is computed simply by multiplying the weighted factor by the rating in each column for each criterion (see Table 13-2).

Performance questionnaires and rating systems can improve rapport between in-house staffs and their clients. Open communication helps clarify each other's needs and leads to a strengthening of an in-house operation or a switch to an

Table 13-2. In-house performance rating guide.
Rating scale: 1–10 (10=excellent)

Criterion	Composite Rating	Weight	Weighted Rating Points
Competence	8	.9	7.2
Creative Excellence	10	.9	9.0
Knowledge of Client Needs	9	.8	7.2
Pricing of Services	6	.8	4.8
Fast Turnaround	5	.7	3.5
Product Knowledge	7	.6	4.2
Performance Standards	7	.6	4.2
Market Knowledge	7	.6	4.2
Cost Control	6	.6	3.6
Motivation	8	.5	4.0
Total Rating 51.9 points out of a possible 70			51.9

Creative excellence scored high as did knowledge of client needs. Improvement is required on moving work faster and on cost efficiencies.

Performance criteria established and weights assigned will vary depending on the direct marketing functions evaluated and the in-house manager's opinion of the relative value of each criterion.

outside service. Beyond this, the rating guide based on actual client evaluations minimizes the tendency of managers to defend that which they have built long after its value has eroded.

OUTSIDE RESOURCE OPTIONS

The Direct Marketing Agency

Another of the marketer's resource options is the direct marketing agency or general advertising agency that has business-to-business accounts. However, since direct marketing embraces many different functions that must be performed by people who have specialized expertise, it is not always cost effective for an agency to have all the functions performed by the personnel within the agency.

Some agencies draw on the talents of independent production houses, computer service bureaus, lettershops, and telemarketing services as standard procedure. Some use outside creative boutiques and free-lance copywriters and graphics artists necessitated by peak periods. These agencies usually operate with a minimum of staff, using outside sources for the details of tactical implementation. A business-to-business marketer may or may not feel comfortable with this approach. The mode of operation, however, is not what makes an agency deliver the results that the client marketer is looking for. It's the people who develop the plan and concepts and who know how to select the talent and put it all together. The direct marketing agency account director is a key member of the team that represents the needs of the client to the agency and provides the best the agency has to offer to the client.

When business-to-business marketers search for a direct marketing agency, they look for one that has an understanding of and experience in these seven areas:

- Direct marketing planning
- Segmentation analysis and market targeting
- Data base concepts
- Mailing list sophistication
- Research and testing techniques
- Copy and graphics expertise
- Experience in the marketer's direct marketing application

Business buyers react more positively to businesslike approaches. They have different buying motives and require more justification before making a purchase. Direct marketing agencies that have consumer experience only will tend to build their learning curve on the business-to-business side with the first few business-to-business accounts. The astute business-to-business marketer will avoid being the first.

It is also wise to investigate the area of direct marketing where the agency principals get most of their income and profit. It is in that area of specialization, whether in general counseling, campaign planning, mailing lists, creative services, or testing, that the marketer will get the most value from dealing with that support service.

Size and location are also decisive factors in a direct marketing agency selection. Size is important in terms of budget. When an agency is too large the low-budget client may get minimal attention. The big-budget client, on the other hand, can overwhelm a small agency's facilities and personnel. Location is a key factor because a marketer wants to get service when needed. And, of course, the marketer expects intelligence, good judgment, and intellectual honesty in those who run and work in the agency.

The traditional commission system of compensation for general advertising agencies still functions for many of the larger consumer advertisers who require full service. This system does not apply to direct marketing agencies. Most magazines, newspaper publications, and radio and TV stations grant a 15 percent commission for giving them business. The agency earns this commission because it provides creative and other services to the client.

Marketers who do not require full service negotiate an agency compensation arrangement where the agency receives only a partial commission or establishes a fee for work performed, rebating all or part of the commission to the marketer. Commissions from programs of smaller marketers often must be supplemented by a fee to adequately cover the services required. An advertising agency will also charge an advertiser 15 or 20 percent mark-up on all out-of-pocket expenses such as printing and photography.

Direct marketing agencies handling business-to-business accounts are compensated by a fee usually based on an hourly rate, because the media most prevalently used by business-to-business marketers, direct mail, and telephone are not commissionable. Because of this compensation system—and given the specialized creative skills needed and direct marketing's built-in accountability—the direct marketing segments of most general advertising agencies are organized as separate profit centers.

Most general advertising agencies today own a direct marketing agency. Client marketer demand for skills and talent in this area continues to increase at a rapid rate. Consumer mail order sales volume was up 12 percent in 1987 from 1986, but the business-to-business segment is growing even faster.

The marketer should make sure that agency personnel are available who have experience in the specific type of business-to-business direct marketing application needed, such as solo mail order, catalog selling, inquiry generation, or other types of sales support direct mail and telemarketing. As full service direct marketing agencies continue to proliferate, they offer more and more opportunities for business-to-business marketers to get complete direct marketing programs planned, implemented, and measured.

As will be discussed further later on in this chapter, direct marketing agencies can be located through various sources, including the following:

1. Directory section of direct marketing publications, such as *Direct Marketing, DM News, Catalog Age,* and *Target Marketing*
2. *Standard Register of Advertising Agencies*
3. Direct Marketing Association's membership directory
4. Business colleagues

Figure 13-1 lists 81 direct marketing agencies that volunteered information for

Figure 13-1. Direct response advertising agencies' U.S. gross billings.

Agencies Reporting Fees and Commissions Only

	Billings (in millions) 1986		Billings (in millions) 1986
Wunderman Worldwide	224.5	Central Advertising Agency, Inc.	6.2
Ogilvy & Mather Direct*	207.4	Associates & Larranga, Inc.	5.9
MARCOA DR Group, Inc.	110.0	HBM/Creamer Direct	5.3
Grey Direct International	94.0	JLA Direct	4.6
Kobs & Brady Advertising, Inc.	81.0	Parsons & Kern Advertising, Inc.	4.0
Chapman Stone & Adler, Inc.	80.4	Webb & Co.	4.0
Rapp & Collins Direct Response Group*	80.1	Lortz Direct Marketing, Inc.	3.9
FCB Direct	78.4	Taurus Marketing	3.3
Barry Blau & Partners	63.1	Jacobs & Clevenger, Inc.	3.3
McCann Direct	42.0	Cargill, Wilson & Acree Direct	3.1
McCaffrey & McCall Direct Marketing	41.0	Huber Hoge & Sons Advertising, Inc.	2.9
Lowe Marschalk Direct Marketing	40.9	J.W. Prendergast & Associates, Inc.	2.8
Fairfax Advertising, Inc.	40.0	Egan Advertising, Inc.	2.5
Ayer Direct	37.0	Haynes & Pittenger Direct*	2.2
Bozell, Jacobs, Kenyon & Eckhardt Direct	36.7	Carmichael-Lynch, Inc.*	2.1
GSP Marketing Services*	34.4	Malmo Direct	2.1
Scali, McCabe, Sloves Direct	31.0	Ronald A. Bernstein & Assoc., Inc.	2.0
Hemmings, Birkholm & Grizzard	26.0	Russ Lapso & Associates, Inc.*	1.9
SSC&B: Vos Direct, Inc.	25.2	Gerald Patlis Advertising	1.5

The Reich Group	25.1
Lawrence Butner Advertising, Inc.*	24.3
Fairfax Advertising, Inc.*	24.2
DFS Dorland Direct	21.7
Cramer-Krasselt/Direct*	20.7
Karl Rove & Co.	16.8
Tracy-Locke/Denver & Dallas	15.8
Clark Direct Marketing	15.7
Direct Inc.*	15.3
MacDantz Direct, Inc.	12.5
The Townsend Agency, Inc.*	12.0
Ketchum Direct	10.7
AC & R Direct	10.7
KKB, Inc.	10.5
Peter Vane Advertising	10.4
Muldoon Direct, Inc.	10.2
Evergreen Advertising & Marketing, Inc.	8.7
Wakeman and de Forrest*	8.5
Herring/Newman Direct Advertising*	8.4
Della Femina Travisano & Partners-Direct	8.1
Bloom & Gelb	8.0
Abelson Taylor, Inc.*	6.7
Hal Langerman Co.	6.5
MTD Marketing Direct	6.4

Henderson Direct	1.3
Campbell-Ewald Co.	0.6

Agencies Reporting Fees and Commissions Plus Internal Production Revenues

The Direct Marketing Group, Inc.*	138.7
Krupp/Taylor	64.8
The Direct Marketing Agency, Inc.	60.4
Epsilon	47.8
Customer Development Corp.	40.5
Direct Mail Corporation of America	40.0
Computer Marketing Services, Inc.	37.5
Grizzard Advertising, Inc.*	13.7
Manus Services Corp.*	12.4
Marketing Communications, Inc.*	11.7
Hub Mail Advertising	10.8
Nelson Panullo Jutkins Direct Marketing, Inc.	10.7
Communique, Inc.	9.3
Walter Latham Co.	9.0
Bruce W. Eberle & Assoc.	8.0
Frank/James Direct Marketing Co.	7.5
Creative Direct Marketing Group	3.5

*Audit available on reported figures

Source: Direct Marketing Association, 1987.

the Direct Marketing Association's 1985–1986 billing survey. The greater percentage of these agencies are qualified to handle direct marketing plans and programs for business-to-business marketers. Many small direct marketing agencies are not on this list even though they are successful because they do not want to go public with their billing figures. Such agencies are more difficult to find since they confine themselves to a fairly narrow but profitable client base. They limit their promotion mostly to word-of-mouth advertising.

Scanning the local business-to-business yellow pages may be helpful to the marketer who knows the specific areas of expertise of the firms listed, but to the uninitiated marketer it may take many phone calls to the various direct marketing service firms to find the bona fide full-service direct marketing agency wanted.

Some direct response agencies are listed in direct marketing directories as consultants, a term used loosely in this field. Some specialist firms such as computer service bureaus, lettershops, mailing list suppliers, and even direct response writers not only refer to themselves as consultants but as direct marketing agencies as well.

Consultants

Consultants are another resource group. Specialized consultants have expertise in one function of direct marketing. These specialists, highly knowledgeable in their field, often are financially connected to a service firm in their individual specialty. Independent consultants, on the other hand, offer completely objective advice and recommendations since they have no financial arrangements with other direct marketing service firms.

Outsource Networking

Still another choice is a concept referred to as outsource networking and it is gaining acceptance in some business applications. Its proponents enjoy the control advantages of an in-house function without giving up the benefits of outside resources. And only those individual skills and talents most appropriate for a particular program are used.

The network concept centers around a single outside direct marketing professional under contract to the marketer. This coordinator selects the outside independent talent and resources needed and coordinates all activities among these resources to ensure maximum effectiveness. The coordinator also acts as the planner and strategist as required and is usually retained for a specific program or group of programs. Coordinators are much like general contractors who hire subcontractors to perform most, if not all, of the work but are just as professional as the resource people within the network.

The professional chosen for this job should have the proper experience to help the marketer make the right decisions fast and with little risk. Actually the more outside network people on a project, the broader the range of ideas that can be applied to it. Network resource people have worked on all kinds of projects, using the tools of direct marketing in many applications in different fields and industries.

Networking permits the marketer to profit from the vast experience and the current techniques employed by other marketers—the kind of experience the marketer cannot afford to have on the payroll. The marketer can be more flexible and yet have more overall control. With the right coordinator leading the effort, it can be an effective way for the business-to-business marketer to launch a program and to learn for future use how it is done. The hiring of a professional coordinator full-time by the marketer is a logical extension of this concept if direct marketing volume and program continuity warrant.

LOCATING DIRECT MARKETING SERVICES

Buying independent direct marketing services is nothing new for business-to-business direct marketers. So perhaps the *best* source for searching for such services can be found in other direct marketers who can be trusted and who have had good experience in dealing with an individual service. Checking with the local Better Business Bureau for any obvious complaint problems before making a decision helps ensure the right choice as well.

In addition, there are several published sources that the business-to-business marketer can consult to find the right services to handle specific direct marketing functions. The Direct Marketing Association's Information Central has a Supplier Register and Service Directory series that lists and describes direct marketing service firms in major categories. *Catalog Age* publishes a sourcebook of information on hundreds of suppliers to catalog marketers. Also, each issue of *Direct Marketing, Catalog Age,* and *Target Marketing* contains a paid directory listing of direct marketing service firms. The following list gives contact information for each source:

Direct Marketing
    224 Seventh St.
    Garden City, NY 11530-5771
    Phone: (516) 746-6700; out-of-state (800) 645-6132
    Henry R. Hoke Jr., Publisher

Catalog Age and *Catalog Age Sourcebook*
    6 River Bend
    Box 4949
    Stamford, CT 06907-0949
    Phone: (203) 358-9900
    Charles I. Tanner, Publisher

Direct Marketing Association
    Supplier Register
    6 East 43rd St.
    New York, NY 10017
    Phone: (212) 689-4977
    Ann Zeller, Information Central

Target Marketing
    401 N. Broad St.
    Philadelphia, PA 19108
    Phone: (215) 238-5300

Target Marketing lists more than 2,500 independent direct marketing firms that serve the industry in their *1987 Who's Who of Direct Marketing.* These service organizations assist marketers in all aspects of direct marketing from planning through the many and complex phases of implementation. The listings in *Target Marketing* reflect the growing number and variety of direct marketing services now available to help marketers in every conceivable area. Included next from these listings is a broad range of categories of direct marketing services appropriate for business-to-business marketers. Marketers will find these categories useful when looking for appropriate services in published references, directories, and the Yellow Pages.

Creative Services

Firms that create copy, design graphics, place direct response ads, and offer advice on direct marketing strategy:

    Direct marketing advertising agencies
    Direct marketing art and design services
    Direct marketing consultants
    Direct marketing copywriters

List Marketing Services

Firms responsible for securing and maintaining names and addresses:

    List brokers and consultants
    List compilers
    List management companies
    List manager (in-house)
    Marketing services: Co-op and package inserts
    Service bureaus: credit clearance
    Service bureaus: data base management companies
    Service bureaus: geographic, demographic, psychographic
    Service bureaus: list maintenance

Telemarketing Services

Firms that make calls, receive calls, and tell users the best way to approach calling:

Incoming services
Outgoing services
Telemarketing consultants

Printing and Production Services

Firms that prepare material for the press, process it on the press, and ready it for mail processing:

Printers of:

card decks
catalogs
direct response packages
envelopes
forms
general promotion
labels
personalization
plastic cards
postalgrams
prepress
protective packaging
specialty printing

Mail Processing Services

Firms that convert materials into mailable packages:

Electronic mail
Expedited delivery carriers
Lettershops
Mail monitoring services
Service bureaus
Mail processing computer software

Equipment and Supply Services

Firms that manufacture and distribute equipment and supplies for mail processing lettershops and service bureaus. Included here are computer manufacturers and computer software suppliers:

Addressing/labeling equipment
Computers
Computer software

Inserting and collating equipment
Mail processing equipment
Postage meters
Telemarketing equipment
Peripheral direct marketing equipment

Fulfillment Services

Firms that handle the back-end functions of direct marketing:

Caging and cashiering
Fulfillment services
Lead verification
Order processing
Software systems

SUMMARY

Personnel in charge of business-to-business direct marketing resources require high-level management skills regardless of the direct marketing functions. The sales-support direct-marketing function is fully accountable even though its budgets may be less clearly defined than the mail order budget. Those in charge work in concert with other sales support groups who relate to the same sales goals. In mail order marketing the manager is accountable for profits whether the operation is run as an independent specialty business or a business unit of a multichannel company.

Effective management of the information base has become the key to the mail order direct marketer's success. Analysis and accountability are the basis for successful mail order direct marketing efforts. Financial planning attempts to measure the profitability of each program and attendant risks. Among the planning and evaluation tools used by mail order direct marketers are:

- Profit and loss statement
- Contribution to selling costs and profit analysis
- Calculation of break-even
- Response
- Back-end performance analysis
- Life-time value of a customer

The three major factors that affect direct marketing profitability are unit contribution, selling cost, and response rate.

Sales support direct marketing competes for budget dollars with other support activities that have similar objectives, yet it has an advantage since it is more measurable and can be held more accountable. Of the three popular budgeting approaches, sales maintenance, arbitrary "top-down" guideline, and task, the latter, with its preliminary assessment of opportunities, is the purest approach. Presenting sales-support direct-marketing programs well in advance reduces budget plan rejections later.

Before determining the "make or buy" decision the business-to-business marketer needs to evaluate each of the direct marketing services required. Those most often in demand include creative services, telemarketing, lettershops, computer service bureaus, and response handling services. Each of these functions is performed differently depending on whether the direct marketing objectives are sales support or mail order.

Next, the marketer needs to understand the points of view continually debated between in-house direct marketing proponents and outside resource specialists. Issues center around whether the in-house or outside resource will provide services more creatively and more effectively for less cost.

The consideration of carefully weighed options leads the marketer to intelligent resource choices. Considerations focus on philosophy and style of management, type of business and product, existing capabilities of staff, volume and consistency of services, and dominance of the direct marketing function in the company's objectives.

Centrally organized companies lean toward support of in-house operations. However, these units can thrive in decentralized companies as well, when operated as a profit center.

Abilities of personnel, management incentives, and organizational policies comprise the keys to effective operation of the in-house support center. A mix of talents and skills of staff people, in-house managerial competence, motivation to succeed, freedom of action, and selling know-how raise the in-house support center to a professional level, functioning conceptually as a profit center even though organizationally it may not be one.

A well-thought-out business plan provides an in-house start-up with a disciplined approach and a blueprint for follow-up. High-energy achiever types have start-up successes with early implementation of key action items: charter development and organization of personnel, facilities, and equipment, along with financial plans and a 12-month timetable.

The best evaluation of an ongoing in-house service comes from its clients. Performance criteria can easily be established in the form of questions to be answered by the clients of the service. By consolidating the responses and adding weights, a performance rating guide can be developed that will point out service strengths and weaknesses.

For those business-to-business marketers who elect to use outside resources, there are direct marketing agencies, ad agencies, consultants, and thousands of independent direct marketing specialist firms from which to choose. Services cover the full range of the marketer's needs.

14

RESPONSE-HANDLING SYSTEMS

Responses or inquiries from business-to-business direct marketing promotions demand well-thought-out handling systems and procedures. The way inquiries are handled for sales support objectives is distinctly different from the method needed to follow up on a response for a mail order objective. Sales support inquiries must be qualified and then passed on to salespeople for personal follow-up. This process, which also includes tracking the inquiry through the sale, is normally referred to as inquiry handling. Responses from media used for mail order objectives, on the other hand, deal with orders for products and services. The process that handles these responses through the customer satisfaction phase is known as fulfillment.

SALES SUPPORT INQUIRY HANDLING

More than 100 million inquiries are generated each year from many sources: trade shows, space ads, direct mail, card decks, reader service cards, telephone, and publicity releases. Millions of dollars are spent by industry to get these inquiries but much of this money is wasted because there is either no follow-up or follow-up is delayed too long. If it takes more than four weeks for action on an inquiry, it is more than likely that the inquirer has forgotten about it.

Typically, medium and small business-to-business companies have relied on reader service cards from their advertising in various trade magazines for the bulk of their inquiry-getting activity. These cards are circled and mailed to the publisher by the reader. Publishers in turn deliver them to the appropriate advertisers. Analyses of these reader service cards indicate that most readers who fill them out are only interested in receiving information by mail rather than having a salesperson call.

A secretary or clerk of the advertiser then may sort these by territory along with inquiries from other sources. For many companies the standard inquiry-response package consists of a brochure, and a specification sheet or price list. When this is mailed out to the inquirer a copy of the inquiry is sent to the regional sales manager or salesperson. Any qualification of the inquiry will come from the "bounce-back" response card contained in the inquiry-fulfillment package.

Why Inquiries Go Unanswered

Inquiries are valuable to the direct marketer not only because of sales that may result when they get in the hands of the salespeople but also because even those that do not end up in a sale provide the marketer with important information about customer markets. They can be thought of as the first step in developing new customers and creating long-term relationships. Some marketers follow an inquiry only through the sending of the requested information. Others determine the degree of quality after looking at the inquiry before deciding what they will send to the inquirer. These marketers have two offers—one is less expensive for those inquirers obviously not qualified to be a prospect; the other is a more elaborate package.

Unfortunately, many inquiries end up on a shelf in the home office or in the back of a desk drawer in a sales office. There are many reasons why salespeople don't follow up inquiries. When an inquiry card comes into a sales office, even experienced salespeople have difficulty determining its value simply by looking at it. Many feel their time is better spent calling on and selling prequalified prospects rather than performing the qualifying function. And many feel that unqualified inquiries are not worth following up. Also, some salespeople are expert at face-to-face selling, but fall short when it comes to telephone inquiry qualification. Salespeople have their own sets of priorities and inquiry follow-up can be very low on their list.

Many salespeople have ceased to get excited when so-called "hot" sales leads are sent to them by well-meaning home office personnel because of the salespeoples' past negative experiences with inquiries. Salespeople are proud professionals but most do not think too highly of the home office. Their sales territory is their domain and they feel they know more about it than anybody else. Therefore, they also do not welcome the unsolicited standard form memo from a home office staff member that says, "Here are some great hot leads in your backyard. Follow them up in 30 days and let me know how well you did."

It is a fact that some sales organizations are actually resentful of advertising and sales promotion departments getting onto their turf, canvassing for inquiries and then qualifying them as sales leads for their follow-up. These salespeople, and some field sales managers as well, feel that it is part of their role to identify from their sales territories those potential customers who are worth calling.

Indeed, no one should be able to qualify a prospect better than the salesperson whose objective and motivation are to go for the sale. But, for many marketers, the high cost of field selling mandates that today's salespeople must be more productive. Economic necessity dictates that the early-on steps of the selling process be handled in a more cost-effective way, through the use of direct marketing and advertising. This focuses the salespeople's talents and strengths on what they do best—securing prospect action with convincing demonstrations and persuasive selling techniques.

The main objective of a lead-building program is to eliminate 60 percent of the salesperson's time that would be spent performing the function of finding, identifying, and qualifying prospects. Direct mail and telephone lead-generating programs can perform these tasks quicker and at much less cost.

The Advertising Research Foundation did a study in the early 1980s that confirmed the disdain salespeople have for inquiries that come from direct response efforts. The results indicated that less than a third of the companies represented by the inquiries sent to field salespeople are ever contacted by a salesperson. Yet a majority of the inquirers do buy the product or a similar one because they have a real need for it.

Overcoming Sales Force Apathy Toward Sales Leads

The problem of too many unqualified inquiries going to the field and resultant negative reactions of the salespeople plagues many inquiry-handling operations. The big question, how to get the salesperson to follow up a sales lead and then report on it, remains unanswered until the business-to-business lead planner overcomes objections of the sales force. Following are six tactics that can eliminate sales force apathy toward sales leads.

Establishing Credibility

The prime reason for the success of most lead-generation programs is the planner's ability to establish credibility with the sales force. There is nothing that will establish credibility in a headquarter's lead program better than continually generating leads of a high enough quality that allow the salespeople to convert them to sales at an acceptable ratio. That is the goal. Also, any claims made for the program should be backed by facts.

At the same time, attention should be paid to eliminating any negative experiences salespeople may be having in not getting their questions and requests answered promptly. When a commitment is made to the field by the direct marketing coordinator or advertising manager, it must be kept. By following through on all promises the planner will get the salespeople to pay attention and to look forward to the next commitment. Planners cannot break faith with salespeople in the field and expect them to feel good about it.

Learning the Salesperson's Driving Force

The direct mail planner must learn what makes salespeople tick. What motivates them to action? Is it sales achievement? Recognition? Dollars? Most salespeople are individualistic and they must have sizable egos to make them successful. Also, the planner should demonstrate a willingness to understand the salespeople's job by making sales calls with them to learn their language, how they relate to customers and prospects, and how they use their selling skills.

Typical salespeople get more excited about dramatic illustrated direct mail materials even though plain direct mail letter formats generally work better for inquiry-generating objectives. This fact should be kept in mind by the program planner, especially in the early stages of developing sales force interest and enthusiasm for the program. Graphic direct mail materials and showmanship techniques can be very productive in getting inquiries, but creative and production costs are not always affordable. Striking a balance by producing both types can be an answer.

Communicating to the Field

Often minimized in some direct marketing and advertising departments is the need for the planner to continually stay in touch with the field salespeople. Motivational materials are always of interest, but specifically news and information about what is going on in the lead program and schedules of proposed mailings should be spelled out in organized periodic field communications.

Maintaining interest in a long-term lead-generation program through ongoing communication with the field can take the form of "how-to" booklets, newsletters, and internal direct mail campaigns. Also, planners can take advantage of the fact that most field salespeople today have access to video recorders. They can provide them with taped demonstrations on salient subjects, such as how to integrate direct mail into individual selling strategies and how to get the most out of sales leads. Many sales offices also have PCs, so communicating by electronic mail is a speedy and dramatic way of sending sample letters and research results to a sales force.

Involving the Sales Force in Lead Program Planning

Of course, one-way communication rarely gets the job done. The smart lead planner closes the loop with the sales force by asking for input on current programs and requesting copies of any direct mail materials used in the past. Since field salespeople are the key players in the lead-generation program, the planner should get their ideas and suggestions well before plans have crystallized. Asking for comments about the kinds of leads they perceive are best establishes needed rapport and understanding. This helps guarantee that the program will most closely complement field selling strategy. The introduction of the lead-development program to the field salespeople becomes, in effect, a result of their input. This fact should be emphasized along with the idea that this sales-support lead-development system can augment their selling efforts.

Involving the Sales Force in Each Lead-Generation Mailing

Placing the names of the salespeople on the lists of prospects and customers who will receive mailings will keep the field well informed about what gets mailed and when it is received. Sending copies of the mailing lists to the salespeople in advance of the mailing gives them a chance to make changes or additions. Also, salespeople can better prepare for follow-up of leads that result from mailings when they have advance sample copies of the direct mail fulfillment packages normally mailed to inquirers by headquarters.

Providing Quality Leads

The salesperson is interested in quality of leads first and quantity second. Any new program from the start must generate leads that can be turned into sales at an acceptable rate. A good way to guarantee this is to qualify every inquiry by telemarketing or by an additional direct mail offer. Even though planners are tempted to stress larger numbers of sales leads at the expense of quality during the early stages of a new program, overemphasis on inquiry quality is preferable.

Business-to-business direct marketers must select the right inquiry-handling system for the specific sales support objectives. If the marketer generates inquiries to get information about target markets, the follow-through on the inquiry will be quite different than it would be for sales lead-generation objectives. Telequalifiers generally are interested in getting information for research purposes, so their conversation with the inquirer is not sales-oriented but rather image building.

Some marketers have difficulty setting up systems to track their inquiries because operations within their own company are inefficient and cannot match files of sales orders and inquiries. An effective computer system tracks the inquiry from the time it is received by the marketer to its final disposition. A well-designed system will make handling inquiries simple and easy.

Computerized Inquiry Handling

A state-of-the-art inquiry-handling system can enhance salespeople's appreciation of the overall lead-building sales objectives and get them to follow up every inquiry sent to them and report results back through the system.

Computerized inquiry handling supplies the business-to-business marketer with a wide range of management tools triggered by an inquiry entry transaction and driven by a multifunction process. Lead tracking in this system ensures automatic follow-up with salespeople, inquirers, and order files. If the system is sophisticated enough, prequalification is done by running incoming raw inquiries against data bank criteria of high-, medium, and low-potential prospects.

For instance, Dun's Direct maintains a highly structured on-line file of names of companies and decision makers complete with demographic information. When the marketer receives an inquiry from a direct mailing, for example, the name and company is computer matched, producing a printout of all the data Dun's has on that business. From this information the planner can determine the quality of the inquiry.

Even small marketers can have an efficient system with commercially available software programs that can be used as is or adapted to specific needs. These sophisticated systems generate reports that can give direct marketers just about all the information they need to know. They can provide concise source analyses for each week for all leads. Other reports can analyze inquiries by product or sales division or by type. They can report each lead source by cost per lead and cost per sale and can evaluate expenditures and help justify effectiveness of advertising and promotion dollars.

Publishers, as a rule, take between four to six weeks to get inquiry information to the advertiser via the reader response card. Responding to this problem, Cahners Publishing now offers its advertisers an on-line system that allows the advertiser to access inquiries generated by ads on a daily basis. Of course, if a direct marketer places response ads in a magazine that traditionally pulls few inquiries, an on-line system could be very expensive.

Other publishers are using computerized inquiry-handling systems as promotional tools to help their salespeople sell more advertising space. For a fee they send the advertisers their inquiries on magnetic tape or floppy disks. A cost analysis will determine if such a system will be effective for an individual marketer.

Some computer inquiry-handling systems lead telephone sales communicators, using a branched questionnaire as a model, into suggesting a salesperson's visit or even asking for the order. Or the communicator may refer the inquiry to a company specialist or may simply send the requested literature.

Qualifying by Telephone

Telephone communicators must be courteous, knowledgeable, and able to answer questions. A script is key because it enables the communicator to target qualified and interested prospects by covering four areas: money, authority, need, and desire. This helps the prospect get over the buying decision hurdle.

At the outset, the need is pinpointed. After determining the prospect's desire to overcome problems, the communicator helps the prospect to justify taking action by explaining what the product will do to solve the problem. When prospects have the ability to purchase the product, the communicator attempts to lead them to a buying decision. The script provides answers to the main questions a prospect may ask. When the prospect is interested and qualified, the communicator will normally make a referral to a salesperson immediately. This qualification process helps assure that what is sent to the salespeople is not a raw inquiry but a highly qualified sales lead.

Companies that use telequalification find that turnaround time is speeded up. The ideal system will handle an inquiry within 48 hours including prequalification hours. Advertising that has an 800 number facilitates the inquiry-generation process. However, not every inquirer wants to make a telephone call. The 800 numbers in ads usually attract those prospects who are closer to taking buying action. Some less-ready prospects prefer a reader response card. When both are used the needs of the prospect are best met. Allowing the inquirer to choose between making a toll-free call or returning a business reply card lets the advertiser know the degree of urgency a prospect may have for the product or service.

When a marketer continually generates a high volume of inquiries, or the products are very complex and technical, an in-house facility with trained tele-marketing personnel and fulfillment handlers may be needed. Handling the functions in-house maintains control over the prospect data base at all stages in the qualification process, follow-up, and analysis.

Handling Inquiries In-house

When direct marketing management decides to have inquiry requests handled in-house, all personnel involved including salespeople should be trained to ask for and record sources of information. The professional telemarketing manager should share with workers reports detailing inquiry activity and a description of how this data will be used. This involvement helps the workers understand and appreciate the bigger direct marketing picture. Also, everyone in the operation should be alert for unclassified inquiries since the system can break down if there are too many.

Most marketers operate an inquiry-handling system in-house with mixed results. Most larger operations are computerized; very small companies may have a manual system in place. For it to be successful the marketer cannot think that just because a system is in place anyone can run it. In some companies this function is delegated to an employee as a part-time job and is treated incidentally.

When starting up a system, the sales-support direct-marketing manager must decide which reports to generate, the maximum and minimum work loads, and the complexity of the system. The manager must know what the system can do, when it can be operational, and who will be responsible for it. Development costs have to be kept to a minimum. There must be sufficient power for processing especially during peak time needs. Management must understand needs of other departments using the computer. The inquiry-handling system should be tested as it is being put together to ensure that it will work as planned.

Handling Inquiries Outside

Since pressure is always on to get prospect inquiries processed immediately, and since inquiry production can vary widely day to day and week to week, a flexible manpower pool is vital. Independent inquiry-handling service firms have little problem shifting personnel or tapping an established, experienced manpower pool of their own. A marketer's in-house inquiry-handling operation, on the other hand, may not be able to meet important turnaround time objectives with consistency because of its inflexible company policy of not allowing overtime or temporary workers as needed. This often forces marketers during these periods to use "a la carte" services offered by independent firms.

If an advertiser historically generates a small number of inquiries and does not make mailings very often, chances are it may be advantageous to use an outside service bureau to at least respond with the first fulfillment package.

Because of the business-to-business marketer's wide range of inquiry-handling requirements, from simple to complex, independent firms also offer their standard computer programs and other inquiry-handling services on a piecemeal basis. Many marketers take advantage of this. However, regardless of where the elements of the inquiry-handling system are performed, the wise marketer does not plan for an evaluation of a new system until sales conversion figures are known. This can take a full year or more.

An organized approach to choosing an outside bureau starts with a written checklist from the marketer. The marketer's needs must be specified precisely, indicating:

- Marketer's present volume of orders
- Description of how all calls and correspondence must be handled
- Description of the reports needed
- Results expected along with future projections

The marketer should request proposals from several bureaus indicating specific information wanted, such as:

- Names of present clients and nature of services performed
- Brief history of the firm and its capabilities and equipment
- Background of the personnel
- Samples of reports that personnel generate
- Indications of the time required to meet addressing requests
- Average time to process an inquiry
- Procedures for handling complaints
- Pricing policies and costs of additional services

The Business/Professional Advertising Association is most helpful in suggesting names of inquiry-handling firms experienced in business-to-business operations. Some of the more well known include:

Inquiry Systems and Analysis
    Division of Hub Mail Advertising
    25 Drydock Avenue
    Boston, MA 02210
    Gerald Posner, President
    (617) 542-6290

LCS Industries, Inc.
    120 Brighton Road
    Clifton, NJ 07012
    Arnie Schiene, President
    (201) 778-5588

On-Line Business Systems, Inc.
    2801 North Western Parkway
    Santa Clara, CA 95051
    Carl Frye, Branch Manager
    (408) 987-4444

Inquiry Handling/Telemarketing Services

If an outside telemarketing firm is hired to handle sales support inquiry handling, the manager should look for one that has had experience in the same field. Most telemarketing service bureaus do not have much experience in the complex industrial arena. Any telemarketing operation under consideration should be reviewed closely, especially the projects the firm has worked on.

Since telephone service bureaus are essentially data processing firms, they do not interpret data or recommend action. Full-service telephone marketing agencies, however, can implement complete inquiry-handling programs or can act as consultants for a client's in-house operation.

Telemarketing operations costs are determined by the complexity of the application. Some fulfillment applications are simple, such as order processing and customer service. But with some products, telemarketing applications can be very complex, especially for sales support objectives.

Key charges include cost per phone hour, cost per call, and cost per order or response. Additional costs are incurred for handling literature requests, customer service, and gathering information for research purposes.

A decision to go with an outside fulfillment group should, in many cases, be preceded by a complete comparative cost analysis of in-house versus outside services. The manager must also know what type of reports will be useful, such as analyses of cost per inquiry. Using estimated volume figures, the direct marketing manager should request estimated costs for a single month and a 12-month period.

Special requirements should be listed and discussed, such as the extent of liability the bureau will assume for work done in error, the name and background of the client representative, and the control procedures that will be in place to assure accuracy and security for lists and materials. All good service bureaus improve and add capabilities to meet client needs. Visits to prime candidate bureaus should confirm this.

MAIL ORDER FULFILLMENT

Handling responses in business-to-business mail order falls under the heading of fulfillment and has a different meaning from response handling for sales support objectives. In selling by catalog or telephone, the fulfillment operation is concerned with processing customer orders and resolving customer problems after the order is shipped.

A complete fulfillment cycle has many steps and each one must be performed correctly or the reputation and eventually the profitability of the mail order effort can be damaged. Computers provide the only economical means to capture all the important high-quality information generated by a fulfillment system. This vital information feeds the prospect and customer data base. Because there is such a great need for data collection, data processing, data analysis, and complete management report systems, a fulfillment operation simply cannot function efficiently without computerization.

The extensive number of elements of an operation include dozens of tasks that fall within these basic services:

- Order receipt and entry
- Credit and order processing

- Inventory control
- Payment processing
- Warehousing
- 800 number service
- Shipping
- Customer service handling
- List maintenance
- Sales management reports
- Marketing analysis

Of course, the value of any fulfillment system lies in the computer software program that drives it. Modular software contributes to an effective system that must grow and change as the mail order program objectives grow and change to maximize profit potential.

In-house vs. Outside Services

The fulfillment cycle begins when a prospect places an order by mail or telephone. More and more use is being made of the telephone by business-to-business mail order marketers (although some have yet to be convinced of the value of the 800 toll-free number). Because of this extensive use a large number of marketers have installed in-house telemarketing operations. In-house telephone communicators usually perform with more dedication and confidence than outside services, drawing on a wide knowledge of the company and its products.

Some marketers go in-house with only a segment of the fulfillment function. For instance, credit approval is of special importance to business-to-business marketers since most sales are made by extending credit and billing the customer. Here, the volume of orders will determine if credit screening can be more cost effectively done outside. Costs, however, are not the only consideration. A marketer who feels the need for hands-on control may opt for an in-house fulfillment center even though a cost comparison shows less cost outside.

Some marketers go to an outside resource to take advantage of the latest technological software and hardware systems for fulfillment applications. This reduces the risk of having an inadequate computer system inside. Other marketers simply do not want to be involved with the highly detailed procedural aspects of the fulfillment operation. They would rather concentrate on the merchandising and marketing end of the business, dealing with catalog development, control of inventory, and analysis of the evolving customer base.

The *Direct Marketing Association's 1987 Membership Directory* lists 18 fulfillment service firms, such as the HYAID Group, a full-service fulfillment firm of over 450 employees. *Target Marketing's Annual Directory* lists Who's Who in Fulfillment firms that handle back-end functions, caging and cashiering, fulfillment services, lead verification, order processing, and software systems.

The way a business-to-business mail order marketer's fulfillment operation is managed can spell profit or loss. And it is the direct marketing manager's job to make sure the center collects the kind of information needed to compile the required management reports. Sales predictions should be in a form that will enable results to be measured. A fulfillment manager's primary responsibility is to make sure that the offer made in the promotional material contains no fulfillment promises that cannot be kept.

Managing the fulfillment process begins with receipt of orders and inquiries by mail or by telephone. The manager should capture all relevant data coming into the fulfillment center: orders, inquiries, product returns, and shipping time frames with appropriate demographic breakdowns. The processing steps of entering, coding, credit checking, and data capture for the data base are followed by appropriate shipping, billing, and inventory documentation. Inventory availability governs shipping schedules. Good control here keeps expensive back orders to a minimum. Also, picking, packing, and shipping, unless performed correctly, can result in costly returns. Timely and accurate billing is an additional function of fulfillment, as well as handling customer complaints and inquiries.

Fulfillment policies and procedures must be efficient and productive because they impact directly on current profits, as well as on future sales. Because of this, fulfillment operations must be customer service oriented. Impeccable service makes customers want to reorder. The best kind of service allows a short time span between order entry and order shipment. For example, a marketer selling supply items that are delivered in 24 to 48 hours can have a competitive edge.

For any product, a shipping time frame should be stipulated in the promotion to avoid customer dissatisfaction. Of course, fulfillment managers are in a better position to make decisions or to recommend changes that will improve the operation when they have a complete understanding of the direct marketing objectives.

Managers of those mail order fulfillment operations that are completely automated should have a working knowledge of various fulfillment systems, manual as well as electronic, and be computer literate. However, the fulfillment manager manages the total operation—not just a computer. Knowledge of postal regulations, performance standards, forms design, work layout, and work flow are all part of the fulfillment manager's job.

Before any fulfillment mailing is made, the mail order package should go through a complete cycle of mailing and fulfillment to catch any problems and correct them. Also, the actual mailing should include a special address from which the direct marketing manager can place an order to evaluate how well and fast the orders are being handled.

Direct marketing managers find it advantageous to visit the fulfillment center before fulfillment begins to discuss the order form with the center's personnel. They can also discuss with the fulfillment manager the possibility of including a printed piece promoting other products in the fulfillment package. The visit will also enable the direct marketing manager to observe how complaints are handled. Fulfillment centers often use form letters to reply to customers and inquirers. A check on these may turn up a need for custom communications.

When the mailings have been completed the direct marketing manager should again visit the center to collect any leftover materials or to arrange for proper storage for a future effort. The direct marketing manager monitors the productivity of the fulfillment operation whether it is in-house or outside, and makes it accountable.

SUMMARY

A fulfillment system differs markedly from an inquiry-handling system. Inquiries from a response-generation program for sales support applications represent only one step in the selling process. Those inquiries must be qualified before they can become a sale. Responses from a mail order promotion, for the most part, represent the entire sale.

Sales leads from the home office are not always received with open arms by salespeople. This resistance must be overcome for a lead-generation program to succeed. The lead-generation manager can help eliminate this apathy by establishing credibility with the sales force, learning what motivates salespeople, communicating to the field, involving salespeople in program planning and in each lead-generation mailing, and providing quality leads that will have a high rate of conversion.

A computerized inquiry-handling system links all informational aspects of the inquiry program, recording each transaction, as well as qualifying inquiries and interacting with salespeople, customers, and inquirers. Different software programs are required for each sales support objective but this software has become affordable for even the small marketer.

The telephone and the computer have speeded up the handling of inquiries by those business-to-business marketers who have learned to use them profitably. Telequalifiers aided with a script help ensure that salespeople get only qualified sales leads.

When searching for an outside inquiry-handling service, marketers look for those that have experience in applications similar to theirs.

Mail order fulfillment includes the basic functions of receiving and processing orders and inquiries, shipping, billing, and customer service. Since fulfillment is one of the critical steps in a mail order operation, direct marketing managers need to know how a customer service-oriented operation should be run and they should be involved in the details of the fulfillment center operation. Computerized operations require highly knowledgeable management personnel.

15

LETTERSHOPS AND POSTAL MATTERS

LETTERSHOPS

Business-to-business direct marketers who mail in volume can find all the services necessary to implement a complete direct mailing in most lettershops. In addition to basic processing of printed materials such as packaging, addressing, postage affixing, and delivery to the post office, some shops offer copywriting, layout, and finished art and lists. Also, list brokers often work through lettershops.

Most direct marketing operations do not have the kind of volume needed to justify an in-house lettershop. The exceptions are the large-volume mailers who have high-frequency multimarket programs on a continual basis.

If an in-house facility is decided on, these marketers will find that locating appropriate personnel for an in-house lettershop is easier than for other direct marketing services because of the production-oriented processes and procedures. A mix of skills is needed. Some personnel are hired on their ability to handle routine functions; others who do well in office work tests handle more complicated procedures. In all cases, employees must score high in accuracy. Apart from this, today's lettershop staff requires a high degree of technical competence because of the accent on higher technology.

The considerable investment in staff, equipment, and facilities may, however, put undue pressure and emphasis on use of the in-house facility. The marketer's direct mail programs, created and designed to augment the marketing and sales manager's dynamic objectives, are frequently planned to conform to the capabilities of the in-house lettershop. As an example, the use of six individual pieces in a mailing package could be the best tactical decision for a program but it may be cut back to four pieces to accommodate the in-house four-station inserter. Timing of a mailing is another example. Rather than mail through an outside lettershop because of in-house work load, the program is held up waiting for available production time. This saves up-front dollars, but perhaps affects tomorrow's sales. For these reasons, many marketers take the least risk and choose an outside lettershop.

What Lettershops Do

The increasing availability of computerization has enabled many lettershops not only to expand their capabilities in letter processing, personalization, list maintenance, inquiry handling, and product and literature fulfillment but also to take on actual data base development and other computer applications for their clients. Most lettershops will handle such details as sending customer or prospect names to the nearest dealer, picking up orders at the post office (caging), as well as processing and logging them in the computer. Much of this work is automated, using software programs designed specifically for lettershops.

But not every lettershop has a computer. Mechanical addressing systems can still be found in some lettershops and continue to function cost effectively for the small-quantity mailer. Scriptomatic's 4000 addressing system, with features similar to a computer's, handles list maintenance in the smaller shops. In fact, some of these shops, very adequate for some small business-to-business mailers, still use Addressograph or Speedaumat machines for addressing. These make use of metal plates imprinting through a moving ribbon.

Preparing a package for mailing requires a variety of equipment, depending on complexity of the package. Binding machinery will cut, trim, fold, collate, stitch, or staple. High-speed Cheshire machines affix computer-generated address labels on mailing envelopes or mailing cards. Postage meter machines hooked to multistation inserters make short work of stuffing letters, cards, and folders into envelopes, sealing the envelopes, and applying postage meter imprints all in one speedy operation.

Coding Capabilities

Business-to-business direct mail planners should visit several lettershops before determining the one to use. Knowing the average size of a mailing that runs through a specific lettershop will help the marketer determine if that shop is large enough to handle the marketer's business. Some mailings can be too small for the larger lettershops to handle efficiently. Knowing the kind of equipment that will be needed and the format it will accommodate will help the marketer find a lettershop that will be able to do the job correctly and competitively.

Sorting

The lettershop's job of sorting is simplified because most mailing lists are already sequenced by zip code, city, and state. However, lettershops must be capable of preparing direct mail to comply with requirements for zip code separation, bundling, and mail sack identification and of taking care of all the forms that are required by the postal service for each mailing. Larger lettershops that specialize in very high-volume mailings have loading platforms to accommodate postal service trucks that pick up the mailings for direct distribution. This is a great convenience for the lettershop and it gets mailings to prospects and customers sooner.

Some large lettershops have electronic sorters and optical character readers. Zip codes on the outgoing envelopes and bar codes on return envelopes using electronically readable font characters enable the mailer to save money. The lettershop eliminates expensive manual labor and the coding allows presort discounts. Electronic scanners and readers also help tally the number of responses received each day, letting the marketer know where the action is.

Printing Services
Many lettershops are now offering printing services. New technological processes have revolutionized the printing industry. Lasers that have many different uses also are found in a new method of printing that is having great success. It is very fast, printing up to 9,500 pages per hour or half a million labels. Laser printing has been cost effective only for marketers mailing in the millions. Increasingly lower costs of high technology are rapidly changing that.

Laser printing is done by a beam of light writing on a photoconductive drum that lays ink on the paper. It then goes through a heat process to bake the ink into the paper. Laser printing is especially good for personalization since it can print in a different size and typeface as well as location throughout a direct mail package. Laser printers offer many different font types, including simulated handwriting, making letters look more personal and therefore more believable.

Ink-jet printing is cheaper than laser printing but it is not letter-quality printing. Ink jet or variable image systems (VIS) printing is a noncontact, plateless, electronically controlled method of printing on standard paper at high speeds. Jet-spray nozzles spurt ink into uniform drops onto the paper.

Ink jet printers are very versatile in the variety of tasks they can perform. In addition to allowing many different type sizes and creative graphics, they can personalize, serialize, address, identify, and code materials on-line, right at the bindery. This process can also apply glue, die-cuts, and sequential numbering. Six lines of address can be printed on the outside of a catalog while printing, serializing, coding, and addressing is being printed on inside order forms directly from the marketer's computer input, on-line, all at bindery speeds.

The Web Printing Process can produce eight colors perfectly registered on both sides of coated papers in one pass at high speed with unvarying quality. This process can also produce two four-color jobs simultaneously. For lower-quantity printing jobs, it can be efficient for six-color sheet-fed printing.

Small business-to-business catalogers now can save money by printing more than one targeted catalog at a time with demographic binding. Catalogs can be custom designed to meet pinpointed targeted marketing goals, reaching only the most profitable customers and best potential prospects. Demographic binding can deliver completely different catalogs or create only minor changes, such as different covers. Binding equipment produces custom catalogs from data received from a computer during the binding process. The fact that different catalogs can be printed at one time and then mailed may earn the cataloger a discounted postal rate. Data base management costs could be justified just by the savings in postage.

There are printing systems now in operation that create complete mailing packages in traditional-looking envelopes, all produced simultaneously on-line. Unique press equipment combines ink and computer-generated printing in multiple colors at the same time on six rolls of paper. As well as being a time saver, this system has the advantage of eliminating overruns. The marketer can print only as many packages as the number of names on the mailing lists. This process, however, is not yet economical for the small mailer.

In some lettershops computers are on the counters to be used by walk-in customers to select and set type style and design a printed page. Some of these shops can link their computers to their customer's office terminals to call up forms, letterhead formats, and artwork.

Tips for Dealing With Lettershops

Normally by the time the direct mail package arrives at the lettershop, big dollars have already been spent and time has just about run out on the schedule. There is no room for hitches at this final stage. These ten suggestions will help guarantee a smooth lettershop experience.

1. Check to make sure the weight of a dummy package is within postal limits.
2. Proofread each element in the package after printing—one more time.
3. Employ quality control on printed pieces. Check for typos and production glitches.
4. Do not date the letter. Unexpected, inevitable mailing delays can render a dated letter obsolete and require a reprinting.
5. Check size of mailing elements; ¼ inch is needed for clearance on each side.
6. Get postal service approval of mailing package.
7. Provide mailing schedules to the lettershop beforehand, along with dummy package with pieces stapled in sequence.
8. Insert mailer's name within the list to receive mailing as an after-the-fact check on mail processing accuracy.
9. Double check the printed quantity of each piece in the package and the envelope to ensure there will be no shortage.
10. When mailing is especially critical or expensive, or consequences of a failure are high, visit with the lettershop supervisor to double-check specific instructions immediately before the lettershop has scheduled the mailing for processing.

Direct marketing managers are aware that the lettershop will waste some materials (called spoilage) so they build into the quantity of envelopes and other materials delivered to the lettershop enough extra to take care of this waste. When the lettershop makes a mailing it will notify the mailer of the date it went out plus the count. Lettershops always return material not used or will store it until another mailing is scheduled.

Lettershops have an association, MASA (Mail Advertising Service Association International, 7315 Wisconsin Avenue, Bethesda, MD 20014), which has printed guidelines for ethical and professional lettershop management.

POSTAL SERVICES

Since direct mail is becoming more and more a major segment in the business-to-business marketer's promotion and selling mix, it is important that not only mail supervisors but planners as well become familiar with the regulations of the United States Postal Service. A thorough understanding of the scope of services and regulations can expand the marketer's creative planning parameters and at the same time avoid expensive mailing problems.

Maximizing the value of the USPS means getting to know the local postal service personnel and the published information they issue. Publication 113, entitled "First Class, Third Class and Fourth Class Bulk Mailings: Permits, Preparation, Regulations," is available from local postmasters. Material especially appropriate for large mailers is contained in "The Domestic Mail Manual" and the "Postal Bulletin," which updates changes in the manual between printings. Bulk mailers can keep informed of proposed changes as well as other information by receiving "Memo to Mailers," a bimonthly mailing in a newsletter format.

The United States Postal Service is divided into 74 divisions. Each division office is located in a major city throughout the country, and is staffed to handle postal problems that business-to-business direct marketers may encounter. If problems arise for the bulk mailer that cannot be satisfied at the local bulk mail acceptance facility, the mailer can discuss the situation at the next level—the U.S. Postal Service Mail Classification Office.

Guidelines of Interest to Marketers

The postal service prides itself on its very strict interpretation of the mailing rules. Mailings are rejected if they are not prepared for postal service handling in accordance with these rules. For instance, when mail bundles are not tied securely, the postal service will reject the mailing. The bundle must stay together through rough handling by postal workers. String or rubber bands may be used as long as they are strong enough to hold the mailing pieces together. Frequent mailers are aware that often the stock used for the printed material can cause the bundle to come apart. In particular, when heavy glossy envelopes are stacked they do not hold together in a bundle as well as other types of envelopes.

Postal service rules also cover sacking. Sacked mail going to a sectional center facility must contain 12 or more bundles of mail with a five-digit zip code to a designated city, and a three-digit zip prefix or a combination of these going to a specific state. Each stack must have a label that uses the correct labeling format for second- or third-class bulk mail. And each label must be legible and written with an indelible pen if prepared by the mailer. Preprinted labels are made available to the mailer from the postal service. An accurate count of the number of mailing pieces is necessary to ensure acceptance when verified by postal clerks.

Mailing package printing standards also must be met on the address side of the envelope or piece. New mailers will find it worthwhile to review proposed mailings with the mail classification office before printing. Potential postal problems can be avoided before costly printing changes have to be made.

Permits must be bought by bulk mailers and these need to be checked against the material to be printed. For instance, if the mailer uses precanceled stamps, a return address must be printed on the envelopes. Return reply envelopes have definite size and format rules to be followed. Reply mail must have the phrase "No postage necessary if mailed in the United States" printed in the upper right hand corner of the front of the mailing piece. The horizontal bars that permit scanning must be placed parallel to the length of the mailing piece and must be printed beneath the permit indicia. The words "FIRST CLASS MAIL PERMIT NO. XXX" and the name of the issuing post office (city and state) must be printed in capital letters.

Sometimes mailers send out mailings from cities other than where their business is located. The bulk mailing permit, however, must be issued from the location where the mailings are made. To get the permit, the mailer must send a sample of the mailing with a form 3602 PC to the specific postal service facility handling the mailing.

The postal service also has envelope guidelines and addressing rules. The words "urgent" and "priority" or any other words that imply expedited delivery are not allowed unless the words "bulk rate" or "nonprofit organization" are more prominently displayed than any other words in the permit imprint. Also there must be at least ⅜ inch of unused space surrounding the permit imprint, which must be easily read.

Sorting different classes of mail can be confusing and is best left to experienced lettershop personnel. For instance, presorted first-class mail with five-digit zip codes must be in bundles of at least ten pieces and identified by a red label D. If the bundles have 50 or more pieces for one particular city, they are identified by a C sticker, and bundles of 50 or more going to a three-digit zip code prefix require a green 3 sticker.

Mail can be rejected if it appears harmful in any way to either the postal handlers or the equipment or even if it can damage other mail. When staples are used they must be completely closed.

A handy reference guide covering postal guidelines and mailing systems is found in Appendix 11.

Automated Services

The postal service, aware of the need to improve mail services, has been developing an automated mail processing system, using high-speed equipment, optical character readers (OCR), and bar code sorters. The handling of bulk mail and business reply mail has always been a problem for business-to-business direct marketing mailers. Much of this mail takes too long to get delivered. The new automated systems being tested now are designed to reduce manual handling, which should get all mail delivered in a shorter time. This equipment will permit reply mail that has a zip plus 4 code and bar code to pass through the bar code sorter where it will automatically calculate the correct postage and fees and also print an itemized bill for the mailer.

The 9 digits of the zip plus 4 code are translated into vertical bars and half bars. They are preprinted by the mailer on the lower right-hand corner of the mailing card or envelope. Only postal service bar code images are permitted. Stats of these images are free of charge to the mailer from USPS division offices. "Facing marks (FIM)" are vertical bars printed in the upper middle portion of mailing pieces. These marks identify mail with preprinted bar codes.

The OCR scans the last line on an address label, and unless there is enough white space around the address information, the OCR cannot read it. When the envelope is read by the automatic sorter it segments the mailings for further processing, transportation, and final delivery. Business-to-business direct marketers who plan large mailings should notify the postal service of upcoming mailings in advance so their processing can be prescheduled.

The Problem of Undeliverables

One of the major problems business-to-business direct marketers have is the sizable percentage of bulk business mailings that never get delivered. This wastes more than the postage for the marketer. Direct marketers may request address changes from the postal service, using form 3547, but every time a mailing is sent to the wrong address it can cost the marketer over a dollar, since direct mail materials as well as original postage and request for address correction must be taken into account.

Some mailers believe that the high percent of nondelivered mail is caused by postal employees who do not have an appreciation for the importance of promotional mail. The USPS is aware of the negative attitude of some workers and is addressing the problem with the help of the Direct Marketing Association by emphasizing the value of promotional mail to the postal services mail handlers.

On the other hand, the postal service believes that much of the problem of nondelivery is caused by mailers themselves. Businesses move and change addresses. Mailers need to analyze the lists they use to get a better feeling for the percentage of delivery they actually can achieve. According to Ed Burnett of Ed Burnett Consultants, 15 percent of the 8 million businesses in the United States moved or changed in 1987; 1.2 million new businesses started up. The USPS processes approximately 140 billion pieces of mail each year and 2.3 billion require some kind of correction to make them deliverable. On some mail the zip code used is incorrect or the address has not been typed correctly.

Address Correction

The postal service offers mailers a change of address service (ACS) via its Address Information Center (AIC) master file located in Memphis, Tennessee. The system was originally designed to give mailers of regularly issued material, such as magazines, changes of address on magnetic tape rather than paper, fast and affordably. Mailers who use this service get an ID number from the postal service, which they print on the face of the mailing package to be mailed. This number lets the postal service know that address change information is wanted by the mailer. The mailer also prints the ID number of the name on the mailing package. This helps the ACS match the old address with the new one.

Letter carriers and other postal workers at delivery points input data changes periodically, manually and electronically, to the 197 Computerized Forwarding System (CFS) sites. From there the information goes to the AIC. This ACS system returns to a mailer the address change or undeliverable-as-addressed information prompted by an actual mailing piece.

However, when the newer National Change Of Address (NCOA) system becomes fully operational, it will provide mailers who have converted their lists to include zip plus 4 codes with the opportunity to get corrections before a mailing is even made. Mailers will also get faster delivery since address changes will be initiated by the USPS. When in operation the NCOA system will provide forwarding addresses of those who have moved in the past 18 months and will eliminate undeliverable addresses from customer lists. This system will also enable the postal service to add missing elements to an address.

The NCOA service list had in mid-1987 about 29 million records, which are updated monthly. This list has been transmitted to a selected licensed group of 20 private service bureaus. Updated master file information will be sent every two weeks to licensees. These companies set their own prices and have minimum charges.

Other change of address products are being developed that may become viable alternatives to those of the postal service. Many large users, when they have the resources, are handling this function on their own computers. Smaller mailers may opt to have a service bureau perform this task. The cost of a service bureau to handle the coding will depend on the size of the file and how concentrated the file is geographically.

Zip Plus 4

The postal service has not been happy with its ability to educate mailers about the benefits of converting their mailing lists to zip plus 4. The success of the USPS's automated delivery system rests with these four digits, which are carrier route codes. This additional information will allow the mail to be sorted and distributed in "chunks" similar to what an individual carrier would deliver on a route. Automation is essential to the postal service because it keeps the cost of handling by manual labor from driving up postal rates. Mailers interested in converting their lists to include zip plus 4 codes can rent or purchase software packages that perform this task.

The postal service is criticized by some mailers for being inflexible with rule interpretations that benefit only a few business-to-business mailers. In the final analysis, costs are always weighed against the bottom line. The postal service views the zip plus 4 discount offered to first-class mailers as an incentive. Yet these discounts are not attractive enough for most third-class mailers to switch from their third-class carrier route presort discount.

The fact that more than half of all third-class mail is presorted is proof that this presort program has been very popular for third-class mailers. One of the reasons for this high use is it allows these mailers to demographically target their messages. The presort helps mailers control their postal costs and they feel they get more efficient mail handling and delivery of third-class mail in 10 to 14 days. However, only a very small portion of business-to-business mail has enough geographic concentration to qualify for carrier route presort.

SUMMARY

Lettershops continue to expand services to meet the increasing needs of large and small business-to-business marketers. The larger lettershops now have systems that optically read OCR codes on mailing pieces, link lettershop computers with customer's office terminals, and provide unique binding for demographic targeting. Also, new methods of printing that offer more efficiencies and more opportunities to personalize and segment are services now being provided by some lettershops. Because of the diversity of services and equipment available, marketers need to shop around for the lettershop that comes closest to filling their specific needs.

Since the United States Postal Service strictly enforces its rules and regulations, it is especially important that the business-to-business direct mail user become familiar with all the rules to avoid potential expensive mistakes.

New automated mail processing systems at the USPS, which use zip plus 4 codes and preprinted postal service bar codes, aim to reduce manual mail handling and improve service to mailers. The NCOA system provides time and cost-saving advantages to those mailers who use zip plus 4 coded lists.

PART III

Direct Marketing Strategies

16

GENERAL SALES SUPPORT
AND MAIL ORDER STRATEGIES

Strategies are the use of plans and methods needed to achieve a specific program objective. Mail order strategies have a single goal—to make a sale. Sales support direct marketing strategies, however, are only one part of the selling process where salespeople actually make the sale. Direct marketing strategies are, in effect, the marketing and sales strategies for mail order. In sales support, they complement the marketing and sales strategies.

MAIL ORDER

When business-to-business marketers choose mail order as a channel of selling they must prepare to commit to a long-range strategic plan. Time and resources must be committed, often for one or two years before the operation becomes profitable. Each mail order promotion has sales goals that become more and more specific as the early stages of testing evolve into a mature operation. Mail-order direct-marketing strategies continue over the life of a specific sales plan for each product. And when a plan changes, strategies usually change also.

Launching a mail order operation requires long-range planning, marketing planning, and creative planning. The major strategies and tactics enumerated in Table 16-1 are those most commonly followed by today's successful business-to-business catalog planners. Marketers can maximize chances of reaching their goals and ensure long-term marketing success by using these proven mail order strategies. Seven of these strategies deserve special attention.

Table 16-1. Direct marketing strategies and tactics in mail order catalogs.

Long-Range Planning

1. Investigate fully with a feasibility study before launching a new catalog operation. Look for a niche to fill.
2. Offer market-driven products.
3. Build a long-term customer, not a one-time sale.
4. Employ customer development techniques.
5. Position the catalog with a unique image in the market to be served.
6. Organize catalog operation as a separate cost center business unit with a solid financial plan.
7. Build a customer data base.
8. Develop a dedicated data processing facility.
9. Organize an entrepreneurial management team committed to the mail order operation.
10. Staff with experienced customer service personnel.
11. Establish marketing orientation in back-end operation, especially financial.

Marketing Planning

1. Use market research to reduce risk.
2. Explore key list sources for best combinations of target markets.
3. Target several markets with different offers to each.
4. Concentrate on one catalog or in a few narrow market segments only if the budget is limited.
5. Don't limit catalog sales to items marketer presently produces.
6. Don't limit catalog sales to present customer base.
7. Seek opportunities to create separate "spin-off" catalogs for selected segments of customer list.
8. Provide high-profit, market-responsive products.
9. Don't depend on price alone as the main selling strategy.
10. Feature products that fit a specified image. The more exclusive or unique, the better.
11. Choose products that have a definable and accessible market.
12. Choose products that have reasonable shipping and handling costs.
13. Choose products that can lead to future sales of supplies, accessories, and replacements.
14. Trade on winners; forget losers.

Creative Planning

1. Write to the specific audience only. Speak the audience's language. Be brief.
2. Look for special reasons why the audience should buy from that catalog.
3. Highlight benefit copy first, then features and functions for each product.

4. Use headlines to tell benefits of one product, a group of products, or a page or spread of related products.
5. Make it easy to determine what the product will do for the reader.
6. Replace editorial puffery with hard-sell editorial.
7. Match copy, graphics, and paper stock with image.
8. Understand reader tendency to view pictures first, price second, and text third.
9. Get closer to the customer with involvement techniques.
10. Convince the prospect that doing business with this catalog is fast, easy, and risk-free.

    a. Eliminate all footnote and "turn-to-page" clarifications.
    b. Repeat the toll-free 800 number often.
    c. Repeat the guarantee on the order form.
    d. Include personal bank card payment options.
    e. Keep the shipping chart simple.
    f. Keep price and other essential specs in designated areas of product layouts.

11. Maximize the value of prime readership pages.
12. Employ a graphic design concept to the entire catalog.
13. Group individual photos of products by customer use.
14. Use graphic symbols to identify product groupings.
15. Take advantage of attention-getting value of photography and graphic dominance.
16. Vary layout and color to fit the product.
17. Keep type 8 point or larger.
18. Give every product in the catalog an opportunity to do its selling job.
19. Do not oversell the catalog or products.

Strategy: Offer Market-Driven Products

Business-to-business mail order marketers find that a market-driven product strategy is best for long-term growth. Products selected should meet the needs of their niche markets. Marketers can get customers to tell them which products should be carried in their catalog by using creative approaches. For instance, Inmac, a leader in the highly competitive computer supplies and accessories catalog field, solicited new product ideas with a contest and received 450 new ideas. Then, 12 months later, it followed up with a questionnaire to its customers, requesting more new product ideas along with demographic information.

    Some innovative catalogers sponsor monthly focus group sessions with customers to improve catalog content and service. Because a large portion of the profit, if not all of it, comes from existing customers, it pays for the marketer to get customer input and continually analyze the variety of products offered.

Strategy: Develop a Long-term Customer, Not a One-time Sale

The cost of getting a new customer often exceeds the gross income received from the first sale made to that customer. It is a common strategy in business-to-business mail order marketing to invest in new customers at an initial loss, since it is the lifetime value of the customer that determines the customer's ultimate profitability to the marketer. And even though business response purchasers tend to be more loyal to suppliers than their consumer counterparts, they cannot be neglected.

A marketer's customer list often produces three or four times more orders than are generated from general prospect lists. The marketer of *Edmond Scientific,* a mail order catalog of optical equipment to engineers, expects six repeat orders from every new customer secured. Building this profitable long-term relationship with potential customers means mailing and calling frequently.

Strategy: Employ Customer Development Techniques

Making every customer contact positive is a solid step in the customer development program. Solo mailings serve as cordial contacts between catalog releases. Keeping customers informed about credit, billing, complaint procedures, shipping, and delivery provides quality service before, during, and after each purchase. Order confirmation by telephone is appreciated by customers and gives the marketer a reason to sell benefits of quantity purchases and explore possible customer needs for accessory items or supplies. Combinations of direct mail and telemarketing promotions encourage increased order size, purchase of additional products, and more frequent purchases.

Strategy: Establish a Unique Image in the Market Served

Product differentiation is one of the best contributors to the unique image a marketer needs for mail order success. Of course, to capitalize on the uniqueness, each promotion must highlight the special feature. For instance, a policy of offering dramatic prices can make a big difference in how a marketer is perceived by the marketplace. Also a policy of providing special customer service, like getting an order to the prospect overnight instead of in 48 hours, can identify a marketer as special. This kind of service can distance a marketer from competitors. For example, Quill ships all stock items in 8 to 32 hours. Demco ships 95 percent of all stocked items in 24 hours.

Strategy: Provide High-Profit, Market-Responsive Products

The most profitable products are those that have features not readily available in other products, reasonable shipping and handling costs, and high-interest turnover (i.e., are purchased fairly often) and are products that lead to additional sales of accessory items, supplies, and replacements. Of course, these products must have real value to the person and company making the purchase. The availability of charge privileges through bank cards and travel and entertainment cards makes sales of some higher-priced, higher-profit products possible. It is a tall order, but if an innovative marketer can find products that fit the mold, customer loyalty can be built, making it very difficult for competition to move in.

Strategy: Target Several Markets with Different Offers to Each

More responses result when mailings speak directly to the interest of each market segment rather than to the larger marketplace as a whole. Reduced version catalogs or solo mailings can highlight high-interest products targeted to narrow markets. Using different copy approaches for different markets, while the product line and product benefits are the same for all markets, is a successful technique used by Bob Dorney, founder of Daytimers. The Seton Name Plate Company has used 25 different offers among various segments in one solo mailing.

Strategy: Explore Key List Sources for Best Combinations of Target Markets

Business-to-business mail order buyers are good names for catalog mailings but generally these lists are neither large enough nor plentiful enough. To compensate for this some catalogers actually rent consumer mail order lists but mail only to those that indicate a company name. Circulation lists of paid trade magazines work well for some products. *R&R Direct,* the catalog arm of Reynolds & Reynolds Company, launched its software and supplies catalog by renting computer trade publication lists and response data bank lists.

Externally compiled lists do not, as a rule, pull well for mail order efforts. Yet some marketers find it profitable to overlay highly structured compiled lists with response data banks. A list strategy of the *Edmond Scientific* catalog is to overlay inquiries for the catalog received from various sources with a list supplier's data bank, like that of Dun's Marketing Services, in order to build SIC code, number of employees, and other demographics into the list. The result is a mail response list structured with characteristics that enable future catalog and telemarketing efforts to become more profitable.

Large manufacturers of capital equipment using their own customer lists can get good response using mail order promotions for supplies, accessories, and other aftermarket products. Marketers should analyze their current lists or data base to identify profiles of best customer companies in key industries of interest. These lists constitute premium catalog mailing lists when the names are overlaid with a business-to-business response name data bank like that of Direct Media.

Some business-to-business catalogers and solo mailers build sizable house lists of customers and inquirers that become a major source of orders for future mailings. Hewlett-Packard, when introducing its pocket calculator, produced in a two-year period 300,000 names that could be mailed profitably. In order to produce that result, over 300 different mailing lists were tested.

SALES SUPPORT

In sales support direct marketing the strategies are normally related to and developed within the major use categories that include research, building awareness, generating inquiries and reinforcing a planned sales call. It is within the context of individual uses and the specific objectives to be met where planners develop their strategies.

Most strategies for sales support direct marketing require more than a "one-shot" mailing piece or telephone call to get the job done. Direct mail campaigns designed to penetrate key accounts, keep present customers sold, and help build customer loyalty need several mailings in a series to make an impact. Continuity of contact with appropriate messages must be maintained in order to build customer and prospect awareness to meaningful levels. This process of educating involves the principle of repetition through a series of messages to each buying influence.

In most cases, inquiry-generation mailings should also be scheduled for more than one mailing during a campaign or a plan period. Actually, as long as responses result and can be profitably processed, additional mailings should continue for extended periods.

Many inquiry planners will schedule waves of three mailings, all with the same offer, spaced weekly or biweekly. On an average, the first mailing of a three-piece inquiry-generation mailing series to business and industrial universes, mailed two weeks apart, each with the same information offer but not the same benefits message, will receive about 45 percent of the total of all inquiries received from all three mailings. Thirty-five percent of responses result from the second mailing and 20 percent from the third.

There are many strategies in the various categories of sales support direct marketing. Table 16-2 lists the major strategies and tactics in use today by leading business-to-business sales-support direct-marketing users. How strategies can apply within the major direct marketing uses is reviewed next for two main objectives of the business-to-business marketer: breaking into a new market with a current product and entering a new product into a current market.

Table 16-2. Direct marketing strategies and tactics in sales support.

Long-Term Strategic Planning

1. Institutionalize direct mail and telemarketing as an integral part of the marketing mix.
2. Build responsibility and accountability for sales support direct marketing into communication division's charter.
3. Build a customer and key prospect data base.
4. Establish resources knowledgeable in business-to-business sales-support direct-marketing techniques.
5. Position the company and its products with a unique image in the market to be served.
6. Help build long-term customers.
7. Merchandise strategic benefits of direct-marketing sales-support programs to field sales force.

8. Bring prospects closer to the company and its salespeople.
9. Measure all inquiries against qualification criteria.
10. Test list segments, offer options, and creative approaches continually as a by-product of making a scheduled mailing.
11. Build measurement yardstick into every indirect response mailing.
12. Spell out measurable objectives for every direct marketing promotion.
13. Conduct a continuing "seminar" with marketing and sales management on advanced principles and procedures of sales support direct marketing.

Marketing Planning

1. Explore key list sources for best prospect markets to target.
2. Create opportunities to contact selected segments of the marketplace.
3. Target only definable and accessible markets.
4. Maintain continuing communications with the customer.
5. Concentrate on mailing to market segments according to a value hierarchy.
6. Provide a continuous flow of sales leads to the sales force.
7. Establish customer-development direct-marketing programs.
8. Use the toll-free 800 number on all promotions.
9. Establish 36-hour turnaround on all inquiry fulfillment.

Creative Planning

1. Build rapport with direct mail reader.
2. Match all elements of direct marketing with corporate image.
3. Design direct mail to appeal to a nonconsumer audience.
4. Think like a buyer, not like a seller.
5. Speak the language of the business audience.
6. Spell out messages in terms of what the reader wants to hear.
7. Maximize the value of personalization.
8. Use reader involvement techniques.
9. Tell the truth—no embellishments, no overselling.
10. Use short words, short sentences, and short paragraphs.
11. Grab attention with unique presentations.
12. Back-up proof convinces cautious business prospects.
13. Stress money-back guarantees.

Sales Objective: Breaking into a New Market with a Current Product

The marketing mix designed to build new marketplaces normally includes many programs, campaigns, events, and activities that involve personnel, equipment, facilities, sales training, advertising, and promotional support tools. All must be coordinated if the program is to succeed.

Research: General Strategies

When expanding into new markets with an existing product, a seasoned marketer has the advantage of past experience in selling the product with the same or similar marketing mix. Where the new market is simply a geographical extension of the present market, no research may be necessary. But where markets are different, the profile of the "best customer" may be different, dictating a change in the marketing mix and tactical implementation of the direct marketing strategies. Research can help set direction for the new promotion.

Market research will also reduce the risks usually associated with a new market launch and will help determine if this objective is even attainable. Sophisticated market research techniques may be unaffordable for some companies, but even the smallest marketer can conduct opinion surveys using a strategy of combining the quantitative advantage of the mail questionnaire with a qualitative in-depth sample survey by telephone. Two essentials are (1) having the surveys directed to a representative cross-section of the potential new market and (2) getting answers to the right series of questions relating to past and present product usage, brand or supplier loyalty, and decision-maker buying behavior.

Even though the product is the same as the one sold successfully in established markets, a brand new market may require different sales-support program-implementation approaches. If the product has different applications, the planner may need mail and telephone surveys to position the direct mail and telemarketing program that will best support the launch. This research will help determine the new "best market" profile, offers, and on-target creative techniques to use. The value of the research expenditure is weighed against the risks of investing many dollars on hiring new salespeople, and furnishing offices and warehouses, equipment, samples, and demonstration products for perhaps a 12-month period.

Awareness: General Strategies

Any entry into a new market raises the question of how the marketer will get prospects who will become buyers. Advertise and publicize, of course! Yet, when a new market may consist of a small geographical entity, there may be few cost-effective media in which to place product releases or announcement ads. Regional issues of trade publications are rare, broadcast is inefficient for most business-to-business marketers, and local club and association newsletters do not have nearly the reach or impact that new launches require.

Awareness direct mail has become a workhorse for getting the marketer's message across to highly selective groups of prospects not only geographically but demographically. Also, for those marketers who find it practical to have an awareness advertising program in trade and business publications, these direct mail campaigns can provide added impact. This strategy not only generates high-quality readership from selected influentials and key decision makers in the top 5, 10, or 20 percent of the marketplace, but also provides it during the specific time periods most suitable to the marketing plan.

Building the prospect's awareness of the marketer's expertise in a product or service in a new marketplace is rarely accomplished with one or only a few contacts. Since most trade publications are issued monthly, relying on print advertising support alone to prepare the way for the sales effort can be a mistake. Direct mail advertising with its innate ability to generate individual reader rapport can dramatically change customers' and prospects' opinions about a marketer or a product in as little as four months. The wisdom of this strategy was demonstrated in seven mailings made by NCR to its financial marketplace (see Chapter 12).

The initial task of an awareness direct mail campaign is short term for this particular sales objective. Its aim is to rapidly establish a mind-share in a specific segment of the new marketplace in preparation for direct response promotional activities that will lead to face-to-face sales calls.

Frequency and timing of awareness campaign mailings is critical to the success of the next stage in the selling plan that includes more mail, telephone contacts, and personal sales calls. Generally, the more message contacts prospects are exposed to within a prescribed time period, the more they will remember the message. However, the marketer should anticipate that a very pronounced drop-off in recall after the awareness campaign can negate much of its value. This can be minimized by beginning the next series of prospect contacts within two or four weeks after the awareness campaign ends.

There are four problem areas where marketers, in their eagerness to enter a new marketplace, have trouble using awareness direct mail. The first concerns reach—the number of people who should be covered by the campaign. Marketers tend to include too many nonprospects on the mailing list. Awareness direct mail should never be used to blanket broad market universes (generally speaking, rarely more than 5,000). Its higher cost cannot compete with other media in getting mass advertising impressions. A marketer's past experience in other marketplaces and research into the new marketplace should pinpoint, at least generally, the high-, the medium-, and the low-profit potential prospect groups. Singling out only the high-profit group to receive the awareness campaign can be the most cost-effective strategy.

The second concern involves mailing frequency. When breaking into a new market where the company name is not well known, if known at all, more awareness mailings will be needed to capture enough mind-share for future lead-generation efforts to pay off. But the number of direct mail advertising impressions is only part of the story since impact also must be counted. Too few mailings in the awareness series can fail to make the needed impact. Mailing frequency depends on how complex, detailed, or technical the message must be. Awareness applications for some products require the use of different creative strategies to make a strong impression. Dimensionals or other showmanship campaigns can do this job. For instance, a series of 6 blockbuster mailings may well outperform 12 plain, personalized letters.

Confusing the objectives of an awareness campaign with those of an inquiry-generation campaign is another commonly made mistake. Some marketers believe that mailings should always include a reason for the recipient to respond. This is, of course, fallacious. The function of an awareness mailing is to get greater reader mind-share. If a direct response request is added, it alters the meaning and the reader's perception of the entire communication and, in effect, negates the strategy.

The fourth concern relates to the natural tendency of optimistic and enthusiastic marketers to overstate the case for the product in direct mail materials, and in awareness letters in particular. So-called brag-and-boast copy is pawned off as awareness copy. There is nothing wrong with a creative strategy that sells the strengths of the product and the company. An awareness campaign can focus on many different objectives depending on the level of understanding the new market may already have of the company's expertise, specialty, quality of service, or other factors that establish a company's credibility. But the copy must be creatively written in ways that readers find extraordinarily interesting and helpful.

Some marketers are able to plan to enter a new marketplace well enough in advance to have a 6- or 12-month direct mail awareness conditioning program precede a formal aggressive sales thrust. This strategy can reflect very positively on the end results.

Inquiry Generation: General Strategies

New marketplaces need sales coverage from the start. But most business-to-business marketing managers know that a sales force blitz of a new market territory with cold canvass calls is no longer practical. The high cost of maintaining a field-selling organization has mandated that the marketer seek only the most effective ways to identify prospects. Identifying the most qualified prospects through response advertising and promotion media is usually the only practical strategy.

Inquiries generated from print publication advertising, product publicity, card decks, press relations, and trade show efforts can be an important part of any new market launch. However, the most selective, versatile, and personal tool for identifying higher-quality prospects in a new marketplace is direct mail. Outbound telemarketing also identifies prospects but is used on a more limited basis because of the higher costs.

For a new market launch of any magnitude the marketer hires and trains new salespeople at considerable cost. A strategy of furnishing these salespeople with a continuing flow of qualified sales leads, starting with their first week in the field, helps protect that marketer's initial investment in these new hires by making them more productive sooner. It also reduces salesperson turnover.

Using telephone marketing to qualify all raw inquiries is one of the better strategies that helps guarantee that these new salespeople follow up only the more interested prospects. There are few things that turn off a new hire in field sales more than a batch of raw inquiries that are purported to be "live" leads. The time and cost for a salesperson to track down 15 inquiries to find the one prospect close to making a purchase can be grossly unprofitable.

Mailing aggressively at the start of the launch with predetermined tight lead-qualification parameters can ensure that only the most highly qualified leads will get into the hands of the new sales people. Costs for these qualified leads may be higher at the start but this form of encouragement is vital to the success of the launch. Once a high level of sales activity has been established, the inquiry quality level and accompanying costs can be effectively lowered to more reasonable levels.

The number of leads a salesperson can handle in a given week will vary depending on the complexity of the product, the salesperson's work load, quality of effort, and other vagaries of selling. A specific quantity of leads to be generated should be established as a weekly goal for each new salesperson. Five to ten leads per week may not be excessive during the early stages of the launch, except for very high-ticket products.

Initial sales goals and budget limitations may warrant inquiry-generation targeting to only representative portions or selected segments of a new marketplace. This strategy—popular with marketers short on time or research dollars and under pressure to produce results—uses initial inquiry-generation direct mail with telephone marketing follow-up as "research." The marketer learns specifically who will respond to a specific offer in the new marketplace. Until research reports are in and a decision is made to hire new salespeople, leads developed from such methods are handled by sales personnel on special assignment from the current sales force. The main strategy here, however, is to use the response as an indication of market interest.

A marketing mix designed to build a share in a new market would normally use all available media to generate inquiries. If the new marketplace is large enough to permit the use of advertising and product publicity programs in the trade or business press, additional inquiries will be generated from the publications' reader response cards. Valuable sales leads can result from these efforts but marketers should proceed cautiously against treating all inquiries alike. Qualifying this particular type of inquiry by telemarketing or further direct mail follow-up before passing it on to a salesperson is mandatory.

Penetrating a new market with a long-term commitment up front presents an opportunity to establish a lead-generation program that will provide a continuous flow of qualified leads for sales force follow-up week by week, month by month, throughout the year. If the program is tentative, however, pending market acceptance of the product, the lead-generation emphasis should be on maximum lead production per se rather than on the long-term commitment that involves testing and fine-tuning for optimal results. But in either instance, cost of a qualified sales lead will usually be higher when canvassing in a new marketplace, because there has not been time for determining the most cost-effective qualified lead.

Sales Objective: Introducing a New Product in the Current Marketplace

The launch of any new product can succeed or fail because the product itself does or does not meet the needs of a major segment of the marketplace. Presuming it does, the burden falls on the tools of marketing and the sales force to get it introduced, accepted, and a specific quantity sold within a given time period. Speed of entry into the market is always important, but especially with products that have short life cycles, such as those in the high-tech office automation fields.

The opportunity for direct marketing to contribute to a successful launch is sizable. There are five major groups of direct marketing strategies that help business-to-business new product introductions to succeed. Research is one. By using mail questionnaires and telephone surveys the marketer can find out if the product is acceptable by the marketplace or how it can better meet its needs. Awareness direct mail is the second that paves the way for more productive subsequent direct response efforts and sales activities. The third and fourth groups involve strategies that provide sales leads through inquiry generation and qualified prospect penetration (or door opener) programs. These identify the best prospects from universes of suspects to bring key prospects and salespeople into face-to-face selling situations. The fifth group involves reinforced selling strategies.

Telemarketing and direct mail working together can get prospect inquiries answered rapidly, and can provide valuable input to the product launch planner helping the program move forward. Telemarketing not only qualifies all inquiries received but also helps build a permanent prospect data base around the new product. It especially speeds communications among all principals in the launch program and helps close the loop between prospects and the sales force.

New product promotions should be preceded by releases to the trade press allowing publicity pick-up while the product is still news. To accomplish this, most product launches use a multimedia communications mix. Of course, maximum market impact can result if a new product release can be arranged during the week of the industry's national or international trade show. To capitalize on the impact value of a new product release, all campaigns should be ready to go on schedule at the time the marketer makes a "go" decision. Immediately identifying and qualifying good sales leads that come from all the publicity and promotions will get the sales organization off to a fast start.

Research: General Strategies

Research is vital to a successful product launch, especially for markets that are large and heterogeneous. For minor new-product releases where there may be less at risk, research may simply consist of making a small test mailing to the marketplace, offering an informative booklet or report and then analyzing the responses. For large companies, before the launch, a strategy of focus group sessions and a mail questionnaire supplemented by a telephone survey can determine the potential market's acceptance of the product and any appearance of hurdles to overcome. Surveys can also help planners determine the best promotion strategies and single out the major segments of the marketplace to pinpoint.

Research explores the current market and new markets along with specific applications for the new product. The research phase should be scheduled to allow enough time in advance of the product release date to be able to analyze and react to the data received so it can impact positively on the direct marketing campaign strategy. Yet, if conducted too early, results may soften.

Although most research efforts in new product launches have mostly short-term benefits, they also have long-term value in that they provide a benchmark from which to compare changes in market attitudes toward the product and the marketer over time. Benchmark studies should be made frequently during the first two years, then annually or biannually until the product cycles out of the market.

Awareness: General Strategies

A major strategy in the use of awareness direct mail in a new product launch is to reach major decision makers and influencers in key segments of the market with informative materials that build their interest and understanding of the new product to high levels. Awareness direct mail campaigns help make sure the important segments of the market know the product has proven value and has industry acceptance in preliminary trials and tests.

An awareness direct mail program has greater scope when the product is a major release in the industry. It is very often used to support print ad campaigns for the new product in selected high-priority audience segments. Preprints of new product announcement ads sent in advance of the ad's appearance in publications tie together the two promotion efforts.

However, even the smallest of companies can use this type of promotion. For many business-to-business marketers the key segment of the marketplace may not consist of more than 12, 50, or 100 prime prospects. This is true especially for high-ticket, high-tech industrial or commercial systems or products. Many direct mail awareness programs designed to reach "the important few" get 100 percent attention and readership and set the stage for response that can go to well above 50 percent. The goal is to prepare the most important present and potential revenue-producing accounts for a later door-opener prequalified prospect penetration campaign.

Direct mail awareness programs are most effective at the beginning stages of the launch when interest and excitement about the new product is greatest. Chances are good that these programs can keep prospect interest and enthusiasm at a high level. However, after early promotional efforts have subsided, awareness levels can drop considerably, necessitating not only more awareness direct mail programs to key prospects but use of other media to broader prospect audiences as well.

Small, key-prospect mailings for new product launches often involve a creative strategy employing relevant dimensional mailings coordinated with carefully scripted telephone interviews.

Awareness mailings scheduled to precede a new product release can materially increase responses to lead-generation efforts that follow. However, mailings made before the official release of the product will not be scheduled too often in most large companies since product managers normally maintain tight control over any efforts to prerelease a new product, system, or service.

Sales support planners are usually able to justify dollars for awareness direct mail in new product release budgets even though direct mail programs are more costly than print publication programs on a cost-per-circulation basis (see Chapter 2).

Inquiry Generation: General Strategies

Inquiry-generation programs are designed to get immediate responses from all appropriate market segments, and to stimulate and motivate the sales organization to sell enough of the new product during the plan period to meet or exceed the sales objective. These campaigns begin a few days or a week after the official announcement of the new product in the marketplace. Markets are often segmented by SIC code and size of business. The most productive segment in terms of inquiries generated could be three or four times higher than the least productive (but still profitable) segment.

Present customer accounts or users having obvious applications for the new product may be defined as prequalified and targeted to receive an awareness campaign followed by a prequalified prospect-penetration response campaign. However, for those customer accounts where the profile shows that a new product application is not readily apparent, an inquiry-generation campaign may be more appropriate. Accounts who have not purchased in 12 months may be worth canvassing by mail or telephone to identify those that justify further follow-up.

One basic objective of this direct marketing strategy is to identify different classes of prospects—the high, medium, and low. Another is to find out who among the present customer and prospect base have the best applications for the product and have the most interest in it. The goal is to end up with quality sales leads for field salespeople to personally follow up. This general goal becomes specific when the marketer looks at the individual market segments.

For instance, one strategy may be to reach Fortune 500 companies who could purchase the product in multiple units. Another may be to reach medium-size companies or divisions of large companies who may purchase one or two product units at a time. Still a third segment may be smaller companies of 50 employees or less who are prospects for their dealer network selling channel. For one marketer there may be any number of individual lead-development campaign mailings running in these different segments simultaneously.

Lead development programs work best when a product, system, or service is new and when prospects can use it in or on the job or it is something that they haven't considered before. This is why more inquiries can be generated during new product introductions than after the product has been established in the marketplace.

Inquiry-generation direct-mail campaigns can be integrated into trade show activities. Mailings are sent to prospective show visitors, suggesting they attend the new product demonstration at the booth or a private suite. VIP lists get custom treatment that often include special incentives to promote attendance. Lead-development mailings also are sent to selected prospects who do not visit the exhibit, offering them another chance to learn from the new product demonstration, this time at the local sales office.

One tactic used by some lead planners to get high quantities of inquiries is to offer, previous to its public release, detailed information about the new product. This mailing normally consists of a letter and a business reply card. It indicates to readers they could be the first to receive this information when the product is released if they act promptly and call the toll-free 800 number or return the reply card. When qualified through telemarketing, results from such promotions usually contain very acceptable numbers of high- and medium-level prospects.

A goal should be set to generate a specific number of qualified sales leads each week. To accomplish this, however, a large number of inquiries may have to be identified and screened. Because of the economic necessity of getting the new product off the ground quickly, marketers have a tendency to generate too many leads in too short a period of time. This can short-circuit the lead handling system. Mailing inquiry-generation campaigns only to sections of the market at one time can prevent this problem. The marketer must take steps to keep the system working. When targeting fairly large markets during a product introduction, the marketer should structure the offer so it is not interesting or valuable to those on the list who would not be qualified prospects. Once the product has proved successful in the marketplace, a long-term continuing lead-generation program should be established, using tests of hardener and softener techniques to fine-tune mailings for optimum results.

Prequalified Prospect Penetration: General Strategies

A percentage of the marketer's current customers may have applications for the new product. These may fall in the prequalified category along with screened inquirers resulting from inquiry development campaigns promoting the new product. Yet there can be a troublesome gap between identifying good prospects from a market universe and physically getting these prospects and salespeople together in a buying/selling environment. The prequalified prospect penetration strategy is designed to close that gap. A series of highly specific messages personalized in the interest of the prospect dovetail with high-impact communication vehicles to motivate and persuade selected prospects to meet with salespeople to learn more about the new product offering.

Reinforced Selling: General Strategies

Reinforced selling direct mail and telemarketing follow-up are especially valuable when the selling objectives emphasize the need to educate the marketplace about a new product. This strategy sends product release promotional materials specifically to the 15 or 20 prospects a salesperson is presently concentrating on. These direct mail programs incorporate messages that reinforce in the minds of the prospects those sales points brought up during a sales call. Telephone scripts are also provided to be used by the salespeople or sales office telecommunicators in concert with the mailings.

DIRECT MARKETING PROGRAM PLANS AND SCHEDULES

A Sales Support Program Plan

The strategies and tactics developed by sales-support direct-marketing planners are often summarized in a calendarized direct marketing schedule. Table 16-3 represents a hypothetical schedule, detailing an overall direct marketing strategy.

The example illustrates a sales-support direct-marketing program schedule for a mid-size manufacturer, calendarized on a 12-month schedule. The program as outlined could indicate 54 multi- or single-piece campaigns, representing 166,000 mail and 9,000 telemarketing contacts, with 38,000 customer and prospect decision makers and other buying influences in a 12-month plan. It reaches 12 separate market segments, each with custom campaigns using 11 different messages, and 7 different direct marketing uses.

Table 16-4 lists specific market segments of varying levels of importance to the marketer. A complete plan (which this schedule does not show) addresses each in terms of actual numbers of companies to be reached and the frequency of contact in relation to sales value.

Table 16-5 indicates the general content and offer strategy of the campaigns scheduled. Actual content and offer would be based on specific objectives. For instance, in this example, the fourth, fifth, and sixth months indicate direct marketing promotion efforts for a major new product.

Built into this plan are three key business-to-business direct marketing considerations: market segmentation, target markets, and creative tactics.

Market Segmentation

Direct mail and telemarketing, being multitask media, can perform different functions for different objectives. One market segment may relate to the same

Table 16-3. Sales support direct marketing schedule: markets by objectives, strategies, and decisionmakers.

Markets/Lists	Months											
	1	2	3	4	5	6	7	8	9	10	11	12
Third-party buying influences Architects	K I		A II		C V		J II		F IV		J II	
Consulting engineers		K I		A II		C V		J II		J II		
Electrical and mechanical contractors									K I	B II	F V	
Customers Customers general		A III		C V		J III		F V		A III		G VII
Key customer accounts	A III		H IV		C VII		E IV		J III		G IV	
Prospects Horizontal Key prospect accounts	K I		A II		C IV		J II		I VII		H IV	
MIS/EDP management		B V	B V	C V								
Facilities management						C V	B V	B V				
Vertical Financial institutions							D II	D II	D V			
Telecommunications										D II	D II	D V
Inquirers High-potential	I IV	K I	I IV						I IV	I IV	I IV	
Medium-potential				C V	C V							F V
Low-potential					C V							
Prospects called on currently by salespeople	VI	VI	VI	VI	VI	VI	VI	VI	VI	VI	VI	VI

Code: Alpha character = campaign content and offer
Roman numeral = direct marketing use

product with a different orientation because the application may be different. The plan takes this into consideration by isolating the target markets into homogeneous mailing segments wherever possible, each to receive different campaigns as may be needed, based on specific objectives. Table 16-6 delineates the major direct marketing uses for the specific objectives planned.

Selective Target Markets
The plan represents selective direct mail and telemarketing coverage of target markets identified by this company. Direct mail and telemarketing are the ideal

media in this case because they can be as selective as the marketer wants them to be without any "waste circulation." One objective during this 12-month plan is to penetrate two new markets, financial institutions and telecommunications, and to identify a specific number of prospect companies, including names and titles of decision makers and influencers.

The most important target lists are the in-house lists of customers and key accounts. These would be actively contacted over the 12-month period. The plan also includes awareness building among third-party buying influences and inquiry generation from other companies that fit the profiles of the current customer. Only unique mailing lists will be built and maintained, but when cost effective, specific selections of compiled lists for lead-generation mailings will be rented.

Creative Tactics

Key accounts warrant personalized high-impact mailings and high-grade tele-marketing follow-up. The program represented by this plan selectively blankets the company's target marketplaces with specific educational, informational, and hard- and soft-sell messages.

The inquiry-generation programs attempt to identify prospects from market-places presently served, and in addition, in new markets in which the marketer wishes to experiment and penetrate. Inquiry mailings consist of a letter and reply card.

Because priorities can change rapidly in any dynamic marketing organization, a detailed 12-month plan may need reformulation before the year is up to conform to changes in sales objectives and budget priorities.

Table 16-4. Market segments: decisionmakers and buying influences.

1. Architects, data center design
2. Mechanical and electrical engineers
3. Mechanical and electrical contractors
4. Customers, general (those who have purchased at least one product and are prospects for more within two years)
5. Key customer accounts (larger companies capable of larger-volume orders, various industries)
6. Key prospect accounts (same profile as key customers but have not yet purchased)
7. Data processing managers
8. Data processing facilities managers
9. Financial institution managers
10. Telecommunication managers
11. Inquirers
12. Prospects and customers currently called on by salespeople

Table 16-5. Mailing content and offer based on marketing, sales, and advertising objectives.

Code	Content	Offer
A	Establish single source	Mind-share, nonresponse
B	Position company as knowledgeable in specific vocation or market	Basic product application brochure
C	Announce new products	Product demonstration
D	Introduce company in two new markets	Successful user case history
E	Emphasize revitalized service group	Service booklet
F	Reintroduce current products	Information packets
G	Highlight leasing program	Leasing program folder
H	National accounts program	Catalog buying guide
I	Highlight advantages of increased knowledge	Seminar
J	Successful user case history	Mind-share, nonresponse
K	Appeal for information	Premium for return of questionnaire

Example of a Schedule for a New Product Launch

In addition to direct mail and telephone marketing, most business-to-business promotions include print advertising, trade shows, special events, displays, exhibits, literature, product publicity, and release materials of many kinds. Each aspect of communication between prospects, salespeople, and line and staff department management must work in concert to maximize response. The program schedule or timetable becomes the enforcer that makes the entire effort flow together.

For a new product introduction, a highly concentrated direct marketing promotion is usually scheduled for the first 12 weeks into the launch period. In this way the marketer takes advantage of the special interest created by the publicity and news value of the new product in the market. The use of direct mail actually begins at least six months in advance of the release date to gather by mail and telephone surveys the information needed for the launch strategies and promotion.

Table 16-7 represents a sales-support direct-marketing schedule. It illustrates generally how direct marketing strategies can impact on various market segments during the initial stage of a major product release. This program consists of 52 separate mailings that would use five basic direct marketing strategies in 14 markets over a 12-week product-introduction. The example allows six months for the research phase. Three to four months before release date would be a minimum, although direct marketing planners have been known to arrange resources to implement complex programs on shorter notice.

Table 16-6. Major direct marketing uses.

Code
I. Research
II. Build awareness
III. Maintain goodwill
IV. Penetrate prequalified prospects
V. Generate inquiries
VI. Reinforce planned sales call
VII. Direct person to seminar

Awareness mailings, coordinated with other release media and events, should begin a few days after the new product release date to allow for press relations efforts to take effect. Because all markets and segments do not have the same potential value to the marketer, not all receive the same number of mail or telephone contacts.

Some multipiece campaign series are designed to have all the mailings perform informational or educational functions of the awareness objectives, except the last, which requests action. In this schedule, awareness and prequalified prospect penetration campaigns are listed separately. In actual practice, this is not always the case.

This type of campaign is used often in new product launches. There is no magic number of mailings in a campaign series. One mailing each week for five weeks can be boring or exciting, depending on the message and manner of presentation. A three-piece mailing series with the first two as awareness nonresponse, and the third as response, can work well when mailed biweekly. The potential value of the list segment targeted will determine whether more than one campaign series will be mailed during the product introduction period.

The number of response mailings to schedule will be governed by the ability of the sales force to effectively follow up the sales leads generated. Since timing and targeting of reinforced-selling mailings are controlled by the individual members of the sales force to coincide with their sales calls, the use of this strategy is on a demand schedule.

SUMMARY

Strategies for mail order marketing are different from strategies involved in sales support direct marketing. Mail order strategies relate to the organizational and operational aspects of running a business, as well as to the marketing aspects. The main strategic concerns for the business-to-business mail order marketer include the offering of market-driven products, the concept of the long-term customer, the customer development techniques, the establishment of a unique image, the provision of high-profit market-responsive products, the targeting of

Table 16-7. Sales support direct marketing schedule for new product introduction.

Direct Mail and Telemarketing Uses by Mailing Segment	Week													
	−26	−25	1°	2	3	4	5	6	7	8	9	10	11	12
Research														
Focus group sessions	x													
Mail questionnaire to all segments		x												
Awareness														
National accounts			x	x	x									
Key prospects														
Market A			x	x	x									
Market B				x	x	x								
Market C					x	x	x							
Past customers						x	x	x						
Prequalified prospect penetration														
National accounts						x		x		x		x		x
Key customers all markets						x		x		x		x		x
Key prospects														
Market A						x		x		x		x		x
Market B							x		x		x		x	
Market C							x		x		x			x
Inquiry generation														
Past customers										x		x		x
General prospects														
High-profit potential				x		x		x						
Medium-profit potential							x		x		x			
Low-profit potential										x		x		x
Reinforced selling (Direct mail campaign materials available for sales force to integrate with sales calls on a daily basis)	On-going													

° Week 1 indicates release of the product.

several markets with different offers, and the exploration of key list sources for best combinations of target markets.

Strategies for sales support objectives emanate from within the major direct marketing use categories of research, building awareness, generating inquiries, and reinforcing a planned sales call. Direct mail efforts for most objectives should consist of more than a "one-shot" mailing. Many direct marketing strategies support sales activities during a marketplace expansion and a product introduction.

PROFILES OF SUCCESSFUL STRATEGIES

How various business-to-business marketers apply direct marketing strategies in pursuit of specific marketing and sales objectives is demonstrated by the Direct Marketing Association's (DMA) Gold and Silver ECHO Award winners of 1985 and 1986. Presented here in capsule form are the highlights of these successful campaigns. They are grouped together by the following direct marketing uses:

- Inquiry generation
- Door-opener
- Traffic building
- Awareness
- Fund raising
- Mail order

The ECHO information that appears in this chapter is reprinted with permission from the Direct Marketing Association, Inc., and originals of the campaigns are on file in the DMA Library, 6 East 43rd Street, New York, NY 10017.

INQUIRY GENERATION

GOLD ECHO 1986

Company: Commonwealth of Massachusetts
Product: Tourism

Direct marketing use: Lead/inquiry generation

Target market: Group tour operators

Objective: To generate qualified inquiries from the operators for the group tour operator guide

Media strategy: Three ⅓-page advertisements in four group tour operator magazines in February and March 1986

Creative strategy: Involve and entertain group tour operators

Offer: Free Massachusetts travel trivia game and group tour manual

Results: All 1,000 group tour operator guides were sold out

Budget: $27,000 for production of three advertisements and the trivia game
$61,000 for media

Agency: Ingalls, Quinn & Johnson

SILVER ECHO 1985

Company: AT&T Information Systems

Product: Seminar

Direct marketing use: Lead/inquiry generation

Target market: Office and corporate management

Objective: To get qualified executives to attend seminars

Media strategy: Catalog self-mailer series
33 targeted lists used, combining demographic market and seminar attendee market
Mailing quantity: 400,000–450,000 per quarter

Creative strategy: Copy was as concrete as possible.

Results: Registrations increased four times from prior experience. Response was three times the seminar industry average.

Budget: $215,000 per quarter

Agency: Chapman Direct Marketing Inc.

SILVER ECHO 1985

Company: Handley & Miller, Inc.

Product: Children's newspaper/publication (nonprofit)

Direct marketing use: Lead/inquiry generation

Target market: Key executives, ad agencies, and influential people in metropolitan Indianapolis

Objective: To generate inquiries for salesperson follow-up

Media strategy: Direct mail: Two mailings consisting of mailing package and press kit followed by a telephone call for an appointment

Creative strategy: To convince advertising executives that the Peanut Butter Press is an affordable buy

Mailing package:

Letter: From the Press's mascot

Brochure: Information about the newspaper

Dimensional: Bag of peanuts

Response card: Stamped response card used

Results: On call-backs, 97 percent of potential contributors/advertisers noted and recalled the mailing.
Mailing generated $57,741 in additional contributions and advertising revenues.

Total budget: Less than $2,500. Agency time, art, and creative time were donated.

Agency: Handley & Miller Advertising

SILVER ECHO 1985

Company: International Minerals & Chemical Corporation

Product: Enviromat, a liquid containment system

Direct marketing use: Lead/inquiry generation

Target market: Irrigation dealers and large irrigators, engineers

Objective: To introduce a new product and generate 500 inquiries for the sales force

Media strategy: Direct response ad in business publications most often read by civil engineers, run twice; run three times in publications read by irrigators and dealers. Total circulation of four publications used, 240,700

Creative strategy: Ad featured cupped hands holding water with inset photo to relate human skin to product.

Offer: More information
Free sample

Fulfillment: Brochures, double-gatefold addressed type of work to be performed
Clear, concise explanations and pictures
Toll-free number for more information

Results: 3,500 responses received from toll-free number and coupons, 700 percent higher than expected. Scheduled ads had to be canceled because the sales force could not handle all the inquiries.

Budget:	$96,000 (included creative, production, media, and fulfillment materials)
Agency:	Miller Meester Advertising Inc.

SILVER ECHO 1985

Company:	West Publishing Company
Product:	158-volume set of *Corpus Juris Secundum,* legal encyclopedia
Direct marketing use:	Multimedia lead/inquiry generation
Target market:	32,000 lawyers
Objective:	To produce quality inquiries for sales force and to maintain the subscription list
Advertising media:	Included a series of five four-color ads in the leading trade publication for attorneys, the *American Bar Association Journal.* The direct mail package followed the space ad "umbrella" campaign.
Media strategy:	Five four-color ads, Oct., Nov., Dec., Jan., Feb. (kick-off with two-page spread) January—Traditional direct mail package (brochure, letter, order card) February—Laser-Gram, order card February—Premium fulfillment package
Creative strategy:	Dramatic comparisons to master crafts developed. Men in other fields to capture the audience's attention and to equate the CJS users with masters of four prestigious arts: handmade violins, stained glass art, race car mechanics, a master chef, and an attorney using CJS
Kick-off ad:	Two-page spread with copy relating to mastering tools of the craft
Graphic:	Inset photo showed six volumes together with a violin
Direct response vehicle:	Reference to bingo card number in magazine
Four Subsequent Ads:	Identical theme and format, different examples
Direct mail:	First mailing Outer envelope: 9-by-12-inch featured offer Broadside brochure with a variation of the space ad, a two-page letter, and a return card Letter: Repeated offer, noting benefits under heading Reinforcement enclosure: Illustrated a typical volume, had perforated response card attached Response card: Check or voucher format perceived as valuable

Offer: Free book, $20 value, *Products Liability and Public Contracts,* one of the volumes of series

Format: Classic, featured "free" prominently along with expiration date

Direct mail: Second mailing

Laser-Gram: Stressed urgency and importance
Printed on stock resembling a telex message
Voucher-type response card was enclosed

Fulfillment package: Specially designed mailing carton with the slogan on side of box
Complimentary volume, and booklet of sample pages from entire set highlighting features and benefits

Schedule: Space ads ran from October 1984 through February 1985.
Two mailings, a standard package in January, and a "Laser-Gram" in February

Results: Initial January direct mail offer received an 8.5 percent response, with cost per inquiry (including postage and all production) of $4.24.
Laser-Gram pulled 3.7 percent, with cost per inquiry of $5.90
Promotion cost to revenue for the January direct mail package was 26 percent and for the Laser-Gram mailing 13 percent.

Budget: $68,907
Strong response caused campaign to come in under budget

Agency: In-house

SILVER ECHO 1985

Company: Citicorp Services

Product: "Wordlink," a new check disbursement system

Direct marketing use: Multimedia lead/inquiry generation

Target market: Chief financial officers and/or international department heads of 400 banks with assets up to $1.5 billion

Objective: To convince "smaller" financial companies they would be able to handle the complexity and up-front expense of the system
To persuade prospects to work with Citicorp
To generate leads

Media strategy: Space ads in banking journals for four months followed by dimensional direct mailing to target audience

Creative strategy: Space ads were slogan-centered. Dispersed throughout the copy were multicolored British pound symbols. Dimensional also used primary slogan.

Mailing:
Offer: Six chocolate bars and invitation to contact Citicorp

Format: Gold wrapped box and card

Results: 18 percent response
Lead generation is being expanded to a broad base of executives in financial and other corporations.

Agency: Cramer-Krasselt/Direct

GOLD ECHO 1985

Company: Dorsey Laboratories

Product: Triaminic Liquid Family over-the-counter line of cough/cold products

Direct marketing use: Direct mail lead/inquiry generation

Target market: 20,000 pediatricians from the American Medical Association list

Objective: To get pediatricians to recommend the product to patients

Media strategy: Series of three direct mailings

Creative strategy: Promote a contest-type program that combines useful and attractive premiums and special prizes to get a high level of physician involvement

Mailing 1: Sent in July 1984
Announcement used "Scratch 'N Sniff" fragrance encapsulated on logo on large outer envelope.
Inside, folded three-panel poster printed on heavy stock, imbedded with about a dozen scented areas. Attractive illustration of young family.
Back of poster displayed product line, welcomed physician into program, and outlined features of premiums and special prize.

Offer: When physicians enter program they receive 12 monthly "Sniff the Season" posters. These were decorative items for reception rooms.
Business reply card attached to lettter-size card along with rules for response
From another sheet, participant could choose three favorite scents from a choice of ten and apply them to the reply card.

Physician had to sign to become eligible and rate the three choices. Postpaid card had to be returned within several weeks.

300 prizes were awarded to each month's entrants. Prizes were quality toys.

Schedule: Similar 20,000 quantity mailings were made in September, October, November, and December.

Results: Response rate was 52 percent.

Budget: $340,644
Creative costs $65,000
Production costs $243,744 (includes cost of purchasing fragrances)
Postage and mailing costs $31,900

Agency: Sieber & McIntyre, Inc.

GOLD ECHO 1985

Company: The Resource Network

Product: Power Charge Battery Treatment (for golf carts)

Direct marketing use: Direct mail lead/inquiry generation

Target market: Test mailing to a list of 500 country clubs and golf courses in three geographic areas
Compiled by client and agency
Full roll-out made nationally to 14,000

Objective: To circumvent apathy in the buyer market and get trial demonstrations for the product

Media strategy: Direct mail

Creative strategy: Self-mailer with a Visual Data Viewer and film strip

Self-mailer: 11-by-4-inch three-fold mailer with attached perforated business reply card
Photographs of golf carts in use on picturesque golf course
Under flap of cover showed closer view.
Middle flap detailed how product worked.
End issued invitation to use viewer to see how product works in battery-powered carts.
Bottom inside flap carried filmstrip, viewer, and instructions
To left of enclosure was invitation to test product in prospect's golf cart.
Reply card attached
The last flap carried six panels of pictures illustrating the benefits.

Schedule: Tested by mailing 500
When full roll-out went into effect, six different mailings were made to test seasonality.

Results: Response rates for test varied by state: 19 percent, 20 percent, and 27 percent. Sales force had to be reorganized to handle the new business.

Budget: $15,000 which included creative costs, list development, follow-up, and production costs ($8,500 for first 1,000 mailers) and postage
Another $10,000 was budgeted after tests were completed.

Agency: Merrell Advertising

GOLD ECHO 1986

Company: Colgate-Palmolive

Product: Fundamentals of direct marketing

Direct marketing use: Direct mail lead/inquiry generation

Target market: The company's 72 international marketing managers in 40 countries

Objective: To educate the international marketers about direct marketing concepts and its benefits

Media strategy: Direct mail

Creative strategy: For mailings with personalized letter and gift that spelled out a specific benefit of direct marketing

Mailing 1: Letter laid groundwork for concept of direct marketing. Introduced marketing data base by making address book analogous to a data base. Gave benefits of having an organized and easily accessible way to reach those who need to be reached.

Format: Two-page letter and address book

Mailing 2: Letter explained benefits of targeting

Format: Letter and brass bulls-eye paper weight

Mailing 3: Review of first two letters and explanation of how direct response can be measured; also how to calculate response rate and return on investment.

Format: Letter and brass desk ruler

Mailing 4: Message related direct marketing to profits

Offer: Idea kit, which included a brochure on how to get started using direct marketing, a list of local consultants who could help them, and a copy of a book on direct marketing

Format:	Survey, reply device, and money clip
Schedule:	One-week intervals
Results:	68 percent of the recipients completed the survey and requested the kit.
Budget:	$7,200
	Mailings were delivered by company's own international pouch, saving postage costs.
Agency:	Kobs & Brady Advertising Inc.

SILVER ECHO 1985

Company:	Rossignol Tennis Company
Product:	Tennis products
Direct marketing use:	Lead/inquiry generation
Target market:	Sporting goods retail dealers, tennis pro shops, court facilities
Objective:	To identify and sign up 300 new dealers in the 14,185 prospect universe. They planned to do this by demonstrating to dealers a commitment to tennis through aggressive dealer support program, aggressive merchandising of product line, and increasing awareness of the product in the consumer marketplace.
Media strategy:	Solo direct mail
Creative strategy:	Direct mail campaign featured a sweepstakes.
Envelope:	Four-color 9-by-12-inch window mailing envelope dramatized offer up front and featured tennis pro Mats Wilander on back.
Letters:	Signed by respective sales representatives in their respective territories
Lift letter:	Signed by U.S. Olympic Tennis Team Coach to validate the offer
Brochure:	Four-color, highlighted prizes and contest rules
Reply card:	Jumbo, with questionnaire to qualify and categorize leads
Results:	6.3 percent response
	Exceeded program objectives by 77.6 percent
Budget:	$55,000
Agency:	Sports Marketing Communications Group, Subsidiary of DMCA, St. Louis

SILVER ECHO 1985

Company:	Sperry Information Systems
Product:	Office automation system specifically designed for government needs
Direct marketing use:	Lead/inquiry generation
Target market:	Government officials
Objective:	Identify government decision makers and address their individual needs.

1. Survey public sector automation needs, identify prospects, convert to qualified leads
2. Establish company as one of the top three suppliers of office automation products in this market
3. Increase awareness of Sperry to allow Sperry to be included in all requests for proposals involving government office automation purchases

Media strategy:	Multimedia

Reach objectives through the use of four media: survey, direct mail, publication advertising, telemarketing

Lists: combined universe of government association memberships, national and regional government publication subscribers, Dunhill's compiled list of government officials. Extensive title selects. Select made by matching county/city prospect address to Metromail population file to eliminate municipalities too small to benefit from products offered. Net mailing quantity, approximately 30,000.

Creative strategy:	Theme of mailings: "Better Government Is Our Business Too"

Survey

Format:	Identified prospects and their information management needs for public sector office
Offer:	Results shared with several local government organizations in return for information
Follow-up:	All respondents received personalized thank-you letter for participating.
Analysis:	Prospects rated for need
	Lowest 20 percent weeded out
Information kit:	Sent to top 80 percent of respondents
Offer:	Information to attend workshop and demonstration
Outbound T/M:	Screened decision makers and estimated interest in workshop demonstration

Names of qualified prospects sent to sales force for follow-up

Direct mail phase: Inquiry follow-up

Mailing 1: Four-color bind-in print insert "Do More For Us at a Lower Cost" watercolor art by Sempe

Mailing 2: "Announcing the Winner of the 1985 Office Automation Systems Awards" featured a Sperry Office Automation system installation in Scottsdale, Arizona

Publication ad: A four-panel center-spread bind-in insert with attached business reply envelope was placed in mixture of eight national and regional publications.

Target: State and local government decision makers
National publications such as *American City* and *County and State Government News* were augmented regionally with the *Empire State Report, Western City,* and others.

Circulation: 106,740

Telemarketing phase: Used to qualify responders of survey
Qualified responders called during first month to generate interest in workshop or demonstration.

Results: 5,400 surveys returned
4,150 from mail or 14 percent
1,250 from print ad or 1.2 percent
2,600 of these or 48 percent converted to leads; half of those requested a demonstration or workshop.
Outbound telemarketing increased positive response to fulfillment kit offer by over 400 percent—250 new prospects were generated.
Cost/response $59
Cost/lead $122
"Positive" lead $244

Budget: $317,200 included all costs: creative development, production, media, lettershop, lead management, telemarketing, tracking and fulfillment

Agency: Kobs & Brady Advertising, Inc.

SILVER ECHO 1985

Company: Boston Five Corporation

Product: Comprehensive line of home mortgages offered through new office opening

Direct marketing use: Lead/inquiry generation

Target market: Real estate brokers

Objective:	To break into a new highly competitive market
Media strategy:	Solo direct mail
Creative strategy:	Sell superior service, products, and rates and to get mortgage referrals from their buyers
Offer:	Indirect
Format:	Letter and dimensional using involvement devices: bottle in mailing tube with paper rolled up inside saying, "help is on the way" and stuffed buffalo in box (company logo is herd of buffalo)
Results:	Response more than 25 percent First month: $2.5 million new mortgages written
Budget:	$15,000
Agency:	Taurus Direct Marketing

SILVER ECHO 1986

Company:	Harris-Lanier Corporation
Product:	Information processing
Direct marketing use:	Lead/inquiry generation
Target market:	Three levels of decision makers in 1,000 companies, 1,000 chief executive officers, 1,000 MIS directors, and 2,400 staff-level managers. Mailing list manually compiled and verified. Sales representatives received duplicate lists for follow-up.
Objective:	To introduce new product in a market where company had a poor image To target three distinct levels of decision makers To generate qualified leads for sales representatives
Media strategy:	Multimedia plan: Full page ad in *Wall Street Journal* two days before delivery of mail packages listed the 1,000 target companies
Creative strategy:	Each group received dimensional using involvement devices.
Offer:	Teaser copy on bottom of mailing label: "Sensitive magnetic material enclosed. Handle with care"
Format:	Cardboard box
Group 1 mailing:	Letter, brochure, and Harris-Lanier Pocket Caddy recorder with four-minute prerecorded microcassette tape and a blank tape for personal use
Group 2 mailing:	Letter, brochure, and 10-minute videotape. Each director was advised a sales representative would contact to

arrange a demonstration. Director would receive an incentive gift if invitation accepted.

Group 3 mailing: Letter, brochure, eight-minute audio cassette, and an offer of incentive gift if they contacted Harris-Lanier for a demonstration

Results: UPS delivered packages. All but 14 were deliverable. Company learned their target market consisted of management information system directors; 28 percent scheduled a meeting; 24 percent had a positive reaction; 31 percent not yet contacted; and 17 percent refused to schedule an appointment.

Agency: Stone & Adler Inc.

SILVER ECHO 1985

Company: Wausau Insurance Companies

Product: Corporate employee benefit retirement plans

Direct marketing use: Lead/inquiry generation

Target market: Personnel directors, office managers, financial officers, and decision makers who manage company assets and insurance needs (a new marketplace for Wausau) in a test market (Detroit)

Objective: To solicit inquiries from Wausau's nontraditional buyers for a face-to-face meeting

Media strategy: A mailing with a built-in incentive premium, a pocket calculator incorporated into the mailing package

Creative strategy: Designed to zero in an aggressive comparison approach. Calculator arrived in a carrying case with the Wausau logo. The copy in the accompanying letter suggested the calculator be used to compare the fund the prospect was presently using with Wausau's.
The calculator enclosure carried "reason-why" copy, along with a business reply card.

Offer: Arrange for a meeting with a salesperson

Format: Dimensional

Schedule: 100 test mailings went out in July 1984 to reach policy holders as well as prospects. Lists were generated by home office sales and management personnel on the basis of qualified customers and prospects not yet participating in Wausau employee benefit plans.

Results: 12 new accounts, which brought in more than $175,000 within 90 days. Sales conversions exceeded original objective by 100 percent.

Budget:	$2,000
	The cost per mailing was $18.
	Cost per conversion was $150.
	Average revenue contribution per conversion amounted to $14,583.
Agency:	Cramer-Krasselt Co.

GOLD ECHO 1986

Company:	Chase Manhattan Bank
Product:	Global payment processing system
Direct marketing use:	Direct mail lead/inquiry generation
Target market:	Heads of worldwide financial institutions: 2,000 in Europe and Asia and 1,500 in the United States
Objective:	To introduce and generate sales leads for a new clearing system in all major languages and currencies
Media strategy:	Direct mail
Creative strategy:	Message delivered in three parts
Part 1:	Telex from head of Chase Europe
Part 2:	Direct mail package

Letter: Signed by local Chase representative, introduced the package and issued invitation for banker to see how the system worked and how a partnership could be mutually beneficial

Brochure: Featured four original modern paintings by a promising young French artist commissioned by Chase. Pocket inside back cover had five pull-outs, one for each currency proposed. A hand was used throughout the brochure as a symbol of Chase system service and trust. Each pull-out cover illustrated a city where services were to be offered in Europe. Specific information was given for the five European cities.

Floppy disk: An original storyboard was specially created for package.

Offer: Invitation to view full-color presentation on an IBM-compatible PC. This tells complete story of how new opportunities and ongoing automation of clearing systems have changed banking in Europe.

Incentive: Prospect offered a signed and numbered and personally dedicated exclusive lithograph specifically created for this campaign by a renowned poster painter.

Reply card: Card with pocket for business card was enclosed in a sealed portfolio-type envelope and marked "Confidential—to be opened by addressee."

Letter with card highlighted the offer. Urged recipient to reply by Telex or SWIFT as only select few would qualify for gift.

Special gift card portrayed the lithograph.

Part 3:   Personal gift delivered by a Chase representative—local Chase representative hand-delivered lithograph to recipient, achieving personal contact needed to start talks.

Format: White box tied with string, colorful postage stamps, sealing wax, handwritten address

Schedule: European and Asian segment done first

Results: Response from Europe and Asia totaled 250 or 12 percent.

60 percent came by Telex or SWIFT.

40 percent came by reply card.

75 percent of reply cards had one or several currency boxes checked.

Meetings were initiated.

Chase hopes for one out of three closure rate.

Chase estimates ten new clients could generate a 40 percent increase in volume of clearing.

Budget: $150,000 or $45 per customer

Agency: MESSAGES

SILVER ECHO 1986

Company:	British Telecom
Product:	Voice/data transmission telecommunication equipment
Direct marketing use:	Direct mail lead/inquiry generation
Target market:	Senior managers and specialists in big buying organizations in British Telecom's West London District holding the seminar
Objective:	To attract senior managers with large purchase potential to attend seminar/presentation
Media strategy:	Direct mail with telephone follow-up
Creative strategy:	To arrest attention and intrigue the person long enough to persuade the prospect to accept the invitation

Transparent design visually suggests the theme of the event—clear, advanced telecommunication. Transparency, shape, and material of the package enhance the retention value of piece to encourage wide circulation among senior managers.

Package: An eight-page brochure, entitled "Immediate Futures." Explained theme and content of exhibition/seminar. Each succeeding page spread progressively adds more detail of a model diagram, which represents the latest in integrated voice and data telecommunications.

Format: A 12-inch square, transparent envelope labeled "Immediate Futures," across the top, also included logo and postage mark.
Invitation screen printed on stiff acetate, also carried the title.

Offer: Invitation to seminar

Reply card: Acetate, gives option of making reservation by phone

Reply envelope: Printed on silver stock, with overprint of "Immediate Futures" slogan

Creative strategy:

Mailing 1: Poster announcing a major new event in ion implantation to occur on September 10, 1985

Mailing 2: On September 8, prospects received a locked wooden box labeled "Look." It contained video cassette featuring the new product. Prospects were instructed not to open it until the next day's mail arrived.

Mailing 3: On September 9, a box labeled "Taste" was delivered. Private label wine and etched wine glasses were enclosed. But the package was locked with similar instructions not to open.

Mailing 4: On September 10, the "Touch" package arrived. This contained a key on a Light Touch Penlight Keychain with instructions to open previous packages, a reprint of the four-page four-color insert that would run in trade publications, and a bounce-back card to get more information.
Response literature was extensive product brochure and data sheet in matching folder.
Product announcement at press conference same day

Schedule: Mailing sent five weeks before each of the four scheduled seminars to allow time for telephone follow-up

Results: Response was 29 percent (290 attendees).
Promotion cost was 1.06 percent of new business resulting from this seminar.

Budget: 27.50 British pounds per response

8,000 British pounds allocated for the campaign. This covered printing, postage, lettershop, and 25 percent of the origination costs. The balance of these costs were to be amortized over subsequent mailings for other British Telecom districts.

Agency: DDM Advertising Ltd.

GOLD ECHO 1986

Company: Applied Materials

Product: "Precision Implant 9000," ion implantation system for semiconductor water fabrication

Direct marketing use: Lead/inquiry generation

Target market: 1,000 key specifiers in 200 semiconductor companies

Objective: New product introduction, inquiry/lead generation

Media strategy: Four-step direct mailing: last mailing coinciding with product announcement at dual press conferences in Horsham, England (where product was developed) and Tokyo, Japan (large customer base).
The press conferences would feature two-way teleconferences between both sites and headquarters in California. Four-page, four-color insert in two publications for three months.

Results: 100 percent of the target market became aware Applied Materials had reentered the ion implantation business.
More than 100 inquiries were received. Three orders have been booked for the $2 million-plus system.
Cost per response is about $2,000.

Budget: $393,000
$60,000 for trade publication media
$140,000 for 1,000 four-stage mailings
$18,000 for space advertising, creative and production
$140,000 for collateral materials, creative and production
$35,000 for guaranteed worldwide courier delivery

Agency: Cortani/Brown/Rigoli

SILVER ECHO 1986

Company: Wyeth Laboratories

Product: Oral contraceptive

Direct marketing use: Lead/inquiry generation

Target market: 36,000 obstetricians/gynecologists and high-volume prescriber family physicians. Lists used were the American

Medical Association list of physicians and the Direct Marketing Agency Databases.

Objective: To position Lo/Ovral as the oral contraceptive of choice for patient comfort and low incidence of side effects

Media strategy: Four-piece direct mail series

Creative strategy: The campaign theme, Records to Remember, "Off Hours" played on the clinical record of low-side effects of Lo/Ovral

Mailing 1: Featured Lou Gehrig's longest consecutive streak of games played
Folder cover showed Gehrig at the plate. Copy inside reviews Lo Ovral's record in controlling side effects.

Offer: Wall poster of Gehrig's farewell at Yankee Stadium and product promotional material, mailed in a tube

Response: 17.3 percent

Mailing 2: Featured "White Christmas," longest selling record in history
2 black arcs in die-cut circular address envelope window to give illusion of phonograph record

Brochure: Four-color, shows winter snow scene and copy describing the record-breaking record
Opened brochure reveals Lo/Ovral's record.

Offer: Special 45 RPM recording of "White Christmas" and product promotional material

Response: 20.7 percent

Mailing 3: Featured Sonja Henie's ten consecutive world figure-skating championships

Offer: Olympic-like medallions and ribbons commemorating Sonja's ice skating records, with product promotional material

Response: 18.3 percent

Mailing 4: Featured Jesse Owens, who broke five world records in one afternoon and equaled a sixth

Offer: Photo montage poster, with product promotion

Response: 7.4 percent

Agency: The Direct Marketing Agency, Inc.

DOOR OPENER

SILVER ECHO 1985

Company: Ameritech Mobile Communications

Product: Cellular car phones and service

Direct marketing use: Direct mail awareness and lead/inquiry generation

Target market: Professionals, senior management, and owners of small-to medium-size businesses in Ameritech Mobile's cellular service area

Objective: To generate prospect leads for sales force and authorized agents

To convince prospects product would make them more productive

To provide prospects with compelling competitive price information, thereby building preference for Ameritech Mobile Service and encouraging prompt purchase action

Media strategy: Multimedia: newspaper, radio, and TV

Results: This campaign replaced a previous introductory campaign. Results were indexed. At the close of Ameritech Mobile's first year of operation, eight months after the first campaign was replaced, average monthly leads nearly tripled (281 index) and company awareness more than doubled (244 index) versus the earlier campaign. Average leads per ad increased 81 percent versus previous campaign.

Budget: Not disclosed

Agency: Ogilvy & Mather Direct

SILVER ECHO 1986

Company: Mature Outlook

Product: Business publication advertising space

Direct marketing use: Direct mail awareness and lead/inquiry generation

Target market: 2,500 media planners/buyers, account supervisors, account executives, and ad managers in large sophisticated agencies/companies

Objective: Increase overall awareness of benefits of advertising in *Mature Outlook*

Media strategy: Reach objective through direct mail; 2,500 prospects divided into two groups. The top group of 1,300 received eight mailings. The remainder received three mailings.

Creative strategy:

Mailing 1:   Both groups received a media kit.

Offer: Indirect

Format: Media kit

Mailing 2:   Both groups received an editorial calendar.
  Offer: Indirect
  Format: Editorial calendar
Mailing 3:   Both groups received a bag of jelly beans (to illustrate assorted benefits of advertising in *Mature Outlook*).
  Offer: Indirect
  Format: Dimensional
             1,300 in first group targeted with five additional mailings. The remainder went to top group only.
Mailing 4:
  Offer: Indirect
  Format: Dimensional: Crate of oranges (to give a taste of fresh new way to reach a mature market)
Mailing 5:
  Offer: Card invitation to call regional sales representative
  Format: Dimensional: Orange sweat shirt ("no-sweat media buy")
Mailing 6:
  Offer: Indirect
  Format: Dimensional: *Mature Outlook* mug (talk about magazine) and orange pekoe tea
Mailing 7:
  Offer: Sign up for advertising
  Format: Dimensional: Candy dispenser (announced circulation growth)
Mailing 8:   Refill package of jelly beans
  Schedule: May 1985 to March 1986
  Results: From January 1985 to March 1986 there was a 627 percent increase in advertising pages. Ad revenue generated from the March/April 1986 issue alone was $142,000.
  Budget: $90,000, 55 percent production, 25 percent creative, 20 percent postage
  Agency: Sandven True Pruitt Advertising

GOLD ECHO 1985

            Company: Citicorp Financial, Inc.
            Product: Financial funding
Direct marketing use: Awareness and lead/inquiry generation
      Target market: 410 key realtors/brokers with sales in excess of $1 million in Philadelphia, Pittsburgh, and Charlotte
          Objective: To announce a new division

	To promote their superior knowledge, greater product depth, and their high flexibility
	To generate leads
Media strategy:	Showmanship direct mail program
Creative strategy:	Three high-impact mailings
Mailing 1:	Announcement mailing
Offer:	Indirect awareness
Format:	Dimensional with letter and business card silk-screened onto a brick
Mailing 2:	Informational
Offer:	Indirect awareness
Format:	Diamond chip dimensional
Mailing 3:	
Offer:	Invitation to call sales representative
Format:	Dimensional: Telephone with representative's phone number posted on it
Results:	223 phone calls were initiated. Response rate was 54.4 percent.
	Of those who called local office, 25.6 percent made mortgage applications and closed loans totaling more than $5 million.
	(Citicorp is using these mail announcements to establish relationships with realtors not presently doing business with Citicorp in already developed markets.)
Budget:	$32,400
Agency:	Yeck Brothers Company

GOLD ECHO 1985

Company:	Ogilvy & Mather Direct Response
Product:	Ogilvy & Mather Direct direct response advertising services
	A "do-it-yourself presentation" portfolio that explained the direct response approach to advertisers
Direct marketing use:	Direct mail awareness and lead/inquiry generation
Target market:	All business people and advertisers in Norway
Objective:	To educate total market and get inquiries
Media strategy:	Single newspaper ad in Norway's largest newspaper, read by almost every businessperson and advertiser in Norway; total circulation, 280,000
Creative strategy:	Full-page ad with coupon
	Ad was conceived as giving tips on what to look for in a good direct response ad.

Offer: Gave three options: A "do-it-yourself presentation," a "live presentation," and a "full-size print of the ad"

The "do-it-yourself" package also included an audio cassette explaining the direct response approach to advertising. The pages in the package coincided with signals on the tape. All pages were in black and white except one red page signifying red carpet treatment by the agency.

Ad: A blank rectangle in the center of the ad page proclaimed to the prospect, "Your ad is here."

Headline invited reader to answer questions that related to the makeup of a good response ad.

Schedule: One time only

Results: 406 coupons were returned (considered a 0.29 percent response).

48 requests for "live presentations" (six new clients signed)

90 percent of coupon returnees asked for ad reprint.

Budget: $30,000 for creative, production, and insertion costs

Agency: In-house

TRAFFIC BUILDING

SILVER ECHO 1986

Company: Du Pont Agricultural Products

Product: Benlate Fungicide

Direct marketing use: Build traffic for dealers

Target market: 12,500 soybean growers of more than 250 acres in six southern states. This list was merged/purged against Du Pont's list of growers identified as having greatest need for this product.

Objective: Hold market share for Benlate Fungicide

Build new life into old product fighting newer competition

Media strategy: Single mailing spectacular

Creative strategy: To turn the relative disadvantage of an older product into an advantage

To focus on Benlate's proven 10-year performance record in controlling disease, and the resulting average additional bushels of soybeans per acre

Format: A professionally designed and packaged long-playing album: six soft-sell songs mentioning product benefits; two songs for entertainment and longer listening time

Offer: Tape cassette versions of the same music farmers could order by phone to play in their trucks and tractors

Schedule: Mailed to coincide with normal fungicide purchase season

Results: 2.3 percent requested tape cassette (During promotion overall fungicide purchase was reduced because of adverse weather conditions and soybean price plunge.) Benlate held its market share against newer products.

Budget: $75,000
$6 per grower

Agency: Rumrill-Hoyt/Rochester

SILVER ECHO 1986

Company: Apple Computer, Inc.

Product: Selected Apple personal computers

Direct marketing use: Traffic building

Target market: 1.3 million kindergarten through twelfth-grade public and private school teachers, their administrators, and university faculties

Objective: To defend and strengthen their dominant market share

Media strategy: Pretested self-mailer

Creative strategy: Program combined the efforts of authorized Apple dealers with a certification of full-time teacher status

Offer: Limited time pricing

Incentive: $75 to $200 rebates on four models

Format: Graphic of Apple logo on a green chalkboard
Inside, four-color photographs depicting capabilities of the four models and short description of features and rebates
Cut-out coupon to be signed by authorized dealer and mailed back

Schedule: Mailing was made in March 1986.

Budget: $475,000 includes all direct mail costs (not the offer). Cost per thousand $365

Results: Sales were 12.91 times the break-even. Program was reported as a major success. The margin revenue was approximately $5.5 million.

Agency: Krupp/Taylor

SILVER ECHO 1986

Company: AT&T Information Systems

Product: Personal computer

Direct marketing use: Traffic building

Target market: Knowledgeable small business customers considering a PC purchase

Objective: To drive PC prospects to retail stores and predispose them to ask for a demonstration of AT&T PC6300

Media strategy: Newspaper advertising in top 20 markets during the third and fourth quarters of 1985
Three full-page newspaper ads were rotated twice a week. Ads also ran in the *Wall Street Journal* and *USA Today.*

Creative strategy: Ads gave the target a real "reason to buy" with customer-driven terminology in attention-getting, nontechnical benefit-oriented ads.
Unique clip-out question checklist encourages readers to visit retailers to get "right answers."

Results: Sales increased significantly in the third quarter. In the fourth quarter share of PC retail market more than doubled.

Budget: $1,500,000

Agency: Ogilvy & Mather Direct

AWARENESS

SILVER ECHO 1985

Company: Helsingin Sanomat

Product: *Helsingin Sanomat,* Finland's biggest daily newspaper (as an advertising medium)

Direct marketing use: Awareness public relations function

Target market: Advertisers, media planners, advertising designers

Objective: To make the current and potential advertiser see the need and potential for brand advertising
To maintain market share of advertising in Finland's largest daily newspaper

Media strategy: Direct mail

Creative strategy: Present picture of the Finnish consumer of today in a book and in a live presentation at a seminar conducted by professional consumer behaviorists
Book was written explaining how well the newspaper reaches the Finnish consumer.
400 books were distributed in seminars.
3,000 books were mailed to those not attending seminar.
500 books were used in salespeople's visits.

Offer: Indirect

Results:	Sales increased 12 percent; strong PR value
Budget:	U.S. $100,000; book, $90,000; and two seminars $10,000
Agency:	Asanti Konttinen Torkler Oy

SILVER ECHO 1985

Company:	Weirton Steel Corporation
Product:	Tin mill products
Direct marketing use:	Awareness
Target market:	115 senior executives in the food can manufacturing industry
Objective:	Increase market share and cement relationships with current customers
Media strategy:	Five-piece series dimensional direct mail campaign
Creative strategy:	Direct mail package, which included letter, folder, and a reply card
	Each mailing was built around a dimensional item relating to the "We hear you" theme that communicated the specific sales message of each mailing: customer service; technical assistance and technological advances; high-quality products; and a complete product line.
	Personalized, hand-signed letters, postage stamps, hand-typed names, and addresses on wrap-around fasson labels
Results:	A 25 percent increase in market share
Budget:	$40,000 for creative and production, dimensional items, boxes, mailing wrappers, fasson labels, folders, letters, reply cards, and postage
Agency:	Robert A. Sherman & Associates, Inc.

FUND RAISING

GOLD ECHO 1985

Company:	Direct Marketing Educational Foundation
Product:	Direct marketing education at college level
Direct marketing use:	Fund raising
Target market:	192 firms engaged in direct marketing who pledged to the original program, which underwrote direct marketing program at the University of Missouri, Kansas City

Objective:	To raise an additional $500,000 from the firms who pledged originally for degree courses in direct marketing
Media strategy:	Personalized letter and pledge/response device
Results:	124 pledges were received, 64.6 percent of the 192 prospects Response cost per pledge was $1.56 per pledge.
Total budget:	$192.00
Agency:	The mailing package was written by Bob Stone (a member of the Direct Marketing Educational Foundation). The pledge form was designed by the Direct Marketing Educational Foundation. Letters were produced and mailed by the Foundation.

MAIL ORDER

SILVER ECHO 1985

Company:	Creative Publications
Product:	Educational materials
Direct marketing use:	Mail order catalog
Target market:	1.3 million teachers
Objective:	To increase catalog sales in a depressed and declining market To capitalize on peak buying periods in the educational publishing industry—spring, summer, and fall
Media strategy:	Three mailings, each with a different cover Distribute catalog at more than 100 trade shows. Smaller mailings are made throughout the year to add incremental sales and bring people back to main catalog.
Creative strategy:	Standard catalog techniques
Schedule:	205,000 catalogs mailed in late December 130,000 in mid-February 125,000 in mid-August
Results:	Sales were up 40 percent compared to industry average of only 10 percent.
Budget:	$500,000 (includes design, photography, typesetting, separations and stripping, paper, printing, binding, mailing preparation, and postage)
Agency:	In-house, free-lance

SILVER ECHO 1985

Company:	Audi of America, Inc.
Product:	Consumer direct mail promotion, "The Spirit of Audi"
Direct marketing use:	Order generation (electronic media)
Target market:	400 Audi dealers
Objective:	To get dealers to subsidize the direct mail promotion introducing the new 5000S passenger car, at a cost of 85 cents per piece mailed to an average of 1,000 prospects each
Media strategy:	Single mailing: ten-minute promotional videorecording based on focus research *Spirit of Audi* magazine, created for dealer's potential customers Dealers received list of local prospects receiving magazine.
Creative strategy:	Video encourages dealer to fill out a form agreeing to have copies of the magazine mailed to selected names in the dealer's locality.
"Minimag":	20-page, glossy, color, features graphic, editorial, and involvement concepts (developed from the focus research interviews) Magazine copy invited interested prospects to contact the dealer whose name and address were included. Designed to build awareness, instill interest, fan that interest into keen desire, and send readers directly to the showroom
Content:	Traces history of company quest for engineering excellence Featured spread on finely designed furniture and appliances in the Museum of Modern Art Center-spread featured full-color double fold-out of the Audi 5000S
Magazine insert:	Test-drive evaluation form for consumer
Results:	339 or 85 percent of dealers paid $0.85 per mailing piece for 1,000 to be mailed in their territories
Agency:	Rapp & Collins

SILVER ECHO 1986

Company:	The Winn Corporation
Product:	Avant-garde art of D. G. Smith Original limited edition prints, framed and unframed, and original framed watercolors

Direct marketing use: Mail order generation

Target market: 183 Smith print buyers, 530 Smith poster buyers, 5,988 other print buyers, 193 Smith inquiries, 3,989 recent gallery inquiries from 19 states.

Rented lists were 5,000 compiled names of art galleries, 5,000 business subscribers of *Architectural Digest,* 5,000 business subscribers of *Interior Design* and business subscribers of *Restaurant and Hotel Design* magazine.

19,850 East Coast names were mailed Dec. 30, 1985, along with names from interior design firms, architectural firms, restaurant chain headquarters, hotel/motel chain headquarters, independent restaurants, and independent hotels/motels.

13,187 (West Coast) mailed a week later. Total rented names mailed was 20,000.

Objective: To find a better way to market artwork of the artist and increase his monthly sales

Catalog would also provide support material to the sales force.

Media strategy: To mail catalog at the end of December in time for galleries to stock up for Valentine's Day to take advantage of the heart motif appearing frequently in the artist's works

Creative strategy: To design a specialty catalog to promote the credibility of the artist and his vision

Prospects would "meet" the artist through copy that reads like personal interview and a positive review by a critic.

Graphics: Photographs of the art in a variety of interiors to show versatility and saleability

Schedule: Two mailings, one week apart

Results: In the six months following the mailing sales were up 398 percent.

Budget: $35,000 (actual cost $35,400)

This includes all production costs, excluding creative costs (direction, design, layout, and paste-up).

Agency: In-house

SILVER ECHO 1985

Company: Frontier Airlines

Product: Air travel summer vacation packages

Direct marketing use: Mail order

Target market: Business market: On-system travel agents

Consumer market: Frontier Airline travelers

Objective: Increase traffic to specific vacation locations

Media strategy: 16,000 sweepstakes packages mailed to travel agents and 500,000 catalogs distributed to Frontier Airline travelers and travel agents

Creative strategy: Sweepstakes filled with incentives motivated travel agents to sell vacation packages out of the catalog.

Results: Response by travel agents to the sweepstakes was 32 percent. All available seating allocated to the program on Frontier aircraft was 100 percent sold out.

Budget: Total allocation for entire program to business and consumer markets was $431,965. Actual costs for catalogs were $366,465, and for sweepstakes, $65,000.

Agency: Design & Image Associates

Appendix 1

DIRECT MARKETING—WHAT IS IT?

An Aspect of Total Marketing - not a fancy term for mail order.

Marketing is the total of activities of moving goods and services from seller to buyer. (See chart). Direct Marketing has the same broad function except that Direct Marketing requires the existence and maintenance of database.

a) to record names of customers, expires and prospects.

b) to provide a vehicle for storing, then measuring, results of advertising, usually direct response advertising.

c) to provide a vehicle for storing, then measuring, purchasing performance.

d) to provide a vehicle for continuing direct communication by mail and/or phone.

THUS

DIRECT MARKETING is interactive, requiring database for controlled activity: By mail, by phone, through other media selected on the basis of previous results.

DIRECT MARKETING makes direct response advertising generally desirable since response (inquiries or purchasing transactions) can be recorded on database for building the list, providing marketing information.

DIRECT MARKETING plays no favorites in terms of Methods of Selling...and there are only three:
a) Where buyer seeks out seller - retailing, exhibits
b) Where seller seeks out buyer - personal selling
c) Where buyer seeks seller by mail or phone - mail order

DIRECT MARKETING requires that a response or transaction at any location be recorded on cards, mechanical equipment or, preferably, on computer.

DIRECT MARKETING can be embraced by any kind of business as defined by the U.S. Census Standard Industrial Classification system:

Agriculture	0100-0999
Mining/Construction	1000-1799
Manufacturing	2000-4999
Wholesale	5010-5199
Retail	5210-5999
Department Stores (5311)	
Financial Services	6010-6799
Services	7010-7999
Advertising Agencies (7311)	
Computer Houses (7372)	
List Brokers (7388)	
Non-Profit	8010-8999
Public Administration	9100-9999

DIRECT MARKETING is an interactive system of marketing which uses one or more advertising media to effect a measurable response and/or transaction at any location.

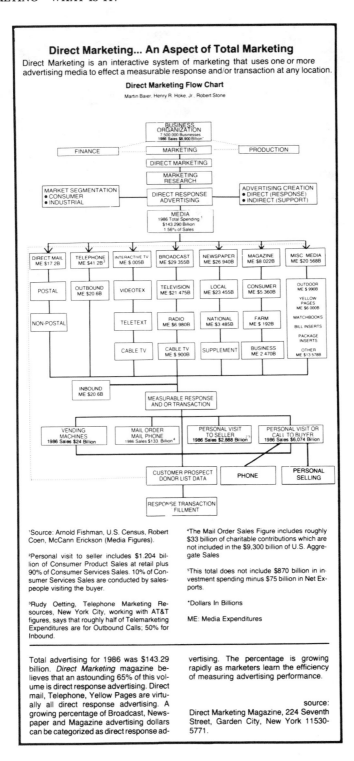

Direct Marketing... An Aspect of Total Marketing

Direct Marketing is an interactive system of marketing that uses one or more advertising media to effect a measurable response and/or transaction at any location.

Direct Marketing Flow Chart

Martin Baier, Henry R. Hoke, Jr. Robert Stone

[¹]Source: Arnold Fishman, U.S. Census, Robert Coen, McCann Erickson (Media Figures).

[²]Personal visit to seller includes $1.204 billion of Consumer Product Sales at retail plus 90% of Consumer Services Sales. 10% of Consumer Services Sales are conducted by salespeople visiting the buyer.

[³]Rudy Oetting, Telephone Marketing Resources, New York City, working with AT&T figures, says that roughly half of Telemarketing Expenditures are for Outbound Calls; 50% for Inbound.

[⁴]The Mail Order Sales Figure includes roughly $33 billion of charitable contributions which are not included in the $9,300 billion of U.S. Aggregate Sales

[⁵]This total does not include $870 billion in investment spending minus $75 billion in Net Exports.

[*]Dollars In Billions

ME: Media Expenditures

Total advertising for 1986 was $143.29 billion. *Direct Marketing* magazine believes that an astounding 65% of this volume is direct response advertising. Direct mail, Telephone, Yellow Pages are virtually all direct response advertising. A growing percentage of Broadcast, Newspaper and Magazine advertising dollars can be categorized as direct response advertising. The percentage is growing rapidly as marketers learn the efficiency of measuring advertising performance.

source:
Direct Marketing Magazine, 224 Seventh Street, Garden City, New York 11530-5771.

Appendix 2

MAIL ORDER

Source: Reprinted from *Direct Marketing Magazine,* 224 7th Street, Garden City, N.Y. 11530. Used by permission.

1985 Business Supplies Mail Order $3.660 Billion Sales

Leaders

Size	Names	Sub-Segments	Sales In Millions
500 + Companies	Digital Equipment Corporation	Business Supplies: Data Processing Oriented	240
	IBM Direct	Business Supplies: Data Processing Oriented	150
	New England Business Service	Business Forms: Full Line	146
	Quill Corporation	Business Supplies: Full Line	120
	INMAC	Business Supplies: Data Processing Oriented	60 (U.S. Only)

Sub-Segment Structure

Characteristics	Leading Companies
Computer Software $940 million	
• Mini- and microcomputer accounting oriented software	
Data Processing Oriented $750 million	
• Computer Accessories • Media • Paper • Magnetic • Storage/Filing Equipment System Supplies	• Digital Equipment Corp. • IBM Direct • INMAC • Burroughs Corp. • Visible • MISCO • Moore Business Forms • Uarco • Wright Line • Pryor Corp. • Devoke • NCR Corp. • Datapoint Corp.
Full Line $450 million	
• Full line of office stationery, forms, writing, storage, filing, binding, equipment and office electronic equipment • Price and sales oriented because of lack of proprietary products	• Quill Corp. • Reliable Corp. • Viking Office Products • Fidelity Products • Grayarc • Amsterdam Printing • M.S. Ginn • Great North American Stationers • Iroquois Products • Woodlyn Office Equipment • Business Envelope Manufacturers • George Stuart
Full Line Business Forms $270 million	
• Standardized functional stationery • Continuous and non-continuous forms • Stationery specialties	• New England Business Service • Drawing Board • Rapid Forms • Stationery House
Office Equipment Specialties: **Appliances/Machines/Filing $270 million**	
• Office Electronics • Accounting hardware • Filing and storage equipment	• Share America • Compugraphic Corp. • Monarch Marking Systems • Corde Business Products • Chiswick Trading Co. • Browncor International • Dictaphone Corp.
Stationery Specialties: Non-Professional $230 million	
• Specialized office products or services cutting across all industries and professions: Office electronics, planning, security, binding, writing, storage equipment, special stationery • Less price and sales sensitive because of proprietary products	• Myron Manufacturing • Day-Timers • BWP • Business Cards, Inc. • Baldwin Cooke • 20th Century Plastics • MNG Professional Services

Characteristics	Leading Companies
Office Advertising Specialties/Executive Gifts $200 million	
• Functional, low price, message-bearing specialties • Gift electronics • Personal accessories • Monogrammed specialties • Home and office decorative accessories in crystal, porcelain and metal	• Bon Vivante Entrepreneurs • Executive Suite • Atlas Pen & Pencil • Union Pen & Pencil • National Pen Corp. • Prudent Publishing • U.S. Pencil & Stationery Co.
Stationery/Equipment Specialties: Professional $180 million	
• Technical products or equipment for a profession or technical field • Accounting • Legal	• Delmart • Colwell • Histacount Corp. • Excelsior Legal Stationery • Alvin & Co. • Frank Paxton Co. • Accountants Supply House • Sycom • Victor W. Eimicke • Medical Arts Press
Office Furniture $120 million	
• Institutional, educational, and small business markets	• Adirondack Chair • Frank Eastern Co. • National Business Furniture • Business & Institutional Furniture • ATD-American Co.
Office Specialties: Scheduling/ **Record Keeping Systems $ 90 million**	
• Office, project, and production control devices and equipment	• Methods Research • Executive Scancard Systems • Caddylak Systems
Business Specialties: Libraries and Schools $ 80 million	
• Institutional stationery • Institutional filing and storage specialties • Institutional supply specialties	• Gaylord Brothers • Brodhead Garrett • Highsmith Co. • Personalized Marketing • Demco • Otto Schmidt
Arts/Drafting/Printing Supplies $ 80 million	
• Technical specialties for art and drafting departments • Printing hardware, accessories, and supplies	

1985 Business Sales Mail Order — $4.890 Billion Sales

Leaders

Size	Names	Sub-Segments	Sales In $Millions
50 + Companies	MCI	Communications	500
	Federal Express	Air Freight	340
	Prentice Hall	Information	283
	McGraw-Hill	Information	225
	Sprint	Communications	220

Sub-Segment Structure

Characteristics	Leading Companies	Characteristics	Leading Companies
Information $1,600 million		**Air Freight $ 730 million**	
• Government regulation related advisory and accounting and legal information updating • Business and personal financial advisory services • Media information updating services • Newsletters	• Prentice Hall • McGraw-Hill • Commerce Clearing House • American Management Association • Standard Rate & Data Service	• Overnight business package delivery services	• Federal Express • Emery • Airborne • Purolator
Communications $1,850 million		**Trade Subscriptions $ 320 million**	
• Inbound and outbound high volume toll call network services	• MCI • Sprint • AT&T	• Technical and trade magazine subscriptions	• McGraw-Hill
		Mailing List Services $ 390 million	
		• Mailing list rental services	

1985 Industrial Mail Order — $1.340 Billion Sales

Leaders

Size	Names	Sub-Segments	Sales In $Millions
250 Companies	McMaster Carr	Industrial Maintenance/Materials Handling	188
	Axia Corp.	Industry/Functional Specific	69
	Global Equipment Co.	Industrial/Maintenance/Materials Handling	45
	Coast Freight Salvage	Industrial Maintenance/Materials Handling	45
	NASCO Farm	Industry/Functional Specific	40

Sub-Segment Structure

Characteristics	Leading Companies	Characteristics	Leading Companies
Industry Functional/Specific $550 million		**Industrial Maintenance/Materials Handling $560 million**	
• Supplier of chemical, farming, ranching, fishing, forestry, mining and other industry specific equipment • Suppliers of libraries, schools, hotels, fraternal lodges	• NASCO Farm • Goldblatt Tool Co. • PCA Industries • Visual Display • Ames Taping Tool Systems • Jensen Tools • TSC Industries • Flaghouse • Stone Art Theatrical Corp. • Snap-on Tools Corp. • Zip Penn • Calumet Photographic • Forestry Suppliers • VI Pipe & Supply Co. • Alfa Products • American Hotel Register • Cordura Publications • Rutland Tool & Supply Co. • Markson Science • Select Service & Supply • Modern Farm • U.S. Plastic Corp. • Adventure Centers	• Suppliers of general and specialized warehousing, assembly line, packaging, plant maintenance and materials handling equipment	• McMaster Carr • Global Equipment Co. • Coast Freight Salvage • COMB Co. • C&H Distributors, Inc. • Harbor Freight Salvage • Santa Fe Salvage • Garon Products • Loctite Corp. • Technical Electronics
		Medical/Pharmaceutical $230 million	
		• Medical, surgical and drug line suppliers to hospitals, clinics and practitioners	• Interstate Drug Exchange • Intra-Medic Formulations • Kent Dental Supply • Veratex • J.A. Preston • Spencer Mead • Banyan International • Allen Dynamics • American Hospital Supply

Appendix 3

BUSINESS-TO-BUSINESS
DIRECT RESPONSE MARKETING

Business to Business direct response marketing is a large and vital segment of our industry. Despite its importance, relatively little information is available to help us develop sound strategies.

To learn more about the behavior and attitudes of executives in regard to Business to Business direct response, Ogilvy & Mather Direct conducted a major research study. We interviewed over 500 business executives across the U.S.

One of our goals was to study the buying behavior and attitudes of executives at different levels of management. Therefore, we conducted the study among top management, middle management and technical executives such as engineers and data processing executives.

Another objective of the study was to determine whether buying behavior and attitudes of executives varied by company size. Therefore, we conducted the study among executives in large, medium and small companies.

Here are some of the things we explored.

- The product categories in which they either bought via direct response or responded to offers for information.
- The product categories in which they would like to receive offers.
- The amount they spent in the last year on products and services brought to their attention by direct response advertising.
- The decision-making process for major purchases.
- The factors that would increase their interest in buying via direct response.

Here's what we learned.

The first thing we discovered is that nearly all executives have bought something as a result of direct response advertising. Nine executives in ten bought a business-related product or service in the past 12 months that was brought to their attention by direct response advertising.

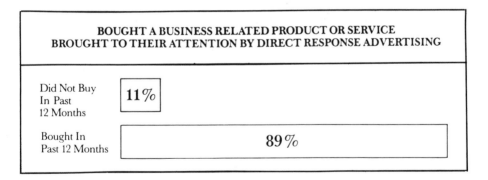

**BOUGHT A BUSINESS RELATED PRODUCT OR SERVICE
BROUGHT TO THEIR ATTENTION BY DIRECT RESPONSE ADVERTISING**

Did Not Buy In Past 12 Months	**11%**
Bought In Past 12 Months	**89%**

We also found that, in the past year, the average executive bought nine different types of business-related

products and services that were brought to his attention
by direct response advertising. And, in fact, twenty
percent bought products and services in fifteen or more
categories.

NUMBER OF PRODUCT CATEGORIES BOUGHT VIA DIRECT RESPONSE IN THE PAST 12 MONTHS	
None	11%
One to three product categories	20%
Four to eight product categories	26%
Nine to fourteen product categories	23%
Fifteen or more product categories	20%
Average number of product categories	Nine

We found that the average executive spent nearly $1,200
in the past year on products and services brought to his
attention by direct response advertising.

But averages tell only part of the story.

We discovered that about half of the executives we spoke
to spent under $1,000 in the past year on products and
services brought to their attention by direct response
advertising. Roughly one quarter spent between $1,000
and $10,000. And another quarter or so spent $10,000 or
more.

But how much does each of these groups contribute to the total dollar volume?

We found that the light spenders account for only 1% of total dollar volume.

The 23% who spent between $1,000 and $10,000 account for only 5% of dollar volume.

Finally, we come to the heavy spenders—those who spent over $10,000 via direct response in the past year. They account for 94% of the dollar volume.

That means we're getting 94% of our business from slightly over one quarter of all executives.

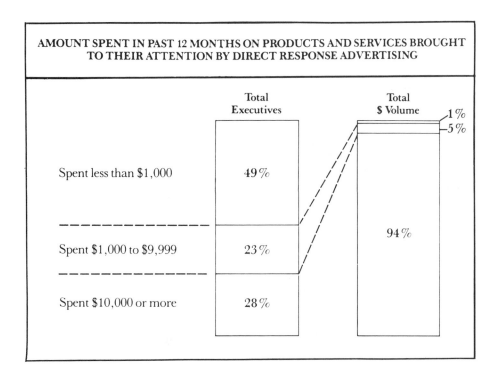

AMOUNT SPENT IN PAST 12 MONTHS ON PRODUCTS AND SERVICES BROUGHT TO THEIR ATTENTION BY DIRECT RESPONSE ADVERTISING

Who are the heavy spenders?

Here are some clues.

We found that the annual sales of a company was a reliable indicator of executive spending via direct response.

An executive of a company that has over 100 million dollars in sales spent nearly six times as much as one from a company with less than 5 million dollars in sales.

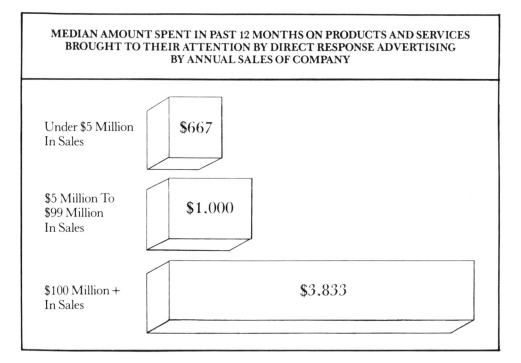

MEDIAN AMOUNT SPENT IN PAST 12 MONTHS ON PRODUCTS AND SERVICES BROUGHT TO THEIR ATTENTION BY DIRECT RESPONSE ADVERTISING BY ANNUAL SALES OF COMPANY

Under $5 Million In Sales — $667

$5 Million To $99 Million In Sales — $1.000

$100 Million + In Sales — $3.833

Region of the country was also an important indicator of spending.

Executives in the west spend the most. And those in the central region spend the least.

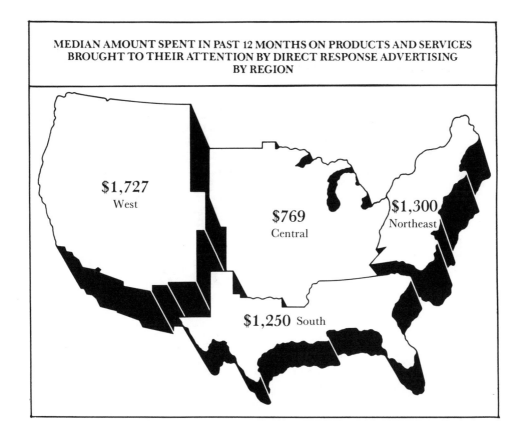

MEDIAN AMOUNT SPENT IN PAST 12 MONTHS ON PRODUCTS AND SERVICES BROUGHT TO THEIR ATTENTION BY DIRECT RESPONSE ADVERTISING BY REGION

$1,727 West

$769 Central

$1,300 Northeast

$1,250 South

Our research also helped us determine which product categories are the most popular.

We read to our respondents a list of 32 categories of products and services. And we asked them to indicate the categories in which they either bought something via direct response or responded to an offer for information, a demonstration or a visit from a sales representative.

As you might expect, business magazines and books, seminars and office supplies are at the top of the list.

However, you might be surprised to learn that two out of
five executives responded to offers regarding manufacturing parts and computer software.

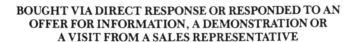

**BOUGHT VIA DIRECT RESPONSE OR RESPONDED TO AN
OFFER FOR INFORMATION, A DEMONSTRATION OR
A VISIT FROM A SALES REPRESENTATIVE**

BUSINESS
MAGAZINES

65%

BUSINESS
BOOKS

54%

SEMINARS,
CONFERENCES AND
CONVENTIONS

54%

OFFICE SUPPLIES
AND STATIONERY

47%

MANUFACTURING
MATERIALS
AND PARTS

44%

COMPUTER
SOFTWARE

43%

AIRLINE
TRAVEL

42%

HOTEL
ACCOMMODATIONS

42%

Here are the figures for the other categories we covered.

**BOUGHT VIA DIRECT RESPONSE OR RESPONDED
TO AN OFFER FOR INFORMATION, A DEMONSTRATION
OR A VISIT FROM A SALES REPRESENTATIVE**

Manufacturing machinery and equipment	40%
Membership in professional associations	40
Business newsletters	38
Personal computers	38
Office equipment such as typewriters and copiers	37
Office furniture such as desks and chairs	34
Packaging materials	32
Long distance telephone service	29
Telephone systems and equipment	27
Delivery services	27
Credit cards	26
Car rentals/leasing	26
Courses via video or audio cassette	24
Gifts for clients or employees	23
Facilities for company meetings	22
Office furnishings such as lamps, pictures and clocks	21
Main frame computers	20
Audio-visual equipment	18
Information systems	18
Vans and trucks	17
Corporate insurance	15
Corporate banking services	13
Leather goods and luggage	6
Real estate or plant relocation	6

	Top Management	Middle Management	Technical Management
BOUGHT VIA DIRECT RESPONSE OR RESPONDED TO AN OFFER IN THE PAST 12 MONTHS			
AIRLINE TRAVEL	38%	47%	41%
OFFICE EQUIPMENT	33	46	31
OFFICE FURNITURE	31	40	32
CREDIT CARDS	25	31	23

As you might imagine, there are differences by the various levels of management.

For example, if you are selling airline travel, office equipment, office furniture or credit cards, you are likely to find that those in middle management represent your best target market.

On the other hand, if you are selling computer software, manufacturing materials, manufacturing machinery or courses on video tape, you are likely to find that technical executives represent a key target market.

BOUGHT VIA DIRECT RESPONSE OR RESPONDED TO AN OFFER IN THE PAST 12 MONTHS			
	Top Management	Middle Management	Technical Management
COMPUTER SOFTWARE	34%	44%	51%
MANUFACTURING MATERIALS AND PARTS	31	45	45
MANUFACTURING MACHINERY AND EQUIPMENT	31	41	48
COURSES VIA VIDEO OR AUDIO CASSETTES	17	25	28

What about the future?

Maybe rapid growth is a lot to expect when you consider that the average executive is already buying products in nine different categories through direct response.

Still, the research does point out ways our industry can keep growing.

One way, of course, is to make sure we are targeting our messages to our best prospects. However, in some cases, identifying the target market is more complex.

For example, we would expect that the purchase of a relatively expensive and complex product or service that would affect the daily operation of a company would require the involvement of a number of executives.

To learn more about the decision-making process, we asked our respondents to assume for a moment that their company was interested in buying a new telephone system. Then we asked them to tell us who would be involved in acquiring this new telephone system.

We found that in a typical company, three to four different individuals would be involved in some aspect of the decision. These individuals range from the Chairman of the Board to the telephone operator.

We were also interested in determining what role each decision maker plays in the buying process.

The chart on the next page indicates who is most likely to get involved in the various decisions and tasks related to obtaining a new telephone system.

In this chart an ○ means that the executive would be involved in at least 20% of the large companies in our sample.

**INDIVIDUALS MOST LIKELY TO BE INVOLVED
IN DECISION TO BUY A NEW TELEPHONE SYSTEM**

	Chairman	Manager	Operations Manager	Technical Engineer	Telephone Supervisor	Financial Officer
Whether new telephone system is needed	○		○			
Gathering information		○	○	○		
Which systems to consider		○	○	○		
Features needed		○	○	○	○	
Price range	○		○			○
Final purchase decision	○					

As you can see, a number of people are involved in the decision and each plays a different role in the buying decision. Therefore, it is important that you reach all those involved in the decision to buy your product or service. And that you address their particular needs and concerns.

One subject that we felt was important to explore is the way that mail is handled at the office.

As you might suspect, most executives in top management do not open their own mail. And the same is true
for half of those in middle management. But let's stick to
top management for a moment.

Three out of five executives in top management do not
open their own mail.

WHO OPENS MAIL			
	Top Management	Middle Management	Technical Management
Executive opens mail	42%	51%	69%
Secretary opens mail	58	49	31

But more importantly, we discovered that half of these
top executives who have their secretaries open their mail
also have their secretaries screen their mail.

Therefore, it is important to devise ways to ensure that
your mailing will survive this screening.

Another question we wanted to answer is whether or not
executives ever forward their direct mail to someone else
in the company. So we asked executives this question:
"Let's say you received an offer for a product or service
that was of no interest to you but might be of interest to
someone else in your company. Would you be more
likely to discard it or forward it to the proper person in
your company?"

Eighty-four percent said they would forward their mail to the proper person in their company.

But we didn't stop there. We asked another question. We said, "In the past month, have you received an offer for a product or service that was forwarded to you by someone else in the company?"

This time only half said yes.

Since we can't always be sure we are mailing to the right person, we ought to devise ways to encourage executives to forward our mail.

However, let's assume for the moment that the executive receives our mailing. What can we do to help ensure that the executive will respond to our offer?

To help answer this question, we asked these executives what it would take to get them to respond to more offers that relate to business products and services.

There are no surprises in what they told us.

- They want good value from companies they know about and trust.

- They want to receive information that's easy to understand, yet contains sufficient technical information.

- They want it promptly.

- And they want to be able to reply easily.

In short, they want more of the basic qualities that underlie any successful direct response operation.

WOULD RESPOND TO MORE OFFERS
FOR INFORMATION IF...

The products were a good value for the money	91%
The offers were from companies they could trust	90
The material received was easy to understand	89
The material contained sufficient technical information	88
They could be sure of a prompt reply	81
Offers came from well known companies	80
Business reply cards or envelopes were provided	74

Appendix 4

POSTAL SERVICE RULES

122 Delivery Address
122.1 Requirements
122.11 General. The purpose of an address is to indicate the specific delivery location of a mailpiece.

122.12 Legible Address. Mail must bear the legible address of the intended recipient on one side only. (See 124.63a(13) for exception on live, day-old poultry.)

122.13 Address Elements. At a minimum, an address must consist of the following elements and appear in the following order (except simplified address mail as prescribed in 122.41):

a. Name or identification of the intended recipient.

b. Street and number and apartment number, or box number, or general delivery, or rural or highway contract route designation and box number, as appropriate (see 122.31).

c. City and state. The "city" is the name of the post office (the delivery post office) serving the intended recipient.

d. ZIP Code (5-digit or ZIP + 4 codes), where required. ZIP Codes (5-digit or ZIP + 4 codes) are required on:

(1) Presort first-class mail (361.3).

(2) ZIP + 4 first-class mail (361.4)

(3) Postal cards and postcards, not mailed as presorted first-class mail, which are mailed under 322.31h, 322.3li, or 322.31j (322.32).

(4) Second-class mail (452 and 455.2f).

(5) Bulk third-class mail (661.2).

(6) Fourth-class mail (761.1).

(7) Business reply mail (917.525).

(8) Merchandise return (919.43, 919.531, and 919.532).

(9) Mail sent to military addresses within the United States (122.82).

(10) Penalty mail (137.263a(3)).

(11) Printed stamped envelopes (141.242).

(12) Return addresses of mail on which postage is paid by stamps precanceled by bars only (143.421a).

(13) The sender's return address, when return service is requested on second-class mail (493).

122.14 Placement of Address
122.141 Letter-Size Mail.

a. The placement of the address on a letter-size mailpiece will determine which dimensions are the length and height of the piece and, consequently, may cause the piece to be either nonmailable or nonstandard. (See 127, 128, 324, 352, 353, 452.1f, 651, and 652.)

b. See 322.3 regarding address placement on postcards.

122.142 Clear Space. A clear space must be provided on all mail for the address, stamps, postmarks, and postal endorsements.

122.143 Other Mail Processing Categories. See 122.141a for all letter-size pieces and 452.1 and Exhibit 452.1 regarding address placement on second-class publications.

122.15 Return Address. The return address contains elements corresponding to those for the destination address in 122.13. The mail listed below must bear, in legible form, the return address of the actual sender:

a. Mail of any class, when its return and/or address-correction service is desired (122.17).

b. Official mail (137.27 and 137.285).

c. Mail matter on which postage is paid by stamps precanceled by bars only (143.421).

d. Matter bearing company permit imprints (145.44).

e. Priority Mail (361.2).

f. Second-class mail in envelopes or wrappers (453.2a).

g. Fourth-class mail (761.12).

h. Registered mail (911.31).

i. Insured mail (913.13e).

j. COD mail (914.131).

k. Certified mail, if a return receipt is requested (912.44b).

l. Express Mail, if a return receipt is requested (297). (Note: The return address on the Express Mail label satisfies this requirement.)

122.16 Special Addressing Instructions. The following mail items must be addressed in accordance with the sections listed below:

a. Overseas military mail (122.8).

b. Department of State mail (126.2).

c. Window envelope mail (129.3).

d. International mail *(International Mail Manual)* 122.1.

122.17 Endorsements. A mailer's specific instructions for forwarding mail (see 159.2), as well as requests for address-correction service or return (see 159.3), must appear below the sender's return address. A full return address must be used with these endorsements. On letter-size mail, the information must appear in the upper left corner of the address side of the piece; on other mail, the information must appear in the upper left corner of the address area. The endorsements must stand out clearly against their background and be large enough to be readily visible. See Exhibit 159.151a-f for specific mailer endorsements authorized for each class of mail.

Examples:

a.   Frank B. White
     2416 Front Street
     St Louis MO 63135-1234

     FORWARDING & RETURN POSTAGE GUARANTEED

b.   Frank B. White
     2416 Front Street
     St Louis MO 63135-1234

     ADDRESS CORRECTION REQUESTED

c.   Frank B. White
     2416 Front Street
     St Louis MO 63135-1234

     FORWARDING & RETURN POSTAGE GUARANTEED ADDRESS CORRECTION REQUESTED

d.   Frank B. White
     2416 Front Street
     St Louis MO 63135-1234

     FORWARDING & ADDRESS CORRECTION REQUESTED

Frank B. White
2416 Front Street
St. Louis, MO 63135-1234

FORWARDING AND RETURN
POSTAGE GUARANTEED

     THREE SOME AUTO
     10 Fixit Street
     Alexandria, VA 22304-2345

122.18 Retaining Mail. At the sender's request, the delivery post office will retain mail, other than registered, insured, and certified, for not less than 3 days nor more than 30 days. To request a specific retention time, the sender, in his return address, must request that mail be held. Requests to lengthen or shorten retention periods to not less than 3 nor more than 30 days will be honored only at the sender's request. (See 159.323 for registered, insured, and certified mail retention periods.)

Examples:

a.   Return in 3 days to:
     Frank B. White
     2416 Front Street
     St Louis MO 63135-2134

b. Return in 30 days to:
Frank B. White
2416 Front Street
St Louis MO 63135-2134

122.2 Restrictions

122.21 Dual Address—Different Lines.
Mail bearing both a street address and a post office box number on different address lines will be delivered to the address element appearing on the line immediately above the city and state. If a ZIP Code (ZIP + 4 or 5-digit code) is used, it must correspond with the address element immediately above the city and state. These restrictions also apply to return address on mail matter.

122.22 Dual Address—Same Line.
Mail bearing both a street address and a post office box number on the same address line will be delivered to the post office box. If a ZIP Code (ZIP+4 or five-digit Code) is used, it must correspond with the post office box number in the address. This type of addressing is not recommended.

Examples:

PREFERRED ADDRESS FORMAT

Mail will be delivered here ———	GRAND PRODUCTS INC. 100 MAJOR STREET PO BOX 200 MORGAN STATION NEW YORK NY 10001-0200
Mail will be delivered here ———	GRAND PRODUCTS INC. PO BOX 200 MORGAN STATION 100 MAJOR STREET NEW YORK NY 10045-2345

NOT RECOMMENDED

Mail will be ——— delivered to PO Box	GRAND PRODUCTS INC. PO BOX 200, 100 MAJOR STREET NEW YORK NY 10001-0200 GRAND PRODUCTS INC.
Mail will be delivered to PO Box ———	100 MAJOR STREET, PO BOX 200 NEW YORK NY 10001-0200

122.23 Dual Address.
Mail bearing the name of more than one post office in either the address or return address is *not* acceptable for mailing.

122.24 Return to Point of Mailing Endorsement.
An endorsement directing return to point of mailing (postmark) will *not* be honored.

122.25 Postage Placement.
Postage (stamps, meter stamps, or permit imprints) must be placed in the upper right corner of the address side for letter-size mail (see 128.2). All other processing categories (see 128.1) must have the postage in the upper right corner of the address area (see 122.142).

122.3 Recommendations

122.31 Address Elements and Return Address.
The address elements in 122.13b (street and number and apartment number, or box number, or general delivery, or rural or highway contract route designation and box number) should be included in the address on all mail matter to ensure delivery and to prevent nondelivery or return due to insufficient addressing. The return address should be included on all mail. The return address on letter-size mail (see 128.2) should be located in the upper left corner of the address side. Other processing categories (see 128.1) should have the return address in the upper left corner of the address area. The return address should not be positioned below the delivery address. It should not appear on the reverse side of a mailpiece.

122.32 ZIP Code Use.
The use of ZIP Codes is recommended on all mail because they enable the Postal Service to achieve greater reliability and efficiency in dispatch and delivery. Although its use is voluntary, except where a ZIP+4 discount is claimed, use of the ZIP+4 Code is preferred over the five-digit ZIP Code.

159.13 Undeliverable Due to Postal Service Adjustments

159.131 Types of Changes

a. Rural route adjustments.

b. Conversion from rural to city delivery service.

c. Renumbering of houses.

d. Renaming of streets.

e. Consolidation of routes.

f. Consolidation of post offices.

g. Readjustment of delivery districts.

159.132 Notice of Change. Customers should notify their correspondents of their correct address, including ZIP Code. Form 3576, *Change of Address Request for Correspondents, Publishers and Businesses,* is available for this purpose. In addition, where practical, postmasters will attempt to notify publishers and other mailers who regularly send bulk mailings into the area. No charge will be made to these mailers for the notices or for corrections to galley lists of address changes due to Postal Service adjustments.

159.133 Disposition of Mail. Mail which is undeliverable due to Postal Service adjustments will be redirected and, if necessary, forwarded to the destination without an additional postage charge (from the end of the month in which the postal change occurs) for the appropriate forwarding period as specified by the class of mail.

Exception: Simplified address (box customer) mail addressed to Rural Route Box Customer, Highway Contract Route Box Customer, or Post Office Box Customer will only be redirected and forwarded free of charge until the next June 30 after the change in service, or until 90 days after the change in service, whichever is later.

159.14 Endorsements. Undeliverable-as-addressed mail will be endorsed by the Postal Service with the reason for nondelivery. See Exhibit 159.14.

159.15 Treatment of Undeliverable-as-Addressed Mail

159.151 Except as provided in 159.153, mail that is undeliverable as addressed may be forwarded, returned to the sender, or treated as dead mail, depending on the treatment authorized for that particular class of mail. A summary of the procedures for handling undeliverable-as-addressed mail is presented in Exhibits 159.151a-f. The chapters covering each class contain more detailed provisions.

159.152 Official mail will be treated the same as mail of the general public, except that no postage due will be rated or collected by post offices on delivery of mail or address-correction notices.

159.153 Return to the sender all non-mailable and nonstandard pieces.

159.16 Processing. It is the policy of the Postal Service to process all undeliverable-as-addressed (UAA) mail within 24 hours of receipt at the markup unit. Forms 3579, *Undeliverable 2nd, 3rd, 4th Class Matter,* will be mailed to publishers once each week. No Forms 3579 are to be retained in a forwarding unit more than seven days from receipt of the publication in the CFS site.

159.2 Forwarding

159.21 Change-of-Address Order

159.211 Forwarding Instructions. Customers should advise their local post office when they are moving. This is done by filing Form 3575, *Change of Address Order,* which is available at any post office or from any carrier. A written and signed order or a telegram sent by the customer, his agent, or person in whose care mail will be addressed is acceptable. Old and new addresses should be furnished. A change of address may not be filed with the Postal Service for mail bearing an employee's name addressed to the place of employment either during or after the termination of the employment relationship. Such mail is delivered in accordance with 153.5. A former employee may leave a forwarding address with the former employer for the purpose of having mail redirected to the former employee under the provisions of 159.224.

Endorsement	Reason for Nondelivery
No Such Office in State.	Addressed to a nonexistent post office.
No Such Street.	Addressed to a nonexistent street and the correct street is not known.
No Such Number.	Addressed to a nonexistent number and the correct number is not known.
Insufficient Address.	Mail from another post office fails to bear a number, street, box number, route number, or geographical section of the city or city and State is omitted and the correct address is not known.
Returned For Better Address.	Mail of local origin is incompletely addressed for distribution or delivery.
Illegible.	Address cannot be read.
Not Deliverable As Addressed—Unable to Forward.	Mail is undeliverable at address given; no Change of Address Order on file; forwarding order has expired; forwarding postage not guaranteed by sender or addressee; or, mail bears sender's instructions DO NOT FORWARD.
Outside Delivery Limits.	Addressed to a location outside the limits of delivery of the post office of address (see 155.5). Mail for Out-of-Bounds customers must be retained in general delivery for the prescribed retention period unless addressee has filed an order.
No Mail Receptacle.	Addressee has failed to provide a receptacle for the receipt of mail.
Returned for Postage.	Mail has no postage and there are no indications that the postage has fallen off.
Moved, Left No Address.	Addressee has moved and has not filed a change of address order.
Temporarily Away.	Addressee is temporarily away and retention period for holding mail has expired.
Attempted—Not Known.	Delivery attempted, addressee is not known at the place of address.
Refused.	Addressee has refused to accept mail or pay postage charges thereon.

Vacant.	House, apartment, office or building is not occupied. Used only on mail addressed Occupant.
Box Closed—No Order.	Post office box has been closed for nonpayment of rent.
Returned to Sender Due to Addressee's Violation of Postal False Representation Law.	Mail is returned to sender under a false representation order.
Unclaimed.	Addressee abandons or fails to call for mail.
Deceased.	Used only when it is known that the addressee is deceased and the mail is not properly deliverable to another person. This endorsement must be made personally by the delivering employee and under no circumstances may it be rubber-stamped. Mail addressed in care of another will be marked to indicate which person is deceased.
Returned to Sender Due to Addressee's Violation of Postal False Representation and Lottery Law.	Mail is returned to sender under a false representation order and a lottery order.
Returned to Sender Due to Addressee's Violation of Postal Lottery Law.	Mail is returned to sender under a lottery order.
In dispute.	Mail is returned to sender by order of the Regional Counsel when it cannot be determined which of disputing parties has better right to the mail.

Exhibit 159.14, Endorsements for Mail Undeliverable-as-Addressed

Exhibit 159.151a
Treatment of Undeliverable Express Mail, First-Class Mail Including Postal and Postcards, and First-Class Zone Rated (Priority) Mail

Mailer Endorsement	USPS Action
No Endorsement.	Forward at no charge (months 1-12). If undeliverable, return to sender with reason for nondelivery.
Address Correction Requested, or Do Not Forward.	Do Not Forward. Provide address correction or reason for nondelivery on mailpiece. Return entire mailpiece at no charge to sender.
Forwarding and Address Correction Requested.	Forward at no charge (months 1-12). If undeliverable, return to sender with reason for nondelivery attached at no charge. Charge the address correction fee if separate address correction is provided to mailer.

Notes:

These regulations apply to mail associated with a customer's change of address. Do not provide temporary change of address information at any time.

The following endorsements or their variations are not authorized for first-class mail:

Forwarding and Return Postage Guaranteed.

Forwarding and Return Postage Guaranteed. Address Correction Requested.

Return Postage Guaranteed.

Exhibit 159.151b
Treatment of Undeliverable Second-Class Mail

Mailer Endorsement	USPS Action
No Endorsement.	Forward at no charge for 60 days. After 60-day period, provide separate address correction or reason for nondelivery; charge address correction fee.
Return Postage Guaranteed.	Forward at no charge for 60 days. After 60-day period, return item to sender with new address or reason for nondelivery attached; charge the single piece third- or fourth-class rate.

Notes:

These regulations apply to mail associated with a customer's change of address. Do not provide temporary change of address information at any time.

The following endorsements or their variations are not authorized for second-class mail:

Address Correction Requested.

Forwarding and Address Correction Requested.

Do Not Forward.

Forwarding and Return Postage Guaranteed.

Forwarding and Return Postage Guaranteed. Address Correction Requested.

Exhibit 159.151c
Treatment of Undeliverable Third-Class Bulk Business Mail—Weighing 1 Ounce or Less (Forwarded up to 12 Months)

Mailer Endorsement	USPS Action
No Endorsement or Do Not Forward.	No forwarding or return service is provided.
Address Correction Requested.	No forwarding service is provided. Return entire mailpiece with address correction or reason for nondelivery; charge the first ounce single piece third-class rate, do not charge the address correction fee.
Forwarding and Return Postage Guaranteed.	Forward at no charge. If mail is not forwardable, return the entire mailpiece with reason for nondelivery; charge the appropriate third-class weighted fee.[1]
Forwarding and Return Postage Guaranteed, Address Correction Requested.[2]	Forward at no charge. If separate address correction notice is provided, charge the address correction fee. If mail is not forwardable, return the entire mailpiece with reason for nondelivery; charge the appropriate third-class weighted fee.[1]
Do Not Forward, Address Correction	Do Not Forward. Return entire mailpiece with the new address or reason for nondelivery; charge

Requested, Return Postage Guaranteed.[3] — the first ounce single piece third-class rate, do not charge the address correction fee.

[1] The weighted fee is the appropriate single piece third-class rate multiplied by a factor of 2.733. The fee is used during months 1-12 when forwarding is unsuccessful and the mailpiece is returned to the sender. During months 13-18 charge this fee on mailpieces endorsed Forwarding and Return Postage Guaranteed or Forwarding and Return Postage Guaranteed, Address Correction Requested.

[2] The authorized abbreviation for this endorsement is FWD & RET Postage Guaranteed—ACR.

[3] The authorized abbreviation for this endorsement is Do Not Forward—ACR-RPG.

Notes:

These regulations apply to mail associated with a customer's change of address. Do not provide temporary change of address information at any time.

The following endorsements or their variations are not authorized for third-class mail:

Forwarding and Address Correction Requested.

Return Postage Guaranteed.

Exhibit 159.151d
Treatment of Undeliverable Third-Class Bulk Business Mail—Weighing Over 1 Ounce (Forwarded up to 12 Months)

Mailer Endorsement	USPS Action
No Endorsement or Do Not Forward.	No forwarding or return service is provided.
Address Correction Requested.	No forwarding service is provided. Address correction is provided via Form 3547 or Form 3579;

charge the address correction fee.

Forwarding and Return Postage Guaranteed.	Forward at no charge. If mail is not forwardable, return the entire mailpiece with reason for nondelivery; charge the appropriate third-class weighted fee.[1]
Forwarding and Return Postage Guaranteed, Address Correction Requested.[2]	Forward at no charge. If separate address correction notice is provided, charge the address correction fee. If mail is not forwardable, return the entire mailpiece with reason for nondelivery; charge the appropriate third-class weighted fee.[1]
Do Not Forward, Address Correction Requested, Return Postage Guaranteed.[3]	Do Not Forward. Return entire mailpiece with the new address or reason for nondelivery; charge the appropriate single piece third-class rate, do not charge the address correction fee.

[1] The weighted fee is the appropriate single piece third-class rate multiplied by a factor of 2.733. The fee is used during months 1-12 when forwarding is unsuccessful and the mailpiece is returned to the sender. During months 13-18 charge this fee on mailpieces endorsed *Forwarding and Return Postage Guaranteed* or *Forwarding and Return Postage Guaranteed, Address Correction Requested.*

[2] The authorized abbreviation for this endorsement is *FWD & RET Postage Guaranteed—ACR.*

[3] The authorized abbreviation for this endorsement is *Do Not Forward—ACR-RPG.*

Notes:

These regulations apply to mail associated with a customer's change of address.

Do not provide temporary change of address information at any time.

The following endorsements or their variations are not authorized for third-class mail:

Forwarding and Address Correction Requested.
Return Postage Guaranteed.

Exhibit 159.151e
Treatment of Undeliverable Third-Class Mail Single Piece Rate (Forwarded up to 12 Months)

Mailer Endorsement	USPS Action
No Endorsement.	No forwarding service is provided. Return the mailpiece to the sender at the single piece third-class rate, with the reason for nondelivery or the new address; do not charge the address correction fee.
Do Not Forward.	No forwarding or return service is provided.
Address Correction Requested.	No forwarding service is provided. If the mailpiece weighs one ounce or less, return the entire piece with the new address or the reason for nondelivery; charge the third-class single piece rate. Pieces over one ounce will receive an address correction notice via Form 3579 or Form 3547; charge the address correction fee.
Forwarding and Return Postage Guaranteed.	Forward at no charge. If mail is not forwardable, return the entire mailpiece with reason for nondelivery, charge the appropriate third-class weighted fee.[1]
Forwarding and Return Postage Guaranteed, Address Correction Requested.[2]	Forward at no charge. If separate address correction notice is provided, charge the address correction fee. If mail is not forwardable, return the entire mailpiece with reason for nondelivery; charge the appropriate third-class weighted fee.[1]
Do Not Forward, Address Correction Requested. Return Postage Guaranteed.[3]	Do Not Forward. Return entire mailpiece with the new address or reason for nondelivery; charge the appropriate single piece third-class rate, do not charge the address correction fee.

[1] The weighted fee is the appropriate single piece third-class rate multiplied by a factor of 2.733. The fee is used during months 1-12 when forwarding is unsuccessful and the mailpiece is returned to the sender. During months 13-18 charge this fee on mailpieces endorsed Forwarding and Return Postage Guaranteed or Forwarding and Return Postage Guaranteed, Address Correction Requested.

[2] The authorized abbreviation for this endorsement is *FWD & RET Postage Guaranteed—ACR.*

[3] The authorized abbreviation for this endorsement is *Do Not Forward—ACR-RPG or DNF-ACR—Return Postage Guaranteed.*

Notes:
These regulations apply to mail associated with a customer's change of address. Do not provide temporary change of address information at any time.

The following endorsements or their variations are not authorized for third-class mail:

Forwarding and Address Correction Requested.
Return Postage Guaranteed.

Exhibit 159.151f
Treatment of Undeliverable Fourth-Class Mail Including Parcel Post (Forwarded up to 12 Months)

Mailer Endorsement	USPS Action
No Endorsement.	Forward locally at no charge; forward out of town postage due. If undeliverable or addressee refuses to pay postage, return mailpiece with new address or reason for nondelivery; charge both forwarding (where attempted) and return postage.
Do Not Forward,[1] Do Not Return.	No forwarding or return service is provided; mailpiece is disposed of by the Postal Service.
Forwarding and Return Postage Guaranteed.	Same as no endorsement.
Forwarding and Return Postage Guaranteed, Address Correction Requested[2]	Forward locally at no charge; forward out of town postage due. If forwarded, provide a separate address correction notice; charge address correction fee. If mailpiece is undeliverable, or addressee refuses to pay postage, return mailpiece with new address or reason for nondelivery, charge both forwarding (where attempted and return postage at the appropriate single-piece fourth class rate.
Do Not Forward, Do Not Return, Address Correction Requested.[3]	No forwarding or return service is provided; provide a separate address correction notice; charge address correction fee; mailpiece is disposed of by Postal Service.
Do Not Forward, Address Correction Requested. Return Postage Guaranteed.[3]	No forwarding service is provided; return mailpiece with the new address or reason for nondelivery. charge return postage at the appropriate single piece fourth-class rate.

[1] Mailers may continue to use the endorsement *Do Not Forwad*, which has been changed to *Do Not Forward-Do Not Return* and the *Address Correction Requested* endorsement until December 24, 1988, when a one year grace period expires.

[2] The authorized abbreviation for this endorsement is *FWD & RET Postage Guaranteed—ACR.*

[3] The authorized abbreviation for this endorsement is *Do Not Forward—ACR-RPG or DNF-ACR—Return Postage Guaranteed.*

Notes:
These regulations apply to mail associated with a customer's change of address. Do not provide temporary change of address information at any time.

Appendix 5

MARKETING DATA BASES—THE DEFINITION AND DEVELOPMENT PROCESS IN BUSINESS

By Richard A. Fredrickson, Vice President, Taurus Marketing Inc., Newburyport, MA, DMA Monograph, vol. 5, 1982

Source: Reprinted by permission of the Direct Marketing Association, Inc.

DEFINITION OF A MARKETING DATA BASE

A marketing data base may be defined as the collection, manipulation, and reporting of financial, operational, and product data from a *marketing* perspective.

It is the development of systems and procedures that perform the following functions for the user:

- Accurate capture of data
- Reporting needs defined by user function, as it relates to the decisions that are made by different users
- Processing procedures for maintaining the master data base and subfile data bases
- Selection of macro and micro segments from the data base for specific direct marketing or direct selling efforts

Each of the following sections will address some of the guidelines that may be used in development of your marketing data base.

Note: The processing methods defined here are capable of being used on almost any size computer system and do not require state-of-the-art data processing techniques or special hardware or software additions to most systems.

DATA CAPTURE

The information required to make effective use of a marketing data base probably already exists within your company. To determine the available sources of data, the following steps may be taken:

1. Collect samples of all documents and forms used by:

   a. accounting
   b. production
   c. sales force (inside and outside)
   d. shipping/receiving
   e. order processing
   f. customer service
   g. marketing, advertising, and public relations

2. Interview key personnel in each of these departments as it relates to customer- and order-based information. Look for pieces of data about the customer or the order that are unique or not part of your normal record-keeping operations.
3. Make a detailed cross-reference chart of the individual pieces of data from the forms and the interview versus the source of that data. If a piece of data is available in many departments (order number, customer name, etc.), post that item under all sources.

This process is both time consuming and somewhat tedious, but it is quite enlightening to find out the massive amounts of available data that can be possibly incorporated into a data base.

Do not overlook the data that may seem insignificant to the planned uses of the data base. In most cases, there is no predefined factor that can be counted on to help you in developing a powerful marketing tool. Therefore, it is necessary to intentionally overcollect data until a dependable factor(s) can be determined and proven in actual use.

With all data, materials, charts, and forms organized, you are ready to process through the next step.

REPORTING NEEDS

With the information gathered from the data capture step, end users of the system can be interviewed to examine the needs of reporting. This would include all of the department identified previously, as well as other layers of management in both staff and line functions.

In helping a user define his or her reporting needs, do not make any restrictions on the content, frequency, volume, or complexity of reports, as long as the information provided is to be used for decision making (versus nice to know). Even if the reporting needs outlined by the user do not seem to have the necessary data available, do not discount the possibility of finding the source of that data, and perhaps incorporating it into the system design and processing.

After all users have had an opportunity to express their needs and desires, all reports should be cross-referenced to the data chart to determine if the data is available, and if there is a correlating piece of data that should be included in the reports. Patterns will develop from varied users that are requesting similar types of reports. Whenever possible, the needs of several can be incorporated into one report, perhaps only changing the sequence in which the data is presented.

DEVELOPING SAMPLE REPORTS

When the needs-definition stage has been completed, sample reports should be typed or dummied on the computer. With each report, attempt to make an estimate of the size of the report based on the level of detail that is being reported. In many cases a user will define a need for data, without realizing the magnitude of the printed report it will develop. This oppressive amount of paper can deter a user from even looking at the report, much less making it a valuable working tool.

In many cases, the volume of a report can be greatly reduced by creating reporting on an exception or ranked basis. For example, a product line manager may be interested in the performance of company products in varied territories. The true interest may only be in the products that are above or below a performance standard, such as plus or minus 25 percent of forecast. In this case, the data can be ranked by sales performance, and all sales that are within target range are bypassed. This reduction of volume and ranking of data makes the real winners and losers stand out on the reports, and provides an action tool for corrective measures on those products.

CODING THE MASTER FILE

The development of a reporting data base within the system is as important as the master file itself. This data base retains the results of individual marketing efforts on a detailed basis. In order to satisfy the reporting needs of varied users and to provide microsegmented reporting, the system must carry many levels of codes in this file. These codes are used for both sorting and for the level breaks.

Through the use of a separate file that retains all of the descriptive, cost, etc., data regarding a marketing effort, you are able to build the reporting data base to almost any level of detail required.

A typical file of this type would contain information such as:

- Effort or adcode number
- Media—direct mail, phone, space, etc.
- Program—new acquisition, upgrade, etc.
- Product group
- Test or rollout codes
- Target market—OEM, End User, CEO's, etc.
- Date
- List or publication code
- Description
- Quantity by list segment
- Cost per 1000 or per insertion
- Campaign
- Audience—customers, prospects, suspects, etc.

This file will be matched to incoming orders, inquiries, etc. on the basis of effort number and list segment (if mail). A file of results that are actually completed computations of such factors as percent response or cost per order will be created. With these calculated results and all of the descriptive coding above, the reporting data base can be sequenced and manipulated to satisfy the reporting defined in step 1 of the development process.

PROCESSING PROCEDURES

In order to effectively serve the needs of the users, the system must conform to meet certain standards of quality of the data to be processed. These standards should include (but not be limited to):

1. Validation of all product codes, part numbers, sales territory, etc.
2. Validation of source codes, dates, name and address data, etc.

After all editing of data has been completed, the actual update of the data base can take place. This process should maintain a set of fields for purchase data, as well as counters for total activity.

An example of some of the data that may be captured would be as follows:

- Source—the source code and date of acquisition of this customer
- First order—the date, source, and dollar amount by product line of the purchases made
- Last order—the date, source, and dollar amount by product line of the purchases made
- Counters—number of orders in total, total dollar amount of all orders, number of orders and dollar amount by product line, etc.

ANALYSIS OF THE MASTER FILE

An effective method that may be useful for analysis of the master file is the creation of a short "cellcode" file that can be used to inventory the number of customers by unique segments. This process is accomplished by converting data fields in the data base to "range codes." Each character of the cellcode has a different meaning as to the content of the data. This technique is helpful in speeding up the processing of varied types of statistical reports.

An example of its use would be as follows:

1. *Create a cellcode count.* Create a cellcode count by source, product line, date of last purchase, and dollar amount of last purchase. The content of these cellcodes may be varied based on the type of reporting data that is required by each user to "inventory" the data base contents.
2. *Conversion of data to the correct codes.* A simple conversion process examines the data base and converts the data to the correct codes. The output is sorted in the proper sequence, and then summarized and totaled as needed.

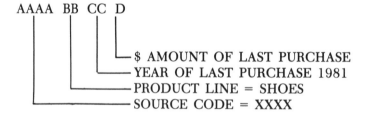

AAAA BB CC D
└─ $ AMOUNT OF LAST PURCHASE
└─ YEAR OF LAST PURCHASE 1981
└─ PRODUCT LINE = SHOES
└─ SOURCE CODE = XXXX

Cellcode report would appear as:

—CELLCODE—				QUANTITY
XXXX	SH	81	A	3,324
XXXX	SH	81	B	1,234
XXXX	SH	81	C	1,098
XXXX	SH	81	° TOTAL	5,566
ETC. . . .				

This method provides a simple way to provide many varied counts on the file. It provides a quick study of the customer base, and it can be easily modified for each user.

SELECTION PROCESSING

To take advantage of the detailed results analysis of your marketing efforts, a selection process that can fulfill requests on a detailed basis is required. To accomplish this, the entire selection process can be based on the defined cellcodes. By retaining these codes in the master file after each update, a matrix selection process can examine each customer record with one simple comparison of cellcodes to be extracted versus cellcodes on file. When they match, the customer record is selected with appropriate data acquired.

This process should also create the counts for each cellcode selected and assign the effort numbers for the planned mailing. In this fashion, you have created both the output required and that section of the reporting data base that contains counts along with detailed outgoing information.

If many cellcodes are required to be selected, a technique of using "wild cards" in the cellcodes can be used. This would be to select all of the records that have any value in the cell. If, for example, you wanted to select all names from the master file that bought shoes, regardless of source, year, or dollar amount, the selection cellcode in our previous section would be °°°° SH °°°, where the asterisk is the wild card and will select only on the basis of product line = SH.

Even though you may select on a broad basis such as this, it is still a good practice to retain the detail of all selected segments in the reporting base. This selection technique is only intended to speed up the processing side of the system.

Appendix 6

HOW TO BUILD A SALES AND MARKETING DATA BASE ON A PERSONAL COMPUTER

Source: Reprinted by permission of Brian Buxton.

(Brian Buxton's use of the personal computer to build a marketing and sales data base is covered from the perspective of companies selling high-ticket items through a sales force. These are products that require a number of face-to-face sales calls.)

Building a sales and marketing data base on a personal computer will require a knowledge of three things: first, a knowledge of data base concepts; second, a knowledge of the types and kinds of files that can constitute a sales and marketing data base; third, a basic knowledge of file importing.

DATA BASE CONCEPTS

The first point, the data base concept, is fairly simple, but it's different from the traditional language of the list manager. A data base is a collection of one or more computer files. Each file contains entries called records. In list terminology *records* mean "names." Each record contains one or more information elements. These are called *fields.* Examples of fields include name, title, company, address, zip code, and so forth. So, in computer language, lists are files, and files contain records, not names.

TYPES OF FILES MAKING UP A SALES AND MARKETING DATA BASE

There are four basic kinds of sales and marketing files that can be used to develop a sales and marketing data base on a PC. (These are files containing 10,000 to 20,000 names, which is the practical limit for most PC systems.)

Customer File

Information on customers is vital to planning future product offerings, promotions, and allocating sales and marketing resources. A simple file, containing only name, address, and total quarterly sales for each customer is an invaluable asset. A file of up to 10,000 customers is usable on an IBM XT or comparable machine (80 millisecond disk access speed); on an IBM AT, or on any disk drive with 20 megabytes of storage and disk access speed under 40 milliseconds, a file of 25,000 customers or more can be used.

A customer file can be obtained in any of several ways:

- It can be downloaded from the company's mainframe.
- A computer tape can be generated from corporate data processing. This tape can then be converted to PC diskettes.
- Hard copy lists (e.g., invoices) can be keypunched to produce a computer tape and PC diskettes.

Sales Prospect File

The next type of marketing information consists of prospect data. Prospects are identified in the specific geographic areas and industry markets served.

Prospect information can be obtained from a number of vendor sources. The best known are those that provide information on United States businesses, those covering special industry markets, and those with data bases of foreign companies. This information can be compiled from sales force reports, industry directories, and research.

Most company information vendors supply prospect information on IBM PC diskettes. These diskettes hold from 1,200 to 3,000 prospects per diskette. If the vendor will only supply a tape, have a service bureau make diskettes from the tape. In some cases it makes sense to order both tape and diskettes.

A number of sales prospect data bases are also available on-line. Most PC modem software packages allow capture of the output of an on-line session on a floppy or hard disk.

Downloading allows a small file to be obtained quickly. There are three restrictions on the use of downloading.

- In some cases it is illegal, or a violation of the service contract to download sales prospect information.
- It is slow and expensive to download large files (more than 2,000 prospects: with a 1,200 baud modem, and a prospect data base of 150 characters per record, a maximum of 48 prospects per minute, or 2,880 per hour can be downloaded).
- Unless the on-line service displays prospect information in a suitable format, the downloaded file cannot be imported into a data base management system. Doing so will require such a large amount of text editing of the downloaded file that it's not worth the effort. Some on-line services, however, will transmit a preformatted file ready for immediate importing into popular software programs.

Sales prospect files can be used internally to generate:

Prospect mailing labels
Personalized letters
Telemarketing lists
Sales territory prospect lists

Respondent Files

Nearly all marketing activities, mailings, telemarketing, trade shows, and print ads generate responses. From these responses any of the following response files can be generated:

Direct mail responses
Telemarketing responses
Trade show leads
Print ad responses
Prospects qualified by the sales force

When sending out business reply cards, or collecting information via telemarketing, a key code (prospect ID number) should be put on each business reply card and each telemarketing sheet. Then keypunch only this prospect ID number and new data on the BRC or telemarketing sheet. A relational data base package will allow "linking" this data back to the information on the original prospect record.

Sales Call Report File

Most companies with sales forces have a sales call reporting system. Often it's hard to get meaningful information from these reports, such as the percent of the sales force's time being spent in industry X or promoting product Y. However, answers to these questions can be found when these sales call reports are converted to files on the PC.

Linked together, files of customers, prospects, respondents and sales call reports can constitute a sales and marketing data base.

FILE IMPORTING

The third point is file importing. All these files on PC diskettes are coming as "text" files. As such, no file manipulation or data base management procedures can be made with them. A data base management software system is needed, either a general-purpose system such as dBase, rBase, Reflex, or DataEase, or a package specifically for use in sales and marketing.

After a data base management package is selected the "text" files will have to be imported into "system" files, which can be used with the data base package. File importing, therefore, is a critical step in building a sales and marketing data base on a PC. An appropriate data base management package will tell how to import files.

Once the files are imported, they can be expanded to contain additional fields such as territory number, industry, mailing campaign code, or industry code.

A TYPICAL LIST ANALYSIS PROBLEM

Problem: Determine the breakdown by industry and by sales region of the names on a 10,000-record mailing list.

Solving this problem will not produce a sales and marketing analysis system. But it will expose the planner to the kind of operations that can be performed on a PC and demonstrate how these operations can be grouped together to produce a marketing analysis or marketing decision support system.

An example of this is as follows: A mailing list of 10,000 names is loaded on an IBM XT. It looks something like this:

Name	George Smith	Mary Lucas	Tom Jones
Title	Manager	President	Director
Company	XYZ Corp	ABC Bank	MCO Corp
Street	123 Main	20 South	66 Fifth
City	Smalltown	Bigtown	Gotham
State	OH	IL	NY
ZIP	44321	66544	10020
SIC	3573	6022	481

A next step is to generate a cross-tab report analyzing the number of these that fall into the following geographic regions (defined by state) and into the following industry groups (defined by SIC Code):

| | Sales Region | | | | | |
Industry	NE	SE	CE	NW	SW	Total
1. Manufacturing	xxx	xxx	xxx	xxx	xxx	xxx
2. Utilities	xxx	xxx	xxx	xxx	xxx	xxx
3. Insurance	xxx	xxx	xxx	xxx	xxx	xxx
4. Commercial banking	xxx	xxx	xxx	xxx	xxx	xxx
5. Investment banking	xxx	xxx	xxx	xxx	xxx	xxx
6. Real estate	xxx	xxx	xxx	xxx	xxx	xxx
7. Business services	xxx	xxx	xxx	xxx	xxx	xxx
8. All other	xxx	xxx	xxx	xxx	xxx	xxx
°°Total°°	xxx	xxx	xxx	xxx	xxx	xxx

The procedure converts the 10,000-record mailing list file to an 8-record file (one record for each industry), containing as fields the number of names on the mailing list in each region. Here's the result:

| | Sales Region | | | | | |
Industry	NE	SE	CE	NW	SW	Total
1. Manufacturing	389	311	421	201	525	1,847
2. Utilities	55	22	66	44	71	258
3. Insurance	244	180	247	154	185	1,010
4. Commercial banking	302	245	299	223	344	1,413
5. Investment banking	101	40	51	21	88	301
6. Real estate	280	225	277	101	206	1,089
7. Business services	404	389	445	277	478	1,993
8. All other	511	346	451	280	501	2,089
°°Total°°	2,286	1,758	2,257	1,301	2,398	10,000

The data base manager "collapses" the mailing list file from 10,000 records to 8 records. It can do this because the field "industry" has only 8 different values across all 10,000 records. As it collapses the mailing list file, it totals up the values in all the numeric fields (i.e., the count, for each region.)

These are the essentials of analyzing a data base on the personal computer. Faster disk drives, faster processors, and new software will provide more power for this purpose.

Other marketing analyses problems that can be performed on the PC generate reports of:

- Prospects by sales territory, industry, company size
- Mail responses by territory, industry, company size
- Mail responses as a percent of total pieces sent by territory, industry, company size
- Customers as a percent of all business-to-business prospects in each territory, industry, size category
- Revenue by geography, industry, company size
- Revenue per customer by geography, industry, company size

Reports like these are available from on-line vendors. When searching for sales prospects by industry, geographic area, and sales volume, the on-line service provides the marketer with the number of records selected. Some on-line services offer report-writing packages to produce more complex reports. Also, some of the sales prospect vendors themselves will produce these reports or sell software for the marketer to produce them.

A TYPICAL SALES-CALL TRACKING PROBLEM

Analysis is critical to the sales and marketing function. But there is an even greater interest in tracking systems. These are systems that monitor the many activities in the sales and marketing departments. For example, who got which leads, who called on which accounts, how many calls did the sales force make in a particular month, and so forth.

Here is an example of a typical tracking problem. How many sales calls did each of the sales reps make last month on prospects in each of the eight industries served? To answer this question, two files are used on the PC. The first file is called PROSPECTS. It contains the information on prospects in each salesperson's territory. The second file is called CALLS. It contains information on each sales call.

PROSPECTS	CALLS
1. ID number------------link----------------	1. Prospect ID number
2. Company name	2. Date
3. Address	3. Territory number
4. City	4. Type of call
5. State	5. Next call date
6. Zip code	6. Next call type
7. SIC code	
8. Industry	

These two files are LINKED on the field ID number and prospect ID number. This allows the marketer to start in the CALLS file and access information in the PROSPECTS file and vice versa. Here is the result:

NUMBER OF CALLS BY INDUSTRY GROUP

Territory #	Industry Group					
	1 MFRG	2 UTILS	3 INSUR	4 BANKG	5 OTHER	TOTAL
101	2	4	3	6	6	21
102	3	5	2	6	1	17
103	4	2	7	3	1	17
104	5	1	6	4	1	17
201	5	1	6	4	1	17
203	6	2	1	2	5	16
204	3	7	4	2	2	18
205	7	6	5	4	1	23
Total	35	28	34	31	18	146
Average	4.38	3.50	4.25	3.88	2.25	18.25
PCT of total	23.97	19.18	23.29	21.23	12.33	100.00

With this problem as an example, procedures can be built for a sales department to generate reports showing:

- The total number of calls made each month in each territory
- The number of calls made cross-tabbed by the size (or purchasing potential) of the prospect company
- The number of direct mail responses to each rep sent versus the number of leads for which the rep has filed a call report
- The number of calls made versus the number of actual sales made (the call-to-close ratio) for each territory
- In ranked-sorted order, the sales rep making the most calls to the sales rep making the least calls

There are a number of software programs that will do these reports, depending on the user's needs and level of familiarity with the PC. Some marketers may want to build a custom system or fit their activities to the requirements of a low-priced "packaged" system. An educated marketer will make the best decision.

Appendix 7

INSTRUCTIONS FOR FILE IMPORTING, LIST ANALYSIS, AND SALES-CALL TRACKING, USING dBASE III ON A PERSONAL COMPUTER

Source: Reprinted by permission of Brian Buxton.

INSTRUCTIONS FOR IMPORTING A TEXT FILE INTO dBASE III

What follows is a set of instructions for file importing; that is, for taking a file which has been copied onto a personal computer diskette and bringing it into dBase III as a system or °.DBF file. File importing is an important function for these reasons:

- It lets you bring information onto your PC; you can take a computer tape from your mainframe or from an outside data entry service, convert it to diskettes, and load these diskettes into your PC;
- It is much easier than manually typing in the information;
- You have to do it to take advantage of any of the data base management functions such as sorting, selecting, copying, adding fields of information—functions you will want to use with sales and marketing information.

1. Format: The first step is to specify the format you will use for your diskettes, files, and records. It is essential to be precise in specifying the format in all three areas; otherwise you may not be able to read, import, or use the data in question.

In this exercise, we are using an IBM PC, XT or AT. Here is the diskette format to specify:

- a. Disk format: double-side, double-density, 362,000 bytes per diskette or 1.2 MB per diskette (high-density) (AT only);
- b. File format: standard ASCII, maximum of 100,000 bytes per file;
- c. Record format: fixed positions, no delimiters, carriage return at the end of each record.

2. Layout: The layout specifies the position of each field in the data file. It is essential to have a layout of the file(s) on PC diskettes which you are using. You should check the files to be sure they correspond to the layout specified in the layout sheet.

In this example, we're going to use a mailing list containing the following information elements (fields) for each name (record) in the mailing list (file):

NAME
TITLE
COMPANY
STREET
CITY
STATE
ZIP
SIC
ID NUMBER

If you open up the file itself on a PC diskette, using a word processing package of the DOS command TYPE, you will see a file that looks like this:

```
Bill Smith    Manager    XYZ Corp    123 Main   Smalltown   OH44321357300001
Mary Lucas    President   ABC Bank    20 South   Bigtown     IL66544602200002
Tom Jones     Director    MCO Corp    66 Fifth   Gotham      NY10020481100003
```

The layout sheet should look like this:

FIELD NAME	TYPE	STARTING POSITION	LENGTH	FILE NAME: LIST01.DAT
NAME	C	1	12	
TITLE	C	13	10	
COMPANY	C	23	10	
STREET	C	33	10	
CITY	C	43	10	
STATE	C	53	2	
ZIP	C	55	5	
SIC	C	60	4	
ID_NUMBER	C	64	5	

TOTAL NUMBER OF CHARACTERS: 68

The "C" means the field type is "character" (also called "text," "alpha" or "alphanumeric"). Other types of fields are N (numeric) and D (date).

Zip code is a character, not a numeric, field because (1) the zip code "02138" should appear as "02138," and not as the number 2138; (2) there is no need to add, subtract, multiply, or divide zip codes; (3) character fields will index, sort, and select as easily as numeric fields. This logic applies to SIC codes and ID numbers.

Checking the file on your diskettes against the layout can be done by bringing the file up on word processing software and adding a "ruler" to the top line, as shown below:

```
0          1          2          3          4          5          6
1234567890123456789012345678901234567890123456789012345678901234567 8
Bill Smith  Manager    XYZ Corp  123 Main   Smalltown   OH44321357300001
Mary Lucas  President   ABC Bank  20 South   Bigtown     IL66544602200002
Tom Jones   Director    MCO Corp  66 Fifth   Gotham      NY10020481100003
```

Here we see that the file does correspond to the layout. The first field, NAME, starts at position 1 and goes on for twelve positions; the field TITLE starts at position 13 and is ten characters long; etc.

3. Importing: Now we are ready to start importing into dBase III.

a. First, at the DOS level (the C> prompt), check out the name of the file you will be working with. In this exercise, the file is called LIST01.DAT. It is a text file—that is, it cannot be used in dBase, or in nearly any data base management system, without importing it first. The file LIST01.DAT will appear when you issue the DOS command DIR (directory) followed by a carriage return (abbreviated as <CR>).

b. If you are using a dual-floppy system, make sure that the file LIST01.DAT
    is no larger than 100,000 bytes. You'll be creating a system or dBase file
    on this same diskette which will take up about 10 percent more space, or
    110,000 bytes, and there are only 362,000 bytes on the floppy diskette.
       If you are using a hard disk system, make sure you copy the text file(s)
    onto the subdirectory where you have the dBase III program.
c. Boot dBase III (i.e., type DBASE <CR>).
d. At the dot prompt, type the command to create a new system file (whose
    suffix will be .DBF):

                         .CREATE LIST01 <CR>

e. This command will take you into a file creation screen. Using the file layout
    sheet, type in the file creation screen so that it looks like this:

C:LIST01.DBF   Bytes remaining: 3841
                                                      Fields defined: 9

	field name	type	width	dec
1	NAME	Char/text	12	
2	TITLE	Char/text	10	
3	COMPANY	Char/text	10	
4	STREET	Char/text	10	
5	CITY	Char/text	10	
6	STATE	Char/text	2	
7	ZIP	Char/text	5	
8	SIC	Char/text	4	
9	ID_NUMBER	Char/text	5	
10		Char/text		

---

f. When you finish typing in the field names, types, and widths, type CONTROL
    W (abbreviated as ∧W)—that is, depress the Ctrl key and type "W." This
    saves the structure you've just created.
g. The dBase III will ask: Input data records now? (Y/N). Type N to signify
    "No."
h. Now go into the system file LIST01.DBF you just created. At the dot prompt,
    type:

                         .USE LIST01 <CR>

i. Check out whether you've created the structure properly. Type:

DISPLAY STRUCTURE <CR>

You can abbreviate and use the first four letters of each word:

.DISP STRU <CR>

The file structure ought to be as follows:

```
Structure for database    : C:file_1.dbf
Number of data records :    0
Date of last update       : 09/03/85

Field   Field name          Type      Width   Dec

  1     NAME                Character   12
  2     TITLE               Character   10
  3     COMPANY             Character   10
  4     STREET              Character   10
  5     CITY                Character   10
  6     STATE               Character    2
  7     ZIP                 Character    5
  8     SIC                 Character    4
  9     ID_NUMBER           Character    5
        °° Total °°                     69
```

The total number of characters in each record is sixty-nine, not sixty-eight, because dBase III takes up an extra character in each record.

j. If you need to change the structure, type MODI STRU <CR> and you'll go back into a file creation menu. When it's correct, type ∧W to save it, and then re-issue the .DISP STRU command.

k. Now you're ready to import. The system file is in exactly the same structure as the text file. Order dBase to use the correct system file:

.USE LIST01

Next you will append the information in the text file (LIST01.DAT) into the system file (LIST01.DBF). You must tell dBase that the information in the text file is in the "Standard Data Format" (SDF). Therefore, the command is:

.APPEND FROM LIST01.DAT SDF

Having received this command, the counter at the bottom of the screen will start running, and when all the records have been read from the text file into the system file, you will see

1500 (OR WHATEVER NUMBER) RECORDS ADDED

at the bottom of your screen.

This completes the instructions for importing a file into dBase III.

dBASE III COMMANDS FOR THE LIST ANALYSIS EXERCISE

In this example, we are going to convert the list file LIST01.DBF created in the file importing exercise that looks like this:

NAME   Bill Smith
TITLE   Manager
COMPANY   XYZ Corp
STREET   123 Main
CITY   Smalltown
STATE   OH
ZIP   44321
SIC   3573
ID NUMBER   00001

into a set of cross-tabs that look like this:

		SALES REGION —				
INDUSTRY	NE	SE	CE	NW	SW	TOTAL
1. MANUFACTURING	xxx	xxx	xxx	xxx	xxx	xxx
2. UTILITIES	xxx	xxx	xxx	xxx	xxx	xxx
3. INSURANCE	xxx	xxx	xxx	xxx	xxx	xxx
4. COMMERCIAL BANKING	xxx	xxx	xxx	xxx	xxx	xxx
5. INVESTMENT BANKING	xxx	xxx	xxx	xxx	xxx	xxx
6. REAL ESTATE	xxx	xxx	xxx	xxx	xxx	xxx
7. BUSINESS SERVICES	xxx	xxx	xxx	xxx	xxx	xxx
8. ALL OTHER	xxx	xxx	xxx	xxx	xxx	xxx
°° TOTAL °°	xxx	xxx	xxx	xxx	xxx	xxx

We're assuming this file (LIST01.dbf) contains 10,000 records or names. Since we've already seen that this file has sixty-nine characters per record, it will take up about 690,000 bytes of space on a hard disk.

First, a bit of general explanation of what we're going to do, and then the step-by-step instructions.

dBase III produces a crosstab file by means of the TOTAL command. It collapses the records in the mailing list file down to a much smaller number of records, based on the field we total on.

In this case, we are going to total on a field called INDUSTRY which has only eight possible values, the ones listed above. Therefore the TOTAL command will collapse the list file, containing 10,000 separate records, into a new file which contains only eight records, one for each possible value of the field totaled on: INDUSTRY. To do this, we will have to add a field called INDUSTRY to LIST01.dbf.

When dBase III totals, it adds up the values in numeric fields in the original file (LIST01.dbf). What do we want dBase to total up? The number of records in the file. Therefore, we will assign the value "1" to a new field in each record. We will call this field CT for "count." The value for CT in each record will be "1." When we total the entire file, the sum of the values in the field CT will be 10,000.

But wait a minute! We also are going to need subtotals by sales region. How are we going to do that? First we are going to add a new field called REGION to the mailing list file (LIST01). Then we are going to add five new "count" fields based on REGION:

NE_CT = the number of records in the NE region
SE_CT = the number of records in the SE region
CE_CT = the number of records in the CE region
NW_CT = the number of records in the NW region
SW_CT = the number of records in the SW region

The correct value for each of these fields will be 1 if the record in LIST01.dbf is in that region, and 0 if it's not.

Therefore, the exercise will be in four steps:

A. Adding the new fields;
B. Placing the correct values in these fields;
C. Preparing the mailing list file for totaling;
D. Totaling the file to produce the totaled file.

An explanation of the commands follows.

Adding the New Fields

1. First we take the mailing list file LIST01 and copy its structure (no data) to a new file LIST02:

        .USE LIST01
        .COPY TO LIST02 STRU

2. The we go into LIST02 and modify the structure:

.USE LIST02
.MODI STRU

We are going to delete some fields we won't be needing, using the $\wedge$U command, and then add the new fields by writing them in at the bottom. The result should look like this:

C:LIST02.dbf

Bytes remaining: 3904
Fields defined: 11

#	field name	type	width	dec	field name	type	width	dec
	MMMMMMMMMMMMMMMMMMMM				MMMMMMMMMMMMMMMM			
1	STATE	Char/text	2					
2	SIC	Char/text	4					
3	ID_NUMBER	Char/text	5					
4	INDUSTRY	Char/text	1					
5	REGION	Char/text	2					
6	NE_CT	Numeric	4	0				
7	SE_CT	Numeric	4	0				
8	CE_CT	Numeric	4	0				
9	NW_CT	Numeric	4	0				
10	SW_CT	Numeric	4	0				
11	CT	Numeric	5	0				
12		Char/text						

Names start with a letter; the remainder may be letters, digits, or —

Then issue the command:

.APPE FROM LIST01

to bring the contents of the LIST01 file into this new, expanded file.

Placing the Correct Values in These Fields

This step has many separate command lines in it. The easiest—and the only practical—way to issue these commands is to create a command file that takes advantage of dBase III's ability to use written command files. We are going to create a command file called LISTREPL to replace the empty values of these new fields with the proper values.

There are two ways to create a command file. One is to issue the command:

.MODI COMM LISTREPL

and dBase III will take you into its text editor. Then type in the commands listed below. Use ∧W to save it. Beware—if you push the Esc key, you destroy everything you've written.

But for long commands, you will want the block creation and copying features of a more robust word processing program such as Wordstar. In this instance, you create a document file called LISTREPL.PRG, and edit it to contain the commands listed below.

Here are the contents of the command file LISTREPL.PRG:

```
SET ECHO ON

USE LIST02

REPLACE ALL INDUSTRY WITH '8'
REPLACE ALL INDUSTRY WITH '1' FOR SIC >= '2000' .AND. SIC <= '3999'
REPLACE ALL INDUSTRY WITH '2' FOR SIC >= '4000' .AND. SIC <= '4999'
REPLACE ALL INDUSTRY WITH '3' FOR SIC >= '6300' .AND. SIC <= '6499'
REPLACE ALL INDUSTRY WITH '4' FOR SIC >= '6000' .AND. SIC <= '6199'
REPLACE ALL INDUSTRY WITH '5' FOR SIC >= '6200' .AND. SIC <= '6299'
REPLACE ALL INDUSTRY WITH '5' FOR SIC >= '6700' .AND. SIC <= '6799'
REPLACE ALL INDUSTRY WITH '6' FOR SIC >= '6500' .AND. SIC <= '6699'
REPLACE ALL INDUSTRY WITH '7' FOR SIC >= '7300' .AND. SIC <= '7399'


REPLACE ALL REGION WITH 'NE' FOR STATE = 'ME'
REPLACE ALL REGION WITH 'NE' FOR STATE = 'NH'
REPLACE ALL REGION WITH 'NE' FOR STATE = 'VT'
REPLACE ALL REGION WITH 'NE' FOR STATE = 'MA'
REPLACE ALL REGION WITH 'NE' FOR STATE = 'RI'
REPLACE ALL REGION WITH 'NE' FOR STATE = 'CT'
REPLACE ALL REGION WITH 'NE' FOR STATE = 'NY'
REPLACE ALL REGION WITH 'NE' FOR STATE = 'NJ'
REPLACE ALL REGION WITH 'NE' FOR STATE = 'PA'
REPLACE ALL REGION WITH 'NE' FOR STATE = 'DC'
REPLACE ALL REGION WITH 'NE' FOR STATE = 'DE'
REPLACE ALL REGION WITH 'NE' FOR STATE = 'MD'


REPLACE ALL REGION WITH 'SE' FOR STATE = 'VA'
REPLACE ALL REGION WITH 'SE' FOR STATE = 'NC'
REPLACE ALL REGION WITH 'SE' FOR STATE = 'SC'
REPLACE ALL REGION WITH 'SE' FOR STATE = 'GA'
REPLACE ALL REGION WITH 'SE' FOR STATE = 'FL'
REPLACE ALL REGION WITH 'SE' FOR STATE = 'TN'
REPLACE ALL REGION WITH 'SE' FOR STATE = 'AL'
REPLACE ALL REGION WITH 'SE' FOR STATE = 'MS'
REPLACE ALL REGION WITH 'SE' FOR STATE = 'LA'
```

```
REPLACE ALL REGION WITH 'CE' FOR STATE = 'OH'
REPLACE ALL REGION WITH 'CE' FOR STATE = 'WV'
REPLACE ALL REGION WITH 'CE' FOR STATE = 'KY'
REPLACE ALL REGION WITH 'CE' FOR STATE = 'IN'
REPLACE ALL REGION WITH 'CE' FOR STATE = 'MI'
REPLACE ALL REGION WITH 'CE' FOR STATE = 'IL'
REPLACE ALL REGION WITH 'CE' FOR STATE = 'WI'
REPLACE ALL REGION WITH 'CE' FOR STATE = 'MO'
REPLACE ALL REGION WITH 'CE' FOR STATE = 'AR'
REPLACE ALL REGION WITH 'CE' FOR STATE = 'KS'
REPLACE ALL REGION WITH 'CE' FOR STATE = 'OK'
REPLACE ALL REGION WITH 'CE' FOR STATE = 'TX'
REPLACE ALL REGION WITH 'CE' FOR STATE = 'MN'
REPLACE ALL REGION WITH 'CE' FOR STATE = 'ND'
REPLACE ALL REGION WITH 'CE' FOR STATE = 'SD'
REPLACE ALL REGION WITH 'CE' FOR STATE = 'NE'
REPLACE ALL REGION WITH 'CE' FOR STATE = 'IA'

REPLACE ALL REGION WITH 'NW' FOR STATE = 'MT'
REPLACE ALL REGION WITH 'NW' FOR STATE = 'WY'
REPLACE ALL REGION WITH 'NW' FOR STATE = 'ID'
REPLACE ALL REGION WITH 'NW' FOR STATE = 'WA'
REPLACE ALL REGION WITH 'NW' FOR STATE = 'OR'
REPLACE ALL REGION WITH 'NW' FOR STATE = 'AK'

REPLACE ALL REGION WITH 'SW' FOR STATE = 'HI'
REPLACE ALL REGION WITH 'SW' FOR STATE = 'CA'
REPLACE ALL REGION WITH 'SW' FOR STATE = 'NV'
REPLACE ALL REGION WITH 'SW' FOR STATE = 'AZ'
REPLACE ALL REGION WITH 'SW' FOR STATE = 'UT'
REPLACE ALL REGION WITH 'SW' FOR STATE = 'NM'
REPLACE ALL REGION WITH 'SW' FOR STATE = 'CO'

REPLACE ALL NE_CT WITH 1 FOR REGION = 'NE'
REPLACE ALL SE_CT WITH 1 FOR REGION = 'SE'
REPLACE ALL CE_CT WITH 1 FOR REGION = 'CE'
REPLACE ALL NW_CT WITH 1 FOR REGION = 'NW'
REPLACE ALL SW_CT WITH 1 FOR REGION = 'SW'

REPLACE ALL CT WITH 1
```

Preparing the Mailing List File for Totaling

dBase III can total only files that have been indexed on the field on which
you want the data totaled. This field is INDUSTRY. So issue the command:

```
.USE LIST02
.INDEX ON INDUSTRY TO INDX
```

Totaling the List File to Produce the Totaled File

To execute the final step (totaling) say:

```
.USE LIST02 INDEX INDX
.TOTAL ON INDUSTRY TO LIST03
```

Then add the text information on each industry through the following steps:

```
.USE LIST03
.COPY TO LIST04 STRU
.USE LIST04
.MODI STRU
```

Add a new CHARACTER field called IND_NAME with a width of 25.

.APPEND FROM LIST03

```
.REPL ALL IND_NAME WITH 'MANUFACTURING'        FOR INDUSTRY = '1'
.REPL ALL IND_NAME WITH 'UTILITIES'            FOR INDUSTRY = '2'
.REPL ALL IND_NAME WITH 'INSURANCE'            FOR INDUSTRY = '3'
.REPL ALL IND_NAME WITH 'COMMERCIAL BANKING'   FOR INDUSTRY = '4'
.REPL ALL IND_NAME WITH 'INVESTMENT BANKING'   FOR INDUSTRY = '5'
.REPL ALL IND_NAME WITH 'REAL ESTATE'          FOR INDUSTRY = '6'
.REPL ALL IND_NAME WITH 'BUSINESS SERVICES'    FOR INDUSTRY = '7'
.REPL ALL IND_NAME WITH 'OTHER'                FOR INDUSTRY = '8'
```

Finally, if you want to further work with this file using Lotus 1–2–3, issue the commands:

```
.USE LIST04
.COPY TO LIST05 DELI
.RENAME LIST05.TXT TO LIST05.PRN
```

This will create a new file, LIST05.TXT, which you rename to LIST05.PRN. This file is compatible with Lotus 1–2–3. Just boot Lotus, issue the command /FIN and pick the file LIST05, and it will come up on the screen ready for you to label the columns and create a worksheet file.

Here is the final worksheet. You can get it either from Lotus 1–2–3, or simply by listing the contents of the file LIST04.DBF as follows:

```
.USE LIST04
.LIST TO PRINT
```

INDUSTRY	NE_ COUNT	SE_ COUNT	CE_ COUNT	NW_ COUNT	SW_ COUNT	TOT_ COUNT
MANUFACTURING	389	311	421	201	525	1847
UTILITIES	55	22	66	44	71	258
INSURANCE	244	180	247	154	185	1010
COMMERCIAL BANK	302	245	299	223	344	1413
INVESTMENT BANK	101	40	51	21	88	301
REAL ESTATE	280	225	277	101	206	1089
BUSINESS SERV	404	389	445	277	478	1993
ALL OTHER	511	346	451	280	501	2089

You can add the TOTAL line using either dBase's CREATE REPORT function, or by importing the file into Lotus 1-2-3 and editing it. The TOTAL line is:

TOTAL	2286	1758	2257	1301	2398	10000

dBASE III COMMANDS FOR THE SALES-CALL TRACKING PROBLEM

In this problem, we are going to use the original mailing list file (LIST01) and link it with a new file called CALLS. Each record in the file CALLS is a sales call report filed by a sales representative.

Then we will create a new file, called LINK01, containing information from both the LIST file on the prospect or customer called, and information from the CALLS file on the sales-call report.

Finally, we are going to go through a similar totaling procedure to the one described above in order to generate the following crosstab:

			Number of Calls by Industry Group			
			INDUSTRY GROUP—			
TERR #	1 MFRG	2 UTILS	3 INSUR	4 BANKG	5 OTHER	TOTAL
101	xxx	xxx	xxx	xxx	xxx	xxx
102	xxx	xxx	xxx	xxx	xxx	xxx
103	xxx	xxx	xxx	xxx	xxx	xxx
104	xxx	xxx	xxx	xxx	xxx	xxx
201	xxx	xxx	xxx	xxx	xxx	xxx
203	xxx	xxx	xxx	xxx	xxx	xxx
204	xxx	xxx	xxx	xxx	xxx	xxx
205	xxx	xxx	xxx	xxx	xxx	xxx
TOTAL	xxx	xxx	xxx	xxx	xxx	xxx
AVERAGE	xxx	xxx	xxx	xxx	xxx	xxx
PCT OF TOTAL	xxx	xxx	xxx	xxx	xxx	xxx

Create the New File CALLS

The first step is to create a new file, CALLS, which will contain information on each sales call. You will notice that this file does not contain the name, title, company name, address, et cetera of the company on which the salesperson called—just the ID number of the prospect (from the file LIST01). The rest of the information on the prospect or customer is extracted from the LIST file. This saves the salesperson a lot of time filling out the call report, and the data entry personnel a lot of time typing in the information.

For the purposes of this exercise, we're going to create a very simple sales-call report, containing only the following information:

IDNUM   —the ID number of the prospect or customer

DATE   —the date of the sales call

TERRNUM   —the salesperson's territory number

CALLTYPE   —the type of call (e.g., initial call, followup call, full-scale presentation)

NEXTTYPE   —the type of the next call to be made

NEXTDATE   —the date by which the next call should be made

Of course, you can use dBase III to design nearly any kind of sales call report you wish.

To create the file CALLS in dBase:

1. Boot dBase (at C>, type: DBASE <CR>).
2. Type: .CREATE CALLS <CR>.
3. When the file creation screen comes up, fill it in so that it looks like this when you have finished:

```
C:CALLS.DBF                              Bytes remaining:    3841
                                         Fields defined:        6


field name              type        width    dec

1  IDNUM               Char/text       8
2  DATE                Date            8
3  TERRNUM             Char/text       4
4  CALLTYPE            Char/text       1
5  NEXTTYPE            Char/text       1
6  NEXTDATE            Date            8
7                      Char/text
```

Type ∧W to save this structure.

4. dBase will then ask: .INPUT DATA NOW? Type NO <CR> if you do not wish to enter new data into this file. Type YES if you plan to type the sales-call reports directly into dBase via the data entry screen. To add new data, just type:

.USE CALLS
.APPEND

To stop adding information, type ∧C. To edit previously entered information, type: .USE CALLS and then: .EDIT 1 (or whatever record you want to edit). The dBase manual explains the codes to use in editing the file.

Conversely, you can have an outside service type the sales-call reports and convert the result to PC diskettes. Then you'll want to use the file importing procedure explained at the beginning of this appendix.

Select the Sales Calls Made in July 1985

To generate a crosstab covering only the calls made in a particular month (e.g., July 1985), type the following sequence:

```
.USE CALLS
.COPY TO CALLS2 FOR DATE >= 7/1/85 .AND. DATE <= 7/31/85
.USE CALLS2
```

This creates a new file, CALLS2, containing only those sales calls made in July 1985.

Create a New File: LINK01

1. As you will recall, the file LIST02 looks like this:

C:LIST02.dbf   Bytes remaining: 3904
                                                Fields defined: 11

	field name	type	width	dec	field name	type	width	dec
	MMMMMMMMMMMMMMMMMMMM				MMMMMMMMMMMMMMMM			
1	STATE	Char/text	2					
2	SIC	Char/text	4					
3	ID–NUMBER	Char/text	5					
4	INDUSTRY	Char/text	1					
5	REGION	Char/text	2					
6	NE–CT	Numeric	4	0				
7	SE–CT	Numeric	4	0				
8	CE–CT	Numeric	4	0				
9	NW–CT	Numeric	4	0				
10	SW–CT	Numeric	4	0				
11	CT	Numeric	5	0				
12		Char/text						

Names start with a letter; the remainder may be letters, digits, or —

It actually contains a little more data than is necessary, but for simplicity's sake, we will use it rather than create another, smaller file—a step you might want to take if the file containing prospect information has many more fields of data than you will need. (This will slow down the running of dBase.)

2. The next step is to create the structure of the file which you will create from the LIST02 and CALLS2 files, and use actually to produce the crosstab. By looking over the crosstab to be produced, you will see that the file must contain the following information for each call:

TERRITORY

INDUSTRY

NUMBER OF CALLS IN MFRG INDUSTRY

NUMBER OF CALLS IN UTILS INDUSTRY

NUMBER OF CALLS IN INSUR INDUSTRY

NUMBER OF CALLS IN BANKG INDUSTRY

NUMBER OF CALLS IN OTHER INDUSTRIES

TOTAL NUMBER OF CALLS

Therefore, create this new file as follows:

    .CREA LINK01

C:LINK.dbf				Bytes remaining: 3841
				Fields defined: 8
field name	type	width	dec	
1 TERR	Char/text	4		
2 INDUS	Char/text	1		
3 CT–MFRG	Numeric	5	0	
4 CT–UTIL	Numeric	5	0	
5 CT–INSU	Numeric	5	0	
6 CT–BANK	Numeric	5	0	
7 CT–OTHR	Numeric	5	0	
8 CT–TOT	Numeric	5	0	
9	Char/text			

Type ∧W to save structure. Type "NO" in response to "Input Data Now?"

Add Information to the New File LINK01.DBF

You will add information to the file LINK01 by creating the following command file, using either the dBase word processor or a separate word processing package. To create this command file, called LINK.PRG using dBase, type:

.MODIFY COMMAND LINK

Here are the contents of the command file LINK.PRG:

```
SET ECHO ON
SELECT 3
USE
SELECT 2
USE
SELECT 1
USE
SELECT 3
  USE LINK 01
SELECT 1
  USE LIST02
  INDEX ON IDNUM TO IDPX
  USE LIST02 INDEX IDPX ALIAS F1
SELECT 2
  USE CALLS2
  INDEX ON IDNUM TO IDCX
  USE CALLS2 INDEX IDCX ALIAS F2
DO WHILE .NOT. EOF ( )
STORE IDNUM TO LOOKUP
SELECT 1
  SEEK LOOKUP
SELECT 3
  APPEND BLANK
  REPLACE TERR WITH F2->TERR
  REPLACE INDUSTRY WITH F1->INDUSTRY
SELECT 2
SKIP
ENDDO
SELECT 3
  USE
SELECT 2
  USE
SELECT 1
  USE LINK01
  REPLACE ALL CT_MFRG WITH 1 FOR INDUSTRY   = '1'
  REPLACE ALL CT_UTIL WITH 1 FOR INDUSTRY   = '2'
  REPLACE ALL CT_INSU WITH 1 FOR INDUSTRY   = '3'
  REPLACE ALL CT_BANK WITH 1 FOR INDUSTRY   = '4'
    .OR. INDUSTRY = '5'
  REPLACE ALL CT_OTHR WITH 1 FOR INDUSTRY   = '5'
    .OR. INDUSTRY = '7' .OR. INDUSTRY = '8'
  REPLACE ALL CT_TOT WITH 1
```

Prepare the File LINK01 for Totaling

To do this, type:

```
.USE LINK01
.INDEX ON TERR TO TERRX
```

Total the File LINK02

To do this, type:

```
.USE LINK01 INDEX TERRX
.TOTAL ON TERR TO LINK02
```

Edit the File LINK02

The file you've just created contains one extraneous field, INDUSTRY. The value in this field is simply the number of the last record that was totaled in the particular territory. You should ignore it. You can create another file, LINK03, from LINK02, as follows:

```
.USE LINK02
.COPY TO LINK03 STRU
.USE LINK03
.MODI STRU
```

and delete the field INDUSTRY with the $\wedge$U and $\wedge$W commands.

Produce the Crosstab Report

You can produce the final crosstab report in any of three ways:

1. Using dBase alone: Simply issue the commands:

```
.USE LINK03
.LIST TO PRINT
```

2. Using the dBase report writing command, type:

```
.USE LINK03
.CREATE REPORT LINK
```

When you've created the report ($\wedge$W to save), type:

```
.REPORT FORM LINK
```

3. Using Lotus 1–2–3, you can make a Lotus-compatible file from LINK03 as follows:

```
.USE LINK03
.COPY TO LINK04 DELI
.QUIT
C> REN LINK04.TXT LINK04.PRN
C> 123
[within 1–2–3, type /FIN and select the file LINK04]
```

If the CALLS file contained 146 sales calls to begin with, the crosstab report would look like this:

Number of Calls by Industry Group

			INDUSTRY GROUP—			
TERR #	1 MFRG	2 UTILS	3 INSUR	4 BANKG	5 OTHER	TOTAL
101	2	4	3	6	6	21
102	3	5	2	6	1	17
103	4	2	7	3	1	17
104	5	1	6	4	1	17
201	5	1	6	4	1	17
203	6	2	1	2	5	16
204	3	7	4	2	2	18
205	7	6	5	4	1	23

If you added the TOTAL, AVERAGE, and PCT OF TOTAL lines with dBase's CREATE REPORT command or Lotus 1–2–3, they would be:

TOTAL	35	28	34	31	18	146
AVERAGE	4.38	3.50	4.25	3.88	2.25	18.25
PCT OF TOTAL	23.97	19.18	23.29	21.23	12.33	100.00

This concludes the instructions on how to complete the two exercises using dBase III.

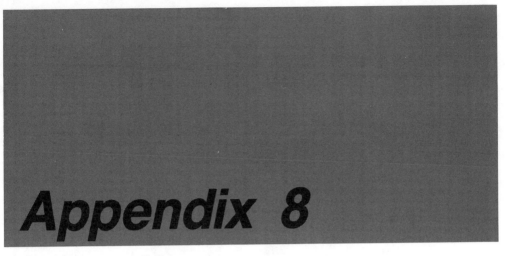

Appendix 8

SAMPLE SIZES FOR RESPONSES

Source: Reprinted by permission of Alan Drey Company, Inc.

SAMPLE SIZES FOR RESPONSES BETWEEN 0.1% and 4.0%
CONFIDENCE LEVEL 95 PERCENT

R (Response)	LIMITS OF ERROR (EXPRESSED AS PERCENTAGE POINTS)						
	.02	.04	.06	.08	.10	.12	.14
.1	95,929	23,982	10,659	5,995	3,837	2,665	1,957
.2	191,666	47,916	21,296	11,979	7,667	5,324	3,911
.3	287,211	71,803	31,912	17,951	11,488	7,978	5,861
.4	382,564	95,641	42,507	23,910	15,303	10,627	7,807
.5	477,724	119,431	53,080	29,858	19,109	13,270	9,749
.6	572,693	143,173	63,632	35,793	22,908	15,908	11,687
.7	667,470	166,867	74,163	41,717	26,699	18,541	13,622
.8	762,054	190,514	84,673	47,628	30,482	21,168	15,552
.9	856,447	214,112	95,160	53,528	34,258	23,790	17,478
1.0	950,648	237,662	105,628	59,415	38,026	26,407	19,401
1.1	1,044,656	261,164	116,072	65,291	41,786	29,018	21,319
1.2	1,138,472	284,618	126,496	71,155	45,539	31,624	23,234
1.3	1,232,097	308,024	136,899	77,006	49,284	34,225	25,145
1.4	1,325,529	331,382	147,280	82,845	53,021	36,820	27,051
1.5	1,418,769	354,692	157,640	88,673	56,751	39,410	28,954
1.6	1,511,818	377,954	167,980	94,489	60,473	41,995	30,853
1.7	1,604,674	401,168	178,297	100,292	64,187	44,574	32,748
1.8	1,697,338	424,334	188,592	106,083	67,894	47,148	34,639
1.9	1,789,810	447,452	198,868	111,863	71,592	49,717	36,526
2.0	1,882,090	470,523	209,121	117,631	75,284	52,280	38,410
2.1	1,974,178	493,544	219,352	123,386	78,967	54,838	40,289
2.2	2,066,074	516,518	229,564	129,129	82,643	57,391	42,165
2.3	2,157,778	539,444	239,753	134,861	86,311	59,938	44,036
2.4	2,249,290	562,322	249,920	140,581	89,972	62,480	45,903
2.5	2,340,609	585,152	260,068	146,288	93,624	65,017	47,767
2.6	2,431,737	607,934	270,192	151,983	97,269	67,547	49,627
2.7	2,522,673	630,668	280,296	157,667	100,907	70,074	51,483
2.8	2,613,416	653,354	290,380	163,339	104,537	72,595	53,335
2.9	2,703,968	675,992	300,440	168,998	108,159	75,110	55,183
3.0	2,794,328	698,582	310,480	174,645	111,773	77,620	57,026
3.1	2,884,495	721,124	320,499	180,281	115,380	80,125	58,867
3.2	2,974,470	743,618	330,496	185,904	118,979	82,623	60,702
3.3	3,064,254	766,063	340,471	191,516	122,570	85,118	62,535
3.4	3,153,845	788,461	350,427	197,115	126,154	87,607	64,364
3.5	3,243,244	810,811	360,360	202,703	129,730	90,089	66,188
3.6	3,332,452	833,113	370,271	208,278	133,298	92,568	68,009
3.7	3,421,467	855,367	380,163	213,842	136,859	95,041	69,825
3.8	3,510,290	877,572	390,031	219,393	140,412	97,507	71,638
3.9	3,598,921	899,730	399,878	224,932	143,957	99,969	73,446
4.0	3,687,360	921,840	409,706	230,460	147,494	102,426	75,252

.16	.18	.20	.30	.40	.50	.60	.70
1,499	1,184	959	426	240	153	106	78
2,994	2,366	1,917	852	479	307	213	156
4,487	3,546	2,872	1,276	718	459	319	234
5,977	4,723	3,826	1,700	956	612	425	312
7,464	5,987	4,777	2,123	1,194	764	530	390
8,948	7,070	5,727	2,545	1,432	916	636	467
10,429	8,240	6,675	2,966	1,669	1,068	741	545
11,907	9,408	7,621	3,387	1,905	1,219	847	622
13,382	10,573	8,564	3,806	2,141	1,370	951	699
14,854	11,736	9,506	4,225	2,376	1,521	1,056	776
16,322	12,897	10,446	4,643	2,611	1,671	1,160	853
17,788	14,055	11,385	5,060	2,846	1,821	1,265	929
19,251	15,211	12,321	5,476	3,080	1,971	1,369	1,006
20,711	16,364	13,255	5,891	3,314	2,121	1,473	1,082
22,168	17,515	14,188	6,305	3,547	2,270	1,576	1,158
23,622	18,664	15,118	6,719	3,780	2,419	1,680	1,234
25,073	19,811	16,047	7,132	4,012	2,567	1,783	1,310
26,521	20,955	16,973	7,543	4,243	2,716	1,886	1,385
27,966	22,096	17,898	7,955	4,474	2,863	1,988	1,461
29,407	23,235	18,821	8,365	4,705	3,011	2,091	1,536
30,846	24,372	19,742	8,774	4,935	3,158	2,193	1,611
32,282	25,507	20,661	9,182	5,165	3,306	2,295	1,686
33,715	26,638	21,578	9,590	5,394	3,452	2,397	1,761
35,145	27,769	22,493	9,997	5,623	3,599	2,499	1,836
36,572	28,896	23,406	10,403	5,851	3,745	2,600	1,911
37,996	30,021	24,317	10,807	6,079	3,891	2,702	1,985
39,416	31,144	25,227	11,211	6,307	4,036	2,803	2,059
40,834	32,264	26,134	11,615	6,534	4,181	2,904	2,133
42,249	33,382	27,039	12,017	6,760	4,326	3,004	2,207
43,661	34,497	27,943	12,419	6,986	4,471	3,105	2,281
45,070	35,611	28,845	12,820	7,211	4,615	3,205	2,355
46,476	36,721	29,745	13,220	7,436	4,759	3,305	2,428
47,878	37,830	30,642	13,619	7,660	4,903	3,404	2,501
49,278	38,936	31,538	14,017	7,884	5,046	3,504	2,574
50,675	40,040	32,432	14,414	8,108	5,189	3,603	2,647
52,069	41,141	33,325	14,811	8,331	5,332	3,702	2,720
53,460	42,240	34,214	15,207	8,554	5,474	3,801	2,793
54,848	43,336	35,103	15,601	8,776	5,616	3,900	2,865
56,233	44,430	35,989	15,995	8,997	5,758	3,998	2,938
57,615	45,522	36,874	16,388	9,218	5,900	4,097	3,010

Appendix 9

SAMPLE TELEPHONE SURVEY—
BUSINESS-TO-BUSINESS MAIL READERSHIP

Hello, I'm Mr./Ms. _____ with Consulting Associates. We have been asked by one of our business-to-business clients to contact people like yourself to get some brief comments of business and industrial direct mail.

1. Do you recall receiving any business or industrial direct mail materials such as sales letters, circulars, broadsides, brochures, folders, new product leaflets, catalogs, bulletins, etc. during the past week?

      1. Yes (Go on to 1a)
      2. No (Skip to 2)

1a. Do you recall any particular piece of direct mail advertising you received at your business office?

      1. Yes (Go on to 1b)
      2. No (Skip to 2)

1b. What was the particular piece? [*Probe*]
Company Sending? Product promoted?
What did the material look like?

      1. Letter
      2. Folder
      3. Brochure
      4. Catalog
      5. Broadside
      6. Other (specify)

1c. Did you read it?

      1. All
      2. Partially
      3. Not at all

1d. What happened to it? Was it

      1. Discarded?
      2. Filed?
      3. Rerouted?

1e. What action was taken on it?

      1. Wrote
      2. Ordered
      3. Called
      4. Other (specify)
      5. No action

2. In general, do you feel that the direct mail advertising received at your business office is

      1. Informative?
      2. Somewhat informative?
      3. Not informative?

3. In general, what percentage of the direct mail advertising received at your business office is

      1. Read more than ½?
      2. Read less than ½?
      3. Not read at all?

4. In general, what percentage of the direct mail material received at your business is

      1. Discarded?
      2. Filed?
      3. Routed?
      4. Some action taken?

Now just a few questions for statistical purposes only.

5. What type of business is this?

6. What is your title?

7. Would you consider your position in management

      1. Top management (chairman, president, vice president)?
      2. Middle management (asst. vice president, manager, director)?
      3. Supervisory or other (assistant to, etc.)?

8. What is your function in the company?

9. Would you consider your organization

      1. Manufacturing?
      2. Wholesaling?
      3. Retailing?
      4. Finance?
      5. Education?
      6. Government?

       7. Institutional?

       8. Other? (specify)

10. And finally, how many employees work at this location?

       1. Under 25

       2. 25 to 49

       3. 50 to 99

       4. 100 to 249

       5. 250 to 499

       6. 500 to 999

       7. 1,000 or more

Respondent's name   _____

Company   _____

Interviewer   _____

Date   _____

Phone #   _____

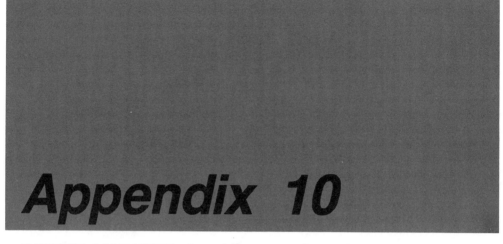

Appendix 10

DIRECT MARKETING ECONOMICS AND BUDGETING

By Pierre A. Passavant, Senior Vice President, Wunderman, Ricotta and Klein

Source: Reprinted by permission of the Direct Marketing Association, Inc.

Direct Marketing is frequently referred to as a "disciplined," "measurable" method of marketing. The reason for this is that, in a well planned and executed direct marketing effort, the cost of an individual promotion and the actual *results* of that promotion can be directly related to each other. This precise information permits the marketer to evaluate the productivity of specific promotions in the past, and to apply that quantitative knowledge to the planning of similar promotions in the future. The result is—or should be—a carefully controlled allocation of promotion dollars to those efforts most likely to produce desired profit results.

Among the planning and evaluation tools used by direct marketers are . . .

- The Profit and Loss statement (both a detailed format for precise profit measurement as well as a summary format for rapid calculations.)
- Contribution to promotion and profit analysis, including calculation of break-even response.
- Back-end performance analysis.
- Return on promotion investment analysis.

Each of these is discussed and demonstrated in the following sections.

THE PROFIT AND LOSS STATEMENT (P&L)

The Profit and Loss statement is a detailed record of sales and costs. It is important to work one out in advance of a promotion (in which case it is called a proforma P&L) as well as after the promotion is over to analyze the results.

Table 1 shows what a detailed P&L might look like for a direct mail offer of an item selling for $29.95.

Explanatory Notes:

Line	Explanation
1)	The price of the item is $29.95. In this example there are no deluxe options or accessories which might increase this price.
2)	If there were a separate deferred payment price (higher than the cash price) it would be entered here. Then line 4 would show the weighted value of cash and installment orders.

	Table 1			
	Detailed P&L Worksheet for Direct Mail Promotion (100,000 packages costing $250 per M. 3.2% response or 3200 orders)			
		Unit Value	No. of Units	Total Dollars
1.	Cash selling price	29.95	3200	95,840
2.	Deferred payment price	—	—	—
3.	+ Shipping/handling	1.75	3200	5,600
4.	Avge. gross order value	31.70	3200	101,440
5.	– Returns (10%)	31.70	320	10,144
6.	Avg. net sale	31.70	2880	91,296
7.	Cost of goods-per sale	7.49	2880	21,571
8.	● per unrefurbished return	7.49	64	479
9.	Order receipt & processing			
10.	● Business reply postage	.18	3200	576
11.	● Order process & customer set up	1.50	3200	4,800
12.	● Credit card fee · 3½%	1.11	1600	1,776
13.	● Credit check	.75	—	—
14.	● Installment billing	—	—	—
15.	● Customer service	7.50	160	1,200
16.	Shipping & handling	1.75	3200	5,600
17.	Returns postage	1.50	320	480
18.	Returns handling	.50	320	160
18A.	Returns refurbishing	.75	256	192
19.	Bad debt (3%)	31.70	86	2,726
20.	● Collection effort	1.00	86	86
21.	Premium	1.00	3200	3,200
22.	Promotion (CPO)	7.81	3200	25,000
23.	Overhead	3.80	2880	10,956
24.	Total expenses			78,802
25.	Profit before taxes		2880	12,494
26.	Profit % to Net Sales			13.7%

Line	Explanation
5)	10% of gross orders received and shipped are returned by the buyer.
6)	Net Sales are orders left *after* returns but *before* bad debt.
7)	The cost of goods delivered to the shipping point is $7.49. Each sale incurs this cost. In addition, it is assumed that 20% of returns cannot be refurbished and therefore become an additional product cost related to each sale.
11)	This line includes mail opening, sorting of orders, credit approval look-up, transfer of checks and charges to bank, capturing customer identification and order history, and creating shipping label.

(Continued on next page)

12) Assumes average charge card fee of 3.5%— lower for bank cards, higher for T&E. Fee applies to 50% of orders that are placed.

13) Because seller is using outside credit cards, he is not doing a retail credit check.

14) Since there is no deferred payment plan, there is no installment billing cost.

15) Complaints, inquiries, special requests by customers. Affects 5% of orders.

16) The actual cost of postage plus shipping department.

17) Seller is refunding return postage to buyer.

18) Cost of processing returned goods and paperwork.

18A) Assumes 80% of returns can be refurbished and put back in inventory.

19) Some checks bounce. And some credit orders are erroneously approved by the company. This amounts to 3% of net orders after returns.

20) Cost of following up on no-pays.

21) The customer keeps the premium—even if he returns the merchandise.

22) The promotion cost assumes 100M packages at $250/M and a response of 32 orders/M or 3.2%.

23) All other expenses (management, plant, equipment, insurance, utilities) etc. not accounted for in items 7-22. The % comes from last year's history or this year's plan.

25) One additional cost that would affect this profit, but which was not allowed for above, is the cost of money—either interest on borrowed funds or the time value of internal capital.

The P&L in Table 1 is very detailed and would be somewhat cumbersome as a means of quickly reviewing alternative marketing plans. Table 2 shows a summarization of some of the detailed expense items.

The numbers in Table 2 are all derived from Table 1. The simplification shown here consists merely of adding together the values for related expense items.

Another way of presenting P&L data is in a per unit format, without reference to any actual total volume. This method can be helpful for quick evaluation of propositions prior to developing full-blown budgets for an actual campaign. Note that the per unit values will be different depending on whether that unit is assumed to be an order (before returns) or a net sale (after returns). This difference is illustrated in Table 3. The values presented in that Table are based on the information presented in Tables 1 and 2.

Both the Per Order and the Per Sale figures are meaningful and useful depending on the analysis being performed. For example, the cost efficiency of order processing and promotion should be evaluated on a per order basis. But when analyzing over-all profitability it is better to look at expenses on a per-sale basis.

Table 2

Summary P&L Statement for Direct Mail Promotion
(100,000 package costing $250 per M.
3.2% response or 3200 orders)

	Unit Value	No. of Units	Total $'s
1. Selling price	29.95	3200	95,840
2. + Shipping/handling	1.75	3200	5,600
3. Gross Order value	31.70	3200	101,440
4. − Returns (10%)	31.70	320	10,144
5. Net Sales	31.70	2880	91,296
6. Cost of goods	7.49	2944	22,050
7. Order process, shipping, returns costs, customer service, credit fee	4.62	3200	14,784
8. Bad debt (3%)	32.70	86	2,812
9. Premium	1.00	3200	3,200
10. Promotion (CPO)	7.81	3200	25,000
11. Overhead	3.80	2880	10,956
12. Total expenses			78,802
13. Profit	4.34	2880	12,494
14. Profit % to Net Sales			13.7%

Table 3

Summary P&L—Per Unit

	Per Order	Per Sale (Assuming 10% returns)
Selling price	29.95	
+Shipping & handling	1.75	
Gross order value	31.70	
− Returns	3.17	
Net Sales	28.53	31.70
Cost of goods (incl. unrefurb. returns)	6.89	7.66
Order process, shipping returns costs, customer service, credit	4.62	5.13
Bad debt	.88	.98
Premium	1.00	1.11
Promotion	7.81	8.68
Overhead	3.42	3.80
Total expenses	24.62	27.36
Profit	3.91	4.34
% to net sales	13.7%	13.7%

The P&L statement also allows the direct marketer to examine the operating *ratios* of a proposition, that is individual items of expense as a percentage of net sales. An example of this is shown in Table 4.

<table>
Table 4

Operating Expense Ratios
</table>

	$	%
Gross Order Value	31.70	
Returns		10%
Net Sale	31.70	100%
Cost of Goods	7.66	24.1%
Order process, etc.	5.13	16.2%
Bad debt	.98	3.1%
Premium	1.11	3.5%
Promotion	8.68	27.4%
Overhead	3.80	12.0%
Total Expense	27.36	86.3%
Profit	4.34	13.7%

Table 5

Contribution to Promotion and Profit

	Total $'s	Per Net Sale
Gross orders	$101,440	
Returns - 10%	10,144	
Net Sales	91,296	31.70
Cost of goods	22,050	7.66
Order process, shipping, returns costs, customer service, credit	14,784	5.13
Bad debt	2,812	.98
Premium	3,200	1.11
Overhead	10,956	3.80
Subtotal-direct expenses	53,802	18.68
Contribution to Promotion and Profit-*per net sale*	37,494	13.02
Contribution *per order* with 10% returns		11.72

The ratios shown above would not be unusual in an offer of a moderate priced item in a solo direct mail package. Cost of goods and cost of promotion in the mid-20% range and order processing, etc., in the mid-teen percent range. For staple products, returns of 10% are typical (they can be much higher in apparel and fashions). The relatively low percent of bad debt in this example reflects the fact that half the orders are being charged to credit cards.

In offers of high-ticket merchandise, as well as in catalogs, cost of goods is often in the mid-40% range, while promotion is in the mid-teens and order processing, etc. well under 10%.

CONTRIBUTION TO PROMOTION AND PROFIT

The development of a pro-forma P&L permits the direct marketer to determine the promotion response that will be needed to achieve break-even or different levels of profitability. This is done by calculating the *contribution to promotion and profit* that is available from each sale after all volume-related expenses have been allowed for.

In the example in **Table 5**, each $31.70 sales has total direct expenses of $18.68—leaving $13.02 per sale for promotion and profit. This is equivalent to $11.72 per order assuming 10% returns.

The relationship between 1) contribution to promotion and profit, 2) profit objective and 3) promotion response is demonstrated in **Table 6**.

If the campaign objective (or minimum acceptable results) were "breakeven" then all of the $13.02 available for promotion *and* profit could be spent on promotion. The result would be that all promotion dollars spent would be recaptured but there would be zero profit. To determine the breakeven promotion response—

• Convert the contribution per sale into a contribution per order by subtracting the value of returns ($13.02 – $1.30 = $11.72)

• Divide the cost per thousand of the promotion by the available contribution per order ($250 ÷ $11.72 = 2.1%).

Table 6 also shows the promotion response re-

Table 6

Relationship Between Contribution to Promotion and Profit and Response Rates Assuming $13.02 Contribution per Sale and $250 per M Package

Campaign Objective	Profit per Net Sale	Available for Promotion ($13.02 — $ Profit) Per Sale	Per Order (10% Rtrns)	Promotion Response Needed ($250 ÷ $ Prom. per Order)
Breakeven	0	13.02	11.72	2.1%
5% profit	$1.59	11.43	10.29	2.4%
10% profit	$3.17	9.85	8.87	2.8%
13.7% profit	$4.34	8.68	7.81	3.2%

quired to achieve 5%, 10% and 13.7% profit. The dollar figures shown in the "Per Order" column in Table 6 are the *Allowable Costs Per Order* at different profit levels, given the direct expense assumptions used in this example. The CPO divided into the promotion CPM gives the response needed as orders per thousand which can then be converted into a per cent response.

BACK-END PERFORMANCE ANALYSIS

Direct marketing promotions must be analyzed in terms of both *front-end response* and *back-end performance.*

Front-end response is the number of orders, the cost per thousand and the resulting cost per order. In the example outlined above the response was 3.2%, the CPM was $250/M and the cost per order was $7.81. It can be dangerous to make future promotion decisions solely on the basis of CPO. For example a lower CPO—say $6.81 instead of $7.81—is not necessarily a more profitable opportunity.

The reason why CPO alone (the front-end) is not necessarily an accurate indicator of profitability is because back-end performance frequently varies as CPO varies. "Back-end" includes returns, bad debt, persistency (how long a customer stays active) and future value (response to other promotions in the future).

Increases in front-end response (and related decreases in CPO) are often promotionally induced—that is more intensive copy, offers, gifts, etc. are used to motivate the prospect to reply. The additional business generated in this way may have lower back-end quality—that is, it may have higher returns and bad debt or lower persistency and future value. Therefore, only a complete analysis of front-end and back-end results can give the answer to the question, "Which is the better promotion approach?"

The following example illustrates the impact that front-end and back-end results have on profitability. It also shows a method for determining what changes in back-end performance can be accepted for a given change in front-end response.

Table 6A

Front-End—Back-End Analysis

	Base Case	Resp. +50% Returns Unchanged	Resp. +50% 13.7% Prof. Returns ?	
Mailing	100,000	100,000	100,000	
CPM	$250/M	$250/M	$250/M	
Prom. $	$25,000	$25,000	$25,000	
% Response	3.2%	4.8%	4.8%	
Cost per Order	$7.81	$5.21	$5.21	
				(1)
Order value	$31.70	$31.70	$31.70	1.
Returns	10%	10%	27.4%	12.
Net Sale	31.70	31.70	31.70	2.
Per Sale				
• Cost of goods	7.66	7.66	7.66	6.
• Ord. Proc. etc.	5.13	5.13	6.36	9.
• Promotion	8.68	5.79	7.18	10.
• Premium	1.11	1.11	1.38	11.
• Overhead 12%	3.80	3.80	3.80	7.
• Bad debt 3.1%	.98	.98	.98	8.
Total	27.36	24.47	27.36	5.
Profit per sale	4.34	7.23	4.34	4.
% to Net $	13.7%	23%	13.7%	3.
(1) Sequence of steps. See explanatory notes.				

Explanatory notes for last column:

1) Enter order value.
2) Enter net sale.
3) Enter % profit target. This can vary.
4) Enter resulting $ profit per sale.
5) Enter total expenses (net sale minus profit).
6) Enter cost of goods (the slight change in unit cost resulting from a different number of unrefurbished returns has been ignored in this example).
7) Enter overhead (12%).
8) Enter bad debt (3.1%) A different assumption could be entered here.
9-11) These numbers are calculated by comparing the last two columns as follows:

Total expenses:	24.47	27.36
Goods, O.H., B.D.:	−12.44	−12.44
Other Exp. (9-11):	12.03	14.92

14.92 ÷ 12.03 = 1.24 which is applied to values of items 9-11 in second column.

12) To determine permissible returns, calculate difference between promotion *cost per order* and *cost per sale* ($7.18 − $5.21 = $1.97). Divide that difference by cost per sale ($1.97 ÷ $7.18 = 27.4%).

In the above example, the "Base Case" uses the same numbers as in Tables 1, 2 and 3. In the second column of figures, the assumption is made that response goes up 50%. Note that consequently promotion cost per sale decreases from $8.68 to $5.79. Since there is no change in back-end performance (an unlikely event) profit increases to $7.23 per sale or 23%.

The third column shows that returns could rise to 27.4% if response increased 50% and the marketer was willing to leave profit at the base rate of 13.7%. The notes at the end of the table show how the calculation was done. Note that the same method could be used to analyze changes in other expense items as well.

RETURN ON
PROMOTION INVESTMENT (ROP)

Another technique used by some companies to analyze alternative promotion opportunities is ROP—or Return on Promotion Investment. The return that is calculated in this instance is the *contribution to overhead and profit.* The promotion investment that this return is related to is limited to media dollars that will be risked up front (premium costs are excluded because they represent a direct expense).

Table 7 shows the calculation of ROP's for two situations. In the left column the response is 3.2%, returns are 10% and the premium costs $1. In the right column response is 3.8%, returns are 15% and the premium costs $1.50. In both cases, total up front promotion cost is $25,000.

The ROP calculation shows that the right column represents a better return on promotion investment (98% vs 94%) even though the profit percent to sales is lower (12% vs 13.7%).

The advantage that the ROP approach offers is that it takes into account differences in contribution to overhead that result from applying a percent overhead factor to different sales volume assumptions. Often the overhead is not actually different, and the additional dollars should be treated as a profit contribution.

Table 7

Return on Promotion Investment or
Contribution to Overhead and Profit

Response:	3.2%	3.8%	
Gross Orders	$101,440	120,460	
Returns	10,144 · 10%	18,069 · 15%	
Net Sales	91,296	102,391	
Cost of goods	22,050	26,185	
Order process, shipping, returns costs, customer service, credit	14,784	17,556	
Bad debt	2,812	3,355	
Premium	3,200 · $1	5,700 $1.50	
Promotion	25,000	25,000	
Subtotal	67,846	77,796	
Contribution to Overhead (12%) and Profit	23,450	24,595	
Return on Promotion (ROP) (Contribution ÷ Promotion)	94%	98%	
$ Profit	12,494	12,308	
% Profit	13.7%	12.0%	

COST OF TESTING

Testing new media, new offers, new formats, etc. is a vital part of direct marketing. It can also be expensive. The reason for the high expense is that tests are usually conducted in relatively small quantities which results in high CPM's. In addition many tests are unsuccessful—that is the response is less than would have been achieved with the control package. The combined effect of higher test CPM's and lower test response rates is to lower profit on the over-all promotion effort in the short run. **Table 8** illustrates this point.

Table 8
Control vs Test Promotion Costs

Package	Quantity	Actual CPM	$ Cost	% Resp.	CPO	Profit
Control	100M	$270/M	27,000	3.5%	7.71	+12%
Test A	10M	$350/M	3,500	2.8%	12.50	− 4%
Test B	10M	$600/M	6,000	4.2%	14.29	−10%
	120M		36,500	3.5%	8.69	+ 9%

In the long run, however, successful tests may lead to higher over-all profits because more productive promotions have been discovered. In the above example, Test B has a response rate 20% higher than the control and, assuming the back end is as good, this will give the seller much higher profits when it becomes the control package in the next campaign.

When analyzing test results, it is important to use the CPM's that will occur when the test is produced in large, roll-out quantities. **Table 9** shows the difference between actual and projected results with the Test B package.

Table 9

Test vs Roll-Out Costs

Test B Package	Quantity	CPM	Resp.	CPO
As Test	10M	$600 M	4.2%	$14.29
As Control	100M	$270 M	4.2%	$ 6.43

In this example, the *projected* CPO for Package B is only $6.43 because, as the control mailing, it would cost only $270/M to produce. Of course, the *actual* cost is important in developing a campaign budget. But the *projected* cost must be used when reading the results of tests.

TWO-STEP MARKETING

The examples used in the beginning of this Release all assumed a one-step direct marketing effort. Some companies use a two-step method of selling. The purpose of Step One is to get an *inquiry* from the prospect. Step Two is the effort to convert that inquiry to a sale. While the final P&L for a two-step effort looks much like that for one-step promotions—there are two separate elements in the promotion expense that should be studied independently. The first is the *cost of an inquiry* and the second is the *conversion rate* of each conversion effort.

Table 10 outlines the economics of two-step marketing.

Table 10

Two-Step Example

1. Inquiry magazine ad CPM	$18 M
2. Response to ad	0.3%
3. Cost per inquiry	$ 6.00
4. Cost per conversion effort	$ .40
5. 4 conversion efforts	$ 1.60
6. Total cost inquiry + conversion	$ 7.60
7. *Cost per order*	
with 10% conversion	$76.00
with 15% conversion	$50.67
with 18% conversion	$42.00

Explanatory Notes:

Line	Explanation
3)	Cost per inquiry is CPM ($18/M) divided by response (3 per thousand).
4)	Assumes that the conversion effort is made by direct mail with a package which cost $400/M or 40 cents each.

5) It is customary to make several conversion efforts in two-step marketing situations.

6) The total cost of acquiring ($6.00) and following up on ($1.60) an inquiry is $7.60.

7) The rate at which inquiries are converted determines the final cost per order. If 10% of inquiries costing $7.60 each are converted to sales, the resulting cost per order is $76. A direct-mail conversion rate of 10% to 18% is not unusual with multiple efforts.

As the final CPO's in Table 10 suggest, two-step marketing is often more appropriate to high-ticket offers than to low-ticket offers.

In two-step marketing, it is important to look at *both* the cost per inquiry *and* the conversion rate before making decisions about a particular campaign. A higher inquiry response (and therefore lower cost per inquiry) is not necessarily beneficial because it may result in a much lower conversion rate (and therefore a higher final cost per order).

Appendix 11

POSTAL GUIDELINES—ONE COMPANY'S REFERENCE GUIDE FOR MAILING SYSTEMS

Source: Reprinted by permission of Moore Response Graphics.

CONTENTS

ALL FEES AND RATES IN THIS PUBLICATION ARE SUBJECT TO CHANGE, ALWAYS CONTACT YOUR POST OFFICE FOR VERIFICATION.

FORWARD COMMENTS

The following information was collected from official U.S. Postal Service publications, discussions from postal officials, and the experiences Moore has had as a major supplier of forms and mailing systems. All information is considered to be accurate and correct. **However, it is recommended that you consult with your local postal officials before manufacturing a piece for use with the postal system.**

A large portion of this publication is dedicated to the machining and OCR reading of mail pieces. At this time, the OCR readability regulations are voluntary. They are designed to assist the U.S. Post Office in handling mail more efficiently, thereby, helping to keep costs at a minimum and service to a maximum. To this end, it is strongly recommended that business mail pieces comply. Other regulations, such as size and thickness, are mandatory and must be followed.

In addition, the following suggested publications are available from the Post Office:

ADDRESSING FOR AUTOMATION	—Notice 221
A GUIDE TO BUSINESS MAIL PREPARATION	—Publication 25
A MANAGER'S GUIDE TO ZIP + 4 CODING	—Publication 149
PREPARING BUSINESS & COURTESY REPLY MAIL	—Publication 12

ADDRESSING FOR AUTOMATION

The United States Postal Service is rapidly modernizing through automation programs.

The new automated equipment includes two main pieces, the OCR scanning equipment and bar code scanners. The OCR scanner reads the city, state and ZIP Code, verifies the ZIP Code, prints a bar code on the mail piece and sorts the piece accordingly. All main post offices and sectional centers now have the OCR scanners in use.

The bar code scanner can be used at the destination post office to further sort the mail for delivery. This equipment scans the bar code that has been printed by the OCR scanner, or preprinted on a return envelope.

Address Read Area   1. For optical scanning of the "mail" to address, it is recommended that the entire address be located within an imaginary rectangle on the front of the mail piece. This area is referred to as the "OCR ADDRESS READ AREA" and is formed by the following boundaries:
   A. 1 inch from the left edge
   B. 1 inch from the right edge
   C. 5/8 inch from the bottom edge (bottom line of Rectangle)
   D. 2¼ inches from the bottom edge (top line of Rectangle)

   At a minimum, the city, state, and Zip Code line(s) must appear within the "OCR ADDRESS READ AREA" in order to be read by optical scanner.

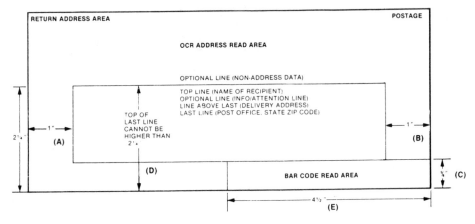

1

Extraneous Data	Within the OCR read area, the entire space below the delivery address line of the address block should be clear of printing other than the address itself. This includes information such as tic marks, underlines, boxes, advertising, computer punch holes, or similar non-address information.
Bar Code Read Area	No printing should appear in the Bar Code read area. This area, 4½″ from the right edge and 5/8″ from bottom edge, should be reserved for the application of Bar Codes. It is recommended the bottom of 5/8″ area across the entire envelope be kept clear. This includes printed perforations and instructions commonly found on self mailer products. (See (E) on diagram, page 1.)
Address Format	The address should have a uniform left margin and be legible. To conserve character spaces, punctuation is not required in the address. The state should be abbreviated using the two-character abbreviation.
Address Content	Use unit, apartment, mail receptacle, office, or suite number in the address. Place that information at the end of the delivery address line. If there is not enough space on this line, place it on the line immediately above the delivery address.
Type Fonts	Italic, artistic, cyrillic, and script-like fonts cannot be read by OCR. Characters or numbers should not touch or overlap within a word or ZIP Code, for any selected fonts. Certain ink jet fonts read satisfactorily. The use of upper case characters is preferred but only required when the line spacing is 8 lines per inch. Preferred spacing is 6 lines per inch.
Character Pitch	The character pitch should be in the range of 7 to 12 characters per inch, but 10 to 12 are preferred
Character Height	The character height must be within the range of .08 inch to .20 inch. All characters on the City, State and ZIP Code line should be of the same height.
Character Spacing	A clear vertical column (.01″ minimum, .05″ maximum) should be maintained between all characters.
Height Ratio	The character height to width ratio should be from 1.1:1 up to 1.7:1.
Word Spacing	The space between words including the State and Zip Code should be 1 or 2 character spaces.
Line Spacing	The space between address lines should be no less than .040 inch (1 millimeter). That is the vertical distance from the bottom most point of either an upper or lower case character to the highest point reached by the tallest character in the line below.
Line Skew (Slant)	Maximum character and line skew relative to the bottom edge of the mailpiece is plus or minus five degrees. Take special care when applying address labels.
Print Contrast	Black ink on a white background is preferred, but color combinations may be used which provide a Print Reflectance Difference of at least 40 percent measured at a wavelength of 650 nanometers. Reverse color printing should not be used.
	It should be kept in mind that anytime we deviate from a white background and black printing, the greater the risk for scanning problems. It's difficult to establish exact parameters in this area since much depends upon how the customer will be printing the address. It is important we stress the need to print as dark as possible (good printer, new ribbon, etc.), and have clear and concise characters with limited background smudging or tracking.
State and ZIP Code	The standard two-letter state abbreviations should be used. The preferred location for the ZIP Code is on the post office, state, and ZIP Code line. However, if this is not possible, the ZIP Code may be placed, at the left margin, on the line immediately below the post office and state.
Window Envelope	The complete address must be the only thing visible through the window. The insert should be positioned to maintain at least 1/8 of inch (1/4 of inch preferred) clearance between the address and the left, right, and bottom edges of the window. Also, avoid background designs which will interfere with the OCR equipment.
Mail to Foreign Country	Mail addressed to a foreign country must have the full name of the post office and country of the destination written in capital letters. The postal delivery zone number (if any) should be included. The address should have a uniform left margin; the country name must be the last item in the address. Also, the mail piece must be sealed on all sides.

2

ARRANGEMENT OF ADDRESS

1. The name and address on mail must be printed clearly and legibly on one side only. The ZIP Code should be included in all addresses and return addresses.

2. Mail must be specifically addressed to the place where the post office is to deliver it. Mail bearing both a street address and post office box number will be distributed for delivery in accordance with the address shown immediately preceding the city, state and ZIP Code. The ZIP Code must correspond with the address immediately preceding the city, state and ZIP Code as well.

3. The proper place for the address is in the OCR address read area.

4. A mailer's specific instructions for forwarding, return or address correction services must appear below the sender's return address. The endorsement should be capitalized and spaced below the return address approximately two line spaces.

5. The ZIP Code should appear on the last line of the address following the city and state. If space or other factors make this position impractical, the ZIP Code may appear below the city and state provided no printing precede it.

6. The return address should be in the upper left corner of the mail piece. **The return address must be above and to the left of the outgoing address.**

EXAMPLES OF ADDRESS RELATIONSHIP

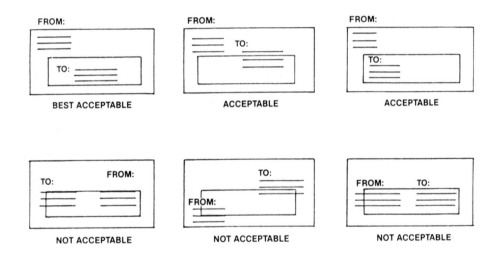

COMMENT

Requirements for the scannability of mail is not a regulation unless the ZIP + 4 discount is being sought. However, it is to the advantage of the business mailer to follow the guidelines for automation so that the mail can be handled in the most efficient manner.

PHYSICAL SIZE REGULATIONS

FIRST CLASS & THIRD CLASS (Single Piece)

Only two classes of mail are affected by the postal regulations for size limitations and surcharge. The two classes are First Class mail, one ounce or less and Third Class, single piece rate weighing two ounces or less (does not include presorted Third Class, BULK MAIL).

The following table is a summary of the physical limitations.

Dimension	STANDARD DIMENSIONS		PENALTY FOR NON-STANDARD	
	Minimum	Maximum	Less than min.	Greater than max.
HEIGHT	3½"	6⅛"	Non-Mailable	Surcharge
LENGTH	5"	11½"	Non-Mailable	Surcharge
THICKNESS	.007"	¼"	Non-Mailable	Surcharge
Aspect Ratio* (Length/Height)	Between 1.3 and 2.5		Surcharge	

*See Template Pages 9-10.

This chart illustrates three important facts to remember:

1. If the mail piece is: a) less than 3-½ " in height or b) less than 5" in width, or c) less than .007" in thickness, it is NON-MAILABLE!

2. If the height or length or thickness of a mail piece exceeds the maximum, it will be SURCHARGED.

3. If the length divided by the height $\frac{\text{Length}}{\text{Height}}$ does not fall within the 1.3 to 2.5 aspect ratio, the mail piece will be SURCHARGED. Refer to the template on pages 9 and 10.

RECOMMENDATIONS—Although, U.S. Regulations do not require a piece to be sealed on all four sides, it is recommended that they be so that it can be handled efficiently by postal service equipment. Open ended pieces are not acceptable for foreign mail.

THIRD CLASS BULK MAIL

Minimum Size   Minimum size standards apply to all Third Class mail. All pieces must be at least .007 inch thick. All pieces ¼ inch or less must be:

      1. Rectangular in shape,
      2. at least 3-½ inches high, and
      3. at least five inches long.

      Any Third Class mail which does not meet these minimums are NON-MAILABLE.

Maximum Size   Maximum size standards apply only to Third Class Bulk Mail that is mailed at the carrier route presort level rate. Those pieces mailed at the carrier route rate must be:

      1. Not more than ¾ inch thick,
      2. not more than 11-½ inches high, and
      3. not more than 13-½ inches long.

Note: Except for Third Class carrier route presort rate mail, there is no maximum size for Bulk Mail. Size surcharges do not apply to Bulk Mail. It is recommended that all mail adhere to the same aspect ratio as First Class mail.

POSTAL PERMITS

A Postal Permit allows a mailer to pay postage with means other than having to affix a stamp or meter imprint. Instead, a permit imprint or Business Reply format is used to identify the permit being used.

OUTGOING MAIL

First Class
Used where speed and efficiency are desired—eliminates the handling and cost of otherwise having to affix postage through the other normal means.
a. Cost of Permit—$50.00 annual fee.
b. Collection of postage—prepayment in full to the local post office is required prior to or at the time of the handling of the mail.
c. Minimum quantity per mailing—200 pieces arranged with addresses all facing the same direction.
d. Required postal permit imprint copy.

Presorted First Class
Used where the sender presorts the mailing by Zip Code before delivering to the post office.
a. Cost of Permit—$50.00 annual fee.
b. Collection of postage—same as normal First Class Permit.
c. Postage price per piece—the applicable First Class rate, less 4¢ per piece for letters and less 2¢ per piece per cards.
d. Minimum quantity per mailing—500 total pieces bundled.
e. Preparation for mailing—minimum of 50 pieces that are sorted to the first three ZIP Code digits or a minimum of 10 pieces sorted to each five-digit ZIP Code. The entire mailing must be bundled into these groups, labeled and presented to the post office in mail trays with a minimum total mailing of 500 pieces. All possible five-digit sortations must be exhausted before proceeding to three-digit bundles.
f. Required postal permit imprint copy—PRESORTED and FIRST CLASS must appear in the imprint. If a meter or stamp is used, PRESORTED FIRST CLASS must appear above the address and immediately below or left of the meter imprint or stamp.

Carrier Route Presort First Class
Used where the sender presorts the mail to the same carrier route before delivering to the post office.
a. Cost of Permit—$50.00 annual fee.
b. Collection of postage—same as normal First Class Permit.
c. Postage price per piece—the applicable full First Class rate, less 5¢ per piece for letters and less 3¢ per piece for cards.
d. Minimum quantity per mailing—500 total pieces bundled.
e. Preparation for mailing—same as Presorted First Class *except*—all mail must be sorted to the full five digit ZIP Code with a minimum of 10 pieces going to each carrier route.
f. Required postal permit imprint copy—must be marked FIRST CLASS and CARRIER ROUTE PRESORT or CAR-RT SORT. If a meter or stamp is used, FIRST CLASS and CARRIER ROUTE PRESORT or CART-RT SORT, must appear above the address and immediately below or left of the meter imprint or stamp.

RETURN MAIL

Business Reply Mail (BRM)
Used where the original sender desires to pay for return postage. Postage is only paid on those "replies" that are actually received. (See BRM section on page 14.)
a. Cost of Permit—$50.00 annual fee (plus $160.00 annual accounting fee if postage fees are "banked" with the local post office).
b. Collection of postage—may be maintained on account "banked" with the local post office or collected at the time the mail piece is delivered back to the original sender.
c. Postage price per piece—standard First Class letter or post card rate.
PLUS
7¢ accounting fee when postage fees are "banked". (Total of 29¢/letter and 21¢/post card.).
23¢ accounting fee without advance deposit of postage fees. (Total of 45¢/letter and 37¢/post card.).
NOTE: If you expect to receive more than 1000 BRM pieces during the year, it is advantages to pay $160.00 accounting fee and bank postage. (1000 is a breakeven point.)
d. Required Business Reply Mail Format.

ACCEPTABLE POSTAL PERMIT IMPRINTS

**Imprint Content
First Class**

Permit Imprints must show CITY and STATE, FIRST CLASS MAIL, U.S. POSTAGE PAID, and PERMIT NUMBER. The mailing date, amount of postage paid, or number of ounces for which postage is paid may also be shown.

STOCK CUT 10-202

STOCK CUT 10-203

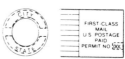

STOCK CUT 10-204

STOCK CUT 10-205

**Imprint Content
Third Class
Bulk Rate
or Nonprofit
Organization**

Permit Imprints must show CITY and STATE, BULK RATE, or NONPROFIT ORG., U.S. POSTAGE PAID, and PERMIT NUMBER. The mailing date, amount of postage paid, or number of ounces for which postage is paid may also be shown.

Alternate Content

An alternate permit imprint may be used so that the pieces can be mailed in may locations using one imprint or so the City and State are not shown. To do this, the Company Name may be used in place of the City and State Permit Number if the following criteria are met:

1. The permit holder must have these permits at two or more post offices.
2. The mail piece must bear a complete return address
3. The Company Name must appear exactly as it does on the permits held.

STOCK CUT 10-204

STOCK CUT 10-205

NOTE: The addition of extraneous matter is not permitted.
Permit imprints must be prepared as shown above.
The broken lines show customer copy area of stock cut.

6

NINE DIGIT ZIP CODE-ZIP + 4

The U.S. Postal Service has introduced use of the ZIP + 4 system. The new system is a voluntary program designed to improve mail service efficiency, thereby holding down costs. Rules have been established which include an incentive discount as follows:

NON-PRESORTED FIRST CLASS WITH ZIP + 4 — 0.9¢/piece ($9/thousand pieces)
PRESORTED FIRST CLASS WITH ZIP + 4 — 0.5¢/piece ($5/thousand pieces)

These discounts apply to post cards as well, however Business Reply Mail and registered mail are excluded.

RULES FOR DISCOUNT RATE

**Non-Presorted
First Class**

ZIP + 4 mail must be tendered in mailings of 250 pieces, each of which must meet all eligibility requirements as to ZIP + 4 code, markings, machinability, and OCR-readability. No fee is required.

**Presorted
First Class**

ZIP + 4 mail must be tendered in mailings of 500 pieces, each of which must meet all eligibility requirements as to ZIP + 4 code, markings, machinability, and OCR-readability. A ZIP + 4 discount is available for carrier route first class mail that meets all ZIP + 4 eligibility requirements. The annual $50 presort fee is required.

REQUIRED MARKINGS

All pieces which are mailed at the ZIP + 4 discounted rate must be marked ZIP + 4 or ZIP + 4 PRESORT. When using a postal permit indicia, it should be included as part of the indicia. When a meter imprint or stamp is used, the identification ZIP + 4 or ZIP + 4 PRESORT, as applicable, must be printed above the address and immediately below or left of the imprint or stamp.

PREPRINTED BAR CODING

The bar coding of reply mail is one of the steps customers can take to maximize the benefits achievable through automation. The nine digits of the ZIP + 4 code are translated into a series of small vertical bars and half bars which are then printed on the lower right hand corner of the envelope. The bar code permits highly reliably sortation of mail through special equipment operating at a much faster rate than manual or conventional. FIM A and FIM C are to be used with a preprinted bar code. Any time a preaddressed envelope is provided for return mail, the addressing should include a preprinted bar code.

A ZIP + 4 discount is allowed for preprinted bar codes corresponding to the ZIP + 4 code.

Quality and location are critical when using preprinted bar codes. Positives are available through your Customer Service Representative at the post office. Postioning must be as follows:

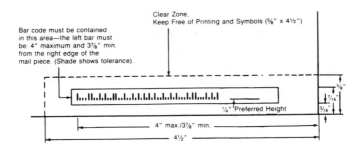

BAR CODE LOCATION

PAPER SPECIFICATION TABLE

PAPER	WEIGHT	MINIMUM CALIPER THICKNESS	TARGET CALIPER THICKNESS
Bond	10	0018	0020
	11.5 Multirite	0019	0021
	12	0021	0024
	15	0028	0030
	16	0031	0033
	18	0035	0037
	20	0037	0039
Safety	24 White	0038	0041
	24 Color	0041	0043
Ledger	24	.0044	0046
	28	0048	0054
	32	0057	0059
Tag	80 White	0055	0060
	80 Manila	0061	0065
	100	0070	0072
	125	0084	0095
Index	90	0070	0072
	110	0082	0087
Tab Card	99	0068	0070
Carbonizing Bond	10	0017	0019
	12	0020	0022
	14	0023	0025
	16	0026	0027
	20	0028	0030
Moore Clean Print	13.1 CB	0028	0030
	13.0 CF	0023	0025
	14.5 CFB	0028	0030
	14.5 CB	0030	0032
	20 CF	0036	0038
	20 CB	0040	.0042
	25 CB	0048	.0053
	33 CF	0062	.0068
	105 CF	0068	.0075
Carbon Tissue			0010
Glue Lines (used in outgoing envelopes only)			0010
Glassine Patch			0011

Minimum Caliper   These calipers are the average lower reject limits used by Moore plants. THEY ARE TO BE USED FOR CALCULATING MINIMUM THICKNESS FOR POSTAL REGULATIONS ONLY. Specifications cannot be rounded up.

Target Caliper   The target calipers are the overall average of papers. USE THESE THICKNESS MEASUREMENTS WHEN CALCULATING THICKNESS FOR OUTPUT PRINTER & OTHER EQUIPMENT RESTRICTIONS.

Glue Lines   Glue line thickness may be used only when calculating minimum thickness of the outgoing portion of a Speedimailer. It may not be used for obtaining minimum standards for return envelopes or pasted pocket construction.

Note: All calipers are averaged and many vary due to allowable tolerances in the paper industry.

LETTER-SIZE MAIL DIMENSIONAL   STANDARDS TEMPLATE

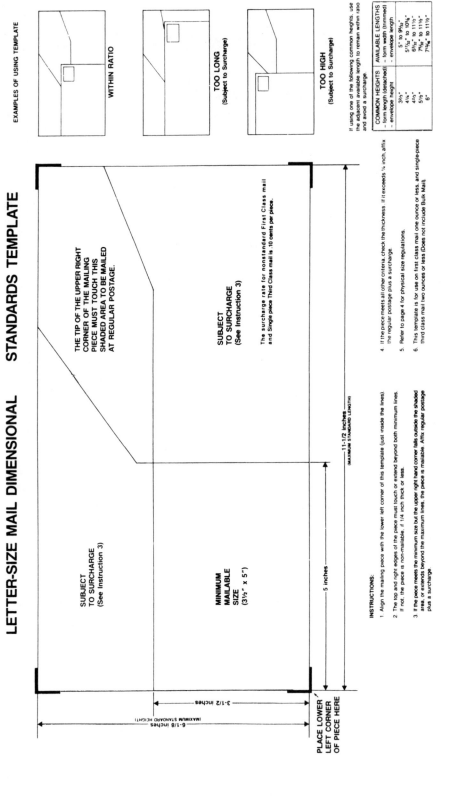

EXAMPLES OF USING TEMPLATE

WITHIN RATIO

TOO LONG
(Subject to Surcharge)

TOO HIGH
(Subject to Surcharge)

If using one of the following common heights, use the adjacent available length to remain within ratio and avoid a surcharge.

COMMON HEIGHTS – form length (detached) – envelope height	AVAILABLE LENGTHS – form width (trimmed) – envelope length
3½"	5" to 9⁵⁄₃₂"
4¼"	5¹¹⁄₃₂" to 10⅝"
4½"	6⁹⁄₃₂" to 11½"
5½"	7⁹⁄₃₂" to 11½"
6"	7³⁄₄" to 11½"

SUBJECT
TO SURCHARGE
(See Instruction 3)

THE TIP OF THE UPPER RIGHT
CORNER OF THE MAILING
PIECE MUST TOUCH THIS
SHADED AREA TO BE MAILED
AT REGULAR POSTAGE.

SUBJECT
TO SURCHARGE
(See Instruction 3)

The surcharge rate for nonstandard First Class mail
and Single piece Third Class mail is .10 cents per piece.

MINIMUM
MAILABLE
SIZE
(3½" x 5")

5 inches

— 11-1/2 inches —
(MAXIMUM STANDARD LENGTH)

3-1/2 inches

6-1/8 inches
(MAXIMUM STANDARD HEIGHT)

PLACE LOWER
LEFT CORNER
OF PIECE HERE

INSTRUCTIONS:

1. Align the mailing piece with the lower left corner of this template (just inside the lines).

2. The top and right edges of the piece must touch or extend beyond both minimum lines.
   If not, the piece is non-mailable, if 1/4 inch thick or less.

3. If the piece meets the minimum size but the upper right hand corner falls outside the shaded
   area, or extends beyond the maximum lines, the piece is mailable. Affix regular postage
   plus a surcharge.

4. If the piece meets all other criteria, check the thickness. If it exceeds ¼ inch, affix
   the regular postage plus a surcharge.

5. Refer to page 4 for physical size regulations.

6. This template is for use on first class mail one ounce or less, and single-piece
   third class mail (two ounces or less (Does not include Bulk Mail).

RATES

First Class Mail   Single Letters (12 oz. or less): This applies to First-Class letters with do not exceed 12 ounces.
First oz. or fraction of an oz. . . . . 25¢
Each additional oz. or fraction of an oz. . . . . . 20¢

Not Exceeding (ounces)	Rate
1.	25¢
2.	45¢
3.	65¢
4.	85¢
5.	$1.05
6.	$1.25
7.	$1.45
8.	$1.65
9.	$1.85
10.	$2.05
11.	$2.25

Post Cards

Single. . . . .   15¢ each
Double. . . . . 30¢ (15¢ each part)
(Reply part does not have to bear postage when
originally mailed.)

Third Class Mail   Single piece rates: The single piece rates are applied to each piece according to its weight.

Ounces	Rate
0 to 1 oz.	$0.25
Over 1 to 2 ozs.	.45
Over 2 to 3 ozs.	.65
Over 3 to 4 ozs.	.85
Over 4 to 6 ozs.	$1.00
Over 6 to 8 ozs.	1.10
Over 8 to 10 ozs.	1.20
Over 10 to 12 ozs.	1.30
Over 12 to 14 ozs.	1.40
Over 14 but less than 16 ozs.	1.50

Regular rates — Bulk: Pieces which weigh more than 3.4948 ounces and are mailed at the 5 digit or basic rate are subject to the per pound rate and are applicable per piece rate. Pieces which are equal to or weigh less than 3.4948 ounces, must be paid at the minimum per piece rate for each presort level.

Presort Level	Per Pound	Minimum Rate Per Piece
Basic	48¢ Plus 4.2¢ per piece	16.7¢
5-digit	48¢ Plus 1.8¢ per piece	13.2¢
Carrier route	48¢	10.1¢

Nonprofit — Bulk: Pieces which weigh more than 3.5213 ounces and are mailed at the 5 digit or basic rate are subject to the per pound rate and are applicable per piece rate. Pieces which are equal to or weigh less than 3.5213 ounces, must be paid at the minimum per piece rate for each presort level.

Presort Level	Per Pound	Minimum Rate Per Piece
Basic	25.0¢ Plus 3.0¢ per piece	8.4¢
5-digit	25.0¢ Plus 1.5¢ per piece	7.6¢
Carrier route	25.0¢	5.3¢

NOTE: ALL RATES ARE SUBJECT TO CHANGE, ALWAYS CONTACT YOUR POST OFFICE FOR VERIFICATION

POST CARDS

A post card is a mail piece made of card stock paper of at least .007 inch thick and no smaller than 3-½ x5 inches. The post card must be made of an unfolded and uncreased piece of paper. Post cards are mailable at a discount First Class rate.

Physical Size   The same requirements for size, thickness and aspect ratio that apply to letter piece mail, apply to post cards. (See the physical size table on page 4.)

Post Card Rate   The post card rate is a special discount First Class rate available to post cards no larger than 4-¼ "x6". Post cards larger than 4-¼ "x6 are mailable at the normal letter piece rates. Presort discounts are deducted from the post card rate or normal letter piece as applicable.

Double Post Card   A double post card consists of two attached post cards, one of which may be detached by the receiver and returned as a reply. Each card is subject to the First Class post card rate.

The general restrictions for a double post card are as follows:

a. Double cards must be folded before mailing. The first half must be detached when the reply half is mailed for return.

b. The reply half on a double card must be used for reply purposes only. It must not be used to convey a message to the original addressee of the double card or to send statements of account.

c. Double cards must be prepared so that the address on the reply half is on the inside when the double card is mailed.

d. Plain stickers, or seals, or a single wire stitch may be used to fasten the edges of double cards, provided they are so fixed that the inner folds of the cards can be readily examined.

CLASSIFICATION NOTES

FIRST CLASS MAIL

All mailable matter may be sent First Class, with the exception of certain undesirable, harmful or dangerous matter. Other features of First Class mail are:

Postal Inspection   First Class mail is closed against postal inspection.

Handling   All First Class mail receives expeditious handling and transportation. The post office does not guarantee delivery in a specified period of time.

Forwarding and Return Service   No permit or fee is required to initiate this service, simply print the appropriate endorsement on the face of the mail piece, directly below the senders return address.
The treatment for all undeliverable first class mail, including post cards, express mail and zone related (Priority) mail bearing the following endorsements.

No endorsement	Forward at no charge (months 1-12).* If undeliverable, return to sender with reason for nondelivery.
Address Correction Requested or Do Not Forward.	Do Not Forward. Provide address correction or reason for nondelivery on mailpiece. Return entire mailpiece at no charge to sender.
Forwarding and Address Correction Requested	Forward at no charge (month 1-12).* If undeliverable, return to sender with reason for nondelivery attached at no charge. Charge the address correction fee if separate address correction is provided to mailer.

NOTES: *Until October 1986, First-Class Mail will be forwarded for 18 months.
The following endorsements are **not** authorized for First Class Mail:
Forwarding and Return Postage Guaranteed.
Forwarding and Return Postage Guaranteed, Address Correction Requested.
Return Postage Guaranteed.

12

THIRD CLASS BULK MAIL

Certain mailable matter may be sent as Third Class mail. Third Class mail includes two discount bulk rate schedules, Bulk Mail and Non-Profit Organizations Bulk Mail. In general terms, Bulk Mail is presorted Third Class mail. Other features and restrictions of Bulk Mail are as follows:

Circulars

Circulars including printed letters which are being sent in identical terms to more than one person, are Third Class mail. A circular does not lose its character as such when a date and the name of the addressee and of the sender are written.

Printed Matter

Printed matter weighing less than 16 ounces may be sent via Third Class mail. Printed matter cannot have the character of a bill or statement, of actual personal correspondence, or be handwritten or typewritten. Computer printed material is considered to be printed matter and is allowed to have:

1. Specific information about a product offered for sale or lease such as the size, color or price.

2. Specific information about a service being offered such as the name, address, and telephone number of a company representative to contact to obtain the service.

3. Information relating the addressee directly to an advertised product or service.

4. Information such as the amount paid for a previous purchase, pledge, or donation, when associated with a sales promotion or solicitation for donations.

Postal Inspection

Third Class mail is not sealed against postal inspection. Sending a mailing by Third Class mail is consent by the mailer to postal inspection of the contents, whether secured or not.

Required Markings

Bulk Rate or the abbreviation Blk Rt must be printed on piece being mailed as Bulk mail. It should be made part of the postal permit indicia; or immediately adjacent to the postage area.

In addition to the endorsement for Bulk Rate, mail being sent at the Carrier Route Presort level must be endorsed Carrier Route Presort or the abbreviation CAR-RT SORT. It should be made part of the postal permit indicia; or immediately adjacent to the postage area. Alternatively, the endorsement may be made part of the address information in accordance with section 662.3 of the DMM.

Forwarding and Return Service

The treatment taken for undeliverable Third Class Bulk Mail, as shown below, bearing the following endorsements.

No Endorsement or Do Not Forward

No forwarding or return service is provided.

Address Correction Requested

No forwarding service is provided. Return entire mailpiece with reason for nondelivery; charge the first ounce single piece third-class rate for mail piece weighing 1 ounce or less and charge the address correction fee for mail piece weighing over 1 ounce.

Forwarding and Return Postage Guaranteed

Forward at no charge. If mail is not forwardable, return the entire mailpiece with raeson for nondelivery; charge the appropriate third class weighted fee. *

Forwarding and Return Postage Guaranteed, Address Correction Requested

Forward at no charge. If separate address correction notice is provided, charge the address correction fee. If mail not forwardable, return the entire mailpiece with reason for nondelivery; charge the appropriate third-class weighted fee. *

Do Not Forward, Address Correction Requested, Return Postage Guaranteed

Do not forward. Return entire mailpiece with new address or raeson for nondelivery; charge the first ounce single piece third-class rate, for mail piece weighing 1 ounce or less and charge the appropriate single piece third-class rate for mail piece weighing over 1 ounce. Do not charge the address correction fee.

13

NOTE: *The weighted fee is the appropriate single piece third-class rate multiplied by a factor of 2.733.
The following endorsements are **not** authorized for third-class mail:
Forwarding and Address Correction Requested.
Return Postage Guaranteed.

BUSINESS REPLY MAIL (BRM)

Business Reply Mail (BRM) service enables permit holders to receive first class mail back from customers by paying postage only on the mail that is returned to them from their original distribution of BRM pieces.

REQUIRED FORMAT ELEMENTS

1. The endorsement NO POSTAGE NECESSARY IF MAILED IN THE UNITED STATES must be printed in the upper right corner of the face of the piece. The arrangement of the endorsement may vary, but it may extend no further than 1-¾ inches from the right edge of the mail piece.

2. The appropriate Business Reply legend must appear above the address and must be in capital letters at least 3/16 inch in height. Authorized legends are:

LEGEND	FOR USE ON
BUSINESS REPLY MAIL	Letters, cartons and cards at letter rate and cards qualifying at the post card rate.
BUSINESS REPLY LABEL	Labels (Business Reply envelopes and cards may not be used as labels to return matter to the permit holder.)

3. Immediately below the Business Reply legend, the words FIRST CLASS MAIL, PERMIT NO., followed by the permit number, and the name of the issuing post office (city and state) must be shown in capital letters.

4. The legend POSTAGE WILL BE PAID BY ADDRESSEE must appear above the address.

5. The complete address, including ZIP Code must appear on face of mail piece. A margin of at least one inch is required between the left edge and the address. A ½ inch clearance must be left between the ZIP Code and the horizontal bars.

6. The address information on BRM must be address in one of the following manners.

   a) The permit holder's name, address, city, state, and zip code. (no authorization required)

   b) The permit holder's name AND the substitute representatives name, address, city, state, and zip code. (no authorization required)

   c) The permit holder's substitute representatives name, address, city, state and zip code. (authorization required)*

   NOTE: Prior to mailing, the permit holder must notify the post office(s) via a written authorization (where the BRM is being returned). In this instance, a separate permit or permit fee is not required.

7. The area 4½ inches from the right edge and 5/8 inches from the bottom edge must be clear of all printing except for the bar code. The bottom line of the address can be no higher than 2¼ inches from the bottom edge.

8. A preprinted bar code is recommended, but not required.

   NOTE: All BRM must comply with the format requirements contained in this section or the BRM will not be accepted for distribution. The permit holder(s) must pay postage for incomplete, blank or empty BRM cards and envelopes.

Facing Identification Mark (FIM) Clear Zone.
(See page 16 for placement.)

14

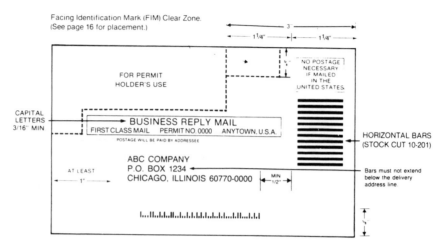

Facing Identification Mark (FIM) Clear Zone.
(See page 16 for placement.)

STANDARD BUSINESS REPLY MAIL

REQUIRED MARKINGS

Horizontal Bars

To facilitate rapid recognition of business reply mail, a series of horizontal bars parallel to the width of the mail piece must be printed immediately below the endorsement, NO POSTAGE NECESSARY IF MAILED IN THE UNITED STATES. The bars must be uniform in length, at least one inch long horizontally. Also, the bars must be between 1/16 and 3/16 inch thick. (Use stock cut 10-201.) The bars must not extend below the delivery address line.

Facing Identification Mark (FIM)

FIM coding of BRM's serves two purposes: 1. It provides automatic facing and cancellation. 2. It provides a means of identifying BRM having a printed bar code. A FIM must be printed on Business Reply Letters and Cards.

An area measuring 5/8 inch in height and 1-¼ inches in width, located along the top edge of the piece and to the left of the endorsement, NO POSTAGE NECESSARY IF MAILED IN THE UNITED STATES is reserved for use of the FIM (See diagram above.)

A print reflective difference of at least 30% is required between the FIM and the paper background for readability. A solid dark color ink is ideal, and problems could occur with light color inks.

The FIM is to be located 2 inches from the right edge, within 1/8 inch of the top of the envelope, and within the FIM CLEAR ZONE. The FIM may extend 1/8 inch below the CLEAR ZONE. No other printing is allowed in the CLEAR ZONE. (See FIM location diagram on page 16.)

Three FIM codes have been defined as follows:

FIM A—to be used only on pre-bar coded **Courtesy Reply** mail. Mail containing FIM A requires the presence of a stamp or meter mark to be accepted in the facer/canceler; otherwise it is rejected. Appropriately equipped facer/cancelers can divert FIM A tagged mail to a special stack, thereby separating pre-bar coded mail for immediate processing on a bar code sorter. FIM A is not required on Courtesy Reply mail but must be used on pre-bar code Courtesy Reply Mail.

FIM B—to be used on **Business Reply** Mail not bearing a preprinted bar code. Mail containing FIM B does not require luminescent indicia; the FIM itself is used for facing and canceling purposes.

FIM C—to be used on **Business Reply** Mail bearing a preprinted bar code. FIM C mail handling exactly parallels FIM A processing, except that no prepaid postage is required.

FACING IDENTIFICATION MARKS (FIM)

Stock Cut 10-206

FIM A
For Pre-Printed
Courtesy Reply
Mail Without Bar Code.

From _____

PLACE
STAMP
HERE

XYZ Sales Company
Attn. Accounts Payable
P.O. Box 1234
Anytown, State 00000-0000

Stock Cut 10-200

FIM B
For Pre-Printed
Business Reply
Mail Without Bar Code.

NO POSTAGE
NECESSARY
IF MAILED
IN THE
UNITED STATES

BUSINESS REPLY MAIL
FIRST CLASS MAIL PERMIT NO. XXXX ANYTOWN, STATE

POSTAGE WILL BE PAID BY ADDRESSEE

Name of Permit Holder
Attn. Accounts Payable
P.O. Box 1234
Anytown, State 00000-0000

Stock Cut 10-207

FIM C
For Pre-Printed
Business Reply
Mail With Bar Code.

NO POSTAGE
NECESSARY
IF MAILED
IN THE
UNITED STATES

BUSINESS REPLY MAIL
FIRST CLASS MAIL PERMIT NO. XXXX ANYTOWN STATE

POSTAGE WILL BE PAID BY ADDRESSEE

Name of Permit Holder
Attn. Accounts Payable
P.O. Box 1234
Anytown, State 00000-0000

See Page 7, for information
on Preprinted Bar Codes.

$2 \pm \frac{1}{8}$

$1\frac{1}{4}$ $1\frac{3}{4}$

Bar top must be within $\frac{1}{8}$ inch
of envelope edge and may
extend to the edge.

Clear zone within
dotted lines

NO POSTAGE
NECESSARY
IF MAILED
IN THE
UNITED STATES

16

SPECIAL CONSIDERATIONS BY PRODUCT

When designing the products listed below, consider the following highlighted information.

SPEEDIMAILER®

Outgoing Envelope

Because there are only two parts pasted in the die cut area (face and back of outgoing envelope) it is essential that this area meet the .007 inch thickness requirement. Glue line thickness may be considered per USPS agreement.

Example	
Face 16# Cbnz Bond	.0026
Back 18# Bond	.0035
	.0061
Glue Line	.0010
Total Thickness	.0071

Postage

The use of a postal permit and indicia eliminates the need to affix or imprint postage. If a postage meter is to be used, consideration must be given to manifolding effects; elimination of carbon coverage in the imprint area is recommended.

Two-Wide Construction

When a two-wide construction is manufactured, both sides must be exactly the same width if presorting will be used. The postal service requires all pieces in a presorted group to be identical.

Return Envelope

The parts forming the return envelope must also be .007 inch thick (Glue line thickness may not be considered).

Example	
Face 18# Bond	.0035
Back 18# Bond	.0035
Total Thickness	.0070

18# Bond is recommended for face and back of return mailer.

Typically, the return envelope feature of a Speedimailer form has the most favorable impact to the user when it is designed for Business Reply Mail. If a BRM is not selected, use of FIM A (Courtesy Reply Mail with preprinted bar code) on the return envelope can improve postal service efficiency.

Pasted Pocket Construction

The parts forming the pasted pocket must be at least .007 inch thick. (Glue line thickness may not be considered.)

Die Cuts & Punch Holes

When designing a form with die cuts or punch holes in the body of the form, be sure the papers behind that area are at least .007 inch thick. Also, all marginal punching must be removed before mailing.

SPEEDISEALER SYSTEM

Outgoing Envelope Copy

When designing the outgoing face copy of Sealermate or Lasermate, opening instructions and printed perforations should be eliminated from the bar code and address read areas. This is required only if ZIP + 4 is utilized.

Return Envelope

Typically, the return envelope feature of a Speedisealer system form has the most favorable impact to the user when it is designed for Business Reply Mail. If BRM is not selected, use of FIM (Courtesy Reply Mail with preprinted bar code) on the return envelope can improve postal service efficiency.

COMPURITE®

Postage

Compurite pieces mailed from a Moore plant require a postal permit. Moore will arrange to purchase the necessary outgoing permit from the post office. If a customer wishes not to have THURMONT, MD or LOGAN, UT in the imprint, they may choose the Company Name permit option (see page 6).

Postage must be received at the plant prior to the mailing (checks made out to the U.S. Postal Service).

Foreign Mail

Foreign mail must be sealed on all sides. Discount rates for presorting, Bulk Mail, etc. are not allowed.

Outgoing Envelope Copy

Opening instructions, printed perforations, and imprints should be eliminated from the bar code and address read areas. This is required if ZIP + 4 is utilized. Also, an OCR readable font should be used to address the outgoing piece.

GLOSSARY OF TERMS

ASPECT RATIO   The relationship of length to height; e.g., 3½ inches x 5 inches (5.0/3.5) = (1.42). The importance of a mail piece having the proper aspect ratio of 1.3 through 2.5 is desirable only to improve automatic mail handling. Those mail pieces not falling within the prescribed aspect ratio of 1.3 through 2.5 will tend to tumble or jam during high speed transport thus making them less machinable. Mail outside of these limits will be surcharged.

BAR CODE   A series of printed parallel bars on a mail piece, used to facilitate automated processing. Copy must be obtained from the post office.

CHARACTER LINE SKEW (SLANT)   Misalignment of any printed character from the horizontal plane of the printed line.

COURTESY REPLY MAIL   Mail generated as a result of a mailer providing a preprinted return envelope or card as a courtesy to customers which requires the customer to affix a stamp or meter imprint.

FIM CODE   Facing Identification Marks—A series of vertical full bars printed in the upper middle portion of the mail piece just to the left of the indicia, used to identify Business Reply Mail, and certain other bar coded mail that allows the USPS equipment to mechanically face, sort and cancel the mail.

INDICIA   Imprinted designation of a postal permit used on mail pieces to denote payment of postage.

LUMINESCENCE   Emission of light that is not directly attributable to incandescence, but is provided by physiological processes, by chemcial action, friction, or by electrical action. Postal Facer/Canceler machines (Mark II or M36) require luminescent materials in the indicia area such as stamps, postage meter labels, etc., in order that upon detection of the luminiscent-bearing mail piece by the Facer/Canceler machines, the mail piece is positioned in a prescribed fashion and a postmark cancellation imprint is made on the mail piece.

MACHINABLE LETTER MAIL PIECE   Envelopes and post cards having the physical and address characteristics recommended in this publication. Example: sizes, thickness and aspect ratio shown on page 5; construction as recommended on page 14; if prepared for OCR processing, those mail pieces having the recommended address characteristics.

METER IMPRINT   An Imprint made by a postal meter denoting payment of postage.

OCR READ AREA   The measured scan area in which postal OCR's look for address information.

OPTICAL CHARACTER READER (OCR)   An automatic mail sorting system consisting of scanner, computer, and letter sorting machine. This system is capable of locating the machine-printed address written on the face of a mail piece, and reading the alpha numeric characters to affect sorting.

PRINT REFLECTANCE DIFFERENCE (PRD)   Reflectance of the paper, minus the reflectance of the ink, expressed as a percentage.

REQUIRED MARKINGS   Required copy and artwork.

STOCK CUT   A stock cut is artwork available at Moore plants.

18

ADDRESS ABBREVIATIONS

STATE ABBREVIATIONS

Alabama .... AL	Kentucky .... KY	Oklahoma .... OK
Alaska .... AK	Louisiana .... LA	Oregon .... OR
Arizona .... AZ	Maine .... ME	Pennsylvania .... PA
Arkansas .... AR	Maryland .... MD	Puerto Rico .... PR
California .... CA	Massachusetts .... MA	Rhode Island .... RI
Colorado .... CO	Michigan .... MI	South Carolina .... SC
Connecticut .... CT	Minnesota .... MN	South Dakota .... SD
Delaware .... DE	Mississippi .... MS	Tennessee .... TN
District of	Missouri .... MO	Texas .... TX
Columbia .... DC	Montana .... MT	Utah .... UT
Florida .... FL	Nebraska .... NE	Vermont .... VT
Georgia .... GA	Nevada .... NV	Virginia .... VA
Guam .... GU	New Hampshire .... NH	Virgin Islands VI
Hawaii .... HI	New Jersey .... NJ	Washington .... WA
Idaho .... ID	New Mexico .... NM	West Virginia .... WV
Illinois IL	New York .... NY	Wisconsin .... WI
Indiana .... IN	North Carolina .... NC	Wyoming .... WY
Iowa .... IA	North Dakota .... ND	
Kansas .... KS	Ohio .... OH	

COMMON ADDRESS ABBREVIATIONS

Apartment .... APT	Meadows .... MDWS	Shore .... SH
Attention .... ATTN	North .... N	South .... S
Avenue .... AVE	Palms .... PLMS	Square .... SQ
East .... E	Park .... PK	Station .... STA
Expressway .... EXPY	Parkway .... PKY	Street .... ST
Heights .... HTS	Plaza .... PLZ	Terrace .... TER
Hospital .... HOSP	Ridge .... RDG	Turnpike .... TPKE
Institute .... INST	River .... RV	Union .... UN
Junction .... JCT	Road .... RD	View .... VW
Lake .... LK	Room .... RM	Village .... VLG
Lakes .... LKS	Route .... RT	West .... W
Lane .... LN	Rural .... R	

INDEX